MYTH
AMERICA

MYTH
AMERICA

Volume II

Edited with an Introduction by
Patrick Gerster
and
Nicholas Cords

BRANDYWINE PRESS • St. James, New York

ISBN 1-933385-13-8

Myth America, Vol. II

Second Edition, 2006

Telephone Orders: 1-800-345-1776

Herein lies the tragedy of the age: not that men are poor—all men know something of poverty; not that men are wicked—who is good? Not that men are ignorant—what is truth? Nay, but that men know so little of men.

William Edward Burghardt Du Bois,
The Souls of Black Folk (1903)

All America lies at the end of the wilderness road, and our past is not a dead past, but still lives in us. Our forefathers had civilization inside them, and the wild outside. We live in the civilization they created, but within us the wilderness still lingers. What they dreamed, we live, and what they lived, we dream.

Thomas King Whipple,
Study Out the Land (1943)

Contents

III
Myths of Progressivism & the 1920s   91

IV
Myths of Politics & Foreign Affairs   145

V

Social Myths of Modern America 211

Preface

The selected historical myths discussed and analyzed in *Myth America* can best be understood as a series of *false beliefs* about America's past. They are false beliefs, however, that have been accepted as true and acted upon as real, and in that acting they have acquired truth. Therefore, myths remain both true and false simultaneously. In fact, the making of myths is a process by which a culture structures its world and perpetuates its grandest dreams.

The idea for *Myth America* grew out of our own teaching experiences. In continuously dealing with students who for the most part were beginning their collegiate study of American history, we found that a thematic approach to the nation's past was stimulating. The theme of myth as threads within the diverse tapestry of cultural experience proved to be especially engaging.

While offering a strong foundation of classic historical writing and interpretation, *Myth America* includes numerous fresh selections on womens' history, southerners and American regionalism, popular culture, African-American stereotyping, urban America, controversial leaders such as Booker T. Washington, progressivism in relation to both conservation and ethnicity, the nature and legacy of the Great War, World War II, and Vietnam, Presidents Kennedy and Reagan, mythic dynamics of the Cold War, Asian-Americans, and multiculturalism. We have been guided in our final selections by a desire to offer articles that voice our mythic theme in a scholarly and provocative way: articles that offer students readability and current interest without sacrificing the demands of thorough historical scholarship. We occasionally refer to historiography, for historians function as the culture's preeminent storytellers and so maintain their seemingly contradictory roles of myth-makers and myth-debunkers.

PATRICK GERSTER
NICHOLAS CORDS

Acknowledgments

As the past itself is a collaborative enterprise, so too is this book. We think the mythic theme applies across the entire landscape of American history, and we gratefully acknowledge those whose efforts came in various ways to be reflected in the final product. Our greatest thanks must be extended to our professional colleagues; their many years of scholarly effort comprise the very heart of this work. Without their passion to explain and interpret the past, their intellectual skills, their narrative talents, this book would not have been possible. Students have helped us both to hone our ideas and to gauge better the critical reception of individual selections. Ms. Patricia Loving of our college library staff abetted computer searches of interpretive literature. Our families have granted us both support and a sounding board for the joys and problems that cumulatively accrue to such a project. The publishing support system of Brandywine Press, and especially the aid and encouragement of David Burner and Thomas R. West, both as historical colleagues and as editors, were indispensable to bringing our ideas through their editorial journey from mind to printed page. To all of these we offer thanks.

PATRICK GERSTER
NICHOLAS CORDS

Introduction:
Myth and History

*"Human Being is a featherless, storytelling animal. . . . We tell stories—myths—
about who we are, where we come from, where we are going and how we should
live. And the myths we tell become who we are and what we believe—as individuals,
families, and cultures."*[1]

In *Myth America: A Historical Anthology*, we address these questions: What
is myth? What is myth's relationship to history? Why study American history by
means of myth?

Myth and history came to life together. In preliterate societies, a sense of origins
and traditions was preserved in cultural memory through stories told by elders
whose task it was to be custodians of the past. While not always—or even often—
factually accurate renditions of the culture's past, myths were able to provide a sense
of cultural continuity. Myths have been the traditional stories a culture tells itself
about itself.

Today the fashion regarding myth is to associate it with the ancient world—as
Greek myths, for example, tell fantastic tales of gods and heroes and collective
cultural accomplishments. Also dating from classical times is the common historical
usage of *myth* as a pejorative term, a synonym for "lie," "fabrication," or "false
belief." Plato declares myths to be "sublime lies," little more than silly beliefs on
false parade. Aristotle, on the other hand, describes myths as a treasury of cultural
stories about the past that provide meaning and hold together a diverse people.
Since Greek times, then, the understanding and use of myth have been ambivalent.
Myth may be dismissed as a mutation of historical fact, more false than true, or
respected as allegorical, discussing cultural values under images containing a
special brand of truth. The use of the term *myth* in American historical studies
mirrors this ambivalence with which Western culture has long contended. The term
myth, as presented in this set of readings, is employed in both ways.

"A historical myth," wrote the American historian Thomas A. Bailey over two
decades ago, "is . . . an account or belief which is demonstrably untrue in whole or
substantial part."[2] Some scholars are determined to isolate and debunk what they
regard as erroneous belief and misguided scholarship. The goal of historical study,
as they would have it, is to record history as clean, unadorned fact. The historian
must stand as a transparent witness to the occurrences of the past. The truth, if
diligently sought and recorded, will out.

An opposite perception of myth has an illustration in Henry Nash Smith's famous study *Virgin Land: The American West as Symbol and Myth.* For Smith, a cultural or social myth, even while often factually false, needs to be sympathetically reckoned with, for it contains an internal treasure—a culture's ideological foundations. Myth, says Smith, is "an intellectual construction that fuses concept and emotion into an image."[3] Myth is, so to speak, a mental movie, with accompanying script, that Americans carry around in their heads regarding their heritage and sense of special destiny. When sensitively deconstructed, myths can be shown to embody American culture's basic beliefs and highest aspirations—honesty, unpretentiousness, optimism, tolerance, hard work, sympathy for the underdog, dedication to perfectionism, an abiding concern for the general well-being, and a special esteem for freedom. The American past is therefore scarcely a dead past. It continues to live within us. Myth lays claim to preserving, repeating, and defending the treasury of wisdom our forebears entrusted to us.

At times both senses of myth are present; on occasion they become nearly indistinguishable. The University of Chicago historian William H. McNeill observes that "myth and history are close kin inasmuch as both explain how things got to be the way they are by telling some sort of story."[4] In the Italian and Spanish languages, for example, the words *history* and *story* are interchangeable. Historians are essentially the storytellers of the tribe, functioning as purveyors of cultural stories. In this sense, historians are mythmakers. And they must be so. Being human, they reflect their personal backgrounds, their times, their methodologies, their current interests including biases and prejudices, and sometimes even their whims. All historical interpretation is both time-bound and ideological—such is the nature of what has been called "the politics of interpretation." Historians, moreover, constantly revise one another's work and sometimes even their own. This process of mythmaking by professional historians—myths as a critical by-product of what historians do—receives major emphasis in this book.

In addition to formal, academic presentation of American history, an assemblage of assumptions, some of them competing, forms a sense of the past. These, too, structure and sustain the illusions and traditional stories—the myths—about America's past. Television and film, two of American culture's favorite media, especially transmit to eager audiences images and re-creations of the past in appealing sight and sound, most often with an eye to drama rather than research and scholarly validity. Historical novels, poetry, political rhetoric, children's literature, paintings, ballads, oral traditions, folklore, political cartoons, tourist shrines, and culturally induced sexist and racist stereotypes contribute in their own ways to our collective impression of the past. In the aggregate they probably represent as consistent and enduring a fund of historical information as is learned in more formal educational settings. As Americans internalize cultural tradition, they fashion a colorful mental mosaic of their history. In acting as if the myths are true, Americans make them true. Policies—even laws—are based on them. The making of myths is a process by which a culture perpetuates its grandest illusions even as it gives substance, order, and stability to its world. The mathematician and philosopher Alfred North Whitehead told a Virginia audience over half a century ago:

> The art of a free society consists first in the maintenance of the symbolic code; and secondly in a fearlessness of revision, to secure that the code serves those purposes which satisfy an enlightened reason. Those societies which cannot combine reverence to their symbols with freedom of revision,

must ultimately decay either from anarchy, or from the slow atrophy of a life stifled by useless shadows.[5]

Seeking to offer cautionary comment as to American culture's many "useless shadows" while still cultivating a decent respect for "the symbolic code," *Myth America* offers much fresh material that illuminates both. Together with classic essays, readings from scholarship of the 1990s and 1980s add to the master narrative of American history. It is hoped that this selective study of myth and the American experience will launch the reader on an especially rewarding journey through America's storied mythic past.

Notes

1. Sam Keen, "Personal Myths Guide Daily Life: The Stories We Live By," *Psychology Today*, 23 (December 1989), p. 44.
2. Thomas A. Bailey, "The Mythmakers of American History," *The Journal of American History*, 55 (June 1968), p. 5.
3. Henry Nash Smith, *Virgin Land: The American West as Symbol and Myth* (New York, 1950), p. v.
4. William H. McNeill, "Mythistory, or Truth, Myth, History, and Historians," *The American Historical Review*, 91 (February 1986), p. 1.
5. Alfred North Whitehead, *Symbolism: Its Meaning and Effect* (New York, 1959), p. 88.

Credits

MYTH
AMERICA

I

Myths of Reconstruction & the Gilded Age

Today the Civil War remains central to the nation's historical experience. The War enjoys the status of an American *Iliad*. It fashioned and defined an American identity and strongly conditioned emergent mythologies.

Former slaves worked to reconstruct both their condition and their self-definition. Some sought to do so by way of sharecropping and tenant farming in the South, while other freedmen, called "exodusters," migrated west in traditional American fashion, to places such as Nicodemus, Kansas, in search of new opportunity and their version of the American Dream.

The South itself had once lived "the roll of frontier upon frontier, and on to the frontier beyond." The early history of western exploration is filled with southern names—from Boone, to Lewis and Clark, to John Charles Frémont. Like the South, the West became a mythic landscape.

But now the vision of many white southerners was transfixed by the past, conditioned by the hypnotic spell still being cast by the mythic shadows of the Old South. They enshrined both cavalier and southern belle, romantically recalling their "Lost Cause," glamorizing the fallen "Knights" of the Confederacy. While the Civil War had saved the Union, it strengthened a sense of regional solidarity among southerners that caused many to court the wish that the mythological South would some day "rise again." For them, reconstruction was the "tragic decade," a kaleidoscope of stereotypical historical characters—villainous Union soldiers, vindictive congressmen, bungling blacks, conniving carpetbaggers, and traitorous scalawags. Still other southerners sought the creation of a New South of economic redevelopment, racial harmony, and political redemption, a regional resurrection from the ashes of Appomattox.

In either case, the South was turning inward, away from the West that was now the repository of myths of freedom for a nation that had rid itself of legal slavery. Meanwhile, the country at large sustained and reiterated its cultural affection for its longstanding idol, the yeoman farmer, refashioning its old frontier hero in the garb of the cowboy. Old romances gave way to new mythologies—rural and urban, male and female, regional and national.

Freedom's Fathers. Painting by J. A. Arthur, 1865. *(Courtesy, Library of Congress)*

The artist of this 1867 glorification of Reconstruction focuses on raising the missing pillars (the returning southern states) to form a rotunda of the reunited Republic. Clasped hands above the American eagle carry the words "Union and Liberty Forever." From heaven, the country's great leaders look down approvingly—Washington, Lincoln, Jefferson, Webster, Calhoun, and many more. Black and white babies (bottom, center), sleeping innocently in baskets, remind the viewer that "All men are born free and equal." Black and white children play together—a nation's noblest dream. *(Courtesy, Library of Congress)*

Myths of Reconstruction

Eric Foner

Generations of American college students, at least those schooled prior to the 1960s, were rather comfortably conveyed the impression that Reconstruction—the era after the Civil War involved with "binding up the nation's wounds" opened by civil conflict—was an era of America's past simply portrayed in shades of black and white. It was said to offer a tale of black rule (the "Africanization" of southern politics), resultant corruption, political subordination of southern whites, military despotism, and radical congressional control of Reconstruction policy. Offering a summary of new research findings, Columbia University professor Eric Foner demonstrates how almost every previous assumption regarding Reconstruction has been overturned. Black supremacy was a myth, the era was far more conservative than radical, southern whites were not categorically disfranchised, and military despotism was hardly the rule. Moreover, recent scholarship has formulated a new agenda for Reconstruction study, emphasizing social rather than political issues, noting the continuing relevance of Reconstruction issues to American society, and, most important, conceding the role of blacks as active agents in the profound changes of the time. The political, economic, and particularly the humanitarian goals of Reconstruction of course failed of achievement. They necessarily remain, however, a critical part of the nation's agenda.

No period in American history has undergone a more complete reevaluation since 1960 than Reconstruction. As with slavery, scholars began by dismantling a long-dominant one-dimensional view and then proceeded to create new and increasingly sophisticated interpretations. According to the portrait that originated with nineteenth-century opponents of black suffrage and achieved scholarly legitimacy early in this century, the turbulent years after the Civil War were a period of unrelieved sordidness in political and social life. Sabotaging Andrew Johnson's attempt to readmit the southern states to full participation in the Union immediately, Radical Republicans fastened black supremacy upon the defeated Confederacy. An orgy of corruption and misgovernment followed, presided over by unscrupulous carpetbaggers (northerners who ventured South to reap the spoils of office), scalawags (southern whites who cooperated with the new govern-

ments for personal gain), and ignorant and childlike freedmen who were incapable of responsibly exercising the political power that had been thrust upon them. After much needless suffering, the South's white communities banded together to overthrow these "black" governments and restore "home rule" (their euphemism for white supremacy).

Resting on the assumption that black suffrage was the gravest error of the entire Civil War period, this traditional interpretation survived for decades because it accorded with firmly entrenched American political and social realities—the disfranchisement and segregation of blacks, and the solid Democratic South. But the "Second Reconstruction"—the civil rights movement—inspired a new conception of the first among historians, and as with the study of slavery, a revisionist wave broke over the field in the 1960s. In rapid succession virtually every assumption of the old viewpoint was dismantled. Andrew Johnson, yesterday's high-minded defender of constitutional principles, was revealed as a racist politician too stubborn to compromise with his critics. By creating an impasse with Congress that Lincoln surely would have avoided, Johnson effectively destroyed his own presidency. Radical Republicans, acquitted of vindictive motives, emerged as idealists in the best nineteenth-century reform tradition. Their leaders, Charles Sumner and Thaddeus Stevens, had worked for black rights long before any conceivable political benefit could have flowed from such a commitment. Their Reconstruction policies were based on principle, not mere political advantage or personal gain. And rather than being the concern of a small band of extremists, the commitment to protecting the civil rights of the freedmen—the central issue dividing Congress and the president—enjoyed broad support within the Republican party.

At the same time, the period of "Black Reconstruction" after 1867 was portrayed as a time of extraordinary progress in the South. The rebuilding of war-shattered public institutions, the establishment of the region's first public school systems, the effort to construct an interracial political democracy on the ashes of slavery—all these were commendable achievements, not elements of the "tragic era" described by earlier historians.

The villains and heroes of the traditional morality play came in for revised treatment. Former slaves did enjoy a real measure of political power, but "black supremacy" never existed: outside of South Carolina blacks held only a small fraction of Reconstruction offices. Rather than unscrupulous adventurers, most carpetbaggers were former Union soldiers seeking economic opportunity in the postwar South. The scalawags were an amalgam of "Old Line" Whigs who had opposed secession in the first place and poorer whites who had long resented the planters' domination of the region's life and saw in Reconstruction a chance to recast southern society along more democratic lines. As for corruption, the malfeasance of Reconstruction governments was dwarfed by contemporary scandals in the North (this was the era of Boss Tweed, Crédit Mobilier, and the Whiskey Ring) and could hardly be blamed on the former slaves. Finally, the Ku Klux Klan, whose campaign of violence against black and white Republicans had been minimized or excused by earlier historians, was revealed as a terrorist organization that beat and killed its political opponents to deprive blacks of their newly won rights.

By the end of the 1960s the old interpretation had been completely reversed. Most historians agreed that if Reconstruction was a "tragic" era, it was so because change did not go far enough; it fell short especially in the failure to distribute land to the former slaves and thereby provide an economic base for their newly acquired political rights. Indeed, by the 1970s this stress on the "conservative" character of Radical Reconstruction was a prevailing theme of many studies. The Civil War did not signal the eclipse of the old planter class and the coming to power of a new entrepreneurial elite, for example. Social histories of communities scattered across the South demonstrated that planters survived the war with their landholdings and social prestige more or less intact.

The denial of substantive change, however, failed to provide a compelling interpretation of an era whose participants believed themselves living through a social and political revolution. And the most recent work on Reconstruction, while fully cognizant of what was not accomplished, has tended to view the period as one of broad changes in southern and national life. In the first modern, comprehensive account of the period, Eric Foner portrays Reconstruction as part of a prolonged struggle over the new system of labor, racial, and political relations that would replace the South's peculiar institution. As in the study of slavery, moreover, some scholars of Reconstruction have sought to place this country's adjustment to emancipation in the broad context of international patterns of development, and to delineate what was and was not unique to the United States, but Reconstruction was; it stands as a dramatic experiment, the only instance in which blacks, within a few years of freedom, achieved universal manhood suffrage and exercised a real measure of political power.

Like recent studies of slavery and the Civil War, current writing on Reconstruction is informed by a recognition of the extent to which blacks themselves helped shape the contours of change. In a kaleidoscopic evocation of black response to the end of slavery, Leon Litwack has shown that freedmen sought to obtain the greatest possible autonomy in every area of their day-to-day lives. Institutions that had existed under slavery, such as the church and family, were strengthened, and new ones sprang into existence. The freedmen made remarkable efforts to locate loved ones from whom they had been separated under slavery. Many black women, preferring to devote more time to their families, refused to work any longer in the fields, thus contributing to the postwar "labor shortage." Continuing resistance to planters' efforts to tie black children to long periods of involuntary labor through court-ordered "apprenticeships" revealed that control over family life was a major preoccupation of the freedmen. Blacks withdrew almost entirely from white-controlled churches, establishing independent religious institutions of their own; and a diverse panoply of fraternal, benevolent, and mutual aid societies also sprang into existence. And though aided by northern reform societies and the federal government, the freedmen often took the initiative in establishing schools. Nor was black suffrage thrust upon an indifferent black population, for in 1865 and 1866 black conventions gathered throughout the South to demand civil equality and the right to vote.

As in every society that abolished slavery, emancipation was followed by a comprehensive struggle over the shaping of a new labor system to replace it. The conflict between former masters aiming to recreate a disciplined labor force and blacks seeking to carve out the greatest degree of economic autonomy profoundly affected economics, politics, and race relations in the Reconstruction South. Planters were convinced that their own survival and the region's prosperity depended upon their ability to resume production using disciplined gang labor, as under slavery. To this end, the governments established by President Johnson in 1865 established a comprehensive system of vagrancy laws, criminal penalties for breach of contract, and other measures known collectively as the "Black Codes" and designed to force the freedmen back to work on the plantations. As Dan T. Carter shows in a study of Presidential Reconstruction, the inability of the leaders of the white South's "self-Reconstruction" to accept the implications of emancipation aroused resentment in the North, fatally weakened support for the president's policies, and made Radical Reconstruction inevitable.

Out of the conflict on the plantations, new systems of labor emerged in the different regions of the South. Sharecropping came to dominate the cotton South. In this compromise between the blacks' desire for land and the planters' for labor discipline, each black family worked its own plot of land, dividing

the crop with the landlord at the end of the year. In the rice-growing areas, with planters unable to attract the outside capital needed to repair wartime destruction and blacks clinging tenaciously to land they had occupied in 1865, the great plantations fell to pieces, and blacks were able to acquire title to small plots and take up self-sufficient farming. And in the sugar region, gang labor survived the end of slavery. In all cases, blacks' economic opportunities were limited by whites' control of credit and by the vagaries of a world market in which the price of agricultural goods suffered a prolonged decline. Nevertheless, the degree to which planters could control the day-to-day lives of their labor force was radically altered by the end of slavery.

The sweeping social changes that followed the Civil War were also reflected in the history of the white yeomanry. Wartime devastation set in motion a train of events that permanently altered these farmers' self-sufficient way of life. Plunged into poverty by the war, ravaged by war casualties, they saw their plight exacerbated by successive crop failures in the early Reconstruction years. In the face of this economic disaster, yeomen clung tenaciously to their farms. But needing to borrow money for the seed, implements, and livestock required to resume farming, many became mired in debt and were forced to abandon self-sufficient farming for the growing of cotton. A region in which a majority of white farmers had once owned their own land was increasingly trapped in a cycle of tenancy and cotton overproduction and became unable to feed itself.

The South's postwar economic transformation profoundly affected the course of Reconstruction politics. As the Black Codes illustrated, state governments could play a vital role in defining the property rights and restricting the bargaining power of planters and laborers. Not surprisingly, when Republicans came to power—largely on the basis of the black vote—they swept away measures designed to bolster plantation discipline and sought to enhance the status of sharecroppers by giving them a first claim on the growing crop. They also launched an ambitious program of aid to railroads, hoping to transform the region into a diversified, modernizing society with enhanced opportunities for white and black alike. But as Mark Summers has shown in an investigation of the program, railroad aid not only failed to achieve its economic aims but produced a sharp increase in taxes, thus exacerbating the economic plight of the yeomanry (attracted in some measure to Reconstruction in its early days by the promise of debtor relief) and preventing the Republican party from broadening its base of white support. Railroad aid also generated most of the corruption that undermined the legitimacy of the Reconstruction governments in the eyes of southern opponents and northern allies alike.

To blacks, however, Reconstruction represented the first time they had ever had a voice in public affairs, and the first time southern governments had even attempted to serve their interests. Recent studies of black politics have stressed both the ways black leaders tried to serve the needs of their constituents and the obstacles that impeded them from doing so effectively. The signal contribution of this new literature has been to reject the idea that Reconstruction politics was simply a matter of black and white. In a broad reevaluation of South Carolina politics, Thomas Holt has argued that many statewide leaders derived from the old Charleston free elite, whose conservative economic outlook rendered them unresponsive to the freedmen's desire for land; studies of Louisiana politics have reached similar conclusions. Free blacks, at the cutting edge of demands for civil and political equality during the Civil War and Reconstruction, failed to find ways of combatting the freedmen's economic plight.

At the local level, however, most black officeholders were former slaves. Although the arduous task of analyzing the local politics of Reconstruction has barely begun, it appears that men who had achieved some special status as slaves—such as ministers and artisans—formed the bulk of black officials. Their ranks were augmented by the little-studied "black carpetbaggers," who looked to the Reconstruction South for opportunities denied them in the North. The presence of sympathetic local officials often made a real difference in the day-to-day lives of the freedmen, ensuring that those accused of crimes would be tried before juries of their peers, and enforcing fairness in such prosaic aspects of local government as road repair, tax assessment, and poor relief. All in all, southern Reconstruction represented a remarkable moment in which the old white elite was stripped of its accustomed political power. It is hardly surprising that its opponents responded not only with criticism but with widespread violence, or that local Republican officials were often the first victims of the Klan and kindred groups.

Recent scholars, indeed, have not only emphasized the role of pervasive violence in the eventual overthrow of Reconstruction but have shown how the problem of law enforcement exposed growing resistance to the expanded federal powers generated by the Civil War. In the war's immediate aftermath Republicans altered the nature of federal–state relations, defining for the first time—in the Civil Rights Law of 1866 and the Fourteenth Amendment—a national citizenship and a national principle of equality before the law, and investing the federal government with the authority to enforce the civil rights of citizens against violations by the states. Then the Fifteenth Amendment prohibited states from infringing upon the right of suffrage for racial reasons, and the Enforcement Acts of 1870–71 gave the federal government the power to protect the civil and political rights of the former slaves against acts of violence.

These were profound changes in a federal system in which the states had traditionally determined and protected the rights of citizens. Yet Reconstruction failed to establish effective means for securing its lofty precepts. The burden of enforcing the new concept of equality before the law was placed upon the federal courts, and it was unrealistic to assume that the courts—even when supplemented on occasion by federal marshals and the army—could bear the major burden of putting down violence in the South. By the 1870s, moreover, many Republicans were retreating from both the racial egalitarianism and the broad definition of federal power spawned by the Civil War. As localism, laissez-faire, and racism—persistent themes of nineteenth-century American history—reasserted themselves, the federal government progressively abandoned efforts to enforce civil rights in the South.

Thus, a complex dialectic of continuity and change affected the ways Americans, black and white, responded to the nation's most profound period of crisis. By the end of the period, slavery was dead, the Union preserved, and both North and South transformed. The social structure populated by masters, slaves, and self-sufficient yeomen was evolving into a world of landlords, merchants, and sharecroppers, both black and white. Also fading into the past was Lincoln's America—a world dominated by the small shop and family farm—as a rapidly industrializing economy took hold in the North. Yet the aspiration galvanized by the Civil War for a society purged of racial injustice had yet to be fulfilled. The end of Reconstruction thrust former slaves into a no-man's-land between slavery and freedom that made a mockery of the ideal of equal citizenship. Scholars, indeed, have yet to assess fully the significance of Reconstruction's failure. That it was a catastrophe for black America is clear, but it also affected the entire structure of American politics, creating a solid Democratic South whose representatives increasingly aligned with northern conservatives to oppose every effort at social change.

It is hardly likely that recent writing represents the final word on slavery, the Civil War, or Reconstruction, for that era raised the decisive questions of America's national existence: the relations between local and national authority, the definition of citizenship, the meaning of equality and freedom. As long as these issues remain central to American life, scholars are certain to return to the Civil War period, bringing to bear the constantly evolving methods and concerns of the study of history.

The Lost Cause Myth in the New South Era

Charles Reagan Wilson

Religion, broadly defined, rests at the heart of southern culture and what it means to be a southerner. Southerners, it is said, are those Americans most "haunted by God." As religion permeated the southern character and southern culture, it structured its regional history and mythology simultaneously. Religion and mythology, declares Charles Reagan Wilson of the University of Mississippi and the Center for the Study of Southern Culture, much affected the shaping of southern attitudes about Confederate defeat in the Civil War and the South's sustaining sense of independent regional identity. As the vanquished Confederacy discovered its cause to be "lost" during the New South era, it sought its reconstruction with the collective sense that the region had been baptized in blood. Thus did the Myth of the Lost Cause find expression in religious vocabulary and religious imagery. Rituals celebrating the Lost Cause not only exploited the southern affinity for ceremonial style, but also made it clear that long-standing southern myth could best be sustained in public consciousness through symbolic remembrance. Through the introduction of such social rituals as Confederate Memorial Day and Confederate reunions, the southern past—particularly as canonized by the United Confederate Veterans and the United Daughters of the Confederacy—became imaginatively reunited with its tragic present.

Scholars have long noted the importance of religion in the South. The predominant evangelical Protestantism and the distinct regional church structures have been key factors in a "southern identity" separate from that of the North. Historians of southern religion have noted the close ties between religion and southern culture itself. Denominational studies have pointed out the role of the churches in acquiescing to the area's racial orthodoxy and in imposing a conservative, moralistic tone on the South since the late nineteenth century, while other works have posited the existence of two cultures in Dixie, one of Christian and one of southern values. At times, it is clear, the churches have been in "cultural captivity," rather than maintaining a judgmental distance, to southern values. The ties between religion and culture in the South have actually been even closer than has so far been suggested. In the years after the Civil War a pervasive southern civil religion emerged. This common religion of the South, which grew out of Confederate defeat in the Civil War, had an identifiable mythology, ritual, and organization. C. Vann Woodward noted long ago that the southern experience of defeat in the Civil War nurtured a tragic sense of life in the region, but historians have overlooked the fact that this profound understanding has been expressed in a civil religion which blended Christian and southern values.

The religion of the Lost Cause originated in the antebellum period. By 1860 a religious culture had been established wherein a religious outlook and tone permeated southern society. The popular sects (Methodists, Baptists, and Presbyterians) provided a

9

sense of community in the individualistic rural areas, which helped to nurture a southern identity. At a time when northern religion was become increasingly diverse, the southern churches remained orthodox in theology and, above all, evangelical in orientation. Despite a conversion-centered theology, ministers played a key role in defending the status quo, and by 1845 the Methodists and the Baptists had split from their northern counterparts, supplying an institutionalized foundation for the belief in southern distinctiveness. The proslavery argument leaned more heavily on the Bible and Christian ministers than on anything else, thus tying churches and culture close together. Because of the religious culture, southern life seemed so Christian to the clerics that they saw threats to their society as challenges to the last bastion of Christian civilization in America.

During the Civil War religion played a vital role in the Confederacy. Preachers nourished the Confederate morale, served as chaplains to the southern armies, and directed the intense revivals in the Confederate ranks. As a result of the wartime experience the religious culture became even more deeply ingrained in the South. Preachers who had been soldiers or chaplains became the celebrants of the Lost Cause religion after the war. By 1865 conditions existed for the emergence of an institutionalized common religion that would grow out of the antebellum-wartime religious culture.

Judged by historical and anthropological criteria, the civil religion that emerged in the postbellum South was an authentic expression of religion. The South faced problems after the Civil War which were cultural but also religious—the problems of providing meaning to life and society amid the baffling failure of fundamental beliefs, offering comfort to those suffering poverty and disillusionment, and encouraging a sense of belonging in the shattered southern community. Anthropologist Anthony F. C. Wallace argues that religion originates "in situations of social and cultural stress," and for postbellum southerners such traditional religious issues as the nature of suffering, evil, and the seeming irrationality of life had a disturbing relevance. Scholars stress that the existence of a sacred symbol system and its embodiment in ritual define religion. As Clifford James Geertz has said, the religious response to the threat of disorder in existence is the creation of symbols "of such a genuine order of the world which will account for, and even celebrate, the perceived ambiguities, puzzles and paradoxes in human experience." These symbols create "long-lasting moods and motivations," which lead men to act on their religious feelings. Mythology, in other words, is not enough to launch a religion. Ritual is crucial because, as Geertz has said, it is "out of the context of concrete acts of religious observance that religious conviction emerges on the human plane." As Wallace concisely expresses it, "The primary phenomenon of religious is ritual." Not all rituals, to be sure, are religious. The crucial factors are rhetoric and intent: whether the language and motivation of a ritual are religious. The constant application of biblical archetypes to the Confederacy and the interpretation of the Civil War experience in cosmic terms indicated the religious importance of the Lost Cause.

The southern civil religion assumes added meaning when compared to the American civil religion. Sociologist Robert Neelly Bellah's 1967 article on the civil religion and his subsequent work have focused scholarly discussion on the common religion of the American people. Bellah argued that "an elaborate and well-institutionalized civil religion" existed that was "clearly differentiated" from the denominations. He defined "civil religion" as the "religious dimension" of a "people through which it interprets its historical experience in the light of transcendent reality." Like Sidney Earl Mead, Bellah saw it as essentially prophetic, judging the behavior of the nation against transcendent values. Will Herberg has suggested that the civil religion has been a folk religion, a common religion emerging out of the life of the folk. He argues that it grew out of a long social and historical experience that established a heterogeneous society. The civil religion came to be the American Way of Life, a set of beliefs that were accepted and revered by Protestants, Catholics, and Jews. "Democracy" has been the fundamental concept of this civil religion. Scholars have identified the sources of the American public faith in the Enlightenment tradition and in the secularized Puritan and revivalist traditions. It clearly was born during the American Revolution, but the American civil religion was reborn with the new theme of sacrifice and renewal, in the Civil War.

In the post–Civil War South the antebellum religious culture evolved into a southern civil religion, differing from the national faith. A set of values arose that could be designated a Southern Way of Life. Dixie's value system differed from that Herberg discussed—southerners undoubtedly were less optimistic, less liberal, less democratic, less tolerant, and more homogeneously Protestant. In their religion southerners stressed "democracy" less than the conservative concepts of moral virtue and an orderly society. Though the whole course of southern history provided the background, the southern civil religion actually emerged from the Civil War experience. Just as the revolution of 1776 caused Americans to see their historical experience in transcendent terms, so the Confederate experience led southerners to a profound self-examination. They understood that the results of the war had clearly given them a history distinct from the northern one. Southerners thus focused the mythic, ritualistic, and organizational dimensions of their civil religion around the confederacy. Moreover, the Enlightenment tradition played virtually no role in the religion of the Lost Cause, but the emotionally intense, dynamic Revivalist tradition and the secularized legacy of idealistic, moralistic Puritanism did shape it.

As a result of emerging from a heterogeneous, immigrant society, the American civil religion was especially significant in providing a sense of belonging to the uprooted immigrants. As a result of its origins in Confederate defeat, the southern civil religion offered confused southerners a sense of meaning, an identity in a precarious but distinct culture. One central issue of the American public faith has been the relationship between church and state, but, since the Confederate quest for political nationhood failed, the southern civil religion has been less concerned with that question than with the cultural issue of identity.

The mythology of the American civil religion taught that Americans are a chosen people, destined to play a special role in the world as representatives of freedom and equality. The religion of the Lost Cause rested on a mythology that focused on the Confederacy. It was a creation myth, the story of the attempt to create a southern nation. According to the mythmakers, a pantheon of southern heroes, portrayed as the highest products of the Old South civilization, had appeared during the Civil War to battle the forces of evil as symbolized by the Yankees. The myth enacted the Christian story of Christ's suffering and death with the Confederacy at the sacred center. But in the southern myth the Christian drama of suffering and salvation was incomplete. The Confederacy lost a holy war, and there was no resurrection.

As Mircea Eliade has said, "it is not enough to *know* the origin myth, one must *recite* it. . . ." While other southern myths could be seen in literature, politics or economics, the Confederate myth reached its true fulfillment after the Civil War in a ritualistic structure of activities that represented a religious commemoration and celebration of the Confederacy. One part of the ritualistic liturgy focused on the religious figures of the Lost Cause. Southern Protestant churches have been sparse in iconography, but the southern civil religion was rich in images. Southern ministers and other rhetoriticians portrayed Robert Edward Lee, Thomas Jonathan ("Stonewall") Jackson, Jefferson Davis, and many other wartime heroes as religious saints and martyrs. They were said to epitomize the best of Christian and southern values. Their images pervaded the South, and they were especially aimed at children. In the first two decades of this century local chapters of the United Daughters of the Confederacy undertook successfully to blanket southern schools with portraits of Lee and Davis. Lee's birthday, January 19, became a holiday throughout Dixie, and ceremonies honoring him frequently occurred in the schools.

An explicit link between Confederate images and religious values was made in the stained-glass windows placed in churches to commemorate Confederate sacrifices. One of the earliest of these was a window placed in Trinity Church, Portsmouth, Virginia, in April 1868, while federal troops still occupied the city. The window portrayed a biblical Rachel weeping at a tomb, on which appeared the names of the members of the congregation who had died during the war. In Mississippi, Biloxi's Church of the Redeemer, "the Westminster of the South," was particularly prominent in this endeavor at the turn of the century. St. Paul's Episcopal church in Richmond, which had been the wartime congregation of many Confederate leaders, established a Lee Memorial Window, which used an Egyptian scene to connect the Confederacy with the stories of the Old Testament. Even a Negro Presbyterian church in Roanoke, Virginia, dedicated a Stonewall Jackson memorial window. The pastor had been a pupil in Jackson's Sunday school in prewar Lexington, Virginia.

Wartime artifacts also had a sacred aura. Bibles that had been touched by the Cause were especially holy. The United Daughters of the Confederacy kept under lock and key the Bible used when Jefferson Davis was sworn in as president of the Confederacy.

More poignantly, a faded, torn overcoat belonging to a young Confederate martyr named Sam Davis was discovered in 1897, and when shown to a United Daughters of the Confederacy meeting the response was, said an observer, first "sacred silence" and then weeping. Presbyterian preacher James Isaac Vance noted that, "like Elijah's mantle of old, the spirit of the mighty dwells within it." Museums were sanctuaries containing such sacred relics. The Confederate Museum in Richmond, which had been the White House of the Confederacy, included a room for each seceding state. These rooms had medals, flags, uniforms, and weapons from the Confederacy, and the Solid South Room displayed the Great Seal of the Confederate States.

The southern civil religion had its reverent images and its sacred artifacts, and it also had its hymns. One group of hymns sung at postwar Confederate gatherings was made up of Christian songs straight from the hymnal. "Nearer My God to Thee," "Abide with Me," and "Praise God from Whom All Blessings Flow" were popular, but the favorite was "How Firm a Foundation." Another group of Confederate sacred songs was created by putting new words to old melodies. The spirit of "That Old-Time Religion" was preserved when someone retitled it "We Are Old-Time Confederates." J. B. Stinson composed new verses for the melody of "When the Roll Is Called up Yonder I'll Be There." A change from the original lyric was the phrase "let's be there," rather than "I'll be there," indicating a more communal redemption in the Lost Cause version. The song used Confederates as evangelical models of behavior: "On that mistless, lonely morning when the saved of Christ shall rise,/ In the Father's many-mansioned home to share;/ Where our Lee and Jackson call to us [sic] their homes beyond the skies,/ When the roll is called up yonder, let's be there." Of special significance was the hymn "Let Us Pass over the River, and Rest under the Shade of the Trees," which was officially adopted by the Southern Methodist church. The words in the title were the last words spoken by the dying Stonewall Jackson. Two other hymns, "Stonewall Jackson's Requiem" and "Stonewall Jackson's Way," made a similar appeal. At some ceremonial occasions choirs from local churches sang hymns. In 1907 southerners organized the United Confederate choirs of America, and soon the young belles from Dixie, clad in Confederate gray uniforms, were a popular presence at ritual events.

These liturgical ingredients appeared during the ritualistic expressions of the Lost Cause. In the years immediately after the war, southern anguish at Confederate defeat was most apparent during the special days appointed by the denominations or the states for humiliation, fasting, prayer, or thanksgiving. These special days could be occasions for jeremiads calling prodigals back to the church, prophesying future battles, or stressing submission to God's mysterious providence in the face of seemingly unwarranted suffering. Southerners, however, usually ignored the national Thanksgiving Day, complaining that northerners used the day to exploit the war issue and to wave the bloody shirt. D. Shaver, the editor of the *Christian Index*, a Baptist newspaper in Atlanta, noted in 1869 that such days too often evoked in the Yankee "the smell (if they do not wake the thirst) of blood." He characterized the northern Christian's behavior on Thanksgiving Day as like that of a Pharisee of old who stood "pilloried through the ages as venting a self-complacent but empty piety." Southerners did celebrate thanksgiving days designated by their denominations, but in general the days of humiliation, fasting, and prayer were more appropriate to the immediate postwar southern mood.

Southern reverence for dead heroes could be seen in the activities of yet another ritual event—Confederate Memorial Day. Southern legend has it that the custom of decorating the graves of soldiers arose in Georgia in 1866 when Mrs. Charles J. Williams, a Confederate widow, published an appeal to southerners to set apart a day "to be handed down through time as a religious custom of the South to wreathe the graves of our martyred dead with flowers." Like true Confederates, southern states could not at first agree among themselves as to which day to honor, but by 1916 ten states had designated June 3, Jefferson Davis's birthday, as Memorial Day. Women played a key role in this ritual since they were in charge of decorating the graves with flowers and of organizing the day's events. It was a holy day, "the Sabbath of the South." One southern woman compared her sisters to the biblical Mary and Martha, who "last at the cross and first at the grave brought their offerings of love...." Another southern woman noted that the aroma of flowers on Memorial Day was "like incense burning in golden censers to the memory of the saints."

A third ritual was the funeral of a wartime hero.

The veterans attending the funerals dressed in their gray uniforms, served as active or honorary pallbearers, and provided a military ceremony. Everything was done according to the "Confederate Veteran's Burial Ritual," which emphasized that the solider was going to "an honorable grave." "He fought a good fight," said the ritual, "and has left a record of which we, his surviving comrades, are proud, and which is a heritage of glory to his family and their descendants for all time to come." These ceremonies reiterated what southerners heard elsewhere—that despite defeat the Confederate experience proved that they were a noble, virtuous people. Moreover, the Confederate funeral included a display of the Confederate flag, the central symbol of southern identity. Often, it was dramatically placed over the hero's casket just before the box was lowered into the ground, while at other times the folded battle flag was removed from the coffin and placed at the head of the grave. Even after Southerners began again to honor the American flag, they continued to cherish the Stars and Bars as well.

The dedication of monuments to the Confederate heroes was the fourth ritualistic expression of the Lost Cause. In 1914 the *Confederate Veteran* magazine revealed that over a thousand monuments existed in the South, and by that time many battlefields had been set aside as pilgrimage sites with holy shrines. Preachers converted the innumerable statues dotting the southern countryside into religious objects, almost idols, that quite blatantly taught Christian religious and moral lessons. "Our cause is with God" and "In hope of a joyful resurrection" were among the most directly religious inscriptions on monuments, but they were not atypical ones. El Dorado, Arkansas, erected a marble drinking fountain to the Confederacy, and its publicity statement said—in a phrase culled from countless hymns and sermons on the sacrificial Jesus—that the water in it symbolized "the loving stream of blood" that was shed by the southern soldiers. Drinkers from the fount were thus symbolically baptized in Confederate blood. The dedication of such monuments became more elaborate as the years went on. Perhaps the greatest monument dedication came in 1907, when an estimated 200,000 people gathered in Richmond for the dedication of a statue to Jefferson Davis on Monument Boulevard. Richmond was the Mecca of the Lost Cause, and Monument Boulevard was the sacred road to it, containing statues of Lee, James Ewell Brown ("Jeb") Stuart, George Washington, and Stonewall Jackson, as well as Davis.

Rituals similar to these existed as part of the American civil religion. In both instances, they were, to use Claude Lévi-Strauss's categories, partly commemorative rites that re-created the mythical time of the past and partly mourning rites that converted dead heroes into revered ancestors. Both civil religions confronted the precariousness and instability of collective life. They were ways for communities to help their citizens meet their individual fears of death. As sociologist William Lloyd Warner has said: "Whenever the living think about the deaths of others they necessarily express some of their own concern about their own extinction." By the continuance of the community, the citizens in it achieve a measure of immortality. For southerners the need for such a symbolic life was even greater than for northerners. Union soldiers sacrificed, but at least the success of their cause seemed to validate their deaths. Postwar southerners feared that the defeat of the Confederacy had jeopardized their continued existence as a distinctively southern people. By participating in the Lost Cause rituals, southerners tried to show that the Confederate sacrifices had not been in vain. Similar rituals existed to honor the Grand Army of the Republic, but the crucial point was that southern rituals began from a very different starting point and had a different symbolic content. Thus, within the United States there was a functioning civil religion not dedicated to honoring the American nation.

The permanence of the Lost Cause religion could be seen in its structural-functional aspect. Three institutions directed its operations, furnishing ongoing leadership and institutional encouragement. One organizational focus was the Confederate veterans' groups. Local associations of veterans existed in the 1870s and 1880s, but southerners took a step forward in this activity with the establishment of the United Confederate Veterans in New Orleans in 1889. The heirs of the Lost Cause formed another group in 1896, the United Sons of Confederate Veterans, which supplied still more energy for the movement. The local chapters of these organizations held frequent meetings, which were an important social activity for southerners, especially those in rural areas. They also had their sacred elements, mostly in the rhetoric used in orations. The highlight of the year for the veterans was the annual regionwide reunion, which was held in a major southern city. It was one of the most highly publicized events in the South. Railroads ran special trains, and the cities gave lavish welcomes to the grizzled old men and their entourage of splendidly dressed young women sponsored by the local chapters. Tens of thousands of people flocked into the chosen city each year to relive the past for a few days. The earliest reunions were boisterous gatherings, but that spirit did not subdue an equally religious tone, especially as the veterans aged. In 1899 the reunion was in Charleston, and a city reporter noted that the veterans were lighthearted at times but that they also were as devout as any pilgrim going "to the tomb of the prophet, or Christian knight to the walls of Jerusalem."

Each day of the reunion began with a prayer, which usually reminded the aging Confederates that religion was at the heart of the Confederate heritage. Presbyterian clergyman Peyton H. Hogue, in a prayer at the tenth reunion in 1900, was not subtle in suggesting his view of the typical Confederate's afterlife. He prayed that those present "may meet in that Heavenly Home where Lee, Jackson and all the Heroes who have gone before are waiting to welcome us there." A hymn was usually sung after the invocation. One favorite was the "Doxology," which ended with the explicitly Christian reference. "Praise Father, Son, and Holy Ghost." A memorial service was held each year at a local church as part of the official reunion program, and it was here that the most direct connections were made between Christianity and the Confederacy. At the 1920 reunion, for example, the Baptist cleric B. A. Owen compared the memorial service to the Christian sacrament, the Holy Communion. In the Communion service, he said, "our hearts are focused upon Calvary's cross and the dying Lamb of God," and in the Confederate sacrament, "we hold sweet converse with the spirits of departed comrades." In order to coordinate their work at memorial services and elsewhere, the ministers of the Lost Cause organized a Chaplains' Association before the Atlanta reunion in 1898.

The Nashville reunion of 1897 was probably the single most religiously oriented Confederate meeting. The veterans met that year at the downtown Union Gospel Tabernacle, later known as Ryman Auditorium, the home of southern music's Grand Old Opry. A new balcony was added to the tabernacle for the 1897 convention, and it was dedicated as a Confederate memorial. Sitting on hard church pews facing the altar and the permanent baptismal font, the veterans had a rollicking but reverent time in 1897 in the sweltering summer heat of the poorly ventilated tabernacle. Each reunion ended with a long parade, and the 1897 procession was one of the most memorable. The reviewing stand was set up on the campus of the Methodists' Vanderbilt University, where the old veterans paused before continuing their march. The reunion coincided with Tennessee's centennial celebration and included the unveiling in Nashville's new Centennial Park of the Parthenon, the replica of the ancient Greek temple, and a mammoth statue to the goddess Athena. The Confederate parade ended in Centennial Park, and as the old soldiers entered the grounds the bells from a nearby tower chimed the old hymn "Shall We Gather at the River?" Apparently unintentionally, the ceremony evoked comparisons with the annual Panathenaic procession in ancient Athens from the lower agora to the Acropolis and then to the Parthenon, the temple of Athena.

If religion pervaded the United Confederate Veterans, it saturated the United Daughters of the Confederacy. The importance of Christianity to the Daughters could be seen in the approved ritual for their meetings. It began with an invocation by the president: "Daughters of the Confederacy, this day we are gathered together, in the sight of God, to strengthen the bonds that unite us in a common cause; to renew the vows of loyalty to our sacred principles; to do homage unto the memory of our gallant Confederate soldiers, and to perpetuate the fame of their noble deeds into the third and fourth generations. To this end we invoke the aid of our Lord." The members responded, "From the end of the Earth will I cry unto Thee, when my heart is overwhelmed; lead me to the rock that is higher than I." After similar chanting exchanges, the hymn "How Firm a Foundation" was sung, followed by the reading of a prayer composed by Episcopal bishop Ellison Capers of South Carolina, who had been a Confederate general before entering the ministry. After the prayer the president then read the Lord's Prayer, and the meeting or convention began its official business.

The Daughters provided an unmatched crusading zeal to the religion of the Lost Cause. The members rarely doubted that God was on their side. Cornelia Branch Stone entitled her 1912 pamphlet on Confederate history *U. D. C. Catechism for Children*, a title that suggested the assumed sacred quality of its contents. The Daughters took an especially aggressive role in preserving the records of the southern past. These were sacred documents that were viewed by the women in a fundamentalist perspective. Mrs. M. D. Farris of Texas urged the organization in 1912 to guard its records and archives, "even as the children of Israel did the Ark of the Covenant."

The Christian churches formed the second organizational focus for the southern civil religion. The postwar development of the religion of the Lost Cause was intimately related to developments in the churches themselves. Before the war an evangelical consensus had been achieved in the South, but it had not been institutionalized. Not until after the war did church membership become pervasive. The evangelical denominations that profited from this enormous expansion of what Samuel Smythe Hill, Jr. calls a "single-option religious culture" taught an inward, conversion-centered religion. Fundamental beliefs on such matters as sin, guilt, grace, judgment, the reality of heaven and hell, and the loving Jesus were agreed upon by all without regard to denominational boundaries. The concept of a civil religion at first glance seems contrary to this inward theology, but the southern churches were not so otherworldly as to ignore society entirely. A southern social gospel existed, as did successful attempts to establish moral reform through state coercion. The combination of a societal interest and the dynamic growth of an evangelical Protestantism was not antithetical to the development of a civil religion.

Unlike the American civil religion, the religion of the Lost Cause did not entirely stand apart from the Christian denominations. They taught similar religious-moral values, and the southern heroes have been directly touched by Christianity. The God invoked in the Lost Cause was a distinctly biblical, transcendent God. Prayers at veterans' gatherings appealed for the blessing of, in John William Jones's words, the "God of Israel, God of the centuries, God of our forefathers, God of Jefferson Davis and Sidney Johnston and Robert E. Lee, and Stonewall Jackson, God of the Southern Confederacy." Prayers invariably ended in some variation of "We ask it all in the name and for the sake of Christ our dear Redeemer." At the 1907 veterans' reunion, the Reverend Randolph Harrison McKim, like other preachers before and after him, invoked the third person of the Christian godhead, praying for "the blessing of the Holy Ghost in our hearts." The references to Christ and the Holy Ghost clearly differentiated the southern civil religion from the more deistic American civil religion. The latter's ceremonies rarely included such Christian references because of potential alienation of Jews, who were but a small percentage of the southern population. In the South, in short, the civil religion and Christianity openly supported each other.

The Agrarian Myth

Richard Hofstadter

For centuries humankind has cherished the notion that agriculture is the basis of all industry and the yeoman farmer the most virtuous of individuals. Though certainly not alone in viewing the farmer as a folk hero, Americans have perhaps been the most persistent in articulating their support for this romantic vision. Americans as diverse as Benjamin Franklin, Thomas Jefferson, Alexander Hamilton, and Calvin Coolidge have held to it. Richard Hofstadter, late Dewitt Clinton Professor of American History at Columbia University, here comments on the yeoman myth as it evolved from a literary to a popular ideal.

The United States was born in the country and has moved to the city. From the beginning its political values as well as ideas were of necessity shaped by country life. The early American politician, the country editor, who wished to address himself to the common man, had to draw upon a rhetoric that would touch the tillers of the soil; and even the spokesman of city people knew that his audience had been in very large part reared upon the farm.

But what the articulate people who talked and wrote about farmers and farming—the preachers, poets, philosophers, writers, and statesmen—liked about American farming was not, in every respect, what the typical working farmer liked. For the articulate people were drawn irresistibly to the noncommercial, nonpecuniary, self-sufficient aspect of American farm life. To them it was an ideal.

Writers like Thomas Jefferson and Hector St. John de Crèvecoeur admired the yeoman farmer not for his capacity to exploit opportunities and make money but for his honest industry, his independence, his frank spirit of equality, his ability to produce and enjoy a simple abundance. The farmer himself, in most cases, was in fact inspired to make money, and such self-sufficiency as he actually had was usually forced upon him by a lack of transportation or markets, or by the necessity to save cash to expand his operations.

For while early American society was an agrarian society, it was fast be coming more commercial, and commercial goals made their way among its agricultural classes almost as rapidly as elsewhere. The more commercial this society became, however, the more reason it found to cling in imagination to the noncommercial agrarian values. The more farming as a self-sufficient way of life was abandoned for farming as a business, the more merit men found in what was being left behind. And the more rapidly the farmers' sons moved into the towns, the more nostalgic the whole culture became about its rural past. Throughout the nineteenth and even in the twentieth century, the American was taught that rural life and farming as a vocation were something sacred.

This sentimental attachment to the rural way of life is a kind of homage that Americans have paid to the fancied innocence of their origins. To call it a "myth" is not to imply that the idea is simply false. Rather the "myth" so effectively embodies men's values that it profoundly influences their way of perceiving reality and hence their behavior.

Like any complex of ideas, the agrarian myth cannot be defined in a phrase, but its component themes form a clear pattern. Its hero was the yeoman farmer, its central conception the notion that he is the ideal man and the ideal citizen. Unstinted praise of the special virtues of the farmer and the special values of rural life was coupled with the assertion that agriculture, as a calling uniquely productive and uniquely important to society, had a special right to the concern and protection of government. The yeoman, who owned a small farm and worked it with the aid of his family, was the incarnation of the simple, honest, independent, healthy, happy human being. Because he lived in close communion with beneficent nature, his life was believed to have a wholesomeness and integrity impossible for the depraved populations of cities.

His well-being was not merely physical, it was moral; it was not merely personal, it was the central source of civic virtue; it was not merely secular but religious, for God had made the land and called man to cultivate it. Since the yeoman was believed to be both happy and honest, and since he had a secure propertied stake in society in the form of his own land, he was held to be the best and most reliable sort of citizen. To this conviction Jefferson appealed when he wrote: "The small land holders are the most precious part of a state."

In origin the agrarian myth was not a popular but a literary idea, a preoccupation of the upper classes, of those who enjoyed a classical education, read pastoral poetry, experimented with breeding stock, and owned plantations or country estates. It was clearly formulated and almost universally accepted in America during the last half of the eighteenth century. As it took shape both in Europe and America, its promulgators drew heavily upon the authority and the rhetoric of classical writers—Hesiod, Xenophon, Cato, Cicero, Virgil, Horace, and others—whose works were the staples of a good education. A learned agricultural gentry, coming into conflict with the industrial classes, welcomed the moral strength that a rich classical ancestry brought to the praise of husbandry.

Chiefly through English experience, and from English and classical writers, the agrarian myth came to America, where, like so many other cultural importations, it eventually took on altogether new dimensions in its new setting. So appealing were the symbols of the myth that even an arch-opponent of the agrarian interest like Alexander Hamilton found it politic to concede in his *Report on Manufactures* that "the cultivation of the earth, as the primary and most certain source of national supply . . . has intrinsically a strong claim to pre-eminence over every other kind of industry." And Benjamin Franklin, urban cosmopolite though he was, once said that agriculture was "the only *honest way*" for a nation to acquire

wealth, "wherein man receives a real increase of the seed thrown into the ground, a kind of continuous miracle, wrought by the hand of God in his favour, as a reward for his innocent life and virtuous industry."

Among the intellectual classes in the eighteenth century the agrarian myth had virtually universal appeal. Some writers used it to give simple, direct, and emotional expression to their feelings about life and nature; others linked agrarianism with a formal philosophy of natural rights. The application of the natural rights philosophy to land tenure became especially popular in America. Since the time of Locke it had been a standard argument that the land is the common stock of society to which every man has a right—what Jefferson called "the fundamental right to labour the earth"; that since the occupancy and use of land are the true criteria of valid ownership, labor expended in cultivating the earth confers title to it; that since government was created to protect property, the property of working land-holders has a special claim to be fostered and protected by the state.

At first the agrarian myth was a notion of the educated classes, but by the early nineteenth century it had become a mass creed, a part of the country's political folklore and its nationalist ideology. The roots of this change may be found as far back as the American Revolution, which, appearing to many Americans as the victory of a band of embattled farmers over an empire, seemed to confirm the moral and civic superiority of the yeoman, made the farmer a symbol of the new nation, and wove the agrarian myth into his patriotic sentiments and idealism.

Still more important, the myth played a role in the first party battles under the Constitution. The Jeffersonians appealed again and again to the moral primacy of the yeoman farmer in their attacks on the Federalists. The family farm and American democracy became indissolubly connected in Jeffersonian thought, and by 1840 even the more conservative party, the Whigs, took over the rhetorical appeal to the common man, and elected a President in good part on the strength of the fiction that he lived in a log cabin.

The Jeffersonians, moreover, made the agrarian myth the basis of a strategy of continental development. Many of them expected that the great empty inland regions would guarantee the preponderance of the yeoman—and therefore the dominance of Jeffersonianism and the health of the state—for an unlimited future. The opening of the trans-Allegheny region, its protection from slavery, and the purchase of the Louisiana Territory were the first great steps in a continental strategy designed to establish an internal empire of small farms. Much later the Homestead Act was meant to carry to its completion the process of continental settlement by small homeowners. The failure of the Homestead Act "to enact by statute the fee-simple empire" was one of the original sources of Populist grievances, and one of the central points at which the agrarian myth was overrun by the commercial realities.

Above all, however, the myth was powerful because the United States in the first half of the nineteenth century consisted predominantly of literate and politically enfranchised farmers. Offering what seemed harmless flattery to this numerically dominant class, the myth suggested a standard vocabulary to rural editors and politicians. Although farmers may not have been much impressed by what was said about the merits of a noncommercial way of life, they could only enjoy learning about their special virtues and their unique services to the nation. Moreover, the editors and politicians who so flattered them need not in most cases have been insincere. More often than not they too were likely to have begun life in little villages or on farms, and what they had to say stirred in their own breasts, as it did in the breasts of a great many townspeople, nostalgia for their early years and perhaps relieved some residual feelings of guilt at having deserted parental homes and childhood attachments. They also had the satisfaction in the early days of knowing that in so far as it was based upon the life of the largely self-sufficient yeoman the agrarian myth was a depiction of reality as well as the assertion of an ideal.

Oddly enough, the agrarian myth came to be believed more widely and tenaciously as it became more fictional. At first it was propagated with a kind of genial candor, and only later did it acquire overtones of insincerity. There survives from the Jackson era a painting that shows Governor Joseph Ritner of Pennsylvania standing by a primitive plow at the end of a furrow. There is no pretense that the Governor has actually been plowing—he wears broadcloth pants and a silk vest, and his tall black beaver hat has been carefully laid in the grass beside him—but the picture is meant as a reminder of both his rustic origin and his present high station in life. By contrast,

Calvin Coolidge posed almost a century later for a series of photographs that represented him as haying in Vermont. In one of them the President sits on the edge of a hay rig in a white shirt, collar detached, wearing highly polished black shoes and a fresh pair of overalls; in the background stands his Pierce Arrow, a secret service man on the running board, plainly waiting to hurry the President away from his bogus rural labors. That the second picture is so much more pretentious and disingenuous than the first is a measure of the increasing hollowness of the myth as it became more and more remote from the realities of agriculture.

Throughout the nineteenth century hundreds upon hundreds of thousands of farm-born youths sought their careers in the towns and cities. Particularly after 1840, which marked the beginning of a long cycle of heavy country-to-city migration, farm children repudiated their parents' way of life and took off for the cities where, in agrarian theory if not in fact, they were sure to succumb to vice and poverty.

When a correspondent of the *Prairie Farmer* in 1849 made the mistake of praising the luxuries, the "polished society," and the economic opportunities of the city, he was rebuked for overlooking the fact that city life *"crushes, enslaves,* and *ruins so many thousands of our young men* who are insensibly made the victims of *dissipation,* of *reckless speculation,* and of *ultimate crime."* Such warnings, of course, were futile. "Thousands of young men," wrote the New York agriculturist Jesse Buel, "who annually forsake the plough, and the honest profession of their fathers, if not to win the fair, at least from an opinion, too often confirmed by mistaken parents, that agriculture is not the road to wealth, to honor, nor to happiness. And such will continue to be the case, until our agriculturists become qualified to assume that rank in society to which the importance of their calling, and their numbers, entitle them, and which intelligence and self-respect can alone give them."

Rank in society! That was close to the heart of the matter, for the farmer was beginning to realize acutely not merely that the best of the world's goods were to be had in the cities and that the urban middle and upper classes had much more of them than he did but also that he was losing in status and respect as compared with them. He became aware that the official respect paid to the farmer masked a certain disdain felt by many city people. "There has . . . a certain class of individuals grown up in our land," complained a farm writer in 1835, "who treat the cultivators of the soil as an inferior caste . . . whose utmost abilities are confined to the merit of being able to discuss a boiled potato and a rasher of bacon." The city was symbolized as the home of loan sharks, dandies, fops, and aristocrats with European ideas who despised farmers as hayseeds.

The growth of the urban market intensified this antagonism. In areas like colonial New England, where an intimate connection had existed between the small town and the adjacent countryside, where a community of interests and even of occupations cut across the town line, the rural-urban hostility had not developed so sharply as in the newer areas where the township plan was never instituted and where isolated farmsteads were more common. As settlement moved west, as urban markets grew, as self-sufficient farmers became rarer, as farmers pushed into commercial production for the cities they feared and distrusted, they quite correctly thought of themselves as a vocational and economic group rather than as members of a neighborhood. In the Populist era the city was totally alien territory to many farmers, and the primacy of agriculture as a source of wealth was reasserted with much bitterness. "The great cities rest upon our broad and fertile prairies," declared Bryan in his "Cross of Gold" speech. "Burn down your cities and leave our farms, and your cities will spring up again as if by magic; but destroy our farms, and the grass will grow in the streets of every city in the country." Out of the beliefs nourished by the agrarian myth there had arisen the notion that the city was a parasitical growth on the country. Bryan spoke for a people raised for generations on the idea that the farmer was a very special creature, blessed by God, and that in a country consisting largely of farmers the voice of the farmer was the voice of democracy and of virtue itself.

The agrarian myth encouraged farmers to believe that they were not themselves an organic part of the whole order of business enterprise and speculation that flourished in the city, partaking of its character and sharing in its risks, but rather the innocent pastoral victims of a conspiracy hatched in the distance. The notion of an innocent and victimized populace colors the whole history of agrarian controversy.

For the farmer it was bewildering, and irritating too, to think of the great contrast between the verbal deference paid him by almost everyone and the real economic position in which he found himself. Improving his economic position was always possible, though this was often done too little and too late; but it was not within anyone's power to stem the decline in the rural values and pieties, the gradual rejection of the moral commitments that had been expressed in the early exaltations of agrarianism.

It was the fate of the farmer himself to contribute to this decline. Like almost all good Americans he had innocently sought progress from the very beginning, and thus hastened the decline of many of his own values. Elsewhere the rural classes had usually looked to the past, had been bearers of tradition and upholders of stability. The American farmer looked to the future alone, and the story of the American land became a study in futures.

In the very hours of its birth as a nation Crèvecoeur had congratulated America for having, in effect, no feudal past and no industrial present, for having no royal, aristocratic, ecclesiastical, or monarchical power, and no manufacturing class, and had rapturously concluded: "We are the most perfect society now existing in the world." Here was the irony from which the farmer suffered above all others: the United States was the only country in the world that began with perfection and aspired to progress.

To what extent was the agrarian myth actually false? During the colonial period, and even well down into the nineteenth century, there were in fact large numbers of farmers who were very much like the yeomen idealized in the myth. They were independent and self-sufficient, and they bequeathed to their children a strong love of craftsmanlike improvisation and a firm tradition of household industry. These yeomen were all too often yeomen by force of circumstance. They could not become commercial farmers because they were too far from the rivers or the towns, because the roads were too poor for bulky traffic, because the domestic market for agricultural produce was too small and the overseas markets were out of reach. At the beginning of the nineteenth century, when the American population was still living largely in the forests and most of it was east of the Appalachians, the yeoman farmer did exist in large numbers, living much as the theorists of the agrarian myth portrayed him.

But when the yeoman practiced the self-sufficient economy that was expected of him, he usually did so not because he wanted to stay out of the market but because he wanted to get into it. "My farm," said a farmer of Jefferson's time, "gave me and my family a good living on the produce of it; and left me, one year with another, one hundred and fifty dollars, for I have never spent more than ten dollars a year, which was for salt, nails, and the like. Nothing to wear, eat, or drink was purchased, as my farm provided all. With this saving, I put money to interest, bought cattle, fatted and sold them, and made great profit." Great profit! Here was the significance of self-sufficiency for the characteristic family farmer. Commercialism had already begun to enter the American Arcadia.

For, whatever the spokesman of the agrarian myth might have told him, the farmer almost anywhere in early America knew that all around him there were examples of commercial success in agriculture—the tobacco, rice, and indigo, and later the cotton planters of the South, the grain, meat, and cattle exporters of the middle states.

The farmer knew that without cash he could never rise above the hardships and squalor of pioneering and log-cabin life. So the savings from his self-sufficiency went into improvements—into the purchase of more land, of herds and flocks, of better tools; they went into the building of barns and silos and better dwellings. Self-sufficiency, in short, was adopted for a time in order that it would eventually be unnecessary.

Between 1815 and 1860 the character of American agriculture was transformed. The rise of native industry created a home market for agriculture, while demands arose abroad for American cotton and foodstuffs, and a great network of turnpikes, canals, and railroads helped link the planter and the advancing western farmer to the new markets. As the farmer moved out of the forests onto the flat, rich prairies, he found possibilities for machinery that did not exist in the forest. Before long he was cultivating the prairies with horse-drawn mechanical reapers, steel plows, wheat and corn drills, and threshers.

The farmer was still a hardworking man, and he still owned his own land in the old tradition. But no longer did he grow or manufacture almost everything he needed. He concentrated on the cash crop, bought more and more of his supplies from the country store. To take full advantage of the possibilities of mechanization, he engrossed as much land as he could and borrowed money for his land and machin-

ery. The shift from self-sufficient to commercial farming varied in time throughout the West and cannot be dated with precision, but it was complete in Ohio by about 1830 and twenty years later in Indiana, Illinois, and Michigan. All through the great Northwest, farmers whose fathers might have lived in isolation and self-sufficiency were surrounded by jobbers, banks, stores, middlemen, horses, and machinery.

This transformation affected not only what the farmer did but how he felt. The ideals of the agrarian myth were competing in his breast, and gradually losing ground, to another, even stronger ideal, the notion of opportunity, of career, of the self-made man. Agrarian sentiment sanctified labor in the soil and the simple life; but the prevailing Calvinist atmosphere of rural life implied that virtue was rewarded with success and material goods. Even farm boys were taught to strive for achievement in one form or another, and when this did not take them away from the farms altogether, it impelled them to follow farming not as a way of life but as a *career*—that is, as a way of achieving substantial success.

The sheer abundance of the land—that very internal empire that had been expected to insure the predominance of the yeoman in American life for centuries—gave the *coup de grâce* to the yeomanlike way of life. For it made of the farmer a speculator. Cheap land invited extensive and careless cultivation. Rising land values in areas of new settlement tempted early liquidation and frequent moves. Frequent and sensational rises in land values bred a boom psychology in the American farmer and caused him to rely for his margin of profit more on the appreciation in the value of his land than on the sale of crops. It took a strong man to resist the temptation to ride skyward on lands that might easily triple or quadruple their value in one decade and then double in the next.

What developed in America, then, was an agricultural society whose real attachment was not, like the yeoman's, to the land but to land values. The characteristic product of American rural society, as it developed on the prairies and the plains, was not a yeoman or a villager, but a harassed little country businessman who worked very hard, moved all too often, gambled with his land, and made his way alone.

While the farmer had long since ceased to act like

a yeoman, he was somewhat slower in ceasing to think like one. He became a businessman in fact long before he began to regard himself in this light. As the nineteenth century drew to a close, however, various things were changing him. He was becoming increasingly an employer of labor, and though he still worked with his hands, he began to look with suspicion upon the working classes of the cities, especially those organized in trade unions, as he had once done upon the urban fops and aristocrats. Moreover, when good times returned after the Populist revolt of the 1890's, businessmen and bankers and the agricultural colleges began to woo the farmer, to make efforts to persuade him to take the businesslike view of himself that was warranted by the nature of his farm operations. "The object of farming," declared a writer in the *Cornell Countryman* in 1904, "is not primarily to make a living, but it is to make money. To this end it is to be conducted on the same business basis as any other producing industry."

The final change, which came only with a succession of changes in the twentieth century, wiped out the last traces of the yeoman of old, as the coming first of good roads and rural free delivery, and mail order catalogues, then the telephone, the automobile, and the tractor, and at length radio, movies, and television largely eliminated the difference between urban and rural experience in so many important areas of life. The city luxuries, once so derided by farmers, are now what they aspire to give to their wives and daughters.

In 1860 a farm journal satirized the imagined refinements and affectations of a city girl in the following picture:

> Slowly she rises from her couch. . . . Languidly she gains her feet, and oh! what vision of human perfection appears before us: Skinny, bony, sickly, hipless, thighless, formless, hairless, teethless. What a radiant belle! . . . The ceremony of enrobing commences. In goes the dentist's naturalization efforts; next the witching curls are fashioned to her "classically molded head." Then the womanly proportions are properly adjusted; hoops, bustles, and so forth, follow in succession, then a profuse quantity of whitewash, together with a "permanent rose tint" is applied to a sallow complexion; and lastly the "killing" wrapper is arranged on her systematical and matchless form.

But compare this with these beauty hints for farmers' wives from the *Idaho Farmer*, April, 1935:

> Hands should be soft enough to flatter the most delicate of the new fabrics. They must be carefully manicured, with none of the hot, brilliant shades of nail polish. The lighter and more delicate tones are in keeping with the spirit of freshness. Keep the tint of your fingertips friendly to the red of your lips, and check both your powder and your rouge to see that they best suit the tone of your skin in the bold light of summer.

Nothing can tell us with greater finality of the passing of the yeoman ideal than these light and delicate tones of nail polish.

Frontierswomen: Myths and Realities

Glenda Riley

As a woman visitor to the Iowa frontier once put it: "People as a general thing clothe the west with too much romance." For later generations, media representations of frontier life have fashioned an enhanced collective mythology regarding the national experience at, or beyond, the fringes of late nineteenth-century American "civilization." Subtly suggesting how one myth often shrouds several levels of reality, Professor Glenda Riley of Iowa State University challenges both sentimental historical portraits of life on the Middle Border, and its counter-mythology—that of the supposed drabness and loneliness of frontier life for women, and their alleged overwhelming fear and hatred of Indians. Noting the numerous "impediments to interpretation" inherent in telling the story of frontierswomen, and using source materials largely drawn from other than public records—letters, diaries and daybooks, memoirs, and various products of material culture—Professor Riley finds mostly short-lived the grievances of women against the often gray dailiness of life. Few frontierswomen were truly isolated, physically, culturally, or spiritually, for very long. Quilting, work events, literary societies, religious meetings, and a great variety of frontier social activities collectively facilitated community, mitigating the harsh impact of the frontier environment. Frontierswomen were especially enterprising in quickly mobilizing the activities and accoutrements of civilization. As for their fears of Indians, most representations are based on celebrated Indian "scares," or assumptions rooted in earlier, over-heated and dramatic captivity narratives. The truth is that such interaction was often fleeting at best, much more often congenial than distressful, and, for most frontier women or men, Indians were little more than stories or pictures in books—to the frontier mind and experience, already "ancient history" of sorts.

The underlying theme of this study has been an attempt to penetrate the myths and legends surrounding Iowa frontierswomen. A realistic and balanced picture of their daily lives emerges from the sources, but stereotypes are elusive amorphous concepts—difficult to dissect and even more troublesome to dispel. Rather than admit the less-than-colorful dailiness of frontierswomen's lives, twentieth-century Americans have found it easier to cling to the dramatic, sentimental portrayal of pioneer women presented by writers such as Hamlin Garland. Presenting his own mother's life on the Middle Border as a representative of pioneer women, he wrote that she was burdened with a "grinding weight of drudgery, enduring a life centered around a "rude little cabin" and desperate poverty. According to Garland, this pathetic woman followed her husband to each new homestead "without complaining word" in spite of the "bitter pangs of doubt and unrest which strike through the woman's heart when called upon to leave her snug, safe fire for a ruder cabin in a strange land."

Disclosing aspects of frontierswomen's lives, other than the brutal ones revealed by Garland, demands recognition that pioneer women are deserving of serious study. It also requires the collection and thorough examination of their source materials, although such use of women's resources is fraught with problems.

Because women customarily spent so much of their time in traditional roles behind hut or cabin walls, the source materials they left behind are usually of a personal, individualized nature. There is little in the way of public records, newspaper accounts, or census data directly related to women. What remains are the artifacts discarded by pioneer women—bits of material culture such as cream skimmers or candle molds. Such items are just beginning to be viewed as valuable tools by historians. If the historian is fortunate enough to resurrect some of the personal papers of frontierswomen, he or she may find that reading them objectively is an almost impossible task. Do letters from women on the frontier represent their true feelings about their makeshift homes, or were the letters intended to elicit sympathy, respect, or urge a move to the West by the home folks? Are reminiscences and memoirs reliable, or are they colored by the glow of passing time to a burnished hue that does not match reality? Did diaries and daybooks record anything of "note," or were they filled to the point of tedium with daily domestic routines—and if so, what does that in itself tell the historian about the writer's life?

As complex as these questions are, they represent only a superficial level of inquiry. One must also ask whether or not nineteenth-century frontierswomen accurately reflected upon their own lives or were they so accepting of a taxing social system that they were unaware and thus unable to adequately articulate the way they felt about the harshness and the limitations of their environment? Did women's running commentaries on the difficulty of men's tasks indicate that women had been socialized to think of their own labor as only supplementary? Or did women genuinely feel sympathetic with the demanding lot of their men?

In addition, frontiersmen's sources must be critically examined in relation to women's lives. Does the fact that men had little to say about women, children, and domestic affairs indicate their unconcern or disdain of them, or does it simply demonstrate that the culture pressured men to be more involved with the accepted "manly" pursuits of business and finance? Or does it only suggest that men were out of the home so much that they were not as cognizant of the nature of women's chores as women were of men's? It is known that at least some men seemed to recognize the crucial role of women's labor in subduing the frontier. At an old settlers' association meeting in Louisa County in 1860, one man noted that "Man has too long monopolized the entire attention of history and of the world. Men occupy themselves in celebrating and perpetuating the deeds and heroic action of men, while those of women are unmentioned and forgotten." But perhaps this was just a sop, for as another male "old settler" tellingly remarked to the women present, "Although not recognized as members of our organization, you are not forgotten."

Complicating these impediments to interpretation are the distorted media images of the last hundred years. Dime novels, newspapers, radio, and television have presented their audiences with the drama and color or the pathos and hardship that they expected of the West. The media representations of frontier life have become so institutionalized that they now form what one historian has called a "collective mythology." How does a scholar who has matured in a country steeped in such mythology discard it in order to enhance his or her own objectivity towards the western experience? Clearly, the questions arising from frontierswomen's source materials are legion and the answers few. Two characteristics of frontierswomen that have been assumed to be archetypal—debilitating loneliness an overwhelming fear of Indians—particularly prove to be at odds with reality. First, in considering the loneliness of frontierswomen, the generalized nature of a statement such as "Isolation and loneliness was the portion of the border woman," must be recognized. It, or a remark much like it, so frequently accompanies a sketch of frontierswomen that it has become trite. Indeed, woman after woman did lament the fact that she did not see another white woman for months at a time after migrating westward. Scores of women sorrowed endlessly over the loss of their friends and relatives; others spent many tearful hours as a result of their solitude.

Such complaints tell only part of the story. In Iowa such grievances were usually short-lived because most pioneers, desirous of companionship and the safety of numbers, settled loosely structured neighborhoods. One Iowa woman, Jessie Newcomb, admitted that "after the first two years things were not quite so bad." Even during her first year on the Iowa frontier another woman "did not feel the least lonely or homesick," and yet another cogently noted, "Not homesick much."

Towns, stage routes, and eventually railroads followed lines of settlement, so that few frontierspeople were truly isolated for very long. One woman described the rapidly changing landscape in Iowa before the Civil War.

> We saw the country change almost overnight, it seemed, from raw, unbroken prairie to a settled community with schools and churches. We saw the coming of the railroad, the building of roads and bridges, and the growth of a nearby county seat from a scraggly village to a thriving, up-to-date town with all the improvements of the city.

Another woman who arrived in Iowa in 1835 offered a similar observation: "The summer of 1837 we raised considerable grain, our health was good and we prospered finally." A decade later, she added the comment that "nothing of importance occurred save that the country was fast improving and settling up . . . all was peace and tranquility in our little home."

Since women were more likely to be tied to their homes, they were less likely than men to be affected by rapid changes in transportation and other technological advancements. Yet, many women managed to create domestic, women-centered activities to relieve their seclusion. Quiltings provided a combination social-work event. Other women organized farmers' wives' societies to create an "opportunity for discussing informally those things pertaining to the duties of a farmer's wife, and a relief from the routine and monotony of such a life." And others formed literary societies to add sociability to their lives while "improving" their minds at the same time. Social activities provided a focal point for many women. Mary J. Mason, daughter of Chief Justice Charles Mason, frequently attended the many balls, circuses, and masquerades held in her home city of Burlington. Virginia Ivins of Keokuk retained pleasant memories of sleighing on the river ice, parties in elegant homes, and dancing "the night away" at fancy dress balls. Even many country women were not necessarily cut off from society. One of these rural women recalled,

> For years after moving to the country I still took part in various activities in town. I often drove to Lue's [her sister] and to my parents' home. In fact I was away in the afternoon almost daily. Marion [her husband] always inquired at noon if I had plans to go. If so, he harnessed a horse and left it hitched to buggy all ready for me.

Another rural woman believed that social life in her area was actually fostered by the slow pace of country living. People "took time for all day visits and the few social gatherings were all the more enjoyed for being held so seldom." She added that in one sense even the difficulties of frontier life aided the pioneers' social interaction for the "hardships they endured together bound them with ties of sympathy and understanding."

Religion formed the basis for social cohesion in many pioneer communities. Camp meetings were well attended, drawing people who pitched tents and remained as long as two or three weeks to participate in the various activities. Formal churches were organized very rapidly in most areas. Congregations first met in the local schoolhouse and later erected a simple log structure shared by several denominations until each could afford its own individual building. Churches sponsored "socials" which involved both good fellowship and bounteous food. They also supported Sunday schools, prayer meetings, singing schools, and musical groups, all of which were regularly attended by the congregation. Wedding ceremonies were often accompanied by a celebration or a raucous charivari which "enlivened the neighborhood until morning" with the noise of "cow-bells, whistles, horse-fiddles, and drumming on tin pans."

Other social gatherings revolved around the settlers' own homes. Log-rollings to clear the land, house-raisings to build a dwelling, and house-warmings to celebrate a home's completion all called for feasting, dancing, and games. Cards, checkers, song-fests, or a Saturday night dance in someone's cabin to the music of the local fiddler also brought friends and neighbors together. And affairs such as apple-parings, husking bees, and harvest days, although demanding women's labor in preparing meals and other refreshments, "gave the farmer's wife an opportunity to exchange ideas with her neighbors, gave her a change of surroundings and scenes and an opportunity to form lifelong friendships."

Christmas was another time of festivity for Iowa pioneers. Although the presents were frequently as simple as a pair of handmade wristlets, frontier people appreciated the day of leisure to share some time with their families as well as to enjoy the inevitable feast. As Matilda Peitzke Paul portrayed the pioneers' Christmas,

> The pioneer enjoyed life much better and had many more good times than people do now and were so much more appreciative than now. Christmas was always a day of great joy. We always got one present which cost from five to ten cents also got a little candy and an apple.

For many years Paul treasured "a little tin pail about the size of a ½ pint cup" which she received one Christmas. "It was painted green," she recalled, "with the word Girl painted on it in yellow. . . . I can still feel the joy I had when I looked at it and to know it was mine."

The Fourth of July was another recognized occasion for conviviality. For some Iowans it meant an elaborate dinner and ball, such as the one held at the Roe House in Fort Madison in 1859. For others it signified impromptu toasts, local orators, singing, and colorful parades. For still others, it brought lemonade, firecrackers, and horse racing. For the very lucky, the Fourth was sometimes even attended by "Fire Works! Fire Works! Confectionary, Nuts, Cigars, and everything else with which to Celebrate the Glorious 4th of July." But for most pioneers, the Fourth was probably much like the one described by a young German woman:

> Father took us to the grove where the crowd was gathered to hear the Declaration of Independence read, band music played, and "My Country Tis of Thee" sung. Then we had a fine lunch from the basket we carried with us and mother and I stayed in the grove and visited with some German women while father took Anna [her sister] to a dance pavilion.

As the Iowa frontier became more settled, a variety of professional entertainments appeared to augment social events and festivities. In 1885, a new dancing school opened in Burlington offering instruction in popular dances such as quadrilles, waltzes, and fancy dances including the Hornpipe and Highland Fling. Later that same year in Burlington a "Grand Balloon Ascension and Exhibition of Fire Works" was accompanied by a contest of "Female Equestrianship."

One of the more exotic amusements was the circus. Many circuses ventured across the Mississippi River into Iowa in the mid-1850s. For fifty cents for a box seat or twenty-five cents for a "pit" seat, one could view the "Grand Olympic Arena and North American Circus" in Davenport in 1855. It was shortly followed by another circus in Burlington, which offered "The Unrivalled Female Equestrian" as its leading attraction. Within the year another circus appeared in Burlington with an Indian exhibition. By the early 1860s, Waterloo was the scene of a "multicerial Combination Circus! And Homohippocal Amphitheatre!" which featured "Madamoiselle Ida—The Fairy Equestrianne." A few years later a Fairfield circus promised "A Magnificent Array of Unparalleled Novelties," and another advertised a display of "Wild Animals and Rare Birds." By 1868, "Yankee Robinson's Consolidated Shows" attempted to outdazzle all its competitors with a "Mass Meeting of all the Rare Specimens of Zoology from both Hemispheres" combined with a "Ballet of Beautiful Ladies, and Other Artistes, which will Completely Revolutionize the Programme."

After Matilda Peitzke Paul attended one of these traveling circuses in Riceville in 1868, she characterized it as "one great event." She and her brothers and sisters almost missed the main show since they lacked the money to buy tickets, but when they hung around the doorway longingly, a kind door-tender invited them inside to see the show. She declared that they "felt well repaid for our trip by seeing an elephant, camel, bear and monkey," all admittedly rather strange sights to early Iowans.

Elaborate and splashy shows on the Iowa prairie during the mid-nineteenth century were welcome entertainments, but some pioneers cherished fonder memories of homey pursuits such as spelling bees or lyceums at the local school. Camaraderie among neighbors and family was a continuing source of contentment. As one woman said, "Sometimes I had to make a bed in the kitchen when company stayed overnight, but although we were crowded, we were all well and happy so it didn't make much difference." Other Iowans thought family times were the best. "There was nothing," one Iowa woman wrote, "which gave us more joy than the long winter evenings when we would all gather around the fire—

mother knitting, father reading aloud, and we children cracking nuts."

When Frances Dana Gage visited Iowa in 1854 she surveyed the situation of frontierswomen and quickly dismissed any notions about their being downcast due to isolation. "Not one—not one desponding wife or mother did we find," she reported, "not one willing to go back and live in the old States." A resident of the state confirmed Gage's assessment, writing to her husband's family in 1856:

> I have not been homesick or felt so awfully as I have heard folks tell of who come out here people as a general thing clothe the west with to much romance I take it its not all gold that shines anywhere I thought this was the best place for a poor man to get a living with nothing but his hands to help himself with and I think so now. I can't say I like the west as well as I do New England yet I think it is better for me to be here.

It appears, then, that feelings of isolation and loneliness are relative. If some of us record that we are lonely in our high-rise, industrialized, technological world of the 1980s, will historians someday praise our fortitude in surviving such a harsh world, or will they pity us our cruel situation? And if they should take either of these positions, would they be accurate in their interpretation? Clearly, they would face the same problems that today's historians confront in attempting to assess the position of the nineteenth-century frontierswomen. Pinpointing the tenor and character of frontierswomen's attitudes toward Native Americans is as elusive as judging their degree of loneliness. The myth is that white women feared and hated Native Americans; that they were raped and carried off by Native Americans in vast numbers; and that they always chose to return to their homes rather than to remain with their captors.

Convictions like these were originally presented to an already prejudiced American public by means of captivity narratives. These were usually based on fact, laced rather liberally with fiction, and sold for profit to an audience thirsty for what Roy H. Pearce calls "penny dreadfuls." They almost always involve the odyssey of a courageous soul torn from civilization who prevails over primitive evil and is eventually restored once again to civilization. In women's captivity narratives, the odyssey is translated into a saga of abduction, rape, and escape; a thrilling story that was meant to titillate Americans of the nineteenth century while venting their hatred of Native Americans.

Here again, the few scholars who have looked beyond captivity narratives have unearthed significant, but seemingly contradictory, views of Native Americans by white women. One scholar argues that white women were socialized by nineteenth-century civilization into seeing Indians as primitive, savage, and dirty. Because society relegated women to the position of "civilizers" they had no choice but to visualize Native Americans as "representative of an alien and depraved culture, decidedly inferior to their own." As guardians of public morality, women were given to understand one basic fact before they left their eastern homes—"The American Indian is a savage." Once on the frontier, women described the Native Americans they encountered as filthy, foolish, degraded; in all ways a "symbol of defeat and failure," the antithesis of the white female, who embodied progress and success.

Researcher Dawn L. Gherman maintained that all white women did *not* see themselves as civilizers and Native Americans as primitive savages. To the contrary, she believed that many women actually had a streak of "wildness" in their makeup which caused them to occasionally long for the natural, the free, and the unrestrained qualities which they perceived in the lives of Native Americans. If indeed she was on the right track in her assertion that some women fantasized themselves as "white squaws," it might be a threatening concept for many Americans to consider, given their anti-Indian attitude.

As with the traditions regarding the loneliness of women on the frontier, such intricacies of interpretation exist that frontierswomen's true feelings towards Native Americans are difficult to detect. In Iowa, only hints are present as to the day-to-day working relationship between white settlers and indigenous peoples. It is true that there were some actual outbreaks of violence when Indian groups attempted to resist white encroachment on their lands. Black Hawk is famous, or infamous, depending on one's perspective, for leading his people in an ill-fated resistance movement against the whites in 1831. The Sauk and the Fox, pressured by their restriction to a small land area, carried on internecine warfare in the 1840s which not only diminished their own numbers, but also largely destroyed the peaceful Winnebago who were placed on the so-called neutral ground between them. And the starving Wahpeton Sioux will long be remembered for their depredation of the white settlement at Spirit Lake in 1857.

But more illuminating are the numerous occasions on which white Iowans panicked as a result of unfounded rumors of Indian attacks. Although the area was actually cleared of its native inhabitants rapidly and with little trouble to the whites, the settlers still harbored inordinate fears of uprisings. Fort Dodge was closed in 1853 after only three quiet years of protecting settlers from Indians, yet frequent alarms were still sounded in the region. Author Ruth S. Beitz points out that "reports of some Indian attacks were greatly exaggerated, but the danger seemed real enough to send the settlers scurrying into stoutly built homes for protection." In another western county in the mid-1850s, the appearance of two hungry Cherokee caused an all-night guard to be posted, the members of which almost shot a wandering cow in their panic.

After the much-publicized "massacre" at Spirit Lake, rumors increased in frequency and intensity. Beitz reported that in 1857 "the rumor that a band of warlike red men was coming caused some families . . . to drive from Ida Grove to take shelter at Benjamin Dobson's and Mason's Grove, where they 'forted up.' " In 1858, other false reports spurred the formation of the Iowa Frontier Guard in Iowa's lake region.

On hearing of the New Ulm, Minnesota, clash between white settlers and displaced Indians in 1862, northwestern Iowa reached a fever pitch of excitement and fear. Federal aid was granted, troops were sent, and blockhouses such as Fort Defiance were built in response to the settlers' demands for protection from the supposedly impending attacks. The building of a Sioux City fort, hastily begun on the strength of a scare story, was discontinued when no attack materialized. The stockade, never completed, was finally sold as building timbers and firewood.

Iowans were also quick to abandon their homes in the face of hysterical reports. In April 1857, a group of families left their homes on the Little Sioux River when one of their number told them that "Indians are up on the Des Moines River and are going to come down to kill us." After camping out overnight, they went on to Sac City where they sent out spies "to see

if there were any Indians around." Sighting no Indians, they finally realized that they had deserted their homes for no reason. In 1858, a group of Webster City settlers similarly fled their homes:

> With the terror of the Spirit Lake massacre vividly in mind mother and we children hastily grabbed a few belongings, packed a basket of food, and father took us in the wagon to Webster City. From there a regular train of wagons, loaded mostly with women and children, started for Boonesboro. Father returned to our home, determined to defend it.

When the party was compelled to stop for the night, they formed their wagons into a circle, built a fire, and "everybody sat up and talked all night." By the following morning "messengers came bearing the good news that the alarm was false, and so the whole company turned around and reached home that night, tired but safe."

These unfounded rumors continued well into the 1870s. When one Pennsylvania family moved to Webster City in 1875 they did so with trepidation. Because of the stories they had heard about Indian raids in Iowa, they determined that three hollow logs would be placed in their front yard, one to hide each member of the family. About the same time, a young man in the Ackley area roused his sleeping neighbors with the cry, "Wild Indians." The next morning it was discovered that the "Indians" were in truth only a hired man carrying a huge featherbed through the late night shadows.

Beyond the apparent fright, other reactions of Iowa pioneer women to Native Americans during Iowa's frontier years are difficult to ascertain. Discounting popularized accounts such as Abbie Gardner-Sharp's *The Spirit Lake Massacre and the Captivity of Miss Abbie Gardner*, women's remarks about Native Americans are fragmentary, yet their general tone is revealing.

Caroline Phelps, a newly married young woman who moved to southeastern Iowa in the 1830s with her husband in order to trade with the Indians, frequently complained that many of them drank to excess. She did not mention that they were violent towards whites when drunk, but only that they were aggravating and troublesome. Although they would sometimes "fight wretchedly" among themselves when drinking, Phelps wrote, "I never was very much afraid of them." On the other hand, Phelps also took note of the many Indian women who befriended her; the Indian doctor who treated her young daughter; the Indian ceremonies, dances, and parades which she attended; and the grief her family felt when their Indian helper was killed in an accident. On his death, she wrote,

> We felt his loss very much, my children cryed for poor John as we called him, as much as though he had been a relative. He was their friend truly they missed his singing, he used to fix a drum and then sing and drum and have them and the little papooses dance.

When Phelps found certain aspects of Native American culture distasteful, she seemed to deal with them in a stoic manner. At one point she found the odor disagreeable around her home because it was near an Indian burial site which had corpses placed upon the ground. "One day we was eating dinner," she recalled, "our doors all open and in came our big dog with a dead indians arm and a hand, right into the house, I took the tongs to take it back to where it belonged." Another time, she sheltered some Indian children until their drunken parents were sober enough to resume cooking and caring for them.

Unlike Phelps, most Iowa women had only brief dealings with their Native American neighbors. A Rodman woman in the mid-1840s said that she could remember groups of them traveling through and camping in the region, but never causing the settlers any difficulty. A Marshall County woman in the late 1840s had a somewhat more detailed story to recount. She and her husband traded food and incidentals regularly with local Indians, one of whom physically attacked her husband over a trade disagreement. Although the altercation ended with little serious damage to either party, she felt rather depressed about the incident until a large group of his people came to her cabin to apologize for his behavior. According to her, "they spoke very indignantly of the Indian who had so badly misused us, and said he was a bad Indian, and often quarreled and fought with his own people." Her recollection was that "most of them treated us kindly as long as they stayed there" in spite of several other quarrels between her family and the tribespeople.

Several women had personal interchanges with Iowa Indians. One received a proposal of marriage from the son of a "powerful Indian chieftain," who in her words, "was willing to give up his wickiup and adopt the ways of a white man if necessary, to win his suit." A relative of hers related another turn of events involving a young woman named Viola who

> . . . used to play with a little Indian girl who asked her to stay for supper one day. She was going to until the old Indian Grandmother heard about it and got up and went over to the pot of food cooking on the stove—lifted the lid and spit in it! Viola ran out the door and didn't stop until she got home! She never asked to eat there again!

During the 1860s a young German woman watched Indians roam the woods around her family's home and camp in tents in the fields between settlers' houses. She was pleased when her Aunt Liz "would come and take us to this Indian village and the squaws gave us beads which we treasured greatly." She also remembered "a very nice Indian" who visited her family and "spoke English very well." Another of her memories centered on "a young buck" who would follow her and other family members in the cornfield as they harvested corn and would amuse them by singing to them in a "monotone" and "rather weird" way.

By the 1870s and 1880s, Native Americans were no more than stories or pictures in books for many Iowa women. One in particular remembered her grandmother's likeness of Black Hawk, a figure that to her seemed to belong to "ancient history." She was amazed that there were still a few people living in Burlington "who had actually seen him in the flesh." She mused, "It makes me realize how immature is our American civilization when I think that, although I, myself, never saw an Indian in my childhood except under a circus tent, there were residents of my home town who had known Iowa when only the so-called savages lived there."

*   *   *

Clearly, the comments cited by early Iowa women belie the usual representation of frontierswomen as perpetual enemies of Native Americans. Certainly some women were negative in their views. As one stated, although she "had no neighbors nor company save a straggling land hunter, or the native Indians, the latter were seldom if ever very welcome visitors" as far as she was concerned. Yet other women demonstrated a more balanced perspective. One woman who migrated to Iowa in 1854 and survived many Indian "scares," commented simply, "Have seen a great many Indians and they used to dance their war dance in our house, but they never offered to harm us in any way."

The examination of these two assumed traits of frontierswomen—loneliness and fear of Native Americans—demonstrates that for every one myth about women, there are several levels of reality. By testing the myths against the conditions of one specific frontier, in this case the Iowa frontier, it is apparent that there are many perceptions of frontierswomen's reality. Despite the usual interpretations of their lives, they did not all resist the westward trek, suffer on the trail, and harbor bitterness against their menfolk. They did not all wither in body and spirit in the demanding surroundings they encountered. They did not all feel exploited by the huge amounts of time and energy required to subdue the prairie. Rather, many frontierswomen looked with favor upon the idea of a western relocation, triumphed over the many challenges presented by the new environment, and prevailed over the additional difficulties imposed by wartime conditions or separation from established homes. Their reactions were as varied as the women themselves. As this study demonstrates, the Iowa frontier evoked a wide range of reactions from frontierswomen rather than generalized, stereotypical ones. To fully understand the lives, concerns, and emotions of frontierswomen, the serious student must continually raise the question, where does myth end and reality begin?

Ten-Gallon Hero: The Myth of the Cowboy

David Brion Davis

The cowboy as folk hero, the product of commercial convention and psychological need, has enjoyed sustained vitality in American mythology since the end of the nineteenth century. The haunting nostalgia the cowboy elicits, so David Brion Davis of Yale University argues, is a synthesis of two American traditions—the myth of the Western scout and that of the antebellum South. Davis' analysis is drawn in part from a novel Owen Wister published in 1902, *The Virginian*. The portrait of the cowboy-hero has been incompletely drawn, and he therefore represents in many ways an essentially false tradition. But he is perhaps among the least obnoxious of folk heroes.

In 1900 it seemed that the significance of the cowboy era would decline along with other brief but romantic episodes in American history. The Long Drive lingered only in the memories and imaginations of old cowhands. The "hoemen" occupied former range land while Mennonites and professional dry farmers had sown their Turkey Red winter wheat on the Kansas prairies. To be sure, a cattle industry still flourished, but the cowboy was more like an employee of a corporation than the free-lance cowboy of old. The myth of the cowboy lived on in the Beadle and Adams paperback novels, with the followers of Ned Buntline and the prolific Colonel Prentiss Ingraham. But this seemed merely a substitution of the more up-to-date cowboy in a tradition which began with Leatherstocking and Daniel Boone. If the mountain man had replaced Boone and the forest scouts, if the cowboy had succeeded the mountain man, and if the legends of Mike Fink and Crockett were slipping into the past, it would seem probable that the cowboy would follow, to become a quaint character of antiquity, overshadowed by newer heroes.

Yet more than a half-century after the passing of the actual wild and woolly cowboy, we find a unique phenomenon in American mythology.

Gaudy-covered Western or cowboy magazines decorate stands, windows, and shelves in "drug" stores, bookstores, grocery stores and supermarkets from Miami to Seattle. Hundreds of cowboy movies and television shows are watched and lived through by millions of Americans. Nearly every little boy demands a cowboy suit and a Western six-shooter cap pistol. Cowboys gaze out at you with steely eye and cocked revolver from cereal packages and television screens. Jukeboxes in Bennington, Vermont, as well as Globe, Arizona, moan and warble the latest cowboy songs. Middle-age folk who had once thought of William S. Hart, Harry Carey, and Tom Mix as a passing phase, have lived to see several Hopalong Cassidy revivals, the Lone Ranger, Tim McCoy, Gene Autry, and Roy Rogers. Adolescents and even grown men in Maine and Florida can be seen affecting cowboy, or at least modified cowboy garb, while in the new airplane plants in Kansas, workers don their cowboy boots and wide-brimmed hats, go to work whistling a cowboy song, and are defiantly proud that they live in the land of lassos and six-guns.

When recognized at all, this remarkable cowboy complex is usually defined as the distortion of once-colorful legends by a commercial society. The obvious divergence between the real West and the idealized version, the standardization of plot and characters, and the ridiculous incongruities of cowboys with automobiles and airplanes, all go to substantiate this conclusion.

However, there is more than the cowboy costume and stage setting in even the wildest of these adventures. Despite the incongruities, the cowboy myth exists in fact, and as such is probably a more influential social force than the actual cowboy ever was. It provides the framework for an expression of common ideals of morality and behavior. And while a commercial success, the hero cowboy must satisfy some basic want in American culture, or there could never be such a tremendous market. It is true that the market has been exploited by magazine, song, and scenario writers, but it is important to ask why similar myths have not been equally profitable, such as the lumbermen of the early northwest, the whale fishermen of New Bedford, the early railroad builders, or the fur traders. There have been romances written and movies produced idealizing these phases of American history, but little boys do not dress up like Paul Bunyan and you do not see harpooners on cereal packages. Yet America has had many episodes fully as colorful and of longer duration than the actual cowboy era.

The cowboy hero and his setting are a unique synthesis of two American traditions, and echoes of this past can be discerned in even the wildest of the modern horse operas. On the one hand, the line of descent is a direct evolution from the Western scout of Cooper and the Dime Novel; on the other, there has been a recasting of the golden myth of the antebellum South. The two were fused sometime in the 1880's. Perhaps there was actually some basis for such a union. While the West was economically tied to the North as soon as the early canals and railroads broke the river-centered traffic, social ties endured longer. Many Southerners emigrated West and went into the cattle business, and of course, the Long Drive originated in Texas. The literary synthesis of two traditions only followed the two social movements. It was on the Great Plains that the descendants of Daniel Boone met the drawling Texas cowboy.

Henry Nash Smith has described two paradoxical aspects of the legendary Western scout, typified in Boone himself. This woodsman, this buckskin-clad wilderness hunter is a pioneer, breaking trails for his countrymen to follow, reducing the savage wilderness for civilization. Nevertheless, he is also represented as escaping civilization, turning his back on the petty materialism of the world, on the hypocritical and self-conscious manners of community life, and seeking the unsullied, true values of nature.

These seemingly conflicting points of view have counterparts in the woodsman's descendant, the cowboy. The ideal cowboy fights for justice, risks his life to make the dismal little cowtown safe for law-abiding, respectable citizens, but in so doing he destroys the very environment which made him a heroic figure. This paradox is common with all ideals, and the cowboy legend is certainly the embodiment of a social ideal. Thus the minister or social reformer who rises to heroism in his fight against a sin-infested community would logically become a mere figurehead once the community is reformed. There can be no true ideal or hero in a utopia. And the civilization for which the cowboy or trailblazer struggles is utopian in character.

But there is a further consideration in the case of the cowboy. In our mythology, the cowboy era is timeless. The ranch may own a modern station wagon, but the distinguishing attributes of cowboy and environment remain. There is, it is true, a nostalgic sense that this is the last great drama, a sad knowledge that the cowboy is passing and that civilization is approaching. But it never comes. This strange, wistful sense of the coming end of an epoch is not something outside our experience. It is a faithful reflection of the sense of approaching adulthood. The appeal of the cowboy, in this sense, is similar to the appeal of Boone, Leatherstocking, and the later Mountain Man. We know that adulthood, civilization, is inevitable, but we are living toward the end of childhood, and at that point "childness" seems eternal; it is a whole lifetime. But suddenly we find it is not eternal, the forests disappear, the mountains are settled, and we have new responsibilities. When we shut our eyes and try to remember, the last image of a carefree life appears. For the nation, this last image is the cowboy.

The reborn myth of the antebellum South also involves nostalgia; not so much nostalgia for something that actually existed as for dreams and ideals. When the Southern myth reappeared on the rolling prairies, it was purified and regenerated by the casting off of apologies for slavery. It could focus all energies on its former rôle of opposing the peculiar social and economic philosophy of the Northeast. This took the form of something more fundamental than mere agrarianism or primitivism. Asserting the importance of values beyond the utilitarian and material, this transplanted Southern philosophy challenged the doctrine of enlightened self-interest and the belief that leisure time is sin.

Like the barons and knights of Southern feudalism, the large ranch owners and itinerant cowboys knew how to have a good time. If there was a time for work, there was a time for play, and the early rodeos, horse races, and wild nights at a cowtown were not occasions for reserve. In this respect, the cowboy West was more in the tradition of fun-loving New Orleans than of the Northeast. Furthermore, the ranch was a remarkable duplication of the plantation, minus slaves. It was a hospitable social unit, where travelers were welcome even when the owner was absent. As opposed to the hard-working, thrifty, and sober ideal of the East, the actual cowboy was overly cheerful at times, generous to the point of waste, and inclined to value friendly comradeship above prestige.

The mythical New England Yankee developed a code of action which always triumphed over the more sophisticated city slicker, because the Yankee's down-to-earth shrewdness, common sense, and reserved humor embodied values which Americans considered as pragmatically effective. The ideal cowboy also had a code of action, but it involved neither material nor social success. The cowboy avoided actions which "just weren't done" because he placed a value on doing things "right," on managing difficult problems and situations with ease, skill, and modesty. The cowboy's code was a Western and democratic version of the Southern gentleman's "honor."

In the early years of the twentieth century, a Philadelphia lawyer, who affected a careless, loose-tied bow instead of the traditional black ribbon and who liked to appear in his shirt-sleeves, wrote: "The nomadic bachelor west is over, the housed, married west is established." In a book published in 1902 he had, more than any other man, established an idealized version of the former, unifying the Southern and Western hero myths in a formula which was not to be forgotten. Owen Wister had, in fact, liberated the cowboy hero from the Dime Novels and provided a synthetic tradition suitable for a new century. *The Virginian* became a key document in popular American culture, a romance which defined the cowboy character and thus the ideal American character in terms of courage, sex, religion, and humor. The novel

served as a model for hundreds of Western books and movies for half a century. In the recent popular movie "High Noon" a Hollywood star, who won his fame dramatizing Wister's novel, reenacted the same basic plot of hero rejecting heroine's pleas and threats, to uphold his honor against the villain Trampas. While this theme is probably at least a thousand years old, it was Owen Wister who gave it a specifically American content and thus explicated and popularized the modern cowboy ideal, with its traditions, informality, and all-important code.

Of course, Wister's West is not the realistic, boisterous, sometimes monotonous West of Charlie Siringo and Andy Adams. The cowboy, after all, drove cattle. He worked. There was much loneliness and monotony on the range, which has faded like mist under a desert sun in the reminiscences of old cowhands and the fiction of idealizers. Owen Wister's Virginian runs some errands now and then, but there are no cattle-driving scenes, no monotony, no hard work. Fictional cowboys are never bored. Real cowboys were often so bored that they memorized the labels on tin cans and then played games to see how well they could recite them. The cowboys in books and movies are far too busy making love and chasing bandits to work at such a dreary task as driving cattle. But then the Southern plantation owner did no work. The befringed hero of the forests did not work. And if any ideal is to be accepted by adolescent America, monotonous work must be subordinated to more exciting pastimes. The fact that the cowboy hero has more important things to do is only in keeping with his tradition and audience. He is only a natural reaction against a civilization which demands increasingly monotonous work, against the approaching adulthood when playtime ends.

And if the cowboy romance banishes work and monotony, their very opposite are found in the immensity of the Western environment. To be sure, the deserts and prairies can be bleak, but they are never dull when used as setting for the cowboy myth. There is always an element of the unexpected, of surprise, of variety. The tremendous distances either seclude or elevate the particular and significant. There are mirages, hidden springs, dust storms, hidden identities, and secret ranches. In one of his early Western novels William MacLeod Raine used both devices of a secret ranch and hidden identity, while Hoffman Birney combined a hidden ranch, a secret trail, and two hidden identities. In such an environment of uncertainty and change men of true genius stand out from the rest. The evil or good in an individual is quickly revealed in cowboy land. A man familiar with the actual cowboy wrote that "brains, moral and physical courage, strength of character, native gentlemanliness, proficiency in riding or shooting—every quality of leadership tended to raise its owner from the common level."

The hazing which cowboys gave the tenderfoot was only preliminary. It was a symbol of the true test which anyone must undergo in the West. After the final winnowing of men, there emerge the heroes, the villains, and the clowns. The latter live in a purgatory and usually attach themselves to the hero group. Often, after stress of an extreme emergency, they burst out of their caste and are accepted in the elite.

While the Western environment, according to the myth, sorts men into their true places, it does not determine men. It brings out the best in heroes and the worst in villains, but it does not add qualities to the man who has none. The cowboy is a superman and is adorable for his own sake. It is here that he is the descendant of supernatural folk heroes. Harry Hawkeye, the creator of an early cowboy hero, Calvin Yancey, described him as:

. . . straight as an arrow, fair and ruddy as a Viking, with long, flowing golden hair, which rippled over his massive shoulders, falling nearly at his waist; a high, broad forehead beneath which sparkled a pair of violet blue eyes, tender and soulful in repose, but firm and determined under excitement. His entire face was a study for a sculptor with its delicate aquiline nose, straight in outline as though chiselled from Parian marble, and its generous manly mouth, with full crimson and arched lips, surmounted by a long, silken blonde mustache, through which a beautiful set of even white teeth gleamed like rows of lustrous pearls.

While the Virginian is not quite the blond, Nordic hero, he is just as beautiful to behold. His black, curly locks, his lean, athletic figure, his quiet, unassuming manner, all go to make the most physically attractive man Owen Wister could describe. Later cowboy heroes have shaved their mustaches, but the great majority have beautiful curly hair, usually blond or red, square jaws, cleft chins, broad shoulders, deep chests, and wasp-like waists. Like the Virginian, they are perfect men, absolutely incapable of doing the wrong thing unless deceived.

Many writers familiar with the real cowboy have criticized Wister for his concentration on the Virginian's love interest and, of course, they deplore the present degeneration of the cowboy plot, where love is supreme. There were few women in the West in the Chisholm Trail days and those few in Dodge City, Abilene, and Wichita were of dubious morality. The cowboy's sex life was intermittent, to say the least. He had to carry his thirst long distances, like a camel, and in the oases the orgies were hardly on a spiritual plane. Since earlier heroes, like the woodsman, led celibate lives, it is important to ask why the cowboy depends on love interest.

At first glance, there would seem to be an inconsistency here. The cowboy is happiest with a group of buddies, playing poker, chasing horse thieves, riding in masculine company. He is contemptuous of farmers, has no interest in children, and considers men who have lived among women as effete. Usually he left his own family at a tender age and rebelled against the restrictions of mothers and older sisters. Neither the Virginian nor the actual cowboys were family men, nor did they have much interest in the homes they left behind. Thus it would seem that courting a young schoolteacher from Vermont would be self-destruction. At no place is the idealized cowboy further from reality than in his love for the tender woman from the East. Like the law and order he fights for, she will destroy his way of life.

But this paradox is solved when one considers the hero cowboy, not the plot, as the center of all attention. Molly Wood in *The Virginian*, like all her successors, is a literary device, a *dea ex machina* with a special purpose. Along with the Western environment, she serves to throw a stronger light on the hero, to make him stand out in relief, to complete the picture of an ideal. In the first place, she brings out qualities in him which we could not see otherwise. Without her, he would be too much the brute for a real folk hero, at least in a modern age. If Molly Wood were not in *The Virginian*, the hero might seem too raucous, too wild. Of course, his affair with a blonde in town is handled genteelly; his boyish pranks such as mixing up the babies at the party are treated as good, clean fun. But still, there is nothing to bring out his qualities of masculine tenderness, there is nothing to show his conscience until Molly Wood arrives. A cowboy's tenderness is usually revealed through his kindness to horses, and in this sense, the Eastern belle's rôle is that of a glorified horse. A woman in the Western drama is somebody to rescue, somebody to protect. In her presence, the cowboy shows that, in his own way, he is a cultural ideal. The nomadic, bachelor cowboys described by Andy Adams and Charles Siringo are a little too masculine, a little too isolated from civilization to become the ideal for a settled community.

While the Western heroine brings out a new aspect of the cowboy's character, she also serves the external purpose of registering our attitudes toward him. The cowboy is an adorable figure and the heroine is the vehicle of adoration. Female characters enable the author to make observations about cowboys which would be impossible with an all-male cast. This rôle would lose its value if the heroine surrendered to the cowboy immediately. So the more she struggles with herself, the more she conquers her Eastern reservations and surmounts difficulties before capitulating, the more it enhances the hero.

Again, *The Virginian* is the perfect example. We do not meet Molly Wood in the first part of the book. Instead, the author, the I, who is an Easterner, goes to Wyoming and meets the Virginian. It is love at first sight, not in the sexual sense, of course (this was 1902), but there is no mistaking it for anything other than love. This young man's love for the Virginian is not important itself; it heightens our worship of the hero. The sex of the worshiper is irrelevant. At first the young man is disconsolate, because he cannot win the Virginian's friendship. He must go through the ordeal of not knowing the Virginian's opinion of him. But as he learns the ways of the West, the Virginian's sublime goodness is unveiled. Though increasing knowledge of the hero's character only serves to widen the impossible gulf between the finite Easterner and the infinite, pure virtue of the cowboy, the latter, out of his own free grace and goodness recognizes the lowly visitor, who adores him all the more for it. But this little episode is only a preface, a symbol of the drama to come. As soon as the Virginian bestows his grace on the male adorer, Molly Wood arrives. The same passion is reenacted, though on a much larger frame. In this rôle, the sex of Molly *is* important, and the traditional romance plot is only superficial form. Molly's coyness, her reserve, her involved heritage of Vermont tradition, all go to build an insurmountable barrier. Yet she loves the Virginian. And Owen Wister and his audience love the Virginian through Molly Wood's love. With the male adorer, they had gone about as far as they could go. But Molly offers a new height from which to love the Virginian. There are many exciting

possibilities. Molly can save his life and nurse him back to health. She can threaten to break off their wedding if he goes out to fight his rival, and then forgive him when he disobeys her plea. The Virginian marries Molly in the end and most of his descendants either marry or are about to marry their lovely ladies. But this does not mean a physical marriage, children, and a home. That would be building up a hero only to destroy him. The love climax at the end of the cowboy drama raises the hero to a supreme height, the audience achieves an emotional union with its ideal. In the next book or movie the cowboy will be the carefree bachelor again.

The classic hero, Hopalong Cassidy, has saved hundreds of heroines, protected them, and has been adored by them. But in 1910 Hopalong, "remembering a former experience of his own, smiled in knowing cynicism when told that he again would fall under the feminine spell." In 1950 he expressed the same resistance to actual marriage:

> "But you can't always move on, Hoppy!" Lenny protested. "Someday you must settle down! Don't you ever think of marriage?" "Uh-huh, and whenever I think of it I saddle Topper and ride. I'm not a marrying man, Lenny. Sometimes I get to thinkin' about that poem a feller wrote, about how a woman is only a woman but—" "The open road is my Fate!" she finished. "That's it. But can you imagine any woman raised outside a tepee livin' in the same house with a restless man?"

The cowboy hero is the hero of the pre-adolescent, either chronologically or mentally. It is the stage of revolt against femininity and feminine standards. It is also the age of hero worship. If the cowboy romance were sexual, if it implied settling down with a real *girl*, there would be little interest. One recent cowboy hero summarized this attitude in terms which should appeal strongly to any ten-year-old: "I'd as soon fight a she-lion barehanded as have any truck with a gal." The usual cowboy movie idol has about as much social presence in front of the leading lady as a very bashful boy. He is most certainly not the lover-type. That makes him lovable to both male and female Americans. There can be no doubt that Owen Wister identified himself, not with the Virginian, but with Molly Wood.

While some glorifiers of the actual cowboy have maintained that his closeness to nature made him a deeply religious being, thus echoing the devoutness of the earlier woodsman hero who found God in nature, this tradition has never carried over to the heroic cowboy. Undoubtedly some of the real cowboys were religious, though the consensus of most of the writers on the subject seems to indicate that indifference was more common. Intellectualized religion obviously had no appeal and though the cowboy was often deeply sentimental, he did not seem prone to the emotional and frenzied religion of backwoods farmers and squatters. Perhaps his freedom from family conflicts, from smoldering hatreds and entangled jealousies and loves, had something to do with this. Despite the hard work, the violent physical conflicts, and the occasional debaucheries, the cowboy's life must have had a certain innocent, Homeric quality. Even when witnessing a lynching or murder, the cowboy must have felt further removed from total depravity or original sin than the farmer in a squalid frontier town, with his nagging wife and thirteen children.

At any rate, the cowboy hero of our mythology is too much of a god himself to feel humility. His very creation is a denial of any kind of sin. The cowboy is an enunciation of the goodness of man and the glory which he can achieve by himself. The Western environment strips off the artifice, the social veneer, and instead of a cringing sinner, we behold a dazzling superman. He is a figure of friendly justice, full of self-reliance, a very tower of strength. What need has he of a god?

Of course, the cowboy is not positively anti-religious. He is a respecter of traditions as long as they do not threaten his freedom. The Virginian is polite enough to the orthodox minister who visits his employer's ranch. He listens respectfully to the long sermon, but the ranting and raving about his evil nature are more than he can stand. He knows that his cowboy friends are good men. He loves the beauty of the natural world and feels that the Creator of such a world must be a good and just God. Beyond that, the most ignorant cowboy knows as much as this sinister-voiced preacher. So like a young Greek god leaving Mount Olympus for a practical joke in the interest of justice, the Virginian leaves his rôle of calm and straightforward dignity, and engages in some humorous guile and deceit. The minister is sleeping in the next room and the Virginian calls him and complains that the devil is clutching him. After numerous sessions of wrestling with his conscience, the sleepy minister acting as referee, morning comes before the divine finds he has been tricked. He leaves the ranch in a rage, much to the delight of all the cowboys. The moral, observes Wister, is that men who are obsessed with evil and morbid ideas of human nature, had better stay away from the cowboy West. As Alfred Henry Lewis put it, describing a Western town the year *The Virginian* was published, "Wolfville's a hard practical outfit, what you might call a heap obdurate, an' it's goin' to take more than them fitful an' o'casional sermons I aloodes to,—to reach the roots of its soul." The cowboy is too good and has too much horse sense to be deluded by such brooding theology. Tex Burns could have been describing the Virginian when he wrote that his characters "had the cow hand's rough sense of humor and a zest for practical jokes no cow hand ever outgrows."

Coming as it did at the end of the nineteenth century, the cowboy ideal registered both a protest against orthodox creeds and a faith that man needs no formal religion, once he finds a pure and natural environment. It is the extreme end of a long evolution of individualism. Even the individualistic forest scout was dependent on his surroundings, and he exhibited a sort of pantheistic piety when he beheld the wilderness. The mighty captain of industry, while not accountable to anyone in this world, gave lip-service to the generous God who had made him a steward of wealth. But the cowboy hero stood out on the lonely prairie, dependent on neither man nor God. He was willing to take whatever risks lay along his road and would gladly make fun of any man who took life too seriously. Speaking of his mother's death, a real cowboy is supposed to have said:

> With almost her last breath, she begged me to make my peace with God, while the making was good. I have been too busy to heed her last advice. Being a just God, I feel that He will overlook my neglect. If not, I will have to take my medicine, with Satan holding the spoon.

While the cowboy hero has a respect for property, he does not seek personal wealth and is generous to the point of carelessness. He gives money to his friends, to people in distress, and blows the rest when he hits town on Saturday night. He owns no land and, in fact, has only contempt for farmers, with their ploughed fields and weather-beaten buildings. He hates the slick professional gambler, the grasping Eastern speculator, and the railroad man. How are these traits to be reconciled with his regard for property rights? The answer lies in a single possession—his horse. The cowboy's horse is what separates him from vagabondage and migratory labor. It is his link with the cavalier and plumed knight. More and more, in our increasingly property-conscious society, the cowboy's horse has gained in importance. A horse thief becomes a symbol of concentrated evil, a projection of all crime against property and, concomitantly, against social status. Zane Grey was adhering to this tradition when he wrote, "In those days, a horse meant all the world to a man. A lucky strike of grassy upland and good water . . . made him rich in all that he cared to own." On the other hand, "a horse thief was meaner than a poisoned coyote."

When a cowboy is willing to sell his horse, as one actually does in *The Virginian*, he has sold his dignity and self-identity. It is the tragic mistake which will inevitably bring its nemesis. His love for and close relationship with his horse not only make a cowboy seem more human, they also show his respect for propriety and order. He may drift from ranch to ranch, but his horse ties him down to respectability. Yet the cowboy hero is not an ambitious man. He lacks the concern for hard work and practical results which typifies the Horatio Alger ideal. Despite his fine horse and expensive saddle and boots, he values his code of honor and his friends more than possessions. Because the cowboy era is timeless, the hero has little drive or push toward a new and better life. He fights for law and order and this implies civilization, but the cowboy has no visions of empires, industrial or agrarian.

One of the American traits which foreign visitors most frequently described was the inability to have a good time. Americans constantly appear in European journals as ill-at-ease socially, as feeling they must work every spare moment. Certainly it was part of the American Protestant capitalistic ethic, the Poor Richard, Horatio Alger ideal, that spare time, frivolous play, and relaxation were sins which would bring only poverty, disease, and other misfortunes. If a youth would study the wise sayings of great men, if he worked hard and made valuable friends but no really confidential ones, if he never let his hair down or became too intimate with any person, wife included, if he stolidly kept his emotions to himself and watched for his chance in the world, then he would be sure to succeed. But the cowboy hero is mainly concerned with doing things skillfully and conforming to his moral code for its own sake. When he plays poker, treats the town to a drink, or raises a thousand dollars to buy off the evil mortgage, he is not aiming at personal success. Most cowboy heroes have at least one friend who knows them intimately, and they are seldom reserved, except in the presence of a villain or nosey stranger.

Both the hero and real cowboy appear to be easy-going and informal. In dress, speech, and social manner, the cowboy sets a new ideal. Every cowboy knows how to relax. If the villains are sometimes tense and nervous, the hero sits placidly at a card game, never ruffled, never disturbed, even when his archrival is behind him at the bar, hot with rage and whisky. The ideal cowboy is the kind of man who turns around slowly when a pistol goes off and drawls, "Ah'd put thet up, if Ah were yew." William MacLeod Raine's Sheriff Collins chats humorously with some train robbers and maintains a calm, unconcerned air which amuses the passengers, though he is actually pumping the bandits for useful information. Previously, he had displayed typical cowboy individualism by flagging the train down and climbing aboard, despite the protests of the conductor. Instead of the eager, aspiring youth, the cowboy hero is like a young tomcat, calm and relaxed, but always ready to spring into action. An early description of one of the most persistent of the cowboy heroes summarizes the ideal characteristics which appeal to a wide audience:

> Hopalong Cassidy had the most striking personality of all the men in his outfit; humorous, courageous to the point of foolishness, eager for fight or frolic, nonchalant when one would expect him to be quite otherwise, curious, loyal to a fault, and the best man with a Colt in the Southwest, he was a paradox, and a puzzle even to his most intimate friends. With him life was a humorous recurrence of sensations, a huge pleasant joke instinctively tolerated, but not worth the price cowards pay to keep it. He had come onto the range when a boy and since that time he had laughingly carried his life in his open hand, and . . . still carried it there, and just as recklessly.

Of course, most cowboy books and movies bristle with violence. Wild fist fights, brawls with chairs and bottles, gun play and mass battles with crashing windows, fires, and the final racing skirmish on horseback, are all as much a part of the cowboy drama as the boots and spurs. These bloody escapades are necessary and are simply explained. They provide the stage for the hero to show his heroism, and since the cowboy is the hero to the pre-adolescent, he must prove himself by their standards. Physical prowess is the most important thing for the ten- or twelve-year-old mind. They are constantly plagued by fear, doubt, and insecurity, in short, by evil, and they lack the power to crush it. The cowboy provides the instrument for their aggressive impulses, while the villain symbolizes all evil. The ethics of the cowboy band are the ethics of the boy's gang, where each member has a rôle determined by his physical skills and his past performance. As with any group of boys, an individual cowboy who had been "taken down a peg" was forever ridiculed and teased about his loss in status.

The volume of cowboy magazines, radio programs and motion pictures would indicate a national hero for at least a certain age group, a national hero who could hardly help but reflect specific attitudes. The cowboy myth has been chosen by this audience because it combines a complex of traits, a way of life, which they consider the proper ideal for America. The actual drama and setting are subordinate to the grand figure of the cowboy hero, and the love affairs, the exciting plots, and the climactic physical struggles present opportunities for the definition of the cowboy code and character. Through the superficial action, the heroism of the cowboy is revealed, and each repetition of the drama, like the repetition of a sacrament, reaffirms the cowboy public's faith in their ideal.

Perhaps the outstanding cowboy trait, above even honor, courage, and generosity, is the relaxed, calm attitude toward life. Though he lives intensely, he has a calm self-assurance, a knowledge that he can handle anything. He is good-humored and jovial. He never takes women too seriously. He can take a joke or laugh at himself. Yet the cowboy is usually anti-intellectual and anti-school, another attitude which appeals to a younger audience.

Above all, the cowboy is a "good joe." He personifies a code of personal dignity, personal liberty, and personal honesty. Most writers on the actual cowboy represented him as having these traits. While many of these men obviously glorify him as much as any fiction writer, there must have been some basis for their judgment. As far as his light-hearted, calm attitude is concerned, it is amazing how similar cowboys appear, both in romances and nonfiction. Millions of American youth subscribed to the new ideal and yearned for the clear, Western atmosphere of "unswerving loyalty, the true, deep affection, and good-natured banter that left no sting." For a few thrilling hours they could roughly toss conventions aside and share the fellowship of ranch life and adore the kind of hero who was never bored and never afraid.

Whether these traits of self-confidence, a relaxed attitude toward life and good humor, have actually increased in the United States during the past fifty years is like asking whether men love their wives more now than in 1900. Certainly the effective influence of the cowboy myth can never be determined. It is significant, however, that the cowboy ideal has emerged above all others. And while the standardization of plot and character seems to follow other commercial conventions, the very popularity of this standard cowboy is important and is an overlooked aspect of the American character. It is true that this hero is infantile, that he is silly, overdone, and unreal. But when we think of many past ideals and heroes, myths and ethics; when we compare our placid cowboy with, say, the eager, cold, serious hero of Nazi Germany (the high-cheekboned, blond lad who appeared on the Reichsmarks); or if we compare the cowboy with the gangster heroes of the thirties, or with the serious, self-righteous and brutal series of Supermen, Batmen, and Human Torches; when, in an age of violence and questioned public and private morality, we think of the many possible heroes we might have had—then we can be thankful for our silly cowboy. We could have chosen worse.

Andrew Carnegie and the Robber Baron Myth

Milton Goldin

One of the most lively and persistent historical controversies pertaining to the Gilded Age concerns the concept of the Robber Barons. According to traditional accounts, based mostly on a famous study in business history by Matthew Josephson, American business leadership from the end of the Civil War until the turn of the century was characterized by corrupt professional practices, unethical exploitation of the working class, and a callous disregard for the public good. Vast fortunes were accumulated through the questionable activities of unsavory business titans. As one social critic at the time said: "Behind every great fortune is a great crime." In turn, the age at large was said to be one of conspicuous consumption and lush, yet crass, extravagance. According to this biographical analysis of one of the business giants of this era—Andrew Carnegie—finding a "typical" robber baron to fit the mold is difficult. Milton Goldin, history scholar from Great Britain, rather finds complexity in lieu of simplicity. While aggressively entrepreneurial in style and execution, Carnegie was magnanimous in his philanthropic enterprises, setting the pattern for foundation and private giving on to the present day. The villainous image of American business leaders at century's end, while an appealing stereotype for those seeking sensational and colorful portraits from the Gilded Age, is something less than a completely useful concept, at least in Carnegie's case. Some members of the business elite—even Carnegie himself at times—give flesh and blood to the knavish image, but Goldin judges that the robber baron image contains much legend and must be applied judiciously.

For thirty-five years after the Civil War, the United States of America sustained the greatest period of economic growth of any country in history. Its wealth quadrupled. Fifth among the world's major powers in 1865, it was first by 1901. Its citizenry came to believe that nothing was impossible and that anything wrong could be made right, provided enough energy was applied to a problem.

One of the great symbols of American wealth and dynamism was a slight, Scottish immigrant with pale, penetrating eyes and a broad nose. Andrew Carnegie rose to fame and fortune in a way that made Horatio Alger look phlegmatic. After retiring from business activity, he donated some $350 million to philanthropic causes and shipped free Scotch whisky to the White House.

What largely accounted for both the surge in American wealth and Carnegie was a development still imperfectly understood today—the extent to which the North's victory affected the capitalist spirit. Nearly all writers on American history now agree that the conflict actually impeded economic growth, instead of stimulating industry as was thought by earlier scholars. But, after 1865, expansionist outlooks characteristic of the country's early history re-emerged, and wartime profiteers invested in railroads, built factories, and, with notable energy, manipulated stocks and bonds. So monumental was their sheer greed that they were called 'robber barons' with justification. By 1890, the United States census bureau estimated that 9 per cent of the nation's families owned 71 per cent of its wealth.

Not unnaturally, the rest of the population noticed significant changes in the distribution of wealth and also grasped that businessmen who wanted to control raw materials, markets, workers, and the legal system might also have greater power than ordinary citizens in local, state, and federal governments. Its assumptions were correct. By 1888, the Pennsylvania Railroad had gross receipts of $115 million and employed 100,000 men. In the same year, the entire State of Massachusetts had gross receipts of $7 million and employed 6,000 persons.

On the face of it, robber barons were so far ahead in the race for power as early as 1870 that the rest of the population feared it would never catch up. Revolution became a distinct possibility. The personal fortunes of the rich beggared anything seen before in America. When George Washington died in 1799, he left an estate of only $500,000 and was accounted one of the richest men of the time. Not until 1847 was the word 'millionaire' used in a New York newspaper to denote a person of unusual wealth, and before the Civil War there were only a handful of multi-millionaires.

Forum magazine estimated 120 men worth over $10 million in 1891, and the following year, the *New York Times* listed 4,047 millionaires. Robert Lincoln, the son of a president whose later life was dedicated to the preservation of the Union, became a corporation lawyer and a multi-millionaire. Apparently because his mother annoyed him, Robert had her committed to an insane asylum.

By the early 1870s, when the unbridled speculation of post-war America reached its first major crisis in a depression, the result was a near-breakdown of society. Hundreds of thousands of people were thrown out of work and off farms. State militias and federal troops mobilized to crush strikes and to put down expected insurrections. In New York, some 70,000 men left their jobs to strike for an eight-hour day at no decrease in pay, as provided for in an 1870 state law. Around them, writes one social historian, 'multitudes of the lowest grades of the city poor' begged for food on the streets, and shelters were overwhelmed by the homeless, who had to be lodged in police stations. Yet, among city fathers, the major question was, 'How can we get rid of the transients at the least cost and trouble to the community?'

This harsh attitude toward the poor reflected a Calvinist philosophy that had informed Americans since Colonial days. During that period, Americans did not interpret poverty as a personal or as a communal failing, mainly because the needy were neighbours. Churches took poor relief as their responsibility, stressed that the existing social order was right and reasonable, and bestowed special praise on generous givers for rising above the common herd with donations for families in need. Typically, colonists cared for dependents in their own homes, disrupting lives as little as possible. This was in sharp contrast to practices in the motherland, where the British had a bewildering array of almshouses, workhouses, and other institutions to house and to feed swarms of beggars.

The Colonial period was an age of emerging humanitarianism, and throughout the western world prosperous citizens led the middle classes in providing succour for the less fortunate. On the other hand, destitute strangers were not welcomed anywhere in North America because of the high costs of maintaining them. The purpose of poor-relief legislation was as much to keep non-residents out as it was to help neighbours. When the first Jews in North America arrived in New Amsterdam from Recife in 1654, Governor Peter Stuyvesant, whole intolerance of Quakers was already notorious, wanted the newcomers ousted at once. The refugees wrote to brethren in Amsterdam, who were directors of the Dutch West India Company, and pleaded to be allowed to stay. The Company finally ordered Stuyvesant to permit them to remain—not because of humanitarian considerations, but because the Jews pledged that they would care for their own in cases of need.

Until the Civil War, philanthropic practices remained largely the same as during the Colonial period, with clerics taking major roles in raising and disbursing funds. What changed was the manner in which funds were raised. In addition to taxes and collections in churches, an Assistance Society in New York, organized in December 1808, raised relief funds via printed appeals and house-to-house solicitations. During the war, a great Metropolitan Fair was held in the city for the benefit of the sick and wounded Union soldiers, which helped set an example for future fund-raising events.

No previous experience prepared anyone for the 1870s, however, thanks to the staggering dimensions of the economic disaster. The State of Massachusetts dumped 7,000 unwanted homeless on the State of New York. In both states, public welfare agencies were permeated not only by gross inefficiency but by the wholesale corruption that marked government at all levels in the post-Civil War years. The gentry, or more specifically the descendants of men and women who had invented America, abandoned hope for government's ability to deal with any problem, let alone charity.

Yet, impressed by post-war strides in industry made possible through technology, a group of militant reformers thought that philanthropy could become 'scientific.' They believed that charity could be rationalized and the poor saved from alcoholism, commonly thought to be the basic cause of impoverishment. Scientific philanthropy would eliminate crafty paupers who took advantage of soup kitchens and cast-off clothing provided by givers. Scientific philanthropy would make better men and women of givers and receivers alike and end poverty altogether. Finally, scientific philanthropy would cut mounting public expenditures for the poor.

But who would pay for philanthropy, scientific or otherwise? The people who had the most money were the robber barons, and so far as reformers could see, robber barons were not so much threatening American standards of living as they were threatening American ways of life.

Inevitably, reformers had two questions to answer. Did robber barons care about the poor? And, if they did care, on what basis would they give?

With amusing regularity, interpretations of the robber barons' business tactics and generosity have changed from generation to generation, since the early years of the twentieth century. The muckrakers, notably Ida Tarbell and Lincoln Steffens, accounted them despoilers, thieves, and threats to the public welfare, whose donations were devices to assuage guilty consciences. A quarter of a century later, President Herbert Hoover acclaimed them industrial statesmen and magnificent benefactors. Then came the Depression of the 1930s and Hoover, himself, fell into disgrace for his economic policies, despite his reputation as a businessman, engineer, and humanitarian organizing relief in Europe during and after the First World War. Writers such as Gustavus Myers (whose earlier *History of the Great American Fortunes*

was updated) and Matthew Josephson again accounted robber barons despoilers and thieves, partly on the basis of Balzac's dictum that behind every great fortune there must lie a great crime.

Early in the 1950s, after the Rockefeller family had given away $2.5 billion since John D. Senior's earliest contributions, former despoilers and thieves received acclaim in the press as business pioneers and model givers. Then came the 1960s, when the doctrines of Social Darwinism and WASP superiority that the rich of the early 1900s espoused were in especially bad repute. The robber barons were hauled out to be demolished yet again in Ferdinand Lundberg's *The Rich and the Super Rich*.

Today, in the midst of untrammeled economic growth, Andrew Carnegie, Jay Gould, John D. Rockefeller, Charles Schwab, J. P. Morgan, Leland Stanford, and Henry Frick—*the créme-de-la-créme* of robber barons—are again described as managerial geniuses and outstanding philanthropists, instrumental in moving mankind forward to its present and exalted status.

In many ways, the most puzzling of these men is Carnegie. The first robber baron to accumulate a fortune of nearly $450 million, he is also accounted the model philanthropist for being the first robber baron to give unprecedented amounts to universities, institutes, libraries, to churches for organs, to a foundation that provides pensions for professors, to a fund that honours 'heroes,' and to innumerable individuals and smaller causes. Admiring contemporaries put his name on hundreds of buildings, avenues, and streets, John D. Rockefeller wrote, 'I would that more men of wealth were doing as you are doing with your money but be assured your example will bear fruit.'

Like so much else in his extraordinary career, the picture of a warm and generous tycoon, which Carnegie assiduously cultivated, is deceptive. All his life, he was a mass of contradictions.

During an eighty-four-year lifetime, he had time to play not only the role of self-made man and multimillionaire but of intellectual and spokesman for the new entrepreneurial classes. His energy, like his duplicity, was limitless. The same man who courageously assailed American imperialism in the Phillipines and sincerely worked for world peace, deceitfully sold overpriced and under done armour plate to the American Navy. Carnegie boasted about his close personal relations with workers and said,

'The best workmen do not think about money.' To reinforce this claim, he constantly demanded that his subordinates reduce wages so that he could earn higher profits.

In 1892, Carnegie ordered Frick, his junior, to cut overheads at the huge Homestead steel plant, near Pittsburgh. He then left for a vacation in the Scottish Highlands. There followed a bloody strike at Homestead during which an anarchist shot Frick, and Irish immigrants fought gun battles with Pinkerton agents. Carnegie later said publicly that he knew nothing about the disorders until they were over but would have handled matters differently had he known. In private, he praised Frick for breaking the strike.

Ironically, Andrew Carnegie's father, William, by trade a linen weaver in Dunfermline, Scotland, was a local leader of the Chartists. His mother, Margaret was the daughter a shoemaker and political and social reformer. After William Carnegie's business failed in 1848, the family, including thirteen-year-old Andrew, emigrated to Allegheny, Pennsylvania (later a suburb of Pittsburgh), where two of Mrs. Carnegie's sisters were living.

William failed for a second time in a handloom business and, with his son, sought work in local cotton mills. Andrew began his labours as a bobbin boy working from 6 a.m. to 6 p.m., earning $1.20 a week. A short time later, his father quit—factory work turned out to be impossible for this small enterpriser—and Andrew got another job dipping newly-made spools in an oil vat. He was paid $3 a week for work in a foul-smelling basement. Thereafter, just a whiff of oil could make him deathly sick.

A game of chequers between his uncle and the manager of the local telegraph office set Carnegie on the road to wealth. The manager mentioned that he was looking for a messenger boy. Andrew got the job and diligently memorised the name of every street in Pittsburgh. He also arrived earlier each day at the telegraph office than any other worker, stayed later, learned the Morse code, and astounded fellow workers by the speed with which he took down words. Among those he impressed was Thomas A. Scott, superintendent of the Pennsylvania Railroad at Pittsburgh. Scott hired him as secretary, telegrapher, and general factotum for $35 a week, a hefty increase over the $800 a year he had been earning.

Carnegie continued to arrive earlier at the office and to leave later than other employees. It is to his hard work and telegraphic skills that biographers ascribe his early successes. But thousands of other young men in hundreds of other places also arrived earlier, stayed later, and learned Morse code but did not become multi-millionaires. The differences between them and Carnegie were that he had business acumen, a willingness to gamble, made salesmanship into art form, and was a born courier, adept at outrageous but irresistible flattery. Applying this talent to Scott, he became the superintendent's favourite. Scott passed on tips on investments, including one to buy $500-worth of Adams Express stock. Carnegie, who probably did not have even $50, told his mother about the offer, and she mortgaged the family home to raise money.

When the first dividend payment arrived, writes Carnegie in his autobiography, 'I shall remember that check as long as I live. It gave me the first penny of revenue from capital—something that I had not worked for with the sweat of my brow. "Eureka!" I cried, "Here's the goose that lays the golden eggs." ' Thus was Andrew Carnegie introduced to capitalist enterprise.

Some time later, Carnegie was riding on a company train when approached by a rustic named T.T. Woodruff who asked whether he was an employee of the Pennsylvania Railroad. Receiving an answer in the affirmative, Woodruff opened a green bag and produced a model of the first sleeping car. An impressed Carnegie arranged for Woodruff to meet Scott. In appreciation, Woodruff offered the go-getter a one-eighth interest in his sleeping-car company, which Carnegie financed with a bank loan of $217.50. The investment was soon to be worth more than $5,000 a year to the young investor.

In 1859, Carnegie replaced Scott as superintendent, Scott having advanced to a vice-presidency. During the Civil War, much too busy with his career to bother with the armed forces, Carnegie bought himself out of the draft. He helped the North use railroads and the telegraph, however, to win a victory.

By 1873, Carnegie already had extensive interests in bridge building, telegraphy, and in sleeping cars, but it was to be during the depression that he would make the move into the steel industry which was to lift him out of the ranks of the rich into those of the super-rich. On a trip to England, he visited a mill in which the new Bessemer converter was being used to manufacture steel. Overnight, he grasped the implications of the process and became a booster of steel products.

Back in the United States, he displayed that sycophantic skill that was his hallmark. His first steel plant was named for J. Edgar Thomson, president of the Pennsylvania Railroad. The name was chosen not only to indicate that there existed no bad blood between the two men (Carnegie left the Railroad in 1865) but because Thomson was a buyer of steel rails and could also transport steel products to customers.

By 1899, a Carnegie Steel Company was making 695,000 tons more of steel every year than the total output of Great Britain. Carnegie had always refinanced internally, through surpluses of earnings, and consequently, he owed nothing to banks. The practice insulated him from the stock mark but left no way to publicly evaluate the worth of his steel company. He rectified the problem by setting his own value on the factories—$157,950,000—which was later artificially inflated to $250 million when John D. Rockefeller indicated interest in buying him out. The price led the oil magnate to drop out of the running.

Charles Schwab, a subordinate, broached the subject of a purchase with J. P. Morgan, who wanted to include Carnegie Steel in a supertrust of steel corporations he was organising. Morgan agreed to a price of $447 million, which was two-thirds more than Carnegie had thought it was worth only months before, and, on January 4th, 1901, the deal was consummated.

Carnegie received $303,450,000 in 5 per cent bonds and stock with a market value of about $144 million. Shrewd to the very end, he also held a mortgage on Morgan's new United States Steel Corporation—a detail that nearly put him back in possession of the whole overpriced monstrosity when it almost went bankrupt a few years later.

In 1868 at the age of thirty-three Carnegie was already earning $50,000 a year, but had given no major gifts to charity. In papers discovered by executors after his death, there was a memorandum that had been written in December of the year. 'By this time two years I can so arrange all my business as to secure at least $50,000 per annum,' he wrote. 'Beyond this never earn—make no effort to increase fortune, but to spend the surplus each year for benevolent purposes. Cast aside business forever, except for others.'

Carnegie did not cast aside business in two years, and his philanthropies began with modest gifts for public baths in Dunfermline, during the late 1860s. What he concentrated on, before he had $447 million to give, was writing about the glories of American business and philanthropy in a series of books and articles. The most influential of these on the philanthropic practices of the American rich was 'Wealth,' an article published in the June 1889 issue of the *North American Review* and republished shortly afterwards in Great Britain in the *Pall Mall* Gazette, under the title, 'The Gospel of Wealth,' The American publication of the article was followed six months later in the *North American Review* by 'The Best Uses of Philanthropy' and in 1890 by a collection of his essays in book form, *The Gospel of Wealth*.

Carnegie's masterful salesmanship is immediately evident in these writings. A true Dr. Pangloss, he does not even suggest the possibility that his may not be the best of all possible worlds. His basic assumptions in 'Wealth' are that the rich deserve their money and know what is best for society. What, then, is there left to discuss? In Carnegie's view, how the rich should spend their fortunes.

Considering the orgies, banquets on horseback, sixty-room mansions, and works of art with which his fellow robber barons happily indulged themselves, this would seem to have been a pressing issue only to Carnegie. But he shifts the argument from the present to the future and from idle frivolities to matters of moral substance. Because no one can take his fortune with him when he dies, Carnegie argues, the man of great wealth (and virtue) actually has only three ways to dispense his fortune: he can leave it to his family; he can bequeath it for public purposes; or he can spend it during his lifetime for public purposes and take an active pleasure in the good that he does.

In Carnegie's view, the first mode is undesirable because its consequences are to make a god of money ('The thoughtful man must shortly say, "I would as soon leave my son a curse as the almighty dollar . . ." '), and the second mode will inevitably result in disappointed heirs contesting wills in courts. 'There remains, then, only one mode of using great fortunes,' he concludes, 'and in this we have the true antidote for the temporary unequal distribution of wealth, the reconciliation of rich and the poor and a reign of harmony. . . .'

The rich man, he believes, should spend his fortune during his lifetime in ways that will benefit mankind and influence society for the better, and:

> under its sway we shall have an ideal State, in which the surplus wealth of the few will become, in the best sense, the property of the many, because administered for the common good, and this wealth passing through the hands of the few, can be made a much more potent force for the elevation of our race than if distributed in small sums to the people themselves.

His views did not go unchallenged. In London, the Reverend Hugh Price Hughes agreed that if tensions between haves and have-nots grew in intensity, social disaster threatened. In an article, 'Irresponsible Wealth,' in the magazine *Nineteenth Century*, Hughes also wrote:

> In a really Christian country—that is to say, in a community reconstructed upon a Christian basis— a millionaire would be an economic impossibility. Jesus Christ distinctly prohibited the accumulation of wealth.

In Massachusetts, the Reverend William Jewett Tucker, professor of religion at Andover Seminary and later president of Dartmouth College, acknowledged in the June 1891 issue of the *Andover Review:*

> ... the great benefit to society from the gifts of the rich, from those which have been received and from those which are likely to be received. But I believe that the charity which this gospel enjoins is too costly, if taken at the price which the author puts upon it; namely the acceptance of his doctrine of the relation of private wealth to society.

Tucker concluded:

> The assumption . . . that wealth is the inevitable possession of the few, and is best administered by them for the many, begs the whole question of economic justice now before society. . . . But charity, as I have claimed, cannot solve the problems of the modern world.

When Morgan bought him out, Carnegie was sixty-five years old, and generosity was still not his strong suit. Donations had hardly made a dent in his fortune—except for gifts to libraries in the United States and in Great Britain. He insisted that receiving libraries match his building donations by providing annual operating expenses and purchasing books.

He also donated organs to churches, for which the applying church had to prove that it was not in debt.

Carnegie rejected contributions to medical causes, a field in which John D. Rockefeller was specialising, and social reform, for which he thought government should be the prime giver, to concentrate on education. His first great benefaction was for a Carnegie Institute in Pittsburgh. His second was to the Carnegie Trust for the Universities of Scotland, but many Scots were suspicious. *Blackwood's Edinburgh Magazine* flatly thought him nothing but an American money-making machine, adding, 'In old days, a rich man enjoyed his wealth—and if he did the community "no good," at least he did not insult it with patronage.'

As usual ignoring criticism, Carnegie gave the trust a $10 million endowment, half of which was to be used to finance the education of 'students of Scottish birth or extraction.' But this, too, inspired protest. British upper classes feared that lower orders would forget 'their proper station in life,' if given free access to education.

When he returned to the United States from his annual trip to Scotland in 1901—from this point on, the British would be just as happy to see him travel west each year as to welcome him back—Carnegie found a host of volunteers, including every college president in the country, ready to help him spend his money. At his new mansion in New York, he thought about creating a national university in Washington, DC, an idea that went back to the country's founding fathers. The university took form, however, as the Carnegie Institution of Washington, an establishment without students but with departments of research in evolution, marine biology, history, economics, and sociology.

The Carnegie Institution, which established an outstanding reputation, required large contributions to sustain operations but did not use up the bulk of Carnegie's fortune. One of his philanthropic tenets was to avoid 'indiscriminate charity' and Carnegie still faced the problem of where to make a really large gift. In 1905, he endowed a Carnegie Teachers Pension Fund Foundation with $10 million. From this seed grew the Carnegie Foundation for the Advancement of Teaching, which eventually received a national charter by Act of Congress and $125 million from Carnegie himself.

Carnegie demanded that educational institutions that applied to the Foundation, which was originally conceived to provide pensions for underpaid professors, meet certain standards. Among them, no school could have an endowment of less than $200,000, no school could receive a substantial portion of its operating funds from public sources, and no school could accept applicants with less than minimum preparation for college studies. Above all, he prohibited colleges under sectarian control from receiving grants.

By insisting on these criteria, and certainly with no plan beforehand to reform education in America, Carnegie did more to advance standards of higher education in the United States than any contemporary educator or government official. As usual, he was roundly attacked for his efforts, this time by heads of institutions who wished to be included but wanted denominational controls maintained. One such was Abram W. Harris, president of Northwestern University, who wrote that his institution was 'really non-sectarian in spirit,' although a majority of its trustees were Methodists. Carnegie responded:

> I [have seen] in my travels around the world what denominationalism really [means]—several sects each claiming to proclaim the truth and by inference condemning the others as imperfect.

Northwestern did not get a grant.

The $125 million he gave to the Foundation was by far the largest single amount that he would give to any of the organisations he founded, or to which he contributed. Thereafter, large-scale philanthropy ceased to be of prime interest to him. Carnegie had discovered that giving away money gave him no special place in the hearts of recipients. For the public, there were two classes of men—those who were rich and had money to give and those who were poor and needed contributions from the rich. Those who wanted money were interested in immediate and direct benefits, not in the philosophy of the giver.

By 1910, Carnegie was increasingly involved in problems of world peace. Benefactions went to the Peace Palace at the Hague (1903) and to the Carnegie Endowment for International Peace (1910). It would come as a shock to him in 1914 that the world's great powers had as little interest in his exertions for peace as the public had had earlier in his philosophy of philanthropy.

On those who had money to give, however, Carnegie's philantropy had a profound influence. His benefactions offered proof that no single private sector giver or group of givers, no matter how rich, could decide for a whole community the terms of its welfare programmes.

On the other hand, the philanthropic foundation, which Carnegie pioneered, became the standard giftgiving vehicle for the rich. After Carnegie, every self-respecting robber baron had to have at least one foundation. There were only five such entities at the end of the nineteenth century. Six more were created in the first decade of the century, twenty-two during the second decade, and forty-one in the third. Today, there are over 25,000 foundations in the United States.

The most dedicated students of Carnegie's philanthropy were John D. Rockefeller, his son, John, Jr., and his five grandsons. It would not only be the enormous wealth of this family that made it the core of the American Establishment, but a network of think-tanks, institutes and experts financed through Rockefeller grants. Andrew Carnegie could indirectly be thanked for these results.

II

American Myths at Century's End

During the 1890s, claims Henry Steele Commager's *The American Mind,* a transformation in American culture took place with particular clarity:

> On the one side . . . lies an America predominantly agricultural; concerned with domestic problems . . . an America still in the making, physically and socially; an America on the whole self-confident, self-contained, self-reliant, and conscious of its unique character and of a unique destiny. On the other side lies the modern America, predominantly urban and industrial; inextricably involved in world economy and politics . . . experiencing profound changes in population, social institutions, economy, and technology; and trying to accommodate its traditions and institutions and habits of thought to conditions new and in part alien.

At century's end, the nation's self-image was being strongly conditioned by a curious mixture of hope and nostalgia, of confidence and doubt. Such conditions were especially conducive to myth-building by both contemporaries and future historians. The cluster of myths that appears in the late nineteenth century speaks not only to the country's confrontation with newness, but also perhaps to its desire to secure something that seemed about to be lost. A flurry of myths concerning the self-made man, the winning of the West, the American working class, Booker T. Washington's famous Atlanta speech, and America's supposed new role in foreign affairs all grew in the complex cultural alchemy of the twilight years of the nineteenth century.

Driving the Golden Spike on May 10, 1869, at Promontory Point, Utah, joining the Union Pacific and Central Pacific lines and completing the first transcontinental railroad. Chinese workers had furnished much of the labor for the Central Pacific. Note the absence of Chinese faces in this photograph. *(Courtesy, Union Pacific Railroad Museum Collection, Omaha, Nebraska)*

Booker T. Washington, founder of Tuskegee Institute in Alabama in 1881. Some criticized his gradualist, conciliatory approach to race relations, but he was very much a man of action who often defied traditional racial conventions. *Courtesy, Library of Congress)*

The Winning of the West and the Sioux: A Myth

Richard White

The image of the fierce mounted warrior astride his fleet pony—silhouetted against an austere western landscape, surveying the inexorable advance of white civilization's "manifest destiny"—is surely the most enduring stereotype of the American Indian. The "winning of the West," however, involves a set of historical complexities that fit the strictures of the stereotype scarcely at all. The process whereby the Plains Indians came to be dispossessed of their lands and cultures during the Plains Wars, argues Professor Richard White of the University of Utah, needs to be more methodically scrutinized and reassessed. Violent episodes between Indians and whites—often bred by cultural misunderstandings—were both a symptom and a foreshadowing of the false beliefs that continued to haunt relations between the two. Most needed as a historical corrective, White concludes, is a proper understanding of intertribal relations, especially the rise of the western Sioux to imperial supremacy. Before the period of white advance the western Sioux had already "won the West" by intertribal warfare. Traders, and then settlers, *followed* the Sioux. The "winning of the West" was in great measure, then, a conflict between the two remaining major expanding powers in the area—the Sioux and the white Americans.

Western historians usually present intertribal warfare as a chaotic series of raids and counter-raids; an almost irrelevant prelude to the real story: Indian resistance to white invasion. The exaggerated focus on the heroic resistance of certain plains tribes to white incursions has recently prompted John Ewers, an ethnologist, to stress that Indians on the plains had fought each other long before whites came and that intertribal warfare remained very significant into the late nineteenth century.

The neglect by historians of intertribal warfare and the reasons behind it has fundamentally distorted the historical position of the Plains Indians. As Ewers has noted, the heroic resistance approach to plains history reduces these tribes who did not offer organized armed resistance to the white American invaders, and who indeed often aided them against other tribes, to the position of either foolish dupes of the whites or of traitors to their race. Why tribes such as the Pawnee, Mandan, Hidatsa, Oto, Missouri, Crow, and Omaha never took up arms against white Americans has never been subject to much historical scrutiny. The failure of Indians to unite has been much easier to deplore than to examine.

The history of the northern and central American Great Plains in the eighteenth and nineteenth centuries is far more complicated than the tragic retreat of the Indians in the face of an inexorable white advance. From the perspective of most northern and central plains tribes the crucial invasion of the plains during this period was not necessarily that of the whites at all. These tribes had few illusions about American whites and the danger they presented, but the Sioux remained their most feared enemy.

The Teton and Yanktonai Sioux appeared on the edges of the Great Plains early in the eighteenth

48

century. Although unmounted, they were already culturally differentiated from their woodland brothers, the Santee Sioux. The western Sioux were never united under any central government and never developed any concerted policy of conquest. By the mid-nineteenth century the Plains Sioux comprised three broad divisions, the Tetons, Yanktons, and Yanktonais, with the Tetons subdivided into seven component tribes—the Oglala, Brulé, Hunkpapa, Miniconjou, Sans Arc, Two Kettles and Sihaspas, the last five tribes having evolved from an earlier Sioux group—the Saones. Although linked by common language, culture, interest, and intermarriage, these tribes operated independently. At no time did all the western Sioux tribes unite against any enemy, but alliances of several tribes against a common foe were not unusual. Only rarely did any Teton tribe join an alien tribe in an attack on another group of Sioux.

Between approximately 1685 and 1876 the western Sioux conquered and controlled an area from the Minnesota River in Minnesota, west to the head of the Yellowstone, and south from the Yellowstone to the drainage of the upper Republican River. This advance westward took place in three identifiable stages: initially a movement during the late seventeenth and early eighteenth centuries onto the prairies east of the Missouri, then a conquest of the middle Missouri River region during the late eighteenth and nineteenth centuries, and, finally, a sweep west and south from the Missouri during the early and mid-nineteenth century. Each of these stages possessed its own impetus and rationale. Taken together they comprised a sustained movement by the Sioux that resulted in the dispossession or subjugation of numerous tribes and made the Sioux a major Indian power on the Great Plains during the nineteenth century. . . .

*   *   *

The conquests of the western Sioux during the nineteenth century were politically united in only the loosest sense. The various Sioux tribes expanded for similar demographic, economic, and social reasons, however, and these underlying causes give a unity to the various wars of the Sioux.

Unlike every other tribe on the Great Plains during the nineteenth century, the Sioux appear to have increased in numbers. They were not immune to the epidemics that decimated the other tribes, but most of the Tetons and Yanktonais successfully avoided the disastrous results of the great epidemics, especially the epidemic of 1837 that probably halved the Indian population of the plains. Through historical accident the very conquests of the Sioux protected them from disease. This occurred in two opposite ways. The advance of Oglalas and Brulés to the southwest simply put them out of reach of the main epidemic corridor along the Missouri. Furthermore, Pilcher, the Indian agent on the Missouri, succeeded in giving them advance warning of the danger in 1837, and, unlike the Blackfeet and other nomadic tribes that suffered heavily from the epidemic, they did not come in to trade. The Tetons were infected, and individual tribes lost heavily, but the losses of the Sioux as a whole were comparatively slight. The Yanktons, Yanktonais, and portions of the Saone Tetons, however, dominated the Missouri trade route, but paradoxically this probably helped to save them. In 1832 the Office of Indian Affairs sent doctors up the river to vaccinate the Indians. Many of the Sioux refused to cooperate, but well over a thousand people, mostly Yanktonais, received vaccinations. Only enough money was appropriated to send the doctors as far upriver as the Sioux; so the Mandans and Hidatsas further upriver remained unvaccinated. As a result, when smallpox came, the Yanktonais were partially protected while their enemies in the villages once again died miserably in great numbers. The renewed American efforts at mass vaccination that followed the epidemic came too late for the Mandans, but in the 1840s thousands more Sioux were given immunity from smallpox.

The combination of freedom from disease, a high birth rate (in 1875 estimated as capable of doubling the population every twenty years), and continued migration from the Sioux tribes further east produced a steadily growing population for the western Sioux. Although the various censuses taken by the whites were often little more than rough estimates, the western Sioux appear to have increased from a very low estimate of 5,000 people in 1804 to approximately 25,000 in the 1850s. This population increase, itself partly a result of the new abundance the Sioux derived from the buffalo herds, in turn fueled an increased need for buffalo. The Sioux used the animals not only to feed their expanding population, but also to trade for necessary European goods. Since pemmican, buffalo robes, hides, and tongues had replaced beaver pelts as the main Indian trade item on the Missouri, the Sioux needed secure and profitable hunting grounds during a period when the buffalo were steadily moving west and north in response to hunting pressure on the Missouri.

Increased Indian hunting for trade contributed to the pressure on the buffalo herds, but the great bulk of the destruction was the direct work of white hunters and traders. The number of buffalo robes annually shipped down the Missouri increased from an average of 2,600 between 1815 and 1830 to 40,000 to 50,000 in 1833, a figure that did not include the numbers slaughtered by whites for pleasure. In 1848 Father Pierre-Jean De Smet reported the annual figure shipped downriver to St. Louis to be 25,000 tongues and 110,000 robes.

Despite what the most thorough student of the subject has seen as the Indians' own prudent use of the buffalo, the various tribes competed for an increasingly scarce resource. By the late 1820s the buffalo had disappeared from the Missouri below the Omaha villages, and the border tribes were already in desperate condition from lack of game. The Indians quickly realized the danger further up the Missouri, and upper Missouri tribes voiced complaints about white hunters as early as 1833. By the 1840s observations on the diminishing number of buffalo and increased Indian competition had become commonplace. Between 1833 and 1844 buffalo could be found in large numbers on the headwaters of the Little Cheyenne, but by the mid-1840s they were receding rapidly toward the mountains. The Sioux to a great extent simply had to follow, or move north and south, to find new hunting grounds. Their survival and prosperity depended on their success.

But buffalo hunting demanded more than territory; it also required horses, and in the 1820s, the Sioux were hardly noted for either the abundance or the quality of their herds. Raids and harsh winters on the plains frequently depleted Sioux horse herds, and the Sioux had to replenish them by raiding or trading farther to the south. In this sense the economy of the Sioux depended on warfare to secure the horses needed for the hunt. As Oscar Lewis has pointed out in connection with the Blackfeet, war and horse raiding became important economic activities for the Plains Indians.

The Yanktonais, Yanktons, and Saone Tetons had a third incentive for expansion. Power over the sedentary villagers secured them what Tabeau had called their serfs. Under Sioux domination these villages could be raided or traded with as the occasion demanded, their corn and beans serving as sources of supplementary food supplies when the buffalo failed. A favorite tactic of the Sioux was to restrict, as far as possible, the access of these tribes to both European goods and the hunting grounds, thus forcing the village peoples to rely on the Sioux for trade goods, meat, and robes. To escape this exploitation, the villagers, in alliance with the nomadic tribes who traded with them, waged a nearly constant, if often desultory, war.

It is in this context of increasing population, increasing demand for buffalos and horses, the declining and retreating bison populations, and attempted domination of the sedentary villagers that the final phase of Sioux expansion during the nineteenth century took place. And, as the Omahas had found out, the loose structural organization of the western Sioux worked to make the impetus of their advance even more irresistible. Accommodation with one band or tribe often only served to increase inroads from others. There was no way for a tribe to deal with the whole Sioux nation.

On the Missouri the Sioux had long feared the logical alliance of all the village tribes against them, and they worked actively to prevent it. After 1810, the Arikaras sporadically attempted to break away from Sioux domination by allying themselves with the Mandans and Hidatsas. In response, the Sioux blockaded the villages, cutting them off from buffalo and stopping the white traders who came up the Missouri from supplying them. The Mandan-Arikara alliance, in turn, sent out war parties to keep the river open. But these alliances inevitably fell apart from internal strains, and the old pattern of oscillating periods of trade and warfare was renewed.

But if the Sioux feared an alliance of the sedentary village tribes, these tribes had an even greater fear of a Sioux-American partnership on the Missouri. The Arikaras, by attacking and defeating an American fur trading party under William Ashley in 1823, precipitated exactly the combination from which they had most to fear. When 1,500 Sioux warriors appeared before their village that year, they were accompanied by United States troops under Colonel Henry Leavenworth. This joint expedition took the Arikara village and sacked it, but the Sioux were disgusted with the performance of their American auxiliaries. They blamed American cautiousness for allowing the Arikaras to escape further upstream. Although they remained friendly to the United

States, the whole affair gave them a low estimation of the ability of white soldiers that would last for years. They finished the removal of the Arikaras themselves, forcing them by 1832 to abandon both their sedentary villages and the Missouri River and to move south to live first with, and then just above, the Skidi Pawnees. The Yanktonais, 450 lodges strong, moved in from the Minnesota River to take over the old Arikara territory.

With the departure of the Arikaras, the Mandans and Hidatsas alone remained to contest Sioux domination of the Missouri. In 1836 the Yanktonais, nearly starving after a season of poor hunts, began petty raids on the Mandans and Hidatsas. In retaliation, a Mandan-Hidatsa war party destroyed a Yanktonai village of forty-five lodges, killing more than 150 people and taking fifty prisoners. The Sioux counterattacks cost the Mandans dearly. During the next year they lost over sixty warriors, but what was worse, when the smallpox hit in 1837, the villagers could not disperse for fear of the hostile Yanktonais who still occupied the plains around the villages. The Mandans were very nearly destroyed; the Hidatsas, who attempted a quarantine, lost over half their people, and even the luckless Arikaras returned in time to be ravaged by the epidemic. The villages that survived continued to suffer from Yanktonai attacks and could use the plains hunting grounds only on sufferance of the Sioux.

The Oglala-Brulé advance onto the buffalo plains southwest of the Missouri was contemporaneous with the push up the Missouri and much more significant. Here horse raids and occasional hunts by the Sioux gave way to a concerted attempt to wrest the plains between the Black Hills and the Missouri from the Arapahos, Crows, Kiowas, and Cheyennes. By 1825, the Oglalas, advancing up the drainage of the Teton River, and the Brulés, moving up the drainage of the White River, had dispossessed the Kiowas and driven them south, pushed the Crows west to Powder River, and formed with the Cheyennes and Arapahos an alliance which would dominate the north and central plains for the next half century.

Historians have attributed the movement of the Sioux beyond the Black Hills into the Platte drainage to manipulations of the Rocky Mountain Fur Company, which sought to capture the Sioux trade from the American Fur Company. But, in fact, traders followed the Sioux; the Sioux did not follow the traders. William Sublette of the Rocky Mountain Fur

Company did not lure the Sioux to the Platte. He merely took advantage of their obvious advance toward it. He was the first to realize that by the 1830s Brulé and Oglala hunting grounds lay closer to the Platte than to the Missouri, and he took advantage of the situation to get their trade. The arrival of the Sioux on the Platte was not sudden; it had been preceded by the usual period of horse raids. Nor did it break some long accepted balance of power. Their push beyond the Black Hills was merely another phase in the long Sioux advance from the edge of the Great Plains.

What probably lured the Sioux toward the Platte was an ecological phenomenon that did not require the total depletion of game in the area they already held and that was not peculiar to the plains. Borders dividing contending tribes were never firm; between the established hunting territory of each people lay an indeterminate zone, variously described as war grounds or neutral grounds. In this area only war parties dared to venture; it was too dangerous for any band to travel into these regions to hunt. Because little pressure was put on the animal populations of these contested areas by hunters, they provided a refuge for the hard-pressed herds of adjacent tribal hunting grounds. Since buffalo migrations were unpredictable, a sudden loss of game in a large part of one's tribe's territory could prompt an invasion of these neutral grounds. Thus, throughout the nineteenth century, there usually lay at the edges of the Sioux-controlled lands a lucrative area that held an understandable attraction for them. In the contest for these rich disputed areas lay the key not only to many of the Sioux wars, but also to many other aboriginal wars on the continent.

These areas were, of course, never static. They shifted as tribes were able to wrest total control of them from other contending peoples, and so often created, in turn, a new disputed area beyond. Between 1830 and 1860, travelers on the plains described various neutral or war grounds ranging from the Sand Hills north of the Loup River in Nebraska down to the Pawnee Fork of the Arkansas. But for the Sioux four areas stand out: the region below Fort Laramie between the forks of the Platte in dispute during the 1830s; the Medicine Bow–Laramie plains country above Fort Laramie, fought over in the 1840s; the Yellowstone drainage of the Powder, Rosebud, and Big Horn rivers initially held by the Crows but reduced to a neutral ground in the 1840s and 1850s;

and portions of the Republican River country contested from the 1840s to the 1870s. Two things stand out in travelers' accounts of these areas: they were disputed by two or more tribes and they were rich in game.

Francis Parkman vividly described and completely misinterpreted an episode of the Sioux conquest of one of these areas, the Medicine Bow Valley, in 1846. He attributed the mustering of the large expedition that went, according to his account, against the Shoshones, and according to others against the Crows, to a desire for revenge for the loss of a son of Whirlwind, an important Sioux chief, during a horse raid on the Shoshones. But in Parkman's account, Whirlwind, who supposedly organized the expedition, decided not to accompany it, and the Oglalas and Saones who went ended up fighting neither the Crows nor the Shoshones. What they did, however, is significant. They moved into disputed Medicine Bow country west of Fort Laramie, land which all of these tribes contested.

The Sioux entered the area warily, took great precautions to avoid, not seek out, Crow and Shoshone war parties, and were much relieved to escape unscathed after a successful hunt. Parkman was disgusted, but the Sioux were immensely pleased with the whole affair. They had achieved the main goal of their warfare, the invasion and safe hunting of disputed buffalo grounds without any cost to themselves. White Shield, the slain man's brother, made another, apparently token, attempt to organize a war party to avenge his loss, but he never departed. The whole episode—from the whites' confusion over what tribe was the target of the expedition, to their misinterpretation of Indian motives, to Parkman's failure to see why the eventual outcome pleased the Sioux—reveals why, in so many accounts, the logic of Indian warfare is lost and wars are reduced to outbursts of random bloodletting. For the Sioux, the disputed area and its buffalo, more that the Shoshones or Crows, were the targets of the expedition; revenge was subordinate to the hunt. Their ability to hunt in safety, without striking a blow, comprised a strategic victory that more than satisfied them. To Parkman, intent on observing savage warriors lusting for blood revenge, all this was unfathomable.

Not all expeditions ended so peacefully, however. Bloodier probes preceded the summer expedition of 1846, and others followed it. When the Sioux

arrived in strength on the Platte in the mid-1830s, their raiding parties were already familiar to peoples from the Pawnee south to the Arkansas and the Santa Fe Trail. As early as the 1820s, their allies, the Cheyennes and Arapahos, had unsuccessfully contested hunting grounds with the Skidi Pawnees. But by 1835, these tribes had agreed to make peace.

The arrival of the Oglalas and Brulés at the Laramie River presented both the Pawnees and the Crows with more powerful rivals. The Crows were by now old enemies of the Tetons. Initially as allies of the Mandans and Hidatsas, and later as contestants for the hunting grounds of the plains, they had fought the Sioux for at least fifty years. By the 1840s, however, the once formidable Crows were a much weakened people. As late as the 1830s they had possessed more horses than any other tribe on the upper Missouri and estimates of their armed strength had ranged from 1,000 to 2,500 mounted men, but the years that followed brought them little but disaster. Smallpox and cholera reduced their numbers from 800 to 460 lodges, and rival groups pressed into their remaining hunting grounds. The Blackfeet attacked them from the north while the Saones, Oglalas, and Brulés closed in on the east and south. Threatened and desperate, the Crows sought aid west of the Rockies and increasingly allied themselves with the Shoshones and Flatheads.

The Pawnees, the last powerful horticultural tribe left on the plains, did not have a long tradition of warfare with the Sioux. The four Pawnee tribes— the Republicans, Skidis, Tapages, and Grands—lived in permanent earth-lodge villages on the Platte and Loup rivers, but twice a year they went on extended hunts in an area that stretched from between the forks of the Platte in the north to the Republican, Kansas, and Arkansas rivers in the south. Sioux horse raids had originally worried them very little, but, after the wars with Arapahos and Cheyennes, the growing proximity of the Sioux and their advantage in firearms had begun to concern the Pawnees enough to ask Americans to act as intermediaries in establishing peace. In the 1830s they remained, in the words of their white agent, along with the Sioux, one of the "two master tribes in the Upper Indian Country . . . who govern nearly all the smaller ones."

Under BullBear the Oglalas spearheaded the conquest of the Platte River hunting grounds of the Skidi Pawnees. By 1838, the Pawnee agent reported that the Skidis, fearing the Sioux would soon dominate the entire buffalo country, were contesting "every inch of ground," and, he added, "they are right for the day is not far off when the Sioux will possess the whole buffalo region, unless they are checked." In 1838, smallpox struck both the Oglalas and the Pawnees, but, as happened further north, the populous horticultural villages of the Pawnees suffered far more than the nomadic Sioux bands. The next year the intertribal struggle culminated in a pitched battle that cost the Pawnees between eighty and one-hundred warriors and led to the *de facto* surrender of the Platte hunting grounds by the Skidis.

The murder of BullBear in 1841 during a factional quarrel prompted a split in the Oglalas. One band, the Kiyuskas, BullBear's old supporters, continued to push into the Pawnee lands along the Platte and Smoky Hill rivers, while the other faction, the Bad Faces, moved west and north often joining with the Saone bands who were pushing out from the Missouri in attacks on the Crows. During these advances the Utes and Shoshones would be added to the ranks of Teton enemies, and further north the Yanktonais and Hunkpapas pushed into Canada, fighting the Metis, Plains Crees, and Assiniboines.

The Oregon, California, and Utah migrations of the 1840s made the Platte River Valley an American road across the plains. Like the traders on the Missouri before them, these migrants drove away game and created a new avenue for epidemic diseases, culminating in the cholera epidemic of 1849–1850. For the first time, the whites presented a significant threat to Sioux interests, and this conflict bore as fruit the first signs of overt Teton hostility since Chouteau's and Pryor's expeditions. But on the whole whites suffered little from the initial Teton reaction to the Oregon trail. The Crows and Pawnees bore the consequences of the decline of the Platte hunting grounds.

The Brulé and Kiyuska Oglalas attacked the Pawnee on the South Platte and the Republican. The Tetons did not restrict their attacks to the buffalo grounds; along with the Yanktons and Yanktonais from the Missouri, they attacked the Pawnees in their villages and disrupted the whole Pawnee economy. While small war parties stole horses and killed women working in the fields, large expeditions with as many as 700 men attacked the villages themselves. This dual assault threatened to reduce the Pawnees to starvation, greatly weakening their ability to resist.

The Sioux struck one of their most devastating blows in 1843, destroying a new village the Pawnees had built on the Loup at the urging of the whites. They killed sixty-seven people and forced the Pawnees back to the Platte, where they were threatened with retribution by whites for their failure to remove as agreed. The Pawnees vainly cited American obligations under the treaty of 1833 to help defend them from attacks by other tribes; and they also repeatedly sought peace. Neither availed. Unlike the Otos, Omahas, and Poncas, who eventually gave up all attempts to hunt on the western plains, the Pawnees persisted in their semiannual expeditions. The tribal census taken in 1859 reveals the price the Pawnees paid. When Zebulon Pike had visited the Pawnees in 1806 he found a roughly equivalent number of men and women in each village. In his partial census, he gave a population of 1,973 men and 2,170 women, exclusive of children. In 1859, agent William Dennison listed 820 men and 1,505 women; largely because of war, women now outnumbered men by nearly two to one.

The final blow came in 1873, three years before the Battle of the Little Bighorn, when the Sioux surprised a Pawnee hunting party on the Republican River, killing about 100 people. The Pawnees, now virtually prisoners in their reservation villages, gave in. They abandoned their Nebraska homeland and, over the protests of their agents, moved to Indian Territory. White settlers may have rejoiced at their removal, but it was the Sioux who had driven the Pawnees from Nebraska.

The experience of the Crows was much the same. Attacked along a front that ran from the Yellowstone to the Laramie Plains, they were never routed, but their power declined steadily. The Sioux drove them from the Laramie Plains and then during the 1850s and 1860s pushed them farther and farther up the Yellowstone. In the mid-1850s, Edwin Denig, a trapper familiar with the plains, predicted their total destruction, and by 1862 they had apparently been driven from the plains and into the mountains. They, too, would join the Americans against the Sioux.

In a very real sense the Americans, because of their destruction of game along the Missouri and Platte, had stimulated this warfare for years, but their first significant intervention in intertribal politics since the Leavenworth expedition came with the celebrated Laramie Peace Conference of 1851. Although scholars have recognized the importance of both intertribal warfare and the decline of the buffalo in prompting this conference, they have, probably because they accepted without question the individualistic interpretation of Indian wars, neglected the Indian political situation at the time of the treaty. They have failed to appreciate the predominance of the Sioux-Cheyenne-Arapaho alliance on the northern and central plains.

By 1851, American Indian officials had recognized that white travel and trade on the Great Plains had reduced the number of buffalo and helped precipitate intertribal wars. They proposed to restore peace by compensating the Indians for the loss of game. Their motives for this were hardly selfless, since intertribal wars endangered American travelers and commerce. Once they had established peace and drawn firm boundaries between the tribes, they could hold a tribe responsible for any depredations committed within its allotted area. Furthermore, by granting compensation for the destruction of game, the government gave itself an entrée into tribal politics: by allowing or withholding payments, they could directly influence the conduct of the Indians.

Although American negotiators certainly did not seek tribal unity in 1851, it is ethnocentric history to contend that the Fort Laramie Treaty allowed the Americans to "divide and conquer." Fundamentally divided at the time of the treaty, the plains tribes continued so afterward. The treaty itself was irrelevant; both the boundaries it created and its prohibition of intertribal warfare were ignored from the beginning by the only tribal participants who finally mattered, the Sioux.

Indeed the whole conference can be interpreted as a major triumph for the Tetons. In a sense, the Fort Laramie Treaty marked the height of Sioux political power. Of the 10,000 Indians who attended the conference, the great majority of them were Sioux, Cheyennes, and Arapahos. Sioux threats kept the Pawnees and all but small groups of Crows, Arikaras, Hidatsas, and Assiniboines from coming to Fort Laramie. The Shoshones came, but the Cheyennes attacked their party and part turned back. With the Sioux and their allies so thoroughly dominating the conference, the treaty itself amounted to both a recognition of Sioux power and an attempt to curb it. But when American negotiators tried to restrict the Sioux to an area north of the Platte, Black Hawk, an Oglala, protested that they held the lands to the south by the same right the Americans held their lands, the

right of conquest: "These lands once belonged to the Kiowas and the Crows, but we whipped those nations out of them, and in this we did what the white men do when they want the lands of the Indians." The Americans conceded, granting the Sioux hunting rights, which, in Indian eyes, confirmed title. The Sioux gladly accepted American presents and their tacit recognition of Sioux conquests, but, as their actions proved, they never saw the treaty as a prohibition of future gains. After an American war with the Sioux and another attempt to stop intertribal warfare in 1855, Bear's Rib, a Hunkpapa chief, explained to Lieutenant G. K. Warren that the Tetons found it difficult to take the American prohibition of warfare seriously when the Americans themselves left these conferences only to engage in wars with other Indians or with the Mormons.

After the treaty, the lines of conflict on the plains were clearly drawn. The two major powers in the area, the Sioux and the Americans, had both advanced steadily and with relatively little mutual conflict. Following the treaty they became avowed and recognized rivals. Within four years of the treaty, the first American war with the Tetons would break out; and by the mid-1850s, American officers frankly saw further war as inevitable. The Sioux, in turn, recognized the American threat to their interests, and the tribes, in a rare display of concerted action, agreed as a matter of policy to prohibit all land cessions and to close their remaining productive hunting grounds to American intrusions. These attempts consistently led to war with the Americans. After a century of conquest the Sioux had very definite conceptions of the boundaries of their tribal territory. Recent historians and some earlier anthropologists contended that Indians never fought for territory, but if this is so, it is hard to explain the documented outrage of the Saones, Oglalas, and Brulés at the cession of land along the Missouri by the Yanktons in 1858. The Tetons had moved from this land decades before and had been replaced by the Yanktons, but from the Teton point of view the whole western Sioux nation still held title to the territory and the Yanktons had no authority to sell it. Fearing that acceptance of annuities would connote recognition of the sale, the Saone tribes refused them, and the cession provoked a crisis on the western plains and hardened Teton ranks against the Americans.

The warfare between the northern plains tribes and the United States that followed the Fort Laramie

Treaty of 1851 was not the armed resistance of a people driven to the wall by American expansion. In reality these wars arose from the clash of two expanding powers—the United States, and the Sioux and their allies. If, from a distance, it appears that the vast preponderance of strength rested with the whites, it should be remembered that the ability of the United States to bring this power to bear was limited. The series of defeats the Sioux inflicted on American troops during these years reveals how real the power of the Tetons was.

Even as they fought the Americans, the Sioux continued to expand their domination of plains hunting grounds, as they had to in order to survive. Logically enough, the tribes the Sioux threatened—the Crows, Pawnees, and Arikaras especially—sided with the Americans, providing them with soldiers and scouts. For white historians to cast these people as mere dupes or traitors is too simplistic. They fought for their tribal interests and loyalties as did the Sioux.

It is ironic that historians, far more than anthropologists, have been guilty of viewing intertribal history as essentially ahistoric and static, of refusing to examine critically the conditions that prompted Indian actions. In too much Indian history, tribes fight only "ancient" enemies, as if each group were doled out an allotted number of adversaries at creation with whom they battled mindlessly through eternity. Historians have been too easily mystified by intertribal warfare, too willing to see it as the result of some ingrained cultural pugnacity. This is not to argue that the plains tribes did not offer individual warriors incentives of wealth and prestige that encouraged warfare, but, as Newcomb pointed out, the real question is why the tribe placed such a premium on encouraging warriors. This is essentially a historical question. Without an understanding of tribal and intertribal histories, and an appreciation that, like all history, they are dynamic, not static, the actions of Indians when they come into conflict with whites can be easily and fatally distorted.

Myths of the American West: Missionaries, Entrepreneurs, and New Identities

Patricia Nelson Limerick

For America the West is far more than a point on the compass. It is a direction of destiny, a mythic landscape, a heroic locale—ultimately, a complex of cultural ideas. The West symbolizes possibility, progress, re-creation as well as recreation, optimism, fulfillment, the future—all prime ingredients of the American Dream. It is a mythic locale where entrepreneurial business people and missionaries—the likes of Narcissa Whitman—shared and charted individual destinies. Resident westerners have always thought they stood for, and practiced, a unique brand of individualism and private enterprise, both economic and religious, free from the constraints of civilization, society, authority, government. From popular culture icons like the Lone Ranger to "pioneer" politicians like Barry Goldwater could consistently be heard a rhetoric of individual independence. "Don't Fence Me In" has become something of a regional anthem, with the consistent refrain that the West represents freedom, independence, and self-reliance—authentic America. Such a chorus of vivid invocations of personal and regional sovereignty, however, simply do not square with the true history of the West. As seen by Patricia Nelson Limerick of the University of Colorado, Boulder, the legacy of the West is also a story of habitual dependence on government, from the region's territorial period to the present. Citing the long-standing reliance on the U.S. Army, an ever-present need for government support and subsidies for railroads, mining rights, land grants, farm credit programs, water and other public projects from Rocky Flats to Los Alamos, and grazing rights for cattle, Limerick sees the West as most always the first in line for government handouts. Ironically, the West, always thought to be adventurous and romantic—and above all *free*—has often functioned as the frontier of the American welfare state.

The Missionary Myth

The idea of the innocent victim retains extraordinary power, and no situation made a stronger symbolic statement of this than that of the white woman murdered by Indians. Here was surely a clear case of victimization, villainy, and betrayed innocence. But few deaths of this kind occurred in American history with such purity; they were instead embedded in the complex dynamics of race relations, in which neither concept—villain or victim—did much to illuminate history.

Narcissa Prentiss Whitman made a very unlikely villain. Deeply moved by the thought of Western Indians living without knowledge of Christianity, Narcissa Prentiss wrote her mission board in 1835, "I now offer myself to the American Board to be employed in their service among the heathen. . . . " In 1836, she left her home in New York to rescue the

Indians in Oregon. An unattached female could hardly be a missionary, and before her departure Narcissa Prentiss hastily married another Oregon volunteer, Marcus Whitman. The Whitmans and Henry and Eliza Spalding set off to cross the country. Pioneers on the overland trail, they faced stiff challenges from nature and some from human nature. The fur trappers and traders with whom they traveled resented the delays and sermons that came with missionary companionship. The missionaries themselves presented less than a united front. They had the strong, contentious personalities of self-appointed agents of God. They also had a history; Henry Spalding had courted Narcissa, and lost. Anyone who thinks of the nineteenth-century West as a land of fresh starts and new beginnings might think of Henry Spalding and Narcissa Whitman and the memories they took with them to Oregon.

Arrived in the Oregon country, the missionaries—like salesmen dividing up markets—divided up tribes and locations. The Whitmans set to work on the Cayuse Indians. Narcissa Whitman's life in Oregon provides little support for the image of life in the West as free, adventurous, and romantic. Most of the time, she labored. She had one child of her own; she adopted many others—mixed-blood children of fur trappers, and orphans from the overland trail. "My health has been so poor," she wrote her sister in 1846, "and my family has increased so rapidly, that it has been impossible. You will be astonished to know that we have eleven children in our family, and not one of them our own by birth, but so it is. Seven orphans were brought to our door in Oct., 1844, whose parents both died on the way to this country. Destitute and friendless, there was no other alternative—we must take them in or they must perish."

Depending on one's point of view, the Whitman mission had a lucky or an unlucky location—along the Oregon Trail, where exhausted travelers arrived desperate for food, rest, and help. Narcissa Whitman's small home served as kitchen, dining hall, dormitory, and church building, while she longed for privacy and rest. She often cooked three meals a day for twenty people. For five years, she had no stove and cooked in an open fireplace.

In the midst of crowds, she was lonely, writing nostalgic letters to friends and family in the East who seemed to answer infrequently; she went as long as two years without a letter from home. Separated by distance and sometimes by quarrels, Narcissa and the other missionary wives in Oregon tried for a time to organize a nineteenth-century version of a woman's support group; at a certain hour every day, they would pause in their work, think of each other, and pray for the strength to be proper mothers to their children in the wilderness.

Direct tragedy added to loneliness, overwork, and frustration. The Whitman's only child, two years old, drowned while playing alone near a stream. Providence was testing Narcissa Whitman's faith in every imaginable way.

Then, in November of 1847, after eleven years with the missionaries among them, when the white or mixed-blood mission population had grown to twenty men, ten women, and forty-four children, the Cayuse Indians rose in rebellion and killed fourteen people—including Marcus and Narcissa Whitman.

Was Narcissa Whitman an innocent victim of brutality and ingratitude? What possessed the Cayuses?

One skill essential to the writing of Western American history is a capacity to deal with multiple points of view. It is as if one were a lawyer at a trial designed on the principle of the Mad Hatter's tea party—as soon as one begins to understand and empathize with the plaintiff's case, it is time to move over and empathize with the defendant. Seldom are there only two parties or only two points of view. Taking into account division within groups—intertribal conflict and factions within tribes and, in Oregon, settlers against missionaries, Protestants against Catholics, British Hudson's Bay Company traders against Americans—it is taxing simply to keep track of the points of view.

Why did Cayuses kill the Whitmans? The chain of events bringing the Whitmans to the Northwest was an odd and arbitrary one. In a recent book, the historian Christopher Miller explains that the Whitman mission was hardly the first crisis to hit the Columbia Plateau and its natives. A "three hundred year cold spell," a "result of the Little Ice Age," had shaken the environment, apparently reducing food sources. Moreover, the effects of European presence in North America began reaching the plateau even before the Europeans themselves arrived. The "conjunction of sickness, with the coming of horses, guns, climatic deterioration and near constant war" added up to an "eighteenth-century crisis." Punctuated by a disturbing and perplexing ash fall from a volcanic explosion, the changes brought many of the Plateau

Indians to the conviction that the world was in trouble. They were thus receptive to a new set of prophecies from religious leaders. A central element of this new worldview came in the reported words of the man known as the Spokan Prophet, words spoken around 1790: "Soon there will come from the rising sun a different kind of man from any you have yet seen, who will bring with them a book and will teach you everything, after that the world will fall to pieces," opening the way to a restored and better world. Groups of Indians therefore began to welcome whites, since learning from these newcomers was to be an essential stage in the route to a new future.

In 1831, a small party of Nez Percé and Flathead Indians journeyed to St. Louis, Missouri. For years, Western historians said that these Indians had heard of Jesuits through contacts with fur traders and had come to ask for their own "Black Robes." That confident claim aside, Christopher Miller has recently written that it is still a "mystery how it all came to pass." Nonetheless, he argues persuasively that the Northwest Indians went to St. Louis pursuing religious fulfillment according to the plateau millennial tradition; it was their unlikely fate to be misunderstood by the equally millennial Christians who heard the story of the visit. A Protestant man named William Walker wrote a letter about the meetings in St. Louis, and the letter was circulated in church newspapers and read at church meetings, leaving the impression that the Indians of Oregon were begging for Christianity.

And so, in this chain of circumstances "so bizarre as to seem providential," in Miller's words, the Cayuses got the Whitmans, who had responded to the furor provoked by the letter. Irritations began to pile up. The Whitmans set out to transform the Cayuses from hunters, fishers, and gatherers to farmers, from heathens to Presbyterians. As the place became a way station for the Oregon Trail, the mission began to look like an agency for the service of white people. This was not, in fact, too far from the founder's view of his organization. "It does not concern me so much what is to become of any particular set of Indians," Marcus Whitman wrote his parents, "as to give them the offer of salvation through the gospel and the opportunity of civilization. . . . I have no doubt our greatest work is to be to aid the white settlement of this country and help to found its religious institutions."

The Cayuses began to suffer from white people's diseases, to which they had no immunity. Finally, in 1847, they were devastated by measles. While the white people at the mission seldom died from measles, the Indians noticed that an infected Cayuse nearly always died. It was an Indian conviction that disease was "the result of either malevolence or spiritual transgression"; either way, the evidence pointed at the missionaries. When the Cayuses finally turned on the Whitmans, they were giving up "the shared prophetic vision" that these newcomers would teach a lesson essential to reshaping the world. The Cayuses were, in other words, acting in and responding to currents of history of which Narcissa Whitman was not a primary determinant.

Descending on the Cayuses, determined to bring light to the "benighted ones" living in "the thick darkness of heathenism," Narcissa Whitman was an intolerant invader. If she was not a villain, neither was she an innocent victim. Her story is melancholy but on the whole predictable, one of many similar stories in Western history that trigger an interventionist's urge. "Watch out, Narcissa," one finds oneself thinking, 140 years too late, "you think you are doing good works, but you are getting yourself—and others—into deep trouble." Given the inability of Cayuses to understand Presbyterians, and the inability of Presbyterians to understand Cayuses, the trouble could only escalate. Narcissa Whitman would not have imagined that there was anything to understand; where the Cayuses had religion, social networks, a thriving trade in horses, and a full culture, Whitman would have seen vacancy or, worse, heathenism.

Narcissa Whitman knew she was volunteering for risk; her willingness to take on those risks is, however, easier to understand because it was based on religion. Irrational faith is its own explanation; one can analyze its components, but the fact remains that extraordinary faith leads to extraordinary action. The mystery is not that Narcissa Whitman risked all for the demands of the deity but that so many others risked all for the demands of the profit motive.

Myths About
Government's Role in the West

Nothing so undermines the Western claim to a tradition of independence as [the] matter of federal support to Western development. The two key frontier activities—the control of Indians and the distribution of land—were primarily federal responsibilities, at times involving considerable ·expense. Federal subsidies to transportation—to freighting companies and to railroads, to harbor improvement and to highway building—made the concept of private enterprise in transportation an ambiguous one. Even apparent inaction could in a way support development. Failing to restrain or regulate access to the public grazing lands or to the timber lands, the federal government in effect subsidized private cattle raisers and loggers with unlimited access to national resources.

Within the territorial framework, the significance of federal money was often dramatic. Federal office provided a valued form of patronage; appropriations for public buildings offered another route to local income. Official government printing, entrusted to a local newspaper of the proper political orientation, could determine a publisher's failure or success. Territorial business involving Indians was another route to federal money. Volunteers in Indian campaigns would expect federal pay. Local Indian hostilities were a mixed blessing; forts and soldiers meant markets for local products and business for local merchants. Similarly, once conquered and dependent on rations, Indians on reservations became a market for local grain and beef.

In its early years, Dakota Territory gave the purest demonstration of this economic dependence. With the delayed development of farming and mining, Dakota settlers rapidly grasped the idea "of the federal government not only as a paternalistic provider of land and governmental organization but also as a subsidizing agency which furnished needed development funds in the form of offices, Indian and army supply orders, and post and land office positions." When Indian troubles increased, white settlement became risky, and hard times came to Dakota, "the federal government remained the only source of revenue and sustenance." In those rough times, "Washington was in essence subsidizing a government which had few citizens, no income, and a highly questionable future." Agricultural development and the mining boom of the Black Hills later relieved the pressure on federal resources, but in the meantime the precedent had been well set. It had become an "old Dakota attitude that government itself was an important paying business."

Nonetheless, Dakotans also took up the standard cry of the oppressed colony. "We are so heartily disgusted with our dependent condition, with being snubbed at every turn in life, with having all our interest subjected to the whims and corrupt acts of persons in power that we feel very much as the thirteen colonies felt," a Dakota newspaper declared in 1877. As they asserted their rights to statehood, Dakota residents did not give much support to the idea that political innovation emanated from the frontier. They used the familiar states' rights arguments; their political ideas were "so much those of the older sections" that "they had not developed any indigenous ones of their own since coming to Dakota." After a close study, Howard Lamar found in the Dakota activists "a singular lack of political originality."

Frederick Jackson Turner's idea that the frontier had been the source of American democracy did receive some support from pioneer rhetoric. Politically involved residents were often gifted speechmakers and petition writers, even if they lacked originality. Western settlers were so abundantly supplied with slogans and democratic formulas that putting our trust in their recorded words alone would be misleading. Only close archival research can reveal what those gifted speakers and writers were actually doing. An early event in Dakota history demonstrates the problem.

In 1857, in unorganized territory to the west of Minnesota, American citizens took part in what appeared to be a classic social illness. The essential project of the American West was to exploit the available resources. Since nature would not provide it all, both speculation and the entrepreneurial uses of government were human devices to supplement nature's offerings.

Consider the dominant political figure of Wyoming, before and after statehood. The imagination supplies a tough and self-reliant rancher—a Cincinnatus in this case leaving his horse, not his plow, to go to the aid of his homeland. The picture is partly true. Francis Warren did invest in ranching, but also in utilities, banks, railroads, and, at first, merchandising. Like many Westerners, he pursued two interchangeable goals—"his own enrichment and the development of Wyoming." What made him a leader in the territory, governor for a time and senator after statehood? "His ability to construct a political machine dedicated to the efficient acquisition of federal subsidies," the historian Lewis Gould has explained, "set him apart from his colleagues." Wyoming "could not rely solely on its own economic resources for growth." Aridity and a short growing season limited agriculture, and cattle raising did not lead to either stable or widely distributed prosperity. Compensating for nature's shortages, Warren's pursuit of federal money—for forts, public building, and other improvements—met the hopes of his constituents, who "were more concerned with economic development than with social protest and as a result favored policies designed to increase their stake in society."

Warren and Wyoming were beneficiaries of the Great Compromise of 1787, by which the American Constitution gave "equal representation to all states, regardless of the disparity of their populations." Proclamations of powerlessness aside, Western states had huge areas of land, few people, and two senators apiece. Given equal standing with their colleagues from more populous states, Western senators had the additional "advantage of representing relatively few major economic interests. They were therefore in a position to trade votes advantageously, in order to pass the relatively few measures which the interests they represented wanted badly." Senator Warren of Wyoming, as his biographer has put it, "left scant positive imprint on American life. He rarely looked up from his pursuit of influence for himself and riches for his state to consider the pressing questions of his time." The opportunity to take up a concern for national affairs always existed for Warren and his Western counterparts, but the workings of Western politics did not push them to it.

*   *   *

Western dependence on federal resources did not end with the territories. Neither did the accepting of help—with resentment. Far from declining in the twentieth century, federal participation in the Western economy expanded. The Reclamation Act of 1902 put the national government in the center of the control and development of water, the West's key resource. President Theodore Roosevelt and Chief Forester Gifford Pinchot pressed the cause of expert management of the national forests, using federal powers to guide resource users toward a longer-range version of utility. The Taylor Grazing Act of 1934 finally centralized the control of grazing on the public domain. Beyond the Taylor Act, many New Deal measures framed to address the national prob-

lems of the Great Depression were especially rewarding for the West.

In early June 1933, Wyoming was proud of its status as "the only state or territory which had not asked for or received any federal assistance for its needy." In late June 1933, the state changed course and took its first federal relief check. Wyoming's "late start," T. A. Larson has pointed out, "proved to be no deterrent. . . . The federal government's nonrecoverable relief expenditures in Wyoming between July 1, 1933, and June 30, 1937, amounted to $330.64 per capita compared with $115.18 in the United States. Meanwhile, per capita internal revenue collected in Wyoming for the years 1934–1937 amounted to $28.94 compared with $109.43 in the United States." This was not an imbalance unique to Wyoming; Colorado "received twice as much as it sent to a government which it considered meddlesome and constitutionally threatening." The New Deal, Leonard Arrington has found, "benefited the West more than other sections of the nation. Indeed, when one lists the states in the order of the per capita expenditures of the federal economic agencies, the top fourteen states in benefits received were all in the West." The West got "sixty percent more" on a per capita basis than the impoverished regions of the South. "Per capita expenditures of federal agencies in Montana from 1933 to 1939, for example, were $710, while they were only $143 in North Carolina.

The New Deal was a good deal for the West. The Civilian Conservation Corps did much of its finest work in the West; the farm credit programs saved numerous farmers and cattlemen from bankruptcy; the Soil Conservation Service tried to keep the West from blowing away; the Farm Security Administration built camps to house the impoverished migrant workers of California. And yet many Western political leaders complained. They took advantage of programs that helped their local interests, and they spent much of their remaining time denouncing the spread of bureaucracy and the give-away quality of the New Deal. The case of the cattlemen was representative: hit by drought, the consequences of overgrazing and of dropping prices, Western cattlemen needed help. But aid "brought regulation, and regulation the cattlemen could not abide." In 1934, in a Drought Relief Service program, the federal government began buying cattle. The sellers "had to agree to any future production-control plans which might be started," and "the prices paid were not high." Still, federal money to the amount of "nearly $525 million" went "to save cattlemen from ruin and starvation," the historian John Schlebecker has written. "For this salvation, many cattlemen never forgave the government. Large numbers of them resented the help."

New Deal assistance went against a number of Western values. T. A. Larson's description of Wyoming residents applied to many other Westerners: "Although they had always been dependent on various types of federal aid, they wanted as little government as possible, and preferred most of that to be in state or local hands. Professing independence, self-reliance, and dedication to free enterprise, they served as vocal, aggressive custodians of what remained of the frontier spirit." In fact, a fair amount of that "frontier spirit" lived on. Parading their independence and accepting federal money, Westerners in the 1930s kept faith with the frontier legacy.

It is common to associate the American West with the future, one of independence and self-reliance. The future that was actually projected in the Western past is quite a different matter. It was in the phenomenon of dependence—on the federal government, on the changeability of nature, on outside investment—that the West pulled ahead. In the course of American history, the central government and its role in the economy grew gradually; years of nonintervention were succeeded by the growing power of the federal government in the Progressive Era, the New Deal, and World War Two. In the West, in land policy, transportation, Indian affairs, border regulation, territorial government, and public projects, it has been possible to see the future and to see that it works—sometimes. Heavy reliance on the federal government's good graces, the example of the West suggests, does expose the two principals to substantial risk—to inefficiency and mismanagement on the part of the benefactor and to resentment and discontent on the part of the beneficiaries. To a striking degree, the lessons of the problems of the American welfare state could be read in the nation's frontier past.

* * *

As powerful and persistent as the fantasy that the West set Americans free from relying on the federal government was the fantasy that westward movement could set one free from the past. The West, for instance, was once a refuge for people who had trouble breathing. Sufferers from asthma, bronchitis, and even tuberculosis believed they chose a therapeutic environment when they chose the clean, dry air of the West.

Respiratory refugees particularly favored Arizona. Tucson's population jumped from 45,454 in 1950 to 330,537 in 1980, in large part an accretion of people who liked the climate—the clear air, the direct sunlight. Understandably, many of these new arrivals missed their homelands. Ill at ease with the peculiar plants and exposed soil of the desert, they naturally attempted to replicate the gardens and yards they had left behind. One popular, familiar plant was the magnificently named fruitless mulberry, the male of the species, which does not produce messy berries. What the fruit-free mulberry produces is pollen.

Re-creating a familiar landscape, Tucson immigrants had also re-created a familiar pollen count. Allergies reactivated. Coping with all the problems of Sun Belt growth, the Tucson City Council found itself debating in 1975 a resolution to ban the fruitless mulberry.

Tucson citizens with allergies had taken part in a familiar Western exercise: replicating the problems they had attempted to escape. It was a twentieth-century version of the Boone paradox. Daniel Boone found civilization intolerable and escaped to the wilderness. His travels blazed trails for other pioneers to follow, and Boone found himself crowded out. His fresh start turned rapidly stale.

Of all the meanings assigned to Western independence, none had more emotional power than the prospect of becoming independent of the past. But Western Americans did what most travelers do: they took their problems with them. Cultural baggage is not, after all, something one retains or discards at will. While much of the Western replication of familiar ways was voluntary and intentional, other elements of continuity appear to have caught Westerners by surprise—as if parts of their own characters were specters haunting them despite an attempt at exorcism by migration. No wonder, then, that emigrants made so much of their supposed new identity; no wonder they pressed the case of their supposed adaptations to the new environment, their earned status as real Westerners. Accenting the factor of their migration and new location, Westerners tried to hold the ghosts of their old, imported identities at bay.

Commanding Performance: Booker T. Washington's Atlanta Compromise Address

David Lionel Smith

Myths about important historical figures die hard. Nowhere is this more true than in the case of the myths surrounding Booker T. Washington. Accordingly, Washington is characterized by words such as "compromise," "moderation," and particularly "accommodation." His great radical and progressive antagonist, of course, was W. E. B. Du Bois. For some time now that mythic picture of Washington has largely been corrected. This major adjustment has centered around the efforts of the historian and biographer, Louis Harlan. Washington now appears as a pragmatist and a powerful politician who literally ruled an empire, including many whites. Accepting and building on the findings of Harlan and others, David Lionel Smith, Professor of English at Williams College, here analyzes what most agree to be Washington's philosophical, rhetorical, and for Smith strategic masterpiece, the "Atlanta Exposition Address." In this address Washington, given the charged times and the southern location, successfully walked the fine line, in speaking to northern and southern whites, as well as blacks. Not only did he successfully walk that line thus "accommodating" all, but revealed as well a calculating, manipulating, myth-controlling style. For example, Washington, in emphasizing Negroes' roles in developing simple craft skills and performing manual labor, clearly excludes participation in the finer arts. Later in the speech, and in another context, he purposely contradicts himself and talks of Negro advancement in those same fine arts. Thus, there is a myth beyond that of Washington the accommodator; he now, behind his humble posture, is stating a contradictory agenda for blacks, and indeed the whole of society. Stated another way, the previous debunking did not go far enough. Finally, Smith notes that however successful Washington's rhetoric at Atlanta, very much of it was anachronistic. His was indeed a "last hurrah"—at least for operating under the cloak of accommodation. In fact the militants, led by Du Bois, were the wave of the future, however rocky that became. Perhaps that is at least one reason for the persistence of the "accommodation" myth associated with Washington. It is instructive to note that Du Bois praised the Atlanta speech in 1895; by 1903 he was decrying it.

Booker T. Washington's classic *Up from Slavery* is unquestionably the finest black autobiography ever written by a European-American. In the final sentence of the book's preface, Washington notes, "without the painstaking and generous assistance of Mr. Max Bennett Thrasher I would not have succeeded in any satisfactory degree." This is a typical Washingtonian understatement. Thrasher wrote the book. Beginning that same paragraph, Washington has declared, "I have tried to tell a simple, straight-forward story, with no attempt at embellishment. My regret is that what I have attempted to do has been done so imperfectly." This is either false modesty or a harsh assessment of his ghost writer. Since Thrasher remained in Washington's employ until his abrupt death (from appendicitis) in 1903, we must infer that "the Wizard" was not so displeased with their collaborative product. Washington had no peers in the use of rhetorical humility as a strategy of manipulation.

Conventional wisdom portrays Washington as a spokesman for compromise, moderation, and "accommodation." This view allows for a neat duality, posing W. E. B. DuBois as Washington's radical and progressive antagonist. A careful reading of Washington's texts, however, reveals a far more complex, ambiguous and calculating figure. Furthermore, Louis Harlan's splendid biographies of Washington and *The Booker T. Washington Papers* published under Harlan's general editorship reveal to us a cynical, efficient, extraordinarily powerful politician: the consummate pragmatist. He ruled an empire, including many white employees, but lest local whites take offense, he concealed this fact and allowed none of his white employees to live in Tuskegee. Washington was not only the most powerful black man of his time, but arguably the most influential Southerner as well. Yet in *Up from Slavery* he portrays himself to be as modest as a field hand.

In his career as in his writing, Washington relied on his exceptional performative skills. His success as an unsurpassed fund-raiser depended largely on his self-representation in speeches, in personal encounters, and in writing. *Up from Slavery* is as much an account of Washington's virtuoso performances as it is a narrative of his life. Indeed, the last quarter of the book—from the "Atlanta Exposition Address" of 1895 onward—degenerates into a virtual scrapbook, complete with tips on how to emulate Washington's success in speaking, self-discipline, and fund-raising. Of course, Washington always cloaks his boasting in understatement and humble gratitude to God, his teachers, his donors, and other white people. Nonetheless, this personal chronicle of one man's progress from slavery to international celebrity is also implicitly a morality tale about the Negro race. Washington emerges as the model Negro; the apt and unassailable representative of his race. *Up from Slavery* both describes and authorizes that status. In practical terms, this self-representation translated into a very effective claim upon absolute authority as the political power broker for black people and the proper recipient of white philanthropy for Negro education. For these endowments, Washington was always humbly grateful.

While *Up from Slavery* is obsessively concerned with effective self-representation, it is also fundamentally preoccupied with reading one's audience and with improvisation and duplicity as essential strategies of effective performance. In this respect, Washington's principles are purely pragmatic. Unlike DuBois and other black intellectuals who saw personal dignity and integrity as crucial traits in their quest to earn from whites respect and acceptance as equals, Washington concentrated on immediate effects and tangible benefits, such as cash contributions and political deals. In other words, he was willing to perform in any way necessary to get what he wanted. Numerous incidents throughout the book illustrate this point and reveal the indissoluble link between humility, duplicity, and ambition in this text. Washington's deft presentation of these incidents also reflects the rhetorical genius that allowed him to be an effective black politician in a period of extraordinarily virulent and violent Negrophobia.

An early example of Washington's pragmatism involves the conflict between his having, as a child, to work in a salt furnace and his desire to attend school. His work schedule makes him always late for school, so he contrives to set the shop clock thirty minutes ahead in order for him to reach school on time. His tampering is eventually discovered, and the clock is made inaccessible. Washington presents this episode as a humorous instance of his youthful naiveté and passion for education. He apologizes profusely, implying that he understands how wrong his tampering had been. But in fact, this episode is perfectly typical of Washington. His humility is not humble, nor his contrition contrite. That he cites such a trivial incident is in itself revealing. Despite his disclaimers, we may view this as an early lesson in Washington's wiliness at subverting social norms in pursuit of his own goals. Perhaps that is why the anecdote pleases him so.

Later, when Washington sets out for Hampton Institute, he is so poor that he has to sleep at night under the plank sidewalks of Richmond, Virginia. Subsequently, he unloads ship cargo to earn money for food. When he arrives at Hampton seeking admission, the head teacher immediately puts him to work sweeping and dusting. Washington recognizes this assignment as an audition, and he performs the task so thoroughly that he earns his admission and a job as school janitor. "The sweeping of the room was my college examination," he gloats, "and never did any youth pass an examination for entrance into Harvard or Yale that gave him more genuine satisfaction." Washington apparently intends both of these anecdotes to demonstrate—in keeping with Hampton's motto, "The Dignity of Labor"—that manual labor brings higher rewards. But we might read these incidents as evidence of his willingness to suffer any indignity in pursuit of his goals. Such anecdotes also help to maintain his mask of humility by allowing his white audience to think of him as a janitor who made good, not as a man driven by ambition.

In any case, neither of these incidents reveals explicit duplicity, yet both suggest undertones of meaning contrary to what Washington attributes to them. The cynical twist of Washington's pragmatism becomes most explicit when he describes his pique with Hampton's Indian students, who refuse to cut their hair and relinquish their own culture. He asserts, "no white American ever thinks that any other race is wholly civilized until he wears the white man's clothes, eats the white man's food, speaks the white man's language, and professes the white man's religion." There is no ambiguity here regarding how he perceives the expectations of his white audience. He emphasizes the importance of self-presentation, but is conspicuously silent on the issue of commitment, belief, or value. This passage leaves no doubt that Washington was first and foremost a rhetorician. Again and again, he reveals himself as a man who can and will perform any verbal or physical gesture necessary to achieve his goals.

Nevertheless, as a black Southerner, Washington's rhetorical options were severely limited by ugly social realities. Lynchings averaged about 150 per year during the 1890s—three per week—and rapes, beatings, house burnings, and other acts of violence against blacks who somehow offended white people were too numerous to count. If a black man spoke at all in public, he was expected to do so quietly, politely, and conservatively. The white South was not

prepared or inclined to accept a black P. T. Barnum, even in jest, and Washington's cynical manipulations had to be carefully masked. They were, indeed, so skillfully masked that Washington continues to deceive us, even now. Washington, the man, is so profoundly enigmatic, even to his most informed scholars, that we may never achieve a satisfactory psychological portrait of him. We can, however, describe the workings of his rhetoric. Nowhere is that rhetoric more startling than in his "Atlanta Exposition Address."

Booker T. Washington's "Atlanta Exposition Address" of 1895 is a masterpiece of American political oratory. This single speech made Washington, who prior to 1895 was not even the most influential black educator in Alabama, a dominant political figure and what Euro-Americans called "the spokesman for his race" for two full decades, until his death in 1915. What it means socially to be the "spokesman for the Negro" in a period of extreme racist violence, political disfranchisement, and increasing segregation is an interesting matter that, regrettably, we cannot pursue in all its social permutations. Nevertheless, an examination of this singular document and its place in *Up from Slavery* will doubtless prove suggestive of social implications, because such implications are naturally entailed by rhetorical inquiry. The "Exposition Address" announced the main themes of Washington's public career and, fittingly, it reiterates the main themes of *Up from Slavery* as well. Furthermore, just as it was the most important event in his public life, it is the formal center of his autobiography: the climax toward which all prior chapters lead and from which all subsequent ones emanate.

The "Address" is in formal terms a fine piece of work, but its true greatness derives from its brilliant response to an inordinately difficult rhetorical situation. Washington himself cogently describes that situation. Always the politician, he focuses immediately upon the problem of facing simultaneously several constituencies with conflicting interests. In his own words, "I knew, too, that this was the first time in the entire history of the Negro that a member of my race had been asked to speak from the same platform with white Southern men and women on any important National occasion." The accuracy of Washington's historical claim depends upon how one defines "important National occasion." Washington, following the discursive norms of his time, habitually ignored or denigrated the history of the

Reconstruction era and Afro-American involvement in all aspects of public life during that time. His doing so both pleased his white audiences and enhanced his own image as a self-made—with help from God and benevolent white people—trailblazer. But in identifying the problem of audience, Washington reveals his own political shrewdness.

Appearing shrewd, however, could itself cause problems, and Washington is always careful to avoid exposing his intelligence. He cloaks himself in a rhetoric of humility and simple common sense. In this specific instance, the problem is doubly complicated because Washington's assessment points to both sectional and racial conflicts. Furthermore, his observation that "an ill-timed address . . . would result in preventing any similar invitation being extended to a black man again for years to come" identifies correctly but inexpediently the racist intemperance of his white audience. In other words, Washington here identifies the danger of his predicament, but to identify it as dangerous is implicitly to indict the racist South. And Washington built an entire career upon publicly evading any statement that might forthrightly describe the reality of American race relations. Honesty on such questions has often been defined by Euro-Americans, then and now, as "bitterness," and Washington frequently reminds readers of *Up from Slavery* that he speaks "without bitterness,"—that is, dishonestly.

With characteristic adeptness, Washington defuses his perception by restating it and placing it in someone else's mouth. He writes,

> In passing through the town of Tuskegee I met a white farmer who lived some distance out in the country. In a jesting manner this man said: "Washington, you have spoken before Northern white people in the South; but in Atlanta, tomorrow, you will have before you the Northern whites, the Southern whites, and the Negroes all together. I am afraid you have got yourself into a tight place." This farmer diagnosed the situation correctly, but his frank words did not add anything to my comfort.

This passage reiterates Washington's sense of danger yet makes a joke of it. What's more, Washington becomes the butt of a poor white farmer's heckling. The great spokesman for his race diminishes suddenly into just another Negro. As always, Washington moves from seriousness to self-parody; and by showing a white farmer's endorsement of his percep-

tion, Washington retains the substance of the analysis without having to claim full credit for it. Finally, this episode with the white farmer allows him to reassert, symbolically, the supposed friendly relationship between white and black Southerners, though his main argument suggests the exact opposite. Even before George Orwell was born, Booker T. Washington had discovered and mastered doublespeak.

The "Atlanta Exposition Address" is one of the most familiar of all African-American documents, and the commentaries on it constitute an entire library. Most commentaries view it as the classic statement of a political philosophy dubbed "accommodation": a policy that surrenders civil rights in exchange for separate development and economic opportunities. The unflattering designation "Atlanta Compromise Address" derives from this interpretation. As a view of Washington's general political behavior, this formulation has some usefulness, though it ultimately obscures Washington's highly complicated, perpetually shifting political involvements. As a key to reading this speech, however, the term "accommodation" distorts and misleads far more than it illuminates. The language of "compromise," "accommodation," and so on, implies a highly rational discursive context in which bargaining occurs on a cooperative basis. Though the "Address" maintains an appearance of rational argument, the most striking thing about it, on closer examination, is how thoroughly illogical it is, how blatantly it lies about past and present social experience, and how cunningly it argues on both sides of issues. If this speech accommodates white people, it deceives and manipulates them as well.

Washington himself provides a clue to his method, stating: "when I am speaking to an audience, I care little for how what I am saying is going to sound in the newspapers, or to another audience, or to an individual. At the time, the audience before me absorbs all my sympathy, thought, and energy." In other words, his standard for his own utterances is the utterly flexible standard of expediency. For Washington, the quintessential pragmatist, the ends always justify the means. This absolute opportunism informs Washington's politics and his prose. The "Address" is utterly illogical, and herein lies its genius. Unlike DuBois, Kelly Miller, and other black intellectuals who wrote as if they were addressing an audience of principled, rational gentlemen, Washington rarely misjudged his public. This speech is not a coherent elaboration of historical facts, social strategies and political principles. Rather it is a cynically calculated appeal to the paranoid ethnochauvinism, crass materialism, and silly nostalgia that dominated the thinking of his Euro-American contemporaries. He was, after all, speaking in the middle of perhaps the most sociopathic decade in this nation's history. Ironically, his unencumbered realist perspective allowed him to compose a rhapsodic oration that brilliantly orchestrates the dominant bigoted themes and social discords of that reactionary decade. Not surprisingly, it was music to white America's ears.

The opening paragraph offers plentiful examples of how Washington combines fact and fiction, flattery and self-deprecation, humble advice and blatant self-aggrandizement. He begins with a simple fact and potentially promising thesis: "[O]ne-third of the population of the South is of the Negro race. No enterprise seeking the material, civil, or moral welfare of this section can disregard this element of our population and reach the highest success." His next sentence, however, is a virtual non sequitur. Claiming to express "the sentiment of the masses of my race," he asserts that "in no way have the value and manhood of the American Negro been more fittingly and generously recognized than by the managers of this magnificent Exposition." While useful as a bit of flattery, this assertion is at best irrelevant. If including Negroes is in the South's best interest, why should blacks be grateful when whites serve their own putative interest? More to the point, Washington does not indicate here or elsewhere how "recognition" facilitates "material, civil, or moral welfare." Indeed, the entire purpose of this introduction is to flatter the white audience and to establish Washington as a legitimate "spokesman for his race," not to make substantive social claims.

What legitimates Washington as a spokesman is not evidence that he accurately represents the views of other Afro-Americans but rather the practical fact that he elicits white people's approval by telling them what they want to hear. The outrageous closing sentence of his first paragraph exemplifies his strictly pragmatic rhetorical designs: "it is a recognition that will do more to cement the friendship of the two races than any occurrence since the dawn of our freedom." In other words, Washington rates participants in an agricultural fair above the Reconstruction Acts, the Thirteenth and Fourteenth Amendments, the Civil Rights Act of 1865, and the creation of Howard and other Negro colleges, including his own Tuskegee Institute—just to cite some obvious landmarks of the specified period. Washington's statement is not merely a lie. It is a repudiation of all the social, legal, and political gains made by Afro-Americans since the Emancipation. This repudiation essentially accedes to the white supremacist assessment of recent history. This unexpected endorsement from a Negro stunned Washington's white audience into euphoria, as the letters, telegrams and editorials available to scholars illustrate.

Historical falsification was a dominant theme of Euro-American intellectual culture in the 1890s, especially regarding black people. Hence it is hardly surprising that Washington devotes another paragraph to such prevarication: "Ignorant and inexperienced, it is not strange that in the first years of our new life we began at the top instead of at the bottom; that a seat in Congress or the state legislature was more sought than real estate or industrial skill, that the political convention of stump speaking had more attractions than starting a dairy farm or a track garden." As a political stump speaker whose entire program was farming and industrial training, Washington wanted to reassure his audience that past sins of black political involvement would not be repeated. Implicitly, experience has taught blacks that their proper place is behind a plow, not in public office. Of course, the national wave of disfranchisement laws was making this claim a foregone conclusion. The falsehood here, obviously, is that all blacks left the farm for the State House and Capitol Hill. As August Meier and other historians have noted, the acquisition and maintenance of farms was the major concern of most Afro-Americans throughout the years.

The real issue was not what the masses were doing. In fact, Afro-Americans were still overwhelmingly an agricultural people. Rather, the issue was whether blacks should exercise the political rights of citizens. To this Euro-Americans, North and South, had begun to answer a resounding "no." Washington's rhetoric here implies that he agrees (though we know that he surreptitiously worked against the disfranchisement laws). Washington claims that blacks will renounce their political digressions and return to working the land. This meant in effect returning to the relations of production that had characterized slavery. Revealingly, his predictions were precisely backward. Within a few years, blacks would become more militantly political than ever and, even as he spoke, tens of thousands were beginning to abandon farms to migrate north. Conveniently, this fallacy points us to the nostalgia, which forms the dominant undercurrent of this speech.

If the call for a return to master-slave relationship does not appear self-evident in this passage I have just discussed, Washington leaves no room for doubt subsequently. He contrasts the disconcerting present to the idyllic past. Having urged blacks to "cast down your bucket" by seeking friendship among Southern whites (as if the 171 lynchings of 1895 did not indicate a defect in the amicability of Southern whites), he makes a parallel, though explicitly humbler, plea to whites:

> To those of the white race who look to the incoming of those of foreign birth and strange tongue and habits for the prosperity of the South, were I permitted I would repeat what I say to my own race, "cast down your bucket where you are." Cast it down among the eight millions of Negroes whose habits you know, whose fidelity and love you have tested in days when to have proved treacherous meant the ruin of your firesides.

Playing upon the xenophobia, anti-Semitism, and anti-Catholicism of his audience, Washington reminds whites that a known Negro is better than a strange-tongued Italian or Pole or Jew. Again speaking as a pragmatist, he endorses what has been proven already by experience.

The sinister undercurrent to this bland assertion is Washington's deeply embedded reference to the alleged sex crimes of black men during the 1890s—acts that in rhetoric, though not in fact, justified the frequent lynching and beatings of the time. For a black man, this topic was publicly unspeakable, yet by invoking the "firesides" of the Civil War years, Washington implicitly refers to the black men who served and protected white women while white men were off defending slavery. These revered paragons, "Uncles" of the past generation, are contrasted implicitly to the unruly young bucks of the post-Reconstruction era. By adopting his program, Washington suggests, the South can efface these ugly realities and return to the Golden Age:

> [Y]ou can be sure in the future, as in the past, that you and your families will be surrounded by the most patient, faithful, law-abiding, and unresentful people that the world has seen. As we have proved our loyalty

to you in the past, in nursing your children, watching by the sick-bed of your mothers and fathers, and often following with tear-dimmed eyes to their graves, so in the future, in our humble way, we shall stand by you with a devotion no foreigner can approach, ready to lay down our lives, if need be, in defence of yours. . . .

Here, black lips utter the nostalgia of Thomas Nelson Page. Nor is it surprising to learn that Page, a couple of weeks later, nominated Washington as secretary of a prize jury on which they both served. This speech demonstrates Washington's flawless skills as an amanuensis.

This sappy nostalgia responds to a profound social crisis, but the politics of nostalgia is inherently counterproductive because it invokes fictionalized versions of an ideal past as alternatives to a troubling present. For a true sentimentalist like Page, this entails persistent self-deception. Washington, however, is a cynical pragmatist who deploys nostalgic rhetoric self-servingly, not credulously. Such calculated manipulation can yield immediate benefits, because it wins the approval of true believers. But those benefits are inevitably transient, because the adherents of nostalgia always espouse strategies that are doomed to fail—are doomed because they evade, not address, reality. They represent what Raymond Williams would call "the residual" rather than "the emergent" historical trend. Hence Washington's policy was a great success for Tuskegee and for himself, but Washington was an historical dead end. Militancy, not passivity, was the emergent historical trend. Migration, not capitulation, was the hope of black Southerners. Multiracial pluralism, not biracial paternalism, was the future of America. Though Washington's opposition did not even exist yet—DuBois was enthusiastic about this speech in 1895—he had already lost the war. His opportunism was bankrupt because it was tied—at least in the case of nostalgia—to a faction already embarked for oblivion.

Washington follows his lyrical fight with a coda, the most celebrated gesture of the speech: "In all things that are purely social we can be as separate as the fingers, yet one as the hand in all things essential to mutual progress." According to contemporary accounts, Washington elicited uproarious applause as he raised his outspread hand, then made a fist to illustrate this precept. In one of history's sweet ironies, this gesture re-emerged two generations later during the 1960s, the period of integration, as the black-power symbol, making a similar separatist claim but with a racially inverted attitude. Appropriately, the white audience of the 1960s responded with a corresponding inversion: howls of outrage. Washington, in any case, enjoyed a momentary triumph because he articulated and illustrated so clearly the newly dominant conception of separate but equal, which the Supreme Court would legally sanction in its *Plessy v. Ferguson* decision within a few months. But illustrating the concept so forthrightly also exposes inadvertently the logical kink in the concept. A close examination of Washington's metaphor will demonstrate its logical incoherence.

At best, separate but equal in its dominant historical manifestation erred in confusing the apparent and the actual; that is, to use Washington's example, the figures appear separate or segregated. But in actuality, there is no more apt—or more traditional —metaphor for social integration than the body itself. Though fingers move independently, the hand embodies a functional interdependence of its constituent parts. Separate but equal is a hierarchical theory, asserting that some parts of the body politic ("white people") are superior to others. By comparison, then, is it sensible to call the thumb or index finger "superior" to its companions? The social theory of separate but equal insists upon preventing the "intermixture of bloods." But the literal body contains only one reservoir of blood, and all parts share equally according to their specific needs. The body is a socialist, not a bourgeois figure.

To suggest that black people ought to survive on scraps that would not sustain white people is like claiming that the thumb needs blood, but that the index finger can thrive on phlegm. In short, Washington presents his metaphor to illustrate the viability of separate but equal, yet on close examination, it reveals the exact opposite, subverting what it claims to prove. Finally, the enthusiasm of Washington's audience for this spurious figure demonstrates once again how thoroughly their commitment to a bankrupt ideology of race had undermined their capacity to employ reason regarding racial claims. This apt metaphor betrays their misbegotten faith and reveals to us a truth that they were unprepared to recognize.

Washington's twisted endeavor to show that Negroes could be simultaneously intimate parts of white domesticity and happily excluded from "all things purely social" followed from his appropriation of the nostalgic mode. He used that mode, with all its irrationalities, to serve his ends; but other aspects of the speech borrow from different cultural tendencies. While the dominant elite of the South comprised sentimental reactionaries and reactionary Negrophobes, whom Washington could seduce with prattle of the good old days and capitulation to white supremacy, his Yankee constituents espoused the gospel of wealth. Indeed, one of Washington's favorite revenue sources, Andrew Carnegie, published a book with this title. Accordingly, Washington has woven in appeals to redemptive investment alongside the declarations of humility, nostalgia, and capitulation. For example, he urges his listeners to commit themselves to encouraging "the fullest growth of the Negro" in order to make him "the most useful and intelligent citizen." This will benefit whites, he insists, because "effort or means so invested will pay a thousand per cent interest. These efforts will be twice blessed—blessing him that gives and him that takes." This bizarre linkage of Christianity and capitalist finance is aimed primarily at Washington's northern constituents, and it has three aspects. First, it is a self-serving gesture by the quintessential fund-raiser, subtly exhorting his benefactors to keep that cash flowing. He shows his hand explicitly near the end of the speech, when he remarks, "our part in this exhibition would fall far short of your expectations but for the constant help that has come to our educational life, not only from the Southern states, but especially from Northern philanthropists, who have made their gifts a constant stream of blessing and encouragement." On this point, Washington's intentions could not be clearer if he distributed pledge envelopes to the crowd.

Secondly, he reiterates that other main themes of the speech are manifested in his economic thinking. "The wisest among my race," he reassures his listeners, "understand that the agitation of questions of social equality is the extremest folly." After all, "no race that has anything to contribute to the markets of the world is long in any degree ostracized." We must ask whether enslavement qualifies as ostracism. Who can deny that African Americans contributed to the markets of the world during over two centuries of involuntary servitude? Linking civil rights to economic productivity is worse than dubious. But truth here is beside the point. Washington's statement primarily aims to reassert his own position as spokesman, to dismiss blacks with a more militant disposition, and to persuade whites that blacks will accept without complaint or contest a position of social and economic inferiority, from which they will endeavor to work their way up. In other words, after two centuries of laboring at the bottom, according to Washington, "the best wisdom of the race" holds that blacks should begin passively at the bottom again. A race in which this passes for wisdom perhaps deserves to be at the bottom.

Third, and finally, Washington's focus on economics entails rejection of liberal humanist values in favor of a pragmatic materialism. Indeed, this question of fundamental values is one of the few philosophical issues in which Washington demonstrates consistent interest throughout *Up from Slavery* and his other works as well. Two of the best sentences in the speech advance this pragmatic doctrine. First, he declares that "no race can prosper till it learns that there is as much dignity in tilling a field as in writing a poem." And near the end he reiterates, "the opportunity to earn a dollar in a factory just now is worth infinitely more than the opportunity to spend a dollar in an opera-house." This latter version, invoking the image of the opera house, is especially provocative because the opera house was one of the most powerful icons of higher aspiration in turn-of-the-century American culture. This proposition epitomizes Washington's popularity among whites and the consternation that he came to elicit from educated blacks. . . .

Fittingly, Washington's last words are his most deviously cynical. To posit the South as a utopian promised land—especially in that moment of profound economic crisis, social conflict, and cultural stagnation—is on one level simply a surrender to the mandates of nostalgic discourse. On another level it voices an extraordinary optimism regarding the South's ability to revitalize itself. But on yet another level, it denies the actual experience of Afro-Americans, who had seen Euro-Southerners grow persistently more violent and oppressive, not more cooperative, during the two preceding decades. Obviously, Afro-Southerners loved their families, their heritage and their homeland just as much as Euro-Southerners did. Yet when Washington embraces it as "our South" in his utopian forecast, he merely abets white chauvinism.

All of this posturing may raise profound ethical and political misgivings, but its rhetorical effectiveness cannot be denied. Despite its apparent clarity and simplicity, the "Atlanta Exposition Address"

does not articulate a definite political position. Rather it issues a blanket authorization to its audience to find in it what they will. That compliant gesture, alongside Washington's claim to represent the best wisdom and leadership of his race, constitutes the submerged "meaning" of his address, if indeed "meaning" can be imputed to such an ambiguous document. Euro-Americans, Northern and Southern, were overwhelmingly united in their conviction that submission, the acceptance of inferiority, was the only tolerable attitude for a Negro. Washington's speech, presented in the name of Negro leadership, was a sustained rhetorical gesture that appeared to offer precisely that.

But needless to say, duplicity is the antithesis of submission. What the speech actually enacts is neither submission nor compromise but manipulation. It is unquestionably among the most effective exercises in rhetorical manipulation ever performed by an American. But to say this is not to imply that the speech represents an uncharacteristic moment, either in Washington's life or in *Up from Slavery*. Quite the contrary, even the title *Up from Slavery* reveals Washington's slipperiness. It reflects, obviously, the banal progressivism of the age: the notion that history develops ever onward and upward. But suppose we ask the question that the title itself implies: up from slavery to where? Though this question may seem glib and impertinent, the text is in fact structured to answer it.

The last sentences of the book are so pregnant that paraphrase will not do them justice. They reveal to us a Washington who has shed his tiresome modesty, exposing instead an agent of Providence and a self-conscious symbol of social transformation:

> As I write the closing words of this autobiography I find myself—not by design—in the city of Richmond, Virginia: the city which only a few decades ago was the capital of the Southern Confederacy, and where about twenty-five years ago, because of my poverty, I slept night after night under a sidewalk.
>
> This time I am in Richmond as the guest of the coloured people of the city; and came at their request to deliver an address last night to both races in the Academy of Music, the largest and finest audience room in the city. This was the first time that the coloured people had ever been permitted to use this hall. The day before I came, the City Council passed a vote to attend the meeting in a body to hear me speak. The state Legislature, including the House of Dele-

gates and the Senate, also passed a unanimous vote to attend in a body. In the presence of hundreds of coloured people, many distinguished white citizens, the state Legislature, and state officials, I delivered my message, which was one of hope and cheer, and from the bottom of my heart I thanked both races for this welcome back to the state that gave me birth.

Needless to say, this contains the usual Washington themes of progress, reconciliation, and humble achievement. As always, he cloaks the assertion of his authority in banal platitudes. But much more interesting are the implications of this concluding tableau, which consummates the autobiography.

If we are to believe Washington's assertion that this symbolic movement does not occur just as he is writing the conclusion of his narrative by his own design, then the design may be Providence's. In this instance, Providence displays a fine sense of narrative closure. Washington has risen from beneath the sidewalk to occupy the most exalted state, but along the way a series of remarkable things happen. No longer is Washington the humble supplicant. Indeed, he appears as a catalyst, whose mere presence transforms traditional social relations. Because of his visit, blacks are allowed to used Richmond's finest auditorium for the first time.

Furthermore, his presence creates an audience of the elites, both white and black. He unifies the races. Both city and state governments gather to absorb Washington's wisdom. In effect, he has made the leaders into the followers. With the ascendancy of this former slave, the last has literally become first. This moment seems to fulfill Washington's own prophecy from the conclusion of the "Atlanta Exposition Address": the South united in "a new heaven and a new earth." But Washington's personal triumph in this is even more pointed. He begins by invoking the Confederacy, but he says nothing about it. Nonetheless, his implication is clear. Just as Jefferson Davis ruled the Confederacy from this city, Washington has arisen in the New South to usurp the dead rebel's authority. In the New South only Washington can attract such an audience as he describes, and only Washington can catalyze such unity between the races. He is the *sine qua non* of interracial harmony. The unity is organized solely around his presence and his leadership—or in different terms, his representation of the Negro.

He blandly asserts that his message was "hope and cheer," to which he adds his usual dose of hum-

ble gratitude. This seems a rather insubstantial "message" for such an occasion, yet Washington's glib evasion of substantive content is wholly appropriate to his rhetorical stance. What Washington really presents in *Up from Slavery* is himself—not a revealed, existential self but rather a representative self. He represents the Negro. To blacks he offers the possibility that they might succeed as he has by following his example and his teachings. To whites he offers a means to handle the Negro Problem without dirtying their own hands: by supporting Washington and his institution. The Washington persona is a figure of mediation through whom both blacks and whites must operate in order to exercise their designs upon the Negro. But that Negro is always implicit, never explicit; always represented, never present; always an object, never a subject; always undeveloped and inscrutable. Like Washington's rhetoric, he is constructed to produce a social effect. Actually, the "message of hope and cheer" is a splendid analogue for what Washington's oratory represents: the promise that blacks might realize themselves and that whites might solve the Negro Problem. That the promise is false does not negate the benefits that Washington gains by proffering it.

A more provocative implication is also embedded in Washington's final tableau. He clearly stands as a figure of unification through mediating activity, but we can also view him as a physical embodiment of unification. Like Frederick Douglass, Washington acknowledges at the beginning of his autobiography that his father was a white man. But Washington, with his kinky hair and Negroid features, does not match our image of a mulatto. Consequently, this detail of his biography has gone largely unremarked. We ought not assume, however, that Washington was oblivious to this fact. Perhaps it seems overly nice to read his phrasing, "I thanked both races" as exempting himself from either race. Nevertheless, he is thanking them for "this welcome back to the state that gave me birth." Invoking his birth in the final line of the text redirects our attention to the opening, which describes his mixed parentage. Whether consciously or not, he reminds us that he unites black and white both in his audience and in his own body.

This is not a solution to the Negro Problem which Euro-Americans liked to consider. On the contrary, they supported Washington because he seemed to affirm racial difference, black inferiority, and separate development. Yet in fact, we know that Washington considered the basic problem of black people to be economic, not racial. He often remarked that the same was true for poor whites. In this materialist age, Washington pursued the implications of materials to conclusions that his equally materialist contemporaries were unable to acknowledge or even recognize. In his rhetoric and in his presence, Washington reiterated the commonplaces of racial discourse even as he simultaneously subverted those commonplaces. He advocated separate development even as he embodied the effectiveness of cooperation and amalgamation. No American politician has ever been so deeply involved with both blacks and whites, Northern and Southern, of all classes and political persuasions. Washington's rhetoric and his figure should remind us how willfully we all read and deploy the discourse of our common culture to perpetuate the familiar categories of race. At the same time, the success of his virtuoso rhetorical performances should also remind us how cynically self-serving and deceptive such performative gestures can be.

The Horatio Alger Myth

Carol Nackenoff

The notion that pluck, luck, and moral rectitude improve one's social and economic station in life—perhaps even to the point of becoming President of the United States, or at least a senator—has long been one of the sacred dogmas of the American creed. More specifically, the ideas of the "self-made man" and "rags to riches" have enjoyed surprising durability within American social and political folklore. Writers and cultural commentators such as Benjamin Franklin—but especially the late nineteenth-century pulp novelist Horatio Alger, Jr.—have professed the belief that at least a move from rags to respectability is possible in America. Indeed, the rise of men and women to higher social and economic status has and continues to occur in America, but perhaps not with the frequency or in the manner generally presumed. Carol Nackenoff, professor of political studies at Bard College in Annandale-on-Hudson, New York, here assesses the upward bound mentality and its sustained cultural vitality—often in the face of contrary social realities. Never, for example, do any of Alger's literary heroes dramatically move from "little tyke to big tycoon." Middle class respectability is both their aspiration and their lot. Similarly, while allowing much mobility, American society has never yielded fortunes commensurate with the nation's capacity to wonder. Still, thoughts of "making it," that "prosperity is just around the corner," remain cultural imperatives to this day. Horatio Alger, for his part, seems less an author than a cultural slogan, who through his formula fiction offered an evocation of values and aspirations ultimately nostalgic, allegorical, and mythic. It remains a culturally powerful formula that informs both individual expectation and almost every political campaign.

More than a century after Horatio Alger, Jr. achieved his greatest fame with *Ragged Dick*, the author's name stands as a symbol that has become associated with central values in the American political creed. Alger, author of over a hundred juvenile novels and stories (plus a few adult romances), which appeared from the late 1850s until roughly the turn of the new century, has become a household name unlike almost any other. It is not because his works are still widely read or known, but because the name itself is a stand-in for ideas supposedly derived from his fiction that "Horatio Alger" has entered the language and discourse of daily life.

Alger is the literary figure most closely associated with the self-help formulas of popular culture.

He has been called one of the two most influential writers in America. To Alger has been attributed an influence on American culture probably broader than any other author except Mark Twain. "To call Horatio Alger, Jr., America's most influential writer may seem like an overstatement . . . but . . . only Benjamin Franklin meant as much to the formation of the American popular mind." The Grolier Club in New York listed *Ragged Dick* among the One Hundred Influential American Books Printed before 1900. The name is invoked to capture something thought to be true about America.

The way in which the Alger story is formulated and the nature of its promises seem to have captured the imagination. Alger heroes are part of our language of discourse about social mobility and economic opportunity, about determination, self-reliance, and success. They are symbols for individual initiative, permeability of economic and social hierarchies, opportunities, and honest dealing. "Horatio Alger" is shorthand for someone who has risen through the ranks—the self-made man, against the odds. The prevailing *form* of this discourse in the United States concerns strong-willed, courageous individuals who struggle against the odds and triumph rather than engage in collective struggle or collective action. They reap rewards for doing what they ought to do. Alger's name is also frequently associated with defense of capitalism and conservative values. (Horatio Alger awards are given annually to prominent Americans associated with the gospel of free enterprise and laissez-faire.) "Self-made" entrepreneurs are held up as examples of the Horatio Alger rags-to-riches story.

The author died on the eve of the new century (1899); his works continued to be read in great number for another two decades. But the routes and methods of the Alger heroes are held up as prescriptions available for late twentieth century individuals, although the social and economic world in which the Alger characters moved has long since vanished.

The stories of this minor American novelist and story writer have been debunked, maligned, and lampooned. Something nevertheless endures. What makes this symbol so compelling and accessible in a much-changed economic environment? Why are its formulations articulated as obvious and natural truths so frequently? In what way did this author of juvenile fiction unwittingly put a finger on a form of expression that could define "the rules of the game" of the economic and social order and enter the political discourse about the meaning of America?

That Alger has been appropriated for use in American political culture is clear; yet the reasons these symbols are so pervasive and the thoughts the narrative can be used to invoke are not as obvious as we have supposed.

The appropriation of Alger is a tale about American political culture, discourse, and imagination. It invites reflection upon the relationship between the language of politics and conditions of material life. It demands attention to the relationship between fact and fiction, texts and readers, audiences and meanings. . . .

*   *   *

Horatio Alger, Jr. has been portrayed alternately as an unabashed booster of capitalism and materialism, a romanticizer of a dying era, a genteel moralist, and a hack writer of cheap, sensational fiction whose moral influence on the young was highly questionable. This literature has tended to treat Alger as a very poor "reader" of the Gilded Age. The pro- or anticapitalist tenor of the vast majority of these portraits is ultimately not very helpful in locating the author, his texts, or their appeal.

The *prevailing* image of Alger's stories is that they celebrate the rise of capitalism and the proliferation of economic opportunities and riches. Typical is the claim that "Horatio Alger can be held largely responsible for instilling into American boys of a former generation purely materialistic ideals." Or, "Alger's fictional heroes started poor and finished rich." Critics see Alger as universalizing a myth of success that at best pertained to only a few. Adventure stories for boys and large pots of gold at the end of the adventure were mere fantasies. This "Alger" universalized aspirations that few could reasonably hope to attain; he is an apologist for the emerging capitalist order.

Some late nineteenth century critics determined that Alger was a vulgar sensationalist in his own day. However, his reputation as capitalist apologist grew in the 1900s, partly through the efforts of his 1928 biographer, upon whose "hoax" work many subsequent interpretations were based. The Herbert Mayes hoax stood virtually uncontested for half a century. It was the vehicle through which many would come to understand Alger heroes in rags-to-riches terms. Alger's fine recent biographer Gary Scharnhorst (with Jack Bales) has contributed a great deal to the understanding of the transformation of Alger's identity and meanings by his biographers and critics.

Another version of "Alger" posits an author who may have wanted to write recipes for success in the new order, but gave antiquated and inappropriate advice or who retreated from change. He was a romanticizer of the dying era who yearned to roll back time. He engaged in deliberate anachronism. Most Alger heroes achieve middle class rewards. The virtues encouraged—punctuality, loyalty, honesty, bookkeeping skills, penmanship, thrift—are more appropriate to middle-level employees than to achieving success in the changing world of the Gilded Age. Alger's world is filled with small shopkeepers, mercantile establishments, and white-collar workers. Rarely do the boys attain extraordinary wealth. Rather than the celebrator of capitalism, we are presented with the "nostalgic spokesman of a dying order." Alger's vision of success "is, in effect, a reassertion of the values of a bygone era in an age of dramatic change and expansion." This Alger was impotent in the new order.

These approaches are more correct in portraying Alger as someone who rejected many of the economic tenets of capitalism and who waged war upon unrestrained accumulation. The best insight to date has come from his biographer, Gary Scharnhorst, who realizes that the "historical Horatio Alger was a Harvard-educated patrician whose moderately popular nineteenth-century morality tracts for boys expressed his genteel abhorrence of the mercenary Gilded Age." At best, we get a portrait of an author who was ambivalent about many of the changes associated with the rise of industrialism. But Alger's stance as a moralist is still seen as largely reactive—and outside capitalism.

One of the most astute readers of Alger, Daniel Rodgers, clearly saw that Alger struggled with the dislocating changes of his era. Rodgers found tension riddling the works of Alger and his patron, Oliver Optic (William T. Adams). Both attempted to capture the child's imagination while engaging in moral instruction. For Rodgers, the synthesis was not successful. These authors, seeking to advise and entertain the young, delivered "split and uncertain," even "schizophrenic," counsel. They claimed their stories illustrated the virtues of self-discipline and hard work, but "the announced story and the one actually told were rarely quite the same; the preface and the tale itself were often disconcertingly out of joint." "If Alger admired the fluidity of his age, he was profoundly distrustful of industrialization itself."

> Absorbing both the extravagant confidences of an expansive economy and its nervous fears, he [Alger] wrote his tales in the teeth of these difficulties, preaching his sober, cautionary lessons and weaving the heady romances that undercut them.

The conclusion is that these stories are seen to have their greatest affinity to the conventions of the classic fairy tales.

Was this, then, a literature of utopian longing? Were Alger—and, by implication, his readers—into "la mode retro," thriving on nostalgia and reviving the good old days when life was simpler, when the community was not coming apart at the seams, and when self-interested men did not triumph? Alger wrote formula stories, and Cawelti has suggested:

> We might loosely distinguish between formula stories and their "serious" counterparts on the ground that the latter tend toward some kind of encounter with our sense of the limitations of reality, while formulas embody moral fantasies of a world more exciting, more fulfilling, or more benevolent than the one we inhabit.

It *is* true that Alger's world is more benevolent than the one we inhabit. But I hope to demonstrate that these are not merely fairy tales and that the Alger narratives endure not simply because of their affinity with some kind of fairy-tale type. Nor will this be a tale about bread and circuses or mass manipulation. These stories struggled to maintain a correspondence with the emerging world that has gone unnoticed.

Alger's blend of fact and fiction affords a more complex response to industrialization than that with which he has been credited. It is not the case that these stories "reflect truth no more accurately than a Coney Island mirror." The tales referred to a world with which the contemporary audience was becoming acquainted; they are rooted in tensions surrounding the Gilded Age transformation of the conditions of material life. Alger offered guidebooks to surviving the economic dislocations occasioned by the rise of capitalism. Figures that reappear constantly in Alger tales work out scripts on major political and economic controversies.

Power is central to this narrative as the author struggles to keep youth from being overpowered by some of the changes in their environment. The struggle for power concerns the power of manipulators and seducers over the morals of youth; the struggle to maintain power over oneself, one's character, and one's labor; illegitimate power and performance in politics and society; the power (or lack thereof) of the author of mass fiction in the literary marketplace, and the struggle to connect certain images of production with manliness. These issues are all addressed in the following pages. So, too, is the power of fiction to guide the young. As tastes, habits, and culture diverged in class-specific ways, Alger did battle over literature, theater, and other entertainments. The battle for the Republic was a struggle to contain the meaning of diversity and class; we were all one estate. This struggle was over the power to define identity and shape political discourse.

Juxtapositions in Alger reveal a constant concern with true or natural value, representation, resemblance, and artifice; substance is distinguished from shadow. Natural value is juxtaposed to manipulated value and manipulators of value. Solid, plain virtues are opposed to fancy and artificial manners and social pretense. Genuine, honest, and sincere characters are contrasted with those who would appear to be so. Those who are human are juxtaposed to those without feeling, who are machinelike and who trample others in pursuit of their self-interest. Those who depend upon themselves, their characters, and efforts for their advancement are juxtaposed to those who depend upon luck and who try to create value out of thin air. As the author upholds traditional values and community, the new men of industry are frequently villains who need to be taught lessons in justice.

The author was part of a struggle over culture, language, habits, class, and meanings in a society in which differences and social distance were becoming ever more apparent. The struggle to maintain the notion that we are all of one estate took place in an era giving the lie to such a message. The identity of the Republic was at stake; its unity was entailed in its identity. Alger's battle against distinctions and class-specific entertainments could be seen as allied with elite and bourgeois attempts to master pleasures— pleasures which "are not only textualised but are also institutionalised and politicised."

As he reacted against amusements, habits, and dispositions that were increasingly class-specific, Alger shared a language and agenda with nineteenth century writers of advice manuals, sermons, religious fiction, and moral reformers.

Alger's course for preserving the identity of the Republic and upholding the virtue of its citizens was deeply indebted to his Harvard training in the texts and lessons of antiquity. He looked to Athens and saw classes sitting side by side in cultural productions, enjoying the same pleasures, engaging in the same discourse. He saw, on these shores, the Astor Place riots.

Religious themes of an ex-minister, trained by Harvard Unitarian moralists steeped in the Scottish Enlightenment, also deeply penetrated this litera-ture. Emphasis on character was testimony to Alger's attachment to rules of success other than those suggested by the emergence of capitalism. Character was fundamentally based on tenets of scripture, but neither church nor other institutions could monopolize access to virtue. And if the young required persuasion that justice was in one's self-interest, Alger arranged a payoff in the currency of the day.

The voices of moral and cultural elites anxiously called out to influence the young, and one prevailing "voice" in Alger texts is that of these cultural guardians concerned for the virtue of the Republic where many new forces and influences threatened their moral leadership. *The Education of Henry Adams* may be a more self-conscious, poignant image of the lack of fit between the Bostonian of privilege and the new world than anything Alger ever wrote or thought, but the two Harvard men, only six years apart, nonetheless shared a great deal. Theirs was a class fraction with declining influence. Alger recognized that many of these genteel voices had lost their chance to be heard.

Alger did not merely replicate their messages. He probably could not have done so and, at the same time, made a living by his pen, which his own exclusion from the ministry and his family's economic position made mandatory. But it is no accident that these genteel voices did not have the impact on popular culture, public discourse, and political vision that Alger did. The particular combination of responses to industrial development, the nature of the literary output, and the vehicles of production themselves helped shape Alger's impact. As his fiction proliferated, it came under attack by those especially fearful for the Republic.

Alger was a participant in the transformation not only of economy and society but in the production of literary arts. He produced mass fiction, contributed to popular culture, and came to stand at the margins of respectable literature. The story papers and cheap magazines in which many of his tales appeared were viewed as working-class vehicles. Dependent upon the market, the author shaped a product that would be consumed. It was not easy to own one's own identity in the genres in which he worked. Alger's own experience pointed out the struggle to define manliness and potency in relationship to production, consumption, and class.

At a time when reading publics were becoming

increasingly class-differentiated, Alger's fiction enters and attempts to address the gap. There were pedagogical as well as economic justifications. We will discover how the texts spoke in overlapping class voices, and, through a brief exploration of the real and likely readership of Alger's fiction, we will see why the different vehicles and means through which Alger fiction reached potential readers suggests that the same Alger story was very likely to have had different communities of readers. There could hardly be one text in this class.

Alger did not write a formula for modern capitalism, but he fashioned one that could be used by diverse class audiences to make sense of, participate in, and even protest against and rectify abuses of modern capitalism. The narrative was not a straight-jacket.

Readers and texts, like words and deeds, and historical subjects and agents of change constitute each other. This project presumes that readers make texts as members of communities. It is important to grasp

> the pluralism of the play of styles, codes and languages which can now be seen to constitute the realm of the popular—the popular, that is, properly understood . . . in terms of a critical repertoire which could assess the significance of 'pleasure' and 'the popular' as at once democratic and socially managed, as contested and controlled, as a structured balance of forces rather than a con-trick.

Locating the narratives and symbols of the Alger text in their historical context is a process of *defamiliarization*, for "meanings and value have been variously constituted over time by changing audiences." The author, literary critics, audiences, and later generations of users of the narrative all constructed Alger. This forces the conclusion that some things about responses to, and meanings of, these narratives remain unavoidably undiscoverable. Although we may not be able to determine why or how particular readers read and enjoyed these texts, this study argues that a great deal more *can* be said about Alger's contribution to the construction of a grammar of American politics.

* * *

This investigation asks how a particular vision and form of discourse became part of the common language. Voices competed in the battle for leading young audiences—for the privilege of defining the universe of discourse about the identity of the Republic and the meaning of American experience. The story of Alger is in part one about how one kind of political vision—articulated by one who was shaped by an intellectual elite with declining moral and economic power—became the dialect of mainstream political discourse, communicating with, while not simply reflecting, worldviews of subaltern classes.

Such an investigation improves our ability to understand how and why the Alger story lends itself to appropriation by different audiences and for different purposes. This investigation recasts the text as a political grammar and permits new reflection on the question of what made Alger as a symbol *available* to express beliefs about the way the American universe works. As we reconsider what *kind* of potential sense this is, we will discover one more piece to its appeal.

In Alger's formulas can be found an allegory. The adolescent of the Republic is the adolescent Republic. In this story, the young Republic faces dangers that threaten its moral fiber, strength, purpose, and identity. The real optimism of the Alger story lies in this story more than in that about wealth.

The Alger hero, whether a New York street boy or a boy from a small village in the hinterland, undertakes a journey that is a rite of passage. He not only promises to attain his manhood and his independence at the end, but his virtue is intact. The dangerous passage, in which the hero is torn from community and family and their moral influence to be thrown among strangers in the city, ends in triumph. The trials and struggle of the young hero standing on the verge of adolescence, when his identity and destiny will be forged, carry a great deal of cultural and political baggage. They are the struggles not merely of Ragged Dick and his acquaintances but of the nation undergoing transition. For this is an allegory of the Republic.

Mythology and Workers' Power

Herbert G. Gutman

The study of the American worker has largely been the study of elites. Much attention has been drawn to the holders of power and their antilabor tactics—the Fisks, Goulds, Vanderbilts, Carnegies, and Rockefellers. Historians have also centered on sensational conflicts between labor and capital—the Haymarket Riot, the exploits of the Molly Maguires, the Homestead steel and Pullman strikes—freighted with brutality and destruction. Following trails blazed by the likes of the historian John R. Commons, the study of organized labor has mostly involved craft unionism, almost exclusively in the form of the American Federation of Labor and its founder and leader, Samuel Gompers. Craft workers, benefiting from the demand for their skills and the paucity of their numbers, needed unions far less than semiskilled and unskilled workers. The structure, goals, and operations of the AFL, moreover, were not unlike those of big business itself and extremely exclusionary toward nonmember laborers. New Left historians and a new social history have sharpened scholarly awareness of the semiskilled and unskilled workers of the period following the Civil War. In this article, the late Herbert Gutman of City College, City University of New York, analyzes the industrial workers against the mythology and finds its many strictures to be much less hardened than previously believed. He does find strong antilabor animosities in large cities such as New York, Boston, and Chicago. In the smaller industrial towns, however, he discovered mutual concern and respect between employer and employee, a neutral and occasionally even prolabor press, and far fewer obstacles to unionism. Gutman wanted a reexamination of stereotypes regarding labor in the Gilded Age, for example its supposed "impotence and division before the iron hand of oppressive capitalism." Also, reflecting the spirit of recent social history, Professor Gutman underscores the need to study the worker per se, not just the power brokers, be they employers or union leaders. Following this advice will yield a much richer social history of American workers and their search for power.

Until very recent times, the worker never seemed as glamorous or important as the entrepreneur. This is especially true of the Gilded Age, where attention focuses more readily upon Jim Fisk, Commodore Vanderbilt, or John D. Rockefeller than on the men whose labor built their fortunes. Most studies have devoted too much attention to too little. Excessive interest in the Haymarket riot, the "Molly Maguires," the great strikes of 1877, the Homestead lockout, and the Pullman strike has obscured the more important currents of which these things were only symptoms.

Close attention has also focused on the small craft unions, the Knights of Labor, and the early socialists, excluding the great mass of workers who belonged to none of these groups and creating an uneven picture of labor in the Gilded Age.

Labor history had little to do with those matters scholars traditionally and excessively emphasize. Too few workers belonged to trade unions to make the unions important. There was a fundamental distinction between wage earners as a social class and the small minority of the working population that belonged to labor organizations. The full story of the wage earner is much more than the tale of struggling craft unions and the exhortations of committed trade unionists and assorted reformers and radicals. A national perspective often misrepresented those issues important to large segments of the postbellum working population and to other economic and social groups who had contact with the wage earners. Most of the available literature about labor in the Gilded Age is thin, and there are huge gaps in our knowledge of the entire period. Little was written about the workers themselves, their communities, and the day-to-day occurrences that shaped their outlook. Excessive concern with craft workers has meant the serious neglect of the impact of industrial capitalism—a new way of life—upon large segments of the population.

A rather stereotyped conception of labor and of industrial relations in the Gilded Age has gained widespread credence, and final and conclusive generalizations about labor abound: "During the depression from 1873 to 1879, employers sought to eliminate trade unions by a *systematic* policy of lockouts, blacklists, labor espionage, and legal prosecution. The *widespread* use of blacklists and Pinkerton labor spies caused labor to organize *more or less* secretly and *undoubtedly* helped bring on the violence that *characterized* labor strife during this period." One historian asserts: "Employers *everywhere* seemed determined to rid themselves of 'restrictions upon free enterprise' by smashing unions." The "*typical* [labor] organization during the seventies," writes another scholar, "was secret for protection against intrusion by outsiders." Such seemingly final judgments are questionable: How *systematic* were lockouts, blacklists, and legal prosecutions? How *widespread* was the use of labor spies and private detectives? Was the secret union the *typical* form of labor organization? Did violence *characterize* industrial relations?

It is widely believed that the industrialist exercised a great deal of power and had almost unlimited freedom of choice when dealing with his workers after the Civil War. Part of this belief reflects the weakness or absence of trade unions. Another justification for this interpretation, however, is more shaky—the assumption that industrialism generated new kinds of economic power which immediately affected the social structure and ideology. The supposition that "interests" rapidly reshaped "ideas" is misleading. "The social pyramid," Joseph Schumpeter pointed out, "is never made of a single substance, is never seamless." The economic interpretation of history "would at once become untenable and unrealistic . . . if its formulation failed to consider that the manner in which production shapes social life is essentially influenced by the fact that human protagonists have always been shaped by past situations."

In postbellum America, the relationship between "interest" and "ideology" was very complex and subtle. Industrial capitalism was a new way of life and was not fully institutionalized. Much of the history of industrialism is the story of the painful process by which an old way of life was discarded for a new one so that a central issue was the rejection or modification of a set of "rules" and "commands" that no longer fitted the new industrial context. Since so much was new, traditional stereotypes about the popular sanctioning of the rules and values of industrial society either demand severe qualification or entirely fall by the wayside. Among questionable commonly held generalizations are those that insist that the worker was isolated from the rest of society; that the employer had an easy time and a relatively free hand in imposing the new disciplines; that the spirit of the times, the ethic of the Gilded Age, worked to the advantage of the owner of industrial property; that workers found little if any sympathy from nonworkers; that the quest for wealth obliterated nonpecuniary values; and that industrialists swept aside countless obstacles with great ease.

The new way of life was more popular and more quickly sanctioned in large cities than in small one- or two-industry towns. Put another way, the social environment in the large American city after the Civil War was more often hostile toward workers than that in smaller industrial towns. Employers in large cities had more freedom of choice than counterparts in small towns, where local conditions often hampered the employer's decision-making power. The ideology of many nonworkers in these small towns was not entirely hospitable toward industrial, as opposed to traditional, business enterprise. Strikes and lockouts in large cities seldom lasted as long as similar disputes outside of urban centers. In the large city, there was almost no sympathy for the city worker among the middle and upper classes. A good deal of pro-labor and anti-industrial sentiment flowed from similar occupational groups in the small towns. Small-town employers of factory labor often reached out of the local environment for aid in solving industrial disputes, but diverse elements in the social structure and ideology shaped such decisions.

The direct economic relationships in large cities and in small towns and outlying industrial regions were similar, but the social structures differed profoundly. Private enterprise was central to the economy of both the small industrial town and the large metropolitan city, but functioned in a different social environment. The social structure and ideology of a given time are not derived only from economic institutions. In a time of rapid economic and social transformation, when industrial capitalism was relatively new, parts of an ideology alien to industrialism retained a powerful hold on many who lived outside large cities.

Men and their thoughts were different in the large cities. "The modern town," John Hobson wrote of the large nineteenth-century cities, "is a result of the desire to produce and distribute most economically the largest aggregate of material goods: economy of work, not convenience of life, is the object." In such an environment, "anti-social feelings" were exhibited "at every point by the competition of workers with one another, the antagonism between employer and employed, between sellers and buyers, factory and factory, shop and shop." Persons dealt with each other less as human beings and more as objects. The *Chicago Times*, for example, argued that "political economy" was "in reality the autocrat of the age" and occupied "the position once held by the Caesars and the Popes." According to the *New York Times*, the "antagonistic . . . position between employers and the employed on the subject of work and wages" was "unavoidable. . . . The object of trade is to get as much as you may and give as little as you can." The *Chicago Tribune* celebrated the coming of the centennial in 1876: "Suddenly acquired wealth, decked in all the colors of the rainbow, flaunts its robe before the eyes of Labor, and laughs with contempt at honest poverty." The country, "great in all the material powers of a vast empire," was entering "upon the second century weak and poor in social morality as compared with one hundred years ago."

Much more than economic considerations shaped the status of the urban working population, for the social structure in large cities unavoidably widened the distance between social and economic classes. Home and job often were far apart. A man's fellow workers were not necessarily his friends and neighbors. Face-to-face relationships became less meaningful as the city grew larger and production became more diverse and specialized. "It has always been difficult for well-to-do people of the upper and middle classes," wrote Samuel Lane Loomis, a Protestant minister, in the 1880s, "to sympathize with and to understand the needs of their poorer neighbors." The large city, both impersonal and confining, made it even harder. Loomis was convinced that "a great and growing gulf" lay "between the working-class and those above them." A Massachusetts clergyman saw a similar void between the social classes and complained: "I once knew a wealthy manufacturer who personally visited and looked after the comforts of his invalid operatives. I know of no such case now." The fabric of human relationships was cloaked in a kind of shadowed anonymity that became more and more characteristic of urban life.

Social contact was more direct in the smaller post–Civil War industrial towns and regions. *Cooper's New Monthly*, a reform trade union journal, insisted that while "money" was the "sole measure of gentility and respectability" in large cities, "a more democratic feeling" prevailed in small towns. "The most happy and contented workingmen in the country," wrote the *Iron Molder's Journal*, "are those residing in small towns and villages. . . . We want more towns and villages and less cities." Except for certain parts of New England and the mid-Atlantic states, the post–Civil War industrial towns and regions were relatively new to that kind of enterprise. Men and women who lived and worked in these areas usually had known another way of life, and they contrasted the present with the past.

The nineteenth-century notion of enterprise came quickly to these regions after the Civil War, but the social distance between the various economic classes that characterized the large city came much more slowly and hardly paralleled industrial developments. In the midst of the new industrial enterprise with its new set of commands, men often clung to older "agrarian" attitudes, and they judged the economic and social behavior of local industrialists by these values.

The social structure of the large city differed from that of the small industrial town because of the more direct human relationships among the residents of the smaller towns. Although many persons were not personally involved in the industrial process, they felt its presence. Life was more difficult and less cosmopolitan in small towns, but it was also less complicated. This life was not romantic, since it frequently meant company-owned houses and stores and conflicts between workers and employers over rights taken for granted in agricultural communities and large cities. Yet the nonurban industrial environment had in it a kind of compelling simplicity. There the inhabitants lived and worked together, and a certain sense of community threaded their everyday lives.

The first year of the 1873 depression sharply suggested the differences between the large urban center and the small industrial town. There was no question about the severity of the economic crisis. Its consequences were felt throughout the entire industrial sector, and production, employment, and income fell sharply everywhere. The dollar value of business failures in 1873 was greater than in any other single year between 1857 and 1893. Deflation in the iron and steel industry was especially severe: 266 of the nation's 666 iron furnaces were out of blast by January 1, 1874, and more than 50 percent of the rail mills were silent. A New York philanthropic organization figured that 25 percent of the city's workers—nearly 100,000 persons—were unemployed in the winter months of 1873–74.

"The simple fact is that a great many laboring men are out of work," wrote the *New York Graphic*. "It is not the fault of merchants and manufacturers that they refuse to employ four men when they can pay but one, and decline to pay four dollars for work which they can buy for two and a half." Gloom and pessimism settled over the entire country, and the most optimistic predicted only that the panic would end in the late spring months of 1873. James Swank, the secretary of the American Iron and Steel Association, found the country suffering "from a calamity which may be likened to a famine or a flood."

A number of serious labor difficulties occurred in small industrial towns and outlying industrial regions during the first year of the depression, revealing much about the social structure of these areas. Although each had its own unique character, a common set of problems shaped them all. Demand fell away and industrialists cut production and costs to sell off accumulated inventory and retain shrinking markets. This general contraction caused harsh industrial conflict in many parts of the country. "No sooner does a depression in trade set in," observed David A. Harris, the conservative head of the Sons of Vulcan, a national craft union for puddlers and boilermen, "than all expressions of friendship to the toiler are forgotten."

The *New York Times* insisted that the depression would "bring wages down for all time," and advised employers to dismiss workers who struck against wage reductions. This was not the time for the "insane imitations of the miserable class warfare and jealousy of Europe." The *Chicago Times* stated that strikers were "idiots" and "criminals." Its sister newspaper, the *Chicago Evening Journal*, said the crisis was not "an unmixed evil," since labor would finally learn "the folly and danger of trade organizations, strikes, and combinations . . . against capital." *Iron Age* was similarly sanguine. "We are sorry for those who suffer," it explained, "but if the power of the trade unions for mischief is weakened . . . the country will have gained far more than it loses from the partial depression of industry." Perhaps "simple workingmen" would learn they were misled by "demagogues and unprincipled agitators." Trade unions "crippled that productive power of capital" and retarded the operation of "beneficent natural laws of progress and development." James Swank was somewhat more generous. Prices had fallen, and it was "neither right nor practicable for all the loss to be borne by the employers." "Some of it," he explained, "must be shared by the workingmen. . . . We must hereafter be contented with lower wages for our labor and be more thankful for the opportunity to labor at all."

In cutting costs in 1873 and 1874, many employers found that certain aspects of the social structure and ideology in small industrial towns hindered their freedom of action. It was easy to announce a wage cut or refuse to negotiate with a local trade union, but it was difficult to enforce such decisions. In instance after instance, and for reasons that varied from region to region, employers reached outside of their environment to help assert their authority.

Industrialists used various methods to strengthen their local positions with workers. The state militia brought order to a town or region swept by industrial conflict. Troops were used in railroad strikes in Indiana, Ohio, and Pennsylvania; in a dispute involving iron heaters and rollers in Newport,

Kentucky; in a strike of Colorado ore diggers; in two strikes of Illinois coal miners; and in a strike of Michigan ore workers.

Other employers aggravated racial and nationality problems among workers by introducing new ethnic groups to end strikes, forcing men to work under new contracts, and destroying local trade unions. Negroes were used in coal disputes. Danish, Norwegian, and Swedish immigrants went into mines in Illinois, and into the Shenango Valley and the northern anthracite region of Pennsylvania. Germans went to coal mines in northern Ohio along with Italian workers. Some Italians also were used in western Pennsylvania as coal miners, and in western and northern New York as railroad workers. A number of employers imposed their authority in other ways. Regional, not local, blacklists were tried in the Illinois coal fields, on certain railroads, in the Ohio Valley iron towns, and in the iron mills of eastern Pennsylvania. Mine operators in Pennsylvania's Shenango Valley and Tioga coal region used state laws to evict discontented workers from company-owned houses in midwinter.

The social structure in these small towns and the ideology of many of their residents, who were neither workers nor employers, shaped the behavior of those employers who reached outside local environments to win industrial disputes. The story was different for every town, but had certain similarities. The strikes and lockouts had little meaning in and of themselves, but the incidents shed light on the distribution of power in these towns, on important social and economic relationships which shaped the attitudes and actions of workers and employers.

One neglected aspect of the small industrial town after the Civil War is its political structure. Because workers made up a large proportion of the electorate and often participated actively in local politics, they influenced local and regional affairs more than wage earners in the larger cities. In 1874, few workers held elected or appointed offices in large cities. In that year, however, the postmaster of Whistler, Alabama, was a member of the Iron Molder's International Union. George Kinghorn, a leading trade unionist in the southern Illinois coal fields, was postmaster of West Belleville, Illinois. A local labor party swept an election in Evansville, Indiana. Joliet, Illinois, had three workers on its city council. A prominent official of the local union of iron heaters and rollers sat on the city council in Newport, Kentucky. Coal and ore miners ran for the state legislature in Carthage, Missouri, in Clay County, Indiana, and in Belleville, Illinois. The residents of Virginia City, a town famous in western mythology, sent the president of the local miners' union to Congress. In other instances, town officials and other officeholders who were not wage earners sympathized with the problems and difficulties of local workers or displayed an unusual degree of objectivity during local industrial disputes.

Many local newspapers criticized the industrial entrepreneur, and editorials defended *local* workers and demanded redress for their grievances. Certain of these newspapers were entirely independent; others warmly endorsed local trade union activities.

The small businessmen and shopkeepers, lawyers and professional people, and other nonindustrial members of the middle class were a small but vital element in these industrial towns. Unlike the urban middle class they had direct and everyday contact with the new industrialism and with the problems and outlook of workers and employers. Many had risen from a lower station in life and knew the meaning of hardship and toil, and could judge the troubles of both workers and employers by personal experience. While they invariably accepted the concepts of private property and free entrepreneurship, their judgments about the *social* behavior of industrialists often drew upon noneconomic considerations and values. Some saw no necessary contradiction between private enterprise and gain and decent, humane social relations between workers and employers.

In a number of industrial conflicts, segments of the local middle class sided with workers. A Maryland weekly newspaper complained in 1876: "In the changes of the last thirty years not the least unfortunate is the separation of personal relations between employers and employees." While most metropolitan newspapers sang paeans of joy for the industrial entrepreneur and the new way of life, the *Youngstown Miner and Manufacturer* thought it completely wrong that the "Vanderbilts, Stewarts, and Astors bear, in proportion to their resources, infinitely less of the burden incident to society than the poorest worker." The *Ironton Register* defended dismissed iron strikers as "upright and esteemed . . . citizens" who had been sacrificed "to the cold demands on business." The *Portsmouth Times* boasted: "We have very little of the codfish aristocracy, and industrious laborers are looked upon here with as much respect as any class of people. . . ."

*   *   *

Nothing better illustrated the differences between the small town and large city than attitudes toward public works for the unemployed. Urban newspapers frowned upon the idea, and relief and welfare agents often felt that the unemployed were "looking for a handout." The jobless, one official insisted, belonged to "the degraded class . . . who have the vague idea that 'the world owes them a living.' " Unemployed workers were lazy, many said, and trifling.

Native-born radicals and reformers, a few welfare officers, ambitious politicians, responsible theorists, socialists, and "relics" from the pre–Civil War era all agitated for public works during the great economic crisis of 1873–74. The earliest advocates urged construction of city streets, parks and playgrounds, rapid transit systems, and other projects to relieve unemployment. These schemes usually depended on borrowed money or fiat currency, or issuance of low-interest-rate bonds on both local and national levels. The government had aided wealthy classes in the past; it was time to "legislate for the good of all not the few." Street demonstrations and meetings by the unemployed occurred in November and December of 1873 in Boston, Cincinnati, Chicago, Detroit, Indianapolis, Louisville, Newark, New York, Paterson, Pittsburgh, and Philadelphia. The dominant theme at all these gatherings was the same: unemployment was widespread, countless persons were without means, charity and philanthropy were poor substitutes for work, and public aid and employment were necessary and just.

The reaction to the demand for public works contained elements of surprise, ridicule, contempt, and genuine fear. The Board of Aldermen refused to meet with committees of jobless Philadelphia workers. Irate Paterson taxpayers put an end to a limited program of street repairs the city government had started. Chicago public officials and charity leaders told the unemployed to join them "in God's work" and rescue "the poor and suffering" through philanthropy, not public employment.

The urban press rejected the plea for public works and responsibility for the unemployed. Men demanding such aid were "disgusting,"

"crazy," "loudmouthed gasometers," "impudent vagabonds," and even "ineffable asses." They were ready "to chop off the heads of every man addicted to clean linen." They wanted to make "Government an institution to pillage the individual for the benefit of the mass." Hopefully, "yellow fever, cholera, or any other blessing" would sweep these persons from the earth. Depressions, after all, were normal and necessary adjustments, and workers should only "quietly bide their time till the natural laws of trade" brought renewed prosperity. Private charity and alms, as well as "free land," were adequate answers to unemployment. "The United States," said the *New York Times,* "is the only 'socialistic,' or more correctly 'agrarian,' government in the world in that it offers good land at nominal prices to every settler" and thereby takes "the sting from Communism." If the unemployed "prefer to cling to the great cities to oversupply labor," added the *Chicago Times,* "the fault is theirs."

None of the proposals of the jobless workers met with favor, but the demand by New York workers that personal wealth be limited to $100,000 was criticized most severely. To restrict the "ambition of building up colossal fortunes" meant an end to all "progress," wrote the *Chicago Times.* The *New York Tribune* insisted that any limitation on personal wealth was really an effort "to have employment without employers," and that was "almost as impossible . . . as to get into the world without ancestors."

Another argument against public responsibility for the unemployed identified this notion with immigrants, socialists, and "alien" doctrine. The agitation by the socialists compounded the anxieties of the more comfortable classes. Remembering that force had put down the Paris Communards, the *Chicago Times* asked: "Are we to be required to face a like alternative?" New York's police superintendent urged his men to spy on labor meetings and warned that German and French revolutionaries were "doing their utmost to inflame the workingman's mind." The *Chicago Tribune* menacingly concluded, "The coalition of foreign nationalities must be for a foreign, non-American object. The principles of these men are wild and subversive of society itself."

Hemmed in by such ideological blinders, devoted to "natural laws" of economics, and committed to a conspiracy theory of social change so often attributed only to the lower classes, the literate nonindustrial residents of large cities could not identify with the urban poor and the unemployed. Most well-to-do metropolitan residents in 1873 and 1874 believed that whether men rose or fell depended on individual effort. They viewed the worker as little more than a factor of production. They were sufficiently alienated from the urban poor to join the *New York Graphic* in jubilantly celebrating a country in which republican equality, free public schools, and cheap western lands allowed "intelligent working people" to "have anything they all want."

The attitude displayed toward the unemployed reflected a broader and more encompassing view of labor. Unlike similar groups in small towns, the urban middle- and upper-income groups generally frowned upon labor disputes and automatically sided with employers. Contact between these persons and the worker was casual and indirect. Labor unions violated certain immutable "natural and moral laws" and deterred economic development and capital accumulation. The *Chicago Times* put it another way in its discussion of workers who challenged the status quo: "The man who lays up not for the morrow, perishes on the morrow. It is the inexorable law of God, which neither legislatures nor communistic blatherskites can repeal. The fittest alone survive, and those are the fittest, as the result always proves, who provide for their own survival."

Unions and all forms of labor protest, particularly strikes, were condemned. The *New York Times* described the strike as "a combination against long-established laws," especially "the law of supply and demand." The *New York Tribune* wrote of "the general viciousness of the trades-union system," and the *Cleveland Leader* called "the labor union kings . . . the most absolute tyrants of our day." Strikes, insisted the *Chicago Tribune*, "implant in many men habits of indolence that are fatal to their efficiency thereafter." Cleveland sailors who protested conditions on the Great Lakes ships were "a motley throng and a wicked one," and when Cuban cigar makers struck in New York, the *New York Herald* insisted that "madness rules the hour."

City officials joined in attacking and weakening trade unions. The mayor forbade the leader of striking Philadelphia weavers from speaking in the streets. New York police barred striking German cigar workers from gathering in front of a factory whose owners had discharged six trade unionists, including four women. Plain-clothes detectives trailed striking Brooklyn plasterers. When Peter Smith, a nonunion barrel maker, shot and wounded four union men—killing one of them—during a bitter lockout, a New York judge freed him on $1,000 bail supplied by his employers and said his employers did "perfectly right in giving Smith a revolver to defend himself from strikers."

Brief review of three important labor crises in Pittsburgh, Cleveland, and New York points out different aspects of the underlying attitude toward labor in the large cities. The owners of Pittsburgh's five daily newspapers cut printers' wages in November, 1873, and formed an association to break the printers' union. After the printers rejected the wage cut and agreed to strike if nonunion men were taken on, two newspapers fired the union printers. The others quit in protest. The *Pittsburgh Dispatch* said the strikers "owe no allegiance to society," and the other publishers condemned the union as an "unreasoning tyranny." Three publishers started a court suit against more than seventy union members charging them with "conspiracy." The printers were held in $700 bail, and the strike was lost. Pittsburgh was soon "swarming with 'rats' from all parts of the country," and the union went under. Though the cases were not pressed after the union collapsed, the indictments were not dropped. In 1876, the *Pittsburgh National Labor Tribune* charged, "All of these men are kept under bail *to this day* to intimidate them from forming a Union, or asking for just wages." A weekly organ of the anthracite miners' union attacked the indictment and complained that it reiterated "the prejudice against workingmen's unions that seems to exist universally among officeholders."

In May, 1874, Cleveland coal dealers cut the wages of their coal heavers more than 25 percent, and between four- and five-hundred men struck. Some new hands were hired. A foreman drew a pistol on the strikers and was beaten. He and several strikers were arrested, and the coal docks remained quiet as the strikers, who had started a union, paraded up and down and neither spoke nor gestured to the new men. Police guarded the area, and a light artillery battery of the Ohio National Guard was mobilized. Lumber heavers joined the striking workers, and the two groups paraded quietly on May 8. Although the strikers were orderly, the police jailed several leaders. The strikers did not resist and dispersed when so ordered by the law. In their complaint to the public, they captured the flavor of urban-industrial conflict:

> The whole thing is a calumny, based upon the assumption that if a man be poor he must necessarily be a blackguard. Honest poverty can have no merit here, as the rich, together with all their other monopolies, must also monopolize all the virtues. We say now . . . we entertain a much more devout respect and reverence for our public law than the men who are thus seeking to degrade it into a tool of grinding oppression. We ask from the generosity of our fellow citizens . . . to dispute [sic] a commission of honest men to come and examine our claims. . . . We feel confident they will be convinced that the authorities of Cleveland, its police force, and particularly the formidable artillery are all made partisans to a very dirty and mean transaction.

The impartial inquiry proved unnecessary; a few days later several firms rescinded the wage cut, and the strikers thanked these employers.

Italian laborers were used on a large scale in the New York building trades for the first time in the spring of 1874. They lived "piled together like sardines in a box" and worked mainly as ragpickers and street cleaners. They were men of "passionate dispositions" and, "as a rule, filthy beyond the power of one to imagine." Irish street laborers and unskilled workers were especially hard on Italians, and numerous scuffles between the two groups occurred in the spring of 1874. In spite of the revulsion toward the Italians as a people, the *New York Tribune* advised employers that their "mode of life" allowed them to work for low wages.

Two non-Italians, civil engineers and contractors, founded the New York Italian Labor Company in April, 1874. It claimed 2,700 members, and its superintendent, an Italian named Frederick Guscetti, announced: "As peaceable and industrious men, we claim the right to put such price upon our labor as may seem to us best." The firm held power of attorney over members, contracted particular jobs, provided transportation, supplied work gangs with "simple food," and retained a commission of a day's wages from each monthly paycheck. The company was started to protect the Italians from Irish "adversaries," and Guscetti said the men were willing to work "at panic prices." The non-Italian managers announced the men would work for 20 percent less in the building trades. Employers were urged to hire them "and do away with strikes."

Protected by the city police and encouraged by the most powerful newspapers, the New York Italian Labor Company first attracted attention when it broke a strike of union hod carriers. Irish workers hooted and stoned the Italians, but the police provided them with ample protection. *Cooper's New Monthly* complained that "poor strangers, unacquainted with the laws and customs and language of the country," had been made "the dupes of unprincipled money sharks" and were being "used as tools to victimize and oppress other workingmen." This was just the start. The firm advertised its services in *Iron Age*. By the end of July, 1874, it had branched out with work gangs in New York, Massachusetts, and Pennsylvania.

There is much yet to learn about the attitude toward labor that existed in large cities, but over all opinion lay a popular belief that "laws" governed the economy and life itself. He who tampered with them through social experiments or reforms imperiled the whole structure. The *Chicago Times* was honest, if callous, in saying: "Whatever cheapens production, whatever will lessen the cost of growing wheat, digging gold, washing dishes, building steam engines, is of value. . . . The age is not one which enquires when looking at a piece of lace whether the woman who wove it is a saint or a courtesan." It came at last almost to a kind of inhumanity, as one manufacturer who used dogs and men in his operation discovered. The employer liked the dogs. "They never go on strike for higher wages, have no labor unions, never get intoxicated and disorderly, never absent themselves from work without good cause, obey orders without growling, and are very reliable."

The contrast between urban and rural views of labor and its fullest role in society and life is clear. In recent years, many have stressed "entrepreneurship" in nineteenth-century America without distinguishing between entrepreneurs in commerce and trade and those in industrial manufacturing. Reflecting the stresses and strains in the thought and social attitudes of a generation passing from the old pre-industrial way of life to the new industrial America, many men could justify the business ethic in its own sphere without sustaining it in operation in society at large or in human relationships. It was one thing to apply brute force in the marketplace, and quite another to talk blithely of "iron laws" when men's lives and well-being were at stake.

Not all men had such second thoughts about the

social fabric which industrial capitalism was weaving, but in the older areas of the country the spirits of free enterprise and free action were neither dead nor mutually exclusive. Many labor elements kept their freedom of action and' bargaining even during strikes. And the worker was shrewd in appealing to public opinion. There is a certain irony in realizing that small-town America, supposedly alien and antagonistic toward city ways, remained a stronghold of freedom for the worker seeking economic and social rights.

But perhaps this is not so strange after all, for pre-industrial America, whatever its narrowness and faults, had always preached personal freedom. The city, whose very impersonality would make it a kind of frontier of anonymity, often practiced personal restriction and the law of the economic and social jungle. As industrialism triumphed, the businessman's powers increased, yet he was often hindered—and always suspect—in vast areas of the nation which cheered his efforts toward wealth even while condemning his methods.

Facile generalizations are easy to make and not always sound, but surely the evidence warrants a new view of labor in the Gilded Age. The standard stereotypes and textbook clichés about its impotence and division before the iron hand of oppressive capitalism do not quite fit the facts. Its story is far different when surveyed in depth, carrying in it overtones of great complexity. And even in an age often marked by lust for power, men did not abandon old and honored concepts of human dignity and worth.

The 'May Day' Myth:
The Emergence of the United States as a World Power

Patrick Gerster and Nicholas Cords

In the interest of forging a measure of order out of chaos, of organizing thinking on a particular subject, historians need labels, categories, periods. Although such generalizations always imply reservations, to those less familiar with their usage they convey certitude. The editors of this volume, Patrick Gerster and Nicholas Cords, in this selection address one of these generalizations—that the United States was not a world power until 1898, when suddenly it emerged full-blown as an international force, and with its characteristic youthful exuberance began immediately to create for itself a well-deserved and dominant global position. They emphasize that from its inception in 1776, the nation was an emergent world power. Internal expressions of manifest destiny, moreover, came to be redirected toward international expansionism. During the four decades following the Civil War, the United States systematically engaged in a concerted and muscular approach to events and territories overseas. This was buttressed chiefly by American businessmen, including farmers, who became convinced of a pressing need for foreign markets, and the recurrence of missionary zeal, resulting from a heightened sense of American power and righteousness. It became our "mission" to take up "the white man's burden." American-style, of course.

A nation that permitted the enslavement of one race of people, conquered another, and persistently refused to grant full citizenship rights to women would scarcely seem in good position internationally to declare itself a model republic. Yet many Americans viewed their nation as such at the turn of the century, as various leaders began to recognize—and exercise—the power the United States could assert in world affairs. Motivated at least in part by feelings of political and cultural superiority, America gained entry to the great power club—that is, began to see itself as a world power and be widely accepted as such—with the symbolic victory of Commodore George Dewey at Manila Bay in the Philippine Islands on May 1, 1898—"May Day."

While many history textbooks, and certainly the majority of Americans, have subscribed to the "May Day" Myth and long accepted the cherished belief that the nation burst onto the stage of world affairs with the explosion of the Battleship *Maine* and the subsequent flash of Dewey's guns in 1898, such a view is in many ways inaccurate. For when the imperialistic activities of the late 1890s are viewed in light of preceding decades, it becomes clear that the nation was not striking out in completely new directions but simply again unleashing its expansionist energies. The "May Day" Myth concerning imperialism, as one historian calls it, fails to recognize both that the United States had been a world power before 1898 and that an appetite for expansion had already been demonstrated and played out in the conquest of the North American continent.

American global ambition is as old as the republic itself. Viewed against the background of the nation's history it can be argued that the United States had been a world power since its birth in 1776. The Declaration of Independence itself was addressed to a "candid world," and stated the desire of the new nation "to assume among the Powers of the earth, the separate and equal station to which the Laws of Nature and of Nature's God entitle them." America's success in securing assistance from France to support the Revolution, as well as the generally favorable treaty with England which concluded revolutionary hostilities, shows the new nation was even at this early date capable of profoundly influencing the direction of world affairs. In addition, American activities throughout the nineteenth century in Europe (successful diplomatic efforts preventing intervention in the Civil War), in Africa (campaigns against Tripoli and other North African states between 1801 and 1815), and in the Far East (Commodore Matthew Perry's missions to Japan in 1853–54) all suggest an active involvement in international trade and politics. The nation also was doing much more than simply tending its domestic garden in the years from the conclusion of the Civil War to the end of the century. Throughout the decades before 1898 the nation was moving gradually—sometimes strenuously—in the direction of world leadership. Blessed with a growing population, an abundance of natural resources, a developing economy, and an expanse of territory well along in the process of white settlement, the country began to assume a high profile in world politics.

Part of the myth of America's quick rise to world power in 1898 involves the idea that foreign affairs can somehow be viewed free and clear from developments within, as if foreign policy and domestic policy were purely distinct enterprises. As the history of the United States during the nineteenth century and especially its "legacy of conquest" in the American West so clearly demonstrates, the foreign policy of a nation is often a direct reflection of forces, values, and attitudes at work in domestic affairs. Manifest Destiny was simply being made manifest in different fashion. As Albert Bushnell Hart observed at the time, the United States already had many "colonies" in its Indian reservations. While the nations of Europe could point to colonial expansion in Africa and the Far East as a basis for prestige and influence in the world, America could claim itself an authentic world power by virtue of its winning of the West, its settlement of the continent under the equally expansionist banner of Manifest Destiny. "The point is often missed," one historian has noted, "that during the nineteenth century the United States practiced internal colonialism and imperialism on a continental scale. When the Western European nations expanded, they had to go overseas; when we expanded we had to go west." Because America gave the appearance of being a power of the future and a youthful nation, the sacred belief that it was the nation's destiny to expand matured to the point where expansion eventually included both the land to the west and even colonies beyond. Though seldom conceded, it was now a case of expansion at home *and* abroad.

During the period 1850 to 1898 "Britannia Ruled the Waves," symbolically drawing attention away from America's emergent role in global affairs. England's historical supremacy on the high seas, Europe's general preoccupation with internal affairs due to unsettled conditions caused by growing feelings of nationalism, and a general desire to sustain a balance of power internationally, in fact did allow the United States a measure of immunity from world problems, a kind of "free security." Even so, however, it should not be assumed that either the will or the means for American involvement in the world community was absent. Witness the acquisitions of the vast Louisiana Territory, portions of Florida, New Mexico and Arizona, as well as Texas, California, and Oregon. Further, regarding world markets, the nation's exports had increased from an average of $116 million annually during the period 1838 to 1849 to a considerably more robust annual rate of $274 million between 1850 and 1873.

Long before the symbolic initiatives of 1898 political leaders began to speak of overseas expansion in terms of the economic advantages which would accrue to the nation should military and political ventures be undertaken. Before this could be accomplished, however, it was necessary to redirect the energies of America's Manifest Destiny into foreign channels. When the limits of America's western frontier appeared to have been reached such adventuresome spirit found international expression, and Hawaii, the Philippines, Guam, and Puerto Rico each in turn became new sites for the nation's expansionist spirit. In light of the nation's proactive ideology of Manifest Destiny and its initiatives in world trade, as one of the leading scholars of this period has concluded, "the familiar story of America isolation becomes a myth."

"We have a record of conquest, colonization, and expansion unequaled by any people in the nineteenth century. We are not to be curbed now." When Massachusetts Senator Henry Cabot Lodge uttered these words in 1895, it articulated his recognition of the measurable distance between the country's often stated McGuffy morality and its practices of *Realpolitik.* Although there were but sixty employees in the State Department in 1885, policymakers had rather consistently displayed an enthusiasm for national expansion and a greater role by the United States in international politics. As early as William H. Seward's tenure as Abraham Lincoln's secretary of state, it was already recognized that America's farming, cattle, and mining frontiers were well on the way to being conquered. It would be necessary, then, to move more vigorously beyond the continent to find suitable foreign markets for agricultural and industrial goods. Thus, Seward was in a major way responsible for charting an early course for the nation's expansion overseas. At his instruction, for example, State Department officials began to explore the possibility of annexing Hawaii. In addition, Seward initiated diplomatic moves designed to bring Cuba, the Danish West Indies (today the U.S. Virgin Islands), Haiti, and Santo Domingo into the American orbit in the Caribbean. But whereas his ambitions often exceeded his accomplishments, he still proved successful in achieving his goals with respect to both the Midway Islands and Alaska. Seeing the fabled markets of China as the nation's ultimate commercial goal, he accomplished the purchase of both in 1867. The Midway Islands, 1,200 miles west of Hawaii, would serve as important outposts for America's eventual economic expansion to the Far East. The Aleutian Islands which spread from Alaska to within some twenty-five miles of Russia were the "drawbridge between America and Asia."

In every succeeding presidential administration to the turn of the century, additional moves were made to bring the United States ever more squarely into international politics. The administration of Ulysses S. Grant, for example, attempted unsuccessfully to annex Santo Domingo. The pattern of American internationalism continued during the presidency of Rutherford B. Hayes. Giving priority to trade expansion, Hayes' secretary of state, William M. Evarts, sought to enlarge America's commercial activities in the Far East, Samoa, Madagascar (off the coast of East Africa), as well as in Canada. His successors in the State Department, first James B. Blaine and then Frederick T. Frelinghuysen, attempted to channel the nation's energies in similar directions, negotiating trade agreements with several Latin American nations into the presidency of Chester A. Arthur. Grover Cleveland's secretary of state Thomas Bayard sought to make both Hawaii and Samoa American way stations on the route to Asia. Indeed at this juncture the direction of American empire was clearly charted. Nothing less than an equal share of China's legendary wealth would do.

Americans turning once again to the trading frontiers of China were handicapped by accumulated layers of misunderstanding and myth concerning that land. Most Americans—policymakers and public alike—held distorted images of China which bore only faint resemblance to fact. A fabricated form of "Orientalism" generally blurred America's vision of Asia. Also, for centuries China had remained almost entirely secluded from the outside world, secure in the belief that the world at large was inhabited by "barbarians." As a result, China remained for most Westerners an estranged land known only through the cultural mists of folklore and myth, a culturally remote region of medieval warlords proclaiming the obscure, inscrutable teachings of Confucius. This view, inspired by Marco Polo's accounts of his journeys to "Cathay" in the thirteenth century, perceived China to be an exotic blend of ancient wisdom and rich economic potential. Had not the storied East been the ultimate destination of Old World explorers and traders as they sailed West?

By the second half of the nineteenth century, however, attitudes had changed noticeably. New attitudes based on rumor and a measure of fact, fed by the encounter in the early 1840s between China and the West known as the Opium War, now turned China into a nation of "barbarians." In describing America's new cultural perception of China, one Far Eastern scholar has explained:

> Merchants and missionaries soon began to see China as a "backward" nation. The exotic now acquired a tinge of the inferior. In almost all of these early American travelogues there are stories about pigtails, bound feet, ancestor worship, female infanticide, and

a host of other sinister practices. Life in China was no longer described as superior but as upside down. The people read from right to left, wrote their surnames ahead of the given names, made soup the last course of a meal, and made a gesture of "come here" when they meant "good-by." The respected Chinese became "Chinamen"; the bearers of a superior civilization became "teeming faceless millions"; and the originators of a profound ethical system became godless heathens.

Both views served American purposes. For those who still saw China through the cloud of ancient legend it was a tantalizing storehouse ready to fulfill the dreams, and fill the pockets, of American merchants. To those convinced of Chinese superstitious backwardness, China seemed desperately in need of democratic and Christian enlightenment—along with a healthy measure of capitalism.

Despite Americans' fascination with China toward century's end, however, it would be a misconception of a different sort to believe that the United States had developed a China policy prior to 1898. According to John K. Fairbank of Harvard's East Asian Research Center, "most studies of American China policy have been pursued as national history. They comb American sources and seek to define American interests, aims, and achievements. This is what Confucius called 'climbing a tree to seek for fish,' acting on a false assumption and using erroneous means." As America expanded its trading activities into China it was in fact following on the coattails of European powers—principally England—which had opened the door to the China trade many decades before. Accordingly, it is clear that the United States did not directly initiate a Far Eastern policy with designs on the fabled commercial trade of China through its Open Door notes in 1899. Later generations of Americans looking for evidence with which to support the legend of America's meteoric rise to world power would assume that the Open Door policy in China was an "American idea" which demonstrated "energy and shrewd skill in negotiation." While it is true that American Secretary of State John Hay dispatched an initial memorandum to the world's leading powers—England, Russia, Germany, France, Italy, and Japan—in late 1899, asking them to leave the door of trade in China open to all nations, like the Monroe Doctrine some seventy-five years earlier the notes did not amount to much in their time. The idea was simply a restatement of

existing British policy and in fact is thought to have been inspired by a British subject in the Chinese Imperial Customs Service. In this fashion, "the myth was established that 'in this episode of the Open Door notes, a tremendous blow had been struck for the triumph of American principles in international society—an American blow for an American idea.' " Ironically, the notion of China's fabled wealth proved to be mythical too. Despite well-honored legend that huge economic benefits lay waiting just beyond the Great Wall, the China trade, even at its peak, never amounted to more than three percent of American exports.

While the development of colonies in the European manner seems never to have been foremost in the minds of expansionists in America, a consistent desire to increase commercial relations, abetted by missionary efforts, was most always present in the minds of the nation's foreign policymakers after the mid-nineteenth century. Washington, and particularly the Department of State, had taken many decades to plant and nurture the seeds of empire. In the course of time commercial ambitions and America's "informal empire" became formalized. Presidents, the business community, the military establishment, institutionalized religion, and eventually public opinion—converted to the faith and began to support the idea of a new empire in the expanding emporium of the Pacific.

Even though America throughout the last half of the nineteenth century often impersonated a domestically-focused nation, exhibiting for all the world a fixation with internal affairs, it did not become a world power in a sudden, spur-of-the-moment fashion with the Spanish-American War. In fact, Commodore Dewey's victory in the Philippines was a rendezvous with destiny—a logical result of much that America had dreamed for the better part of its history. The episode at Manila Bay was of a piece with numerous, accumulating decisions made in the past. The history of American expansionism is ultimately a study in continuity and purpose. More important, the events of May 1, 1898, pointed to the complex fate which America faced in the future. As the nation entered the twentieth century, it would be both beneficiary and victim of a past which had both encouraged and witnessed its rise to world power. In matters of foreign affairs the nineteenth century ended as it had begun—in an explosion of myths.

III

Myths of Progressivism & the 1920s

The study of United States history is in a constant state of revision. Those ever-present revisionists among American historians attempting always to advance the frontiers of interpretation have been particularly active since the end of World War II. Almost every historical personage, event, topic, or period has come in for some sort of reinterpretation; many revisionists have lived to be revised—sometimes even by themselves.

One of the major revisions of twentieth-century historical understanding deals with progressivism, centering its interpretive attention on its origins, its meaning, and the time and circumstances of its "death." The usual exaggeration, distortion, and myth was bound to attach itself to the various views offered to explain the reality of progressivism as historians sought to make their explanations convincing. That professional scholars themselves took a personal hand in shaping the movement has compounded the mythic nature of the period. As one writer has suggested, many of the early attempts to explain progressivism were written by those who were "its partisans in life as well as in print." Indeed at one point, many historians heralded the arrival of a "New Republic" by their contributions to a nascent magazine of the same name. Some in fact found it difficult to engage actively in the shaping of history one week and then to give the movement an objective treatment in their classrooms or writings the next.

As for the movement at large, reformers of different stripes and persuasions all laid claim to being progressive. But what passed for progress to one of them may have seemed retrograde to another. A rural southern progressive might not get excited over eastern urban reform legislation; an urban northeastern progressive might lack a deep interest in midwestern agricultural reform. Thus, while synthesis is difficult, the "movement" was populated largely by middle-class reformers disturbed by the growing power of large corporations, newly organized labor unions, and political bosses. They sought reform not so much out of economic grievance (for most were already reasonably well-to-do), but because some thought their social class was being replaced by a new elite. Progressivism was less a replay of the ancient struggle between democracy and privilege than an effort among the privileged to reassert themselves. It was a "search for order," as Robert Wiebe has termed it, as much as an attempt to carry the banner of American democratic reform on to new liberal horizons.

Lindbergh: the Lone Eagle. *(Courtesy, Library of Congress)*

Theodore Roosevelt: Icon for an Era. *(Courtesy, Library of Congress)*

Woodrow Wilson: Making the World Safe for Democracy. *(Courtesy, Library of Congress)*

In this photograph President Calvin Coolidge represents a bit of the agrarian myth. *(Courtesy, National Archives)*

The Frontier Myth and Teddy Roosevelt's Fight for Conservation

Leroy G. Dorsey

The Frontier Myth has been and continues to be a story much used by rhetorical Presidents to inspire audiences and to energize policies. This essay by Leroy G. Dorsey, Assistant Professor of Speech Communication at Texas A&M University, investigates Theodore Roosevelt's use of the myth. Rather than employ it in a traditional sense to promote a martial or economic policy, he linked it to the notion of conservation. He altered the traditional myth by recasting its conqueror-hero with a farmer-hero, replacing its unlimited frontier with a finite one, and by redefining its values. As a rhetorical leader Roosevelt took his case to the public and promoted conservation not only as a legislative initiative but also as a moral imperative.

As the twentieth century opened, the presidency shifted much of its emphasis from that of an administrative office to more of a bully pulpit. The presidency can now best be characterized as a rhetorical institution, one that reflects Richard Neustadt's axiom that "presidential power is the power to persuade." The "rhetorical presidency" describes a chief executive who employs oratory not only to motivate the public into pressuring Congress to support a legislative agenda, but also to provide moral leadership for the nation.

Faced with an increasingly diverse public and the technology to reach it, modern presidents have sought the means to communicate with the nation in a common yet provocative language. Thus, some chief executives have turned to storytelling. Under this model of rhetorical leadership, presidents may relate stories that feature intriguing characters engaged in epic adventures in an equally fantastic realm. These myths, when merged with stories about "real" peoples' experiences, can act as compelling symbols which the president can use to shape the audience's identity and to prescribe its social behaviors.

The Frontier Myth, in particular, has been a much used story by several rhetorical presidents to inspire audiences and to energize policies. Briefly, the Myth offers an account of how the constant challenge of an unknown and limitless frontier turns some individuals into martial heroes who, because of their epic struggles, come to symbolize American values such as progress and prosperity. For example, both John Kennedy and Ronald Reagan employed key elements of the Myth. According to Justin Gustainis, as a result of Kennedy's "careful image management" of the U.S. Special Forces, the President manipulated the press into portraying the Green Berets as the reincarnation of the frontier hero, turning this military unit into "a particularly potent symbol." William F. Lewis concludes that Reagan's own image as a Western hero enhanced his use of the Myth to portray "American history as a continuing struggle" for both "economic advancement" and "military strength."

Theodore Roosevelt represents yet another chief executive who rhetorically used the Frontier Myth. Foreshadowing his contemporaries, Roosevelt manipulated the press to a degree unheard of at the time, and his image as a frontiersman undoubtedly bolstered his credibility in rearticulating the Myth. However, his use of the Frontier Myth differed substantially from that of Kennedy and Reagan. Rather than employ the Myth in a traditional sense to promote a martial or economic policy, Roosevelt linked it to the notion of conservation. In the process, he radically altered the key elements of the Myth to accommodate and to promote the preservation of the environment. At present, scholarship on Roosevelt's rhetorical presidency, as well as its impact on the issue of environmental conservation, is limited. Therefore, Roosevelt's significant redefinition of the Frontier Myth deserves examination.

As Roosevelt observed in his *Autobiography*, the relationship between the conservation of natural resources and the "National welfare" had not yet "dawned on the public mind." Thus, he found little Congressional support for his conservationist crusade. Congress became increasingly inclined to come between the president and his initiatives, resisting him on almost every major issue regarding conservation. For example, those in Congress constantly questioned the constitutionality of the President's power to make national forest reserves unavailable to the industrial livelihood of the state in which they were established. However, it should come as no surprise that Congress rebelled against the President. Roosevelt made no secret of his belief that the presidency was more powerful than the legislature and he publicly ridiculed accusations that he usurped congressional powers. These attitudes, coupled with the president's habit of personally attacking legislators and his continuous public scorn of Congress for its passive attitude regarding conservation, help to account for Congress' many attempts to frustrate Roosevelt's conservation initiatives.

Despite congressional resistance, Roosevelt accomplished a good deal. From 1901 to 1909, he signed scores of bills into law, including legislation that authorized 80 million dollars for the reclamation of three million acres of land, established the nation's first federal wildlife refuge, transferred the management of the Forest Reserves to his trusted ally Gifford Pinchot in the Department of Agriculture, opened five national parks, and created eighteen national monuments, including California's Muir Woods and Arizona's Grand Canyon.

This essay examines the public discourse of President Roosevelt as he attempted to promote conservation, not only as a legislative initiative, but as a moral imperative. Embracing his role as a rhetorical leader, he took his case to the public to infuse a sense of vision into conservation. This he did by grounding his vision in the drama of the frontier.

Specifically, this essay argues that Roosevelt altered the traditional Frontier Myth in three major ways. First, he recast the hero's role in the Frontier Myth by replacing the Myth's traditional hero, whose relationship to the frontier had been violent and exploitative, with the yeoman farmer-hero, whose wise use of the environment protected it. Second, Roosevelt sought to redefine the "unlimited" frontier. To that end, he linked certain businesses' decreasing economic opportunities to the "finite" nature of the environment. In addition, he argued that while limited, the frontier provided the more valuable opportunity of spiritual regeneration. Finally, Roosevelt redefined the value of "progress" in the frontier narrative to accommodate his revised versions of the hero and the frontier. As a result, progress represented the conservation of nature through common effort rather than by exploitation of the environment by individuals. By these three moves, Roosevelt promoted a substantial redefinition of the relationship between the Frontier Myth and the American people.

* * *

According to Joseph Campbell, myths represent "stories about the wisdom of life." In their retelling from generation to generation, they can teach people how to understand each other and their place in the world. They are the patterns, James Robertson writes, "of behavior, of belief and of perception which people have in common." By emphasizing similarities, these stories can help to reconcile individual inconsistencies in a culture's ideology. Myths can provide the wisdom, Robertson adds, by which "the contrasts and conflicts which normally arise among people, among ideals, among the confusing realities" can be "reconciled, smoothed over, or at least made manageable."

Myths, then, constitute an essential community-building force. They bridge differences and promote commonality among human beings by framing their everyday reality in an almost mystical way. With myths "one ceases to exist in the everyday world," Mircea Eliade notes, "and enters a transfigured auroral world" impregnated with the presence of supernatural entities. These stories transport listeners from their mundane existence to transcendent realms occupied by larger-than-life characters; those mythic beings of a stalwart nature, in particular, serve as role models with which listeners can identify and emulate. In their descriptions of supernormal beings performing epic deeds in a distant and fantastic era, myths provide individuals with what Eliade terms "sacred histories." These mythic histories unify a group of people by offering them an account of their genesis as a culture. According to Campbell, such stories can "integrate the individual into society." Rather than focus on differences, they bind individuals together as a communal organism sharing a supernatural origin that provides social, moral, and pragmatic lessons. As Bronislaw Malinowski concludes, a myth is more than an idle tale; it "expresses, enhances, and codifies belief; it safeguards and enforces morality; it vouches for the efficiency of ritual and contains practical rules for the guidance of man."

One of the longest-lived sacred histories of American culture is the Frontier Myth. Perhaps the most characteristic expression of American culture, this myth tells the origins of how brave individuals contend with an unknown and hostile frontier, coming together as a community to forge a social covenant reflecting its cherished ideals.

During the late nineteenth and early twentieth centuries, the Frontier Myth revealed how intrepid Europeans sought new opportunities on the American frontier. In their challenge of the unknown, these pioneers became Americanized with their transformation into beings who exhibited supernormal resilience, confidence, and steadfastness. Mythic heroes are superior to the rest of humanity, Campbell observes, because they are people who have "done something beyond the normal range of achievement and experience." In a sense, heroes have given their lives to something bigger than themselves. In the traditional Frontier Myth the heroes included the trappers, farmers, Indian-hunters, and others who left civilization to establish communities in a barbaric wilderness. Of all the characteristics these heroes developed on the frontier, it was their determined nature to act alone in the uncharted wilderness that

made them worthy of respect. If they did not "manifest rugged individualism in all of [their] crucial actions," Janice Rushing notes, they could not be heroes. Paradoxically, these rugged individualists had to conform to some degree to the needs of the community. Unless they responded, typically to save a pocket of civilization from evil forces, they would not meet the "goodness" requirement of their heroic status. Rushing concludes that this tension between the hero's individualistic nature and the community's cooperative spirit accounts for part of the "perennial appeal" of the Myth.

The Frontier Myth also revealed the American continent as a place of unlimited majesty and unparalleled ferocity. "The plains, the mountains, the deserts and the forests each have an individual brand of beauty," Jenni Calder writes, but "in each case there is also a cruel power: the beauty is ominous." Beyond the picturesque notions of rolling hills and crystal clear streams, Rushing notes that the frontier manifested itself in the "dark forest," "bleak prairies," and the "burning deserts" explorers faced daily. In addition to these natural challenges, pioneer heroes also struggled with human evil. According to Rushing, this meant the Native American or the outlaw. "Whatever its form," she observes, "evil is to be respected for its fierceness and strength" and its ability to provide "a fitting challenge for the frontier hero." This combination of beauty and cruelty on the limitless frontier also gives the Myth much of its compelling power. "It can inspire ordinary people to conquer immense hazards," Calder writes, or "it can defeat them totally.". . .

Theodore Roosevelt apparently believed that the reduction of America's sacred history to that of a conqueror-hero of an unlimited frontier-universe had brought about severe environmental concerns. As he remarked in his "First Annual Message," the conservation of the land, forest, water, and animals represented "the most vital internal questions of the United States." When he succeeded President McKinley in 1901, Roosevelt saw the environment under siege. At the time, one-half of the country's timber had been cut, with the annual use rate at four times the new growth rate. Furthermore, 200 million acres of forest land had been destroyed with over a billion tons of topsoil washed away. Wasteful mining methods wreaked havoc as well. Not only did they garner four billion tons of coal, but they also destroyed or made inaccessible an equal quantity. Finally, animals such as the heath hen, buffalo, fur seal, passenger pigeon, alligator, elk, bear, and bighorn sheep were either wiped out or neared extinction due to profit-minded hunters.

President Roosevelt attempted a revolutionary alteration of the Frontier Myth icons to promote conservation. Consistent with his rhetorical conception of the presidency, he went to the public with a revised Frontier Myth, one that glorified a preserverhero who acted within a finite, frontier-universe. To disseminate these new mythic elements to the widest audience, Roosevelt not only incorporated them in his addresses from the White House, but he also revolutionized the use of the speaking tour. He gave "swings around the circle," which were even then derided as hackneyed publicity devices, a new sense of purpose and flair. Like later rhetorical presidents, Roosevelt frequently stumped across the country as the nation's preeminent storyteller, using the media to retell his revised versions of the frontier hero and environmental universe. Furthermore, in his Governors' Conference address in 1908, he adapted the third element of the Frontier Myth, the narrative, to accommodate the altered icons of the hero and universe. In that speech he redefined progress in America's covenant so as to provide a new purpose for the country in relation to the environment.

*   *   *

According to David Noble, the yeoman farmer had long been a "figure of superior virtue" in the minds of the American people. By the 1890s, however, the myth of the farmer-hero had been "seriously undermined." The decline in the farmer's image, Noble writes, was due in part to the rise of the city as the primary dwelling place as well as to the "realistic descriptions of the heavy burden of farm work . . . the loneliness of farm life, the dependence of cruelly capricious weather, and the endless financial problems of the farmer." But more than that, the myth of the farmer who used the land in productive ways seemed timid and uninspiring in comparison to the romanticized figure of the Frontier Myth's new heroic icon: the Old West cowboy. By the turn of the century, the cowboy's vices of rootlessness and lawlessness on the frontier had been transformed into virtues, while the "sodbuster" seemed by comparison to lack those American values of courage and adventure.

This ascendance of the rebellious cowboy and

the continuation of the conqueror-hero icon apparently disturbed Roosevelt. As a result, he attempted to buck this trend. A noted rancher, hunter, and naturalist himself, Roosevelt's love of nature promoted a keen sensitivity to the environment and a disdain for those people whose actions threatened it. For example, despite his zeal for hunting, Roosevelt differentiated between hunting to embrace the frontier experience and hunting for the purpose of economic profit; for him, the latter represented wholesale slaughter with inevitable extinction while the former did not. As a result, he had long resisted celebrating the destructiveness of the Frontier Myth's traditional hero. In his works prior to the presidency, most notably *The Winning of the West*, Roosevelt had lionized instead the productive backwoods farmers, crediting them with estimable qualities such as great physical strength, iron resolve, and a strong moral sense.

Roosevelt endorsed the modern yeoman farmers as the true heroes of the Frontier Myth. According to the President, they exhibited the heroic traits of American greatness. It was the farmers, he asserted before a 1902 audience in Maine, "more than any other of our citizens to-day, [that are] called upon continually to exercise the qualities which we like to think of as typical of the United States . . . the qualities of rugged independence, masterful resolution, individual energy, and resourcefulness." Again in his "Sixth Annual Message," Roosevelt likened the contemporary farmer to the traditional frontier heroes. The former, like the latter, were rugged individualists since they "must primarily do most for themselves." Such traditional characteristics as moral resolve and physical strength, Roosevelt declared at a 1907 celebration for the founding of agricultural colleges, were exhibited by contemporary farmers and accounted for their success: "no government aid or direction can take the place of a strong and upright character; of goodness of heart combined with clearness of head, and that strength and toughness of fibre necessary to wring success from a rough workaday world."

Roosevelt's celebratory vision of the contemporary yeoman farmer essentially borrowed the ethos of those mythic frontier farmers who had played a central role in America's sacred history. For example, during a 1903 address in South Dakota, Roosevelt likened the contemporary farmer to those who first built the nation:

the farmer himself still retains, because of his surrounding and the nature of his work, to a pre-eminent degree the qualities which we like to think of as distinctly American in considering our early history. The man who tills his own farm . . . still exists more nearly under the conditions which obtained when the 'embattled farmers' of '76 made this country a nation than is true of any others of our people.

Roosevelt illustrated this point again four years later in his "Seventh Annual Message." "We began our existence as a nation of farmers," he stated, "and in every great crisis of the past a peculiar dependence has had to be placed upon the farming population; and this dependence has hitherto been justified." Now was not the time, Roosevelt charged, for this icon of American culture to be discarded.

Roosevelt believed that what the country needed was not the frontier-conqueror icon of times past, presently incarnated as the lawless cowboy, but the restoration of an American hero that could symbolize the conservation of the nation's resources. Rather than emulate the traditional conqueror-hero of the Frontier Myth who had "but one thought about a tree, and that was to cut it down," Roosevelt declared to the Forest Congress in 1905 that the country needed a symbol that would act as a gatekeeper to America's natural wealth. The frontier figure that Roosevelt charged with providing this example, and through whom the audience could vicariously identify, was the yeoman farmer. According to him, the country needed to recognize that farmers' wise use of the environment formed "the basis of all the other achievements of the American people."

Roosevelt recast the heroic icon of the frontier, calling for a protagonist who embraced the wise use of the environment. As he observed during a 1903 "Address at San Luis Obispo, California," the nation should not revere the people "whose aim it is merely to skin the soil and go on; to skin the country, to take off the timber, to exhaust it, and go on." For too long, he declared in his "Seventh Annual Message," too many people had ignored the fact that failing to conserve the environment constituted "the fundamental problem which underlies almost every other problem in our national life." He asserted that the contemporary farmer provided a practical lesson to the country. Instead of exploiting and ruining the land like certain miners and lumber operators, farmers worked to conserve nature's resources. As Roosevelt stated in his "Eighth Annual Message,"

farmers epitomized the conservationist spirit just as their predecessors did: "a farmer, after all his life making his living from his farm, will, if he is an expert farmer, leave it as an asset of increased value to his son, so we should leave our national domain to our children, increased in value and not worn out."

Farmers who conserved nature's resources through their wise use of them promoted the permanent interests of the country. Just as mythical heroes struggled for a greater good, such as cooperating with the community for its protection, so too did contemporary farmers protect civilization by preserving its resources. Roosevelt told a 1903 Stanford University crowd that it should applaud the farmer as a person "who comes in not to take what he can out of the soil and leave, having exploited the country, but who comes to dwell therein, to bring up his children and to leave them the heritage in the country not merely unimpaired, but if possible even improved." For Roosevelt, the farmer-hero epitomized the conservationist who would use the water, forests, and land "so that by the very fact of the use they will become more valuable as possessions."

Although he replaced the traditional Frontier Myth's hero, Roosevelt's version still reflected the established Myth's familiar and compelling paradox between acting alone and cooperating with a group. The modern farmer-heroes resembled their original counterparts in that they manifested the traditional characteristics of the latter, most notably the trait of rugged individualism. And in order to meet their "goodness" requirement, Roosevelt maintained that these modern heroes opted to protect the community by working to safeguard the environment.

*   *   *

As an icon abstracted from America's sacred history, the frontier has been seen primarily as an unlimited expanse with as many opportunities. However, most of the opportunities afforded by the Myth had reduced the frontier to a source of profit, a commodity to be bought and sold in the marketplace. The frontier's "beauty is associated with riches," Calder notes, "rolling grass lands mean cattle" and "mountains mean gold initially, then later silver, copper and lead." Roosevelt attempted to alter these perceptions of the frontier-universe. In seeking to make the frontier a limited object, he linked its finite nature to the economic opportunities of his audience. Furthermore, he downplayed the capitalistic aspect of the frontier in order to promote its spiritual dimension.

Roosevelt acknowledged the economic necessity of the frontier. According to him, the government's conservation policies would help to ensure the fiscal prosperity of the nation. For example, he stated in his "First Annual Message" the federal laws protecting certain forested areas were not an end in themselves: "it is a means to increase and sustain the resources of our country and the industries which depend upon them." "The preservation of our forests," he granted, was "an imperative business necessity."

However, to act as if there was an unlimited source of frontier-capital, Roosevelt maintained, was reprehensible. On this point, he blamed a human evil in the form of certain private business interests. Unlike the traditional Frontier Myth which featured a primarily "scenic" menace, the President's rhetoric broke with that tradition and identified deliberate, malicious human agents that calculatingly exploited the nation's resources. In particular, Roosevelt depicted the timber barons as little more than reckless looters. In a 1905 Washington, D.C. address, for example, he alleged that loggers had brought the nation to the verge of a timber famine. "The individual whose idea of developing the country is to cut every stick of timber off of it and then leave a barren desert," he warned, was a "curse and not a blessing to the country." Two years later he echoed that charge in his "Seventh Annual Message":

> There are persons who find it to their immense pecuniary benefit to destroy the forests by lumbering. . . . A big lumbering company, impatient for immediate returns and not caring to look far enough ahead, will often deliberately destroy all the good timber in a region, hoping afterward to move on to some new country.

These people, Roosevelt concluded in his "Eighth Annual Message," deliberately engaged in immoral behavior for the sole purpose of purchasing "a little gain for themselves."

Roosevelt played on the fears of those industries that engaged in exploitative practices against the environment by predicting their eventual economic misfortune. Speaking before the Forest Congress in 1905, he warned that for too long forests had been considered obstacles to be cleared. The forests were not limitless, Roosevelt maintained, and it remained only a matter of time before many industries suffered

the consequences of a timber famine. He asserted that "unless the forests of the United States can be made ready to meet the vast demands which [this nation's] growth will inevitably bring, commercial disaster . . . . is inevitable." Roosevelt reminded the audience that not only the loggers would suffer since "the railroads must have ties," "the miner must have timber," and "the stockman must have fence posts." The greed of a few business interests would affect any industry that was "dependent upon the existence of permanent and suitable supplies" from the forests.

But for Roosevelt, conserving the frontier provided more than just an economic benefit to the country. Conservation represented the means to regenerate the American spirit. As a rhetorical president, Roosevelt attempted to elevate the audience's concern beyond material matters to remind it of the sacred power of the frontier.

While the limitless frontier had long since disappeared, Roosevelt maintained, it was imperative that at least small pockets of wilderness be preserved. These pockets helped maintain Americans' physical vigor. The forest reserves, he stated in his "First Annual Message," afforded "free camping grounds for the ever-increasing numbers of men and women who have learned to find rest [and] health in the splendid forests and flower-clad meadows of our mountains." During a tour of the western states in 1903, he asserted that the national parks he established would allow Americans to restore their physical prowess, just as their pioneer ancestors had likewise been transformed. At the gateway to Yellowstone National Park, he assured his audience that conservationists "will be able to ensure to themselves and to their children and to their children's children much of the old-time pleasure of the hardy life of the wilderness and of the hunter in the wilderness." These wilderness refuges, these sanctuaries of the mythologized western lands, still provided the conditions that could spur the "love of adventure" and the "hardihood to take advantage of it."

Despite the limited size of the frontier, Roosevelt believed in its mystical dimension and promoted its power to resuscitate the flagging spiritual nature of the American people. In a larger sense, Roosevelt's rhetoric linked the natural wonder of these isolated frontier areas to a Creator, reestablishing this icon's supernatural quality. During his 1903 visit to California, Roosevelt spoke reverentially about nature and its effect on those who experienced it: "lying out at night under those giant Sequoias was lying in a temple built by no hand of man, a temple grander than any human architect could by any possibility build." For Roosevelt, safeguarding nature's majesty went beyond any practical concerns, as he declared before another California audience:

> Yesterday I saw for the first time a grove of your great trees, a grove which it has taken the ages several thousands of years to build up; and I feel most emphatically that we should not turn a tree which was old when the first Egyptian conqueror penetrated to the valley of the Euphrates . . . into shingles. That, you may say, is not looking at the matter from the practical standpoint. There is nothing more practical in the end than the preservation of beauty, than the preservation of anything that appeals to the higher emotions in mankind.

The conservation of America's wilderness, then, became the practical application of Roosevelt's vision of a great nation. Not only would conservation provide the country's commercial foundation but, equally important, it would also act as an antidote to spiritual malaise in the modern world. . . .

As presidents since Roosevelt have discovered, the use of myths provides them with a powerful rhetorical tool. Part of Roosevelt's short-term success stemmed from his use of myth to transcend specific legislative concerns. For example, while Roosevelt's critics questioned his right to create forest reserves, the President responded with a sacred history that gave his audiences an origin of their greatness. As a result, Roosevelt's storytelling resonated with the audiences' moral being while his opponents' rejoinders seemed irrelevant by comparison. Another element of that success may come from Roosevelt's use of other sacred histories to buoy his new myth. While he did build upon the foundation of the traditional story, bracing his icons upon similar aspects of the traditional Myth's icons, he supplemented the power of his new Frontier Myth by adding other unifying myths such as the creation of the Constitution. Furthermore, with his ability to reach the nation by manipulating the press, as well as having a character consistent with his story, he reinforced his simple, mythic explanations to resolve a complex, "real" problem. Thus, Roosevelt garnered the public support necessary to pressure Congress to accept much of his legislative agenda.

While Roosevelt's short-term success brought legislative gains, his long-term success remains problematic. The lessons of conservation he preached still have not been realized, as illustrated by the nation's continued problems with preserving forested areas and wildlife. One simple explanation may be the fact that for a myth to be effective, it must become embedded in an audience's psyche; it must become a familiar part of the audience's language. For that to occur, it must be retold from generation to generation by rhetors with prominent status. Since Roosevelt, few chief executives have utilized their rhetorical presidency to embrace the conservation of natural resources, let alone repeat the bully pulpiteer's version of the Myth.

Woodrow Wilson, Ethnicity, and the Myth of American Unity

Hans Vought

The subject of immigration and attitudes toward immigrants historically have pervaded American society, and continue to do so. This reflects one of the country's grandest myths—that of American unity, or at least approaching unity. Ethnic concerns appeared early and have persisted. Professor Hans Vought of the University of Connecticut focuses on Woodrow Wilson's attempts to further the ideal of unity, while personally harboring the antithesis—anti-Asian and anti-black prejudices. More specifically, Vought analyzes Wilson's veto of the Burnett Immigration Restriction Bill, which included a literacy test. It seems that Wilson operated with a double standard. On the one hand Asians and blacks were unassimilable; European immigrants were. Europeans carried certain irregularities, such as loyalty to groups (radical political parties and unions), but these could be corrected through the educational process. As a result, Wilson saw an opportunity to follow his hero, President Grover Cleveland, who had, according to Wilson, brought the sections together after the Civil War. Thus the ideal of American unity would be at least furthered—perhaps even realized. The national interest, never dissociated in Wilson's mind from God's will, would be advanced. Finally, Vought sees application to present multicultural concerns. How does the nation progress toward a realization of the mythic ideal of unity, while at the same time maintain a realistic recognition and support of diversity? There may even be some positive lessons to learn from the Wilsonian experience, but assuredly the welcoming, sheltering democratic net must be expanded to include all Americans.

Historians have examined Thomas Woodrow Wilson perhaps more closely than any other United States president. Sixty-five volumes of his papers have now been edited and published, numerous books analyzing his character, administration, and relationship to his times have been written. One would think that nothing remains to be said about the man. But surprisingly, very little attention has been paid to President Wilson's attitude towards immigration. Historians have given passing notice only to his two vetoes of the Burnett Immigration Restriction Bill, without bothering to question why [one] so clearly racist towards blacks and Asians would reject a literacy test to keep ignorant, non-Teutonic foreigners out of the United States. Not only was the bill popular, the very concept of the literacy test was one that he endorsed in his native South to keep blacks disfranchised. Clearly, there is an issue here that needs to be examined.

This essay addresses the issue, and seeks to place Wilson's attitude towards immigration not only in the context of his overall character, but in the larger context of traditional American political attitudes. Specifically, Wilson is pictured in this study as embodying the American political ideal of complete homogeneity. He was upset by the fierce class and ethnic conflict that raged in America in the latter half of the nineteenth and the first two decades of the twentieth century, a struggle that he viewed as a second Civil War and Reconstruction. Wilson saw himself as taking over the role of his hero, Grover Cleveland, the Democrat who, in Wilson's opinion, reunited the sections and brought peace and prosperity to the United States.

Wilson was representative of a moderate progressivism that existed in the latter part of the nineteenth century and the early part of this one. He was reacting negatively to the new, industrialist class, but maintaining a strong belief in the triumph of American ideals and progress. In general, moderate progressives believed that ethnic and class conflict resulted from valuing private interests over the public interest. This in turn led to widespread corruption of the spoils system by political machines. Immigrants living in the major cities had too often been the cogs that kept the machines running. The solution, according to the moderate progressives, was to unify all classes and ethnic groups into a homogeneous middle class. They believed that the majority of Americans, including themselves, belonged to this middle class. Not only did the classes need to be unified, they also needed to be socialized through education to accept the American political, social, and economic ideals. Only with a common basis of belief could the body politic agree upon the national interest.

Wilson, like most progressives, moderate or otherwise, abhorred not only the anarchist and socialist beliefs of some of the foreign born, he failed completely to understand their conception of politics as an exchange of favors. Wilson's heroes were great statesmen, who selflessly served their country's commonweal while rallying the people to patriotic endeavors. Wilson saw himself as another Pitt, another Bismarck who could create an efficient, honest government to which all people would rally.

In all of this, the underlying political idealism was that strange mixture of the Enlightenment and Protestant Christianity, which the founding fathers had incorporated into American political structure and thought. Wilson championed the belief in society as a collection of rational, autonomous men who, given the right education, would always agree as to what was the commonweal and then act upon it. Furthermore, he believed in the inevitability of progress, because he believed in a God who was active

in history. His own deep, personal faith in Jesus Christ led him to temper his belief in autonomous reason with the realization that some truths could only be revealed by the Holy Spirit. But this mattered little, for God's will, in Wilson's mind, was the same as American national interest.

Hyphenated immigrants were unacceptable to Wilson and most progressives because they acted as groups, and put selfish group interests blindly above the national interest, which, in Wilson's thought, was naturally all of humanity's interest. Moderate progressives sought reforms to improve the lives of immigrants, the urban poor, and the working class, but they sought reforms designed scientifically to meet objectively the needs of society as a whole. Hyphenates, suffragettes, unions, and those demanding welfare legislation were thus all grouped together as selfish special interests to Wilson. Later on, he would become more sympathetic to some of these groups, but only when he began to see their special interest as the national interest. The hyphenate groups never fell into this category. Their disloyalty was bad enough in times of peace; in times of war, it was intolerable.

Note, however, that Wilson opposed hyphenate groups, not immigrants in general. Although he was racist towards blacks and Asians, he was only mildly paternalistic towards the former residents of southern and eastern Europe. Wilson thought the literacy test indeed served a valid purpose in preventing the unassimilable blacks and Asians from voting, but it was invalid to deny admittance to people on the basis of ignorance. For Wilson, illiteracy did not equate with unassimilability, despite the great stock that he placed in education. After all, one could hardly expect southern and eastern Europeans to have received a decent education in their homelands. The point was that they were capable of being educated and assimilated into American culture because they shared a similar enough moral and cultural background as well as a similar shade of skin. More importantly, the United States had to allow the "poor, huddled masses, yearning to breathe free" to enter in order to fulfill God's purpose in creating the "land of the free and the home of the brave." . . .

The insistence of hyphenates upon retaining their national loyalty stood directly in the way of the triumphal American century that Wilson envisioned. He had no quarrel with those who wished to remember fondly their heritage. Wilson often referred proudly to his Scotch-Irish background. But he firmly believed that it *was* background, and that all American citizens, whether naturalized or native born, should think and act in the foreground. After all, the United States was the last, best hope of mankind, and hence far more deserving of loyalty than any lesser land. In a 1902 speech, Wilson defined patriotism as not merely a sentiment, but a principle of action: the Biblical command—to "love thy neighbor as thyself." And who was one's neighbor? He answered, "Patriotism comes when a man is of big enough range of affection to take the country in. It is friendship writ large. It is fellowship with many sides, which expends itself in service to all mankind joined in the same citizenship, and who are bound up in the same principles of civilization."

Note once again the theme of unity, a brotherhood of servants of God. In Wilson's view, to take the oath of citizenship was to join this lay order. Immigrants who then insisted on hyphens in their name, and tried to fight out Old World battles in the New World, had broken their vows, and quite literally broken faith with America. He probably remembered his father pronouncing the judgment of Jesus from the pulpit: "No one who puts his hand to the plow and looks back is fit for service in the Kingdom of God." He used similar language when addressing a crowd of several thousand newly naturalized citizens in Philadelphia in 1915:

> You have just taken an oath of allegiance to the United States. Of allegiance to whom? Of allegiance to no one, unless it be God—certainly not of allegiance to those who temporarily represent this great Government. You have taken an oath of allegiance to a great ideal, to a great body of principles, to a great hope of the human race. . . . And while you bring all countries with you, you come with a promise of leaving all other countries behind you—bringing what is best of their spirit, but not looking over your shoulder and seeking to perpetuate what you intended to leave behind in them. I certainly would not be one even to suggest that a man cease to love the home of his birth and the nation of his origin—these things are very sacred and ought not to be put out of our hearts—but it is one thing to love the place where you were born and it is another thing to dedicate yourself to the place to which you go. You cannot dedicate yourself to America unless you become in every respect and with every purpose of your will thorough Americans. *You cannot become thorough Americans if you think of yourselves in groups. America does not consist of groups.* A man who thinks of

himself as belonging to a particular national group in America has not yet become an American.

The fate of immigrants who continued to look to the past would be that of Lot's wife, according to Wilson. Of course, he desired unity of American spirit at all times. But the efforts of hyphenated Americans, whether Irish, German, Italian, or English, to draw the United States into World War I on behalf of their homelands particularly infuriated Wilson, violating as it did his proclamation of neutrality. It is not by accident that in the same speech quoted above, Wilson made his famous declaration that America was "too proud to fight."

Joe Tumulty, Wilson's Irish Catholic secretary (who today would be called chief of staff), recorded Wilson's anger at Irish Americans who wanted the United States to support Germany in order to force Great Britain to give Ireland her freedom, an anger which Tumulty claims to have shared. When Irish agitator Jeremiah O'Leary wrote to Wilson in 1916, threatening the loss of the Irish vote, Wilson replied angrily in a published letter, "I would feel deeply mortified to have you or anybody like you vote for me. Since you have access to many disloyal Americans and I have not, I will ask you to convey this message to them." Although he thus repudiated the hyphenate vote in 1916, Wilson was not ready to silence all disloyal opposition completely, as Roosevelt was. That would come with the United States' entry into the war, one year later.

Wilson most clearly enunciated his views on this subject when giving an address at the unveiling of a statue of Irish-American Commodore John Barry:

> John Barry was an Irishman, but his heart crossed the Atlantic with him. He did not leave it in Ireland. And the test of all of us—for all of us had our origins on the other side of the sea—is whether we will assist in enabling America to live her separate and independent life, retaining our ancient affections, indeed, but determining everything that we do by the interests that exist on this side of the sea. Some Americans need hyphens in their names, because only part of them has come over, but when the whole man has come over, heart and thought and all, the hyphen drops of its own weight out of his name. This man was not an Irish-American; he was an Irishman who became an American. I venture to say that if he voted he voted with regard to the questions as they looked on this side of the water and not as they affected the other side; and that is my infallible test of a genuine American.

Wilson had indeed long supported the Irish nationalists in their struggle for independence, but it must not come at the expense of United States neutrality or interests.

His campaign against hyphenism coincided with ever-present nativism and the growing pro-Allied war movement to produce a backlash against immigration. This backlash led to the Burnett Immigration Restriction Bill passing Congress in 1915 and 1917, and becoming law in 1917 over the president's veto.

Wilson was genuinely opposed to nativism, and he viewed the unions' position as merely selfish interest, which he could not tolerate. To assuage the fears of average Americans, he portrayed the hyphenates as a minor faction, comparable in their disloyalty to the most outspoken Allied supporters, such as Theodore Roosevelt. In a stump speech on preparedness in 1916, Wilson said of the immigrants, "Their intimate sympathies are with some of the places now most affected by this titanic struggle. You can not [sic] wonder—I do not wonder—that their affections are stirred, old memories awakened and old passions rekindled. The majority of them are steadfast Americans, nevertheless." He noted that by contrast, many nativist Americans had been disloyal in seeking to draw the United States into the war on the Allied side, and concluded that all disloyal favoritism must be put down.

Again, in an address to the Daughters of the American Revolution (an organization that was notoriously nativist) in 1915, entitled, "Be Not Afraid of Our Foreign-Born Citizens," Wilson cautioned them, "There is too general an impression, I fear, that very large numbers of our fellow-citizens born in other lands have not entertained with sufficient intensity and affection the American ideal. But the number is, I am sure, not large. Those who would seek to represent them are very vocal, but they are not very influential." He went on to remind these ancestor-worshipping women that "Some of the best stuff in America has come out of foreign lands, and some of the best stuff in America is in the men who are naturalized citizens. . . . The vast majority of them came here because they believed in America, and their belief in America has made them better citizens than some people who were born in America."

The fact that Wilson equated his struggle to bring unity to warring ethnic groups with Abraham Lincoln's struggle to bring unity to the warring states was made explicit in Wilson's Flag Day address of 1916. By an earlier proclamation, he had made Flag Day an official, nationwide celebration, seeking to use this obvious patriotic symbol to end the "influences which have seemed to threaten to divide us in interest and sympathy," by saying to his "fellow countrymen," "Let us on that day rededicate ourselves to our Nation, 'one and inseparable,' from which every thought that is not worthy of our fathers' first vows of independence, liberty, and right shall be excluded and in which we shall stand with united hearts, for an America which no man can corrupt, . . . no force divide against itself." Here was an obvious reference to Lincoln's immortal maxim, "A house divided against itself cannot stand." In the June 14 address itself, Wilson explicitly compared the current test of unity to that of the Civil War, and stated, "There is disloyalty active in the United States, and it must be absolutely crushed." Unfortunately, all dissent was indeed to be crushed under the weight of George Creel's Committee on Public Information and other wartime measures.

All of these themes came together in Wilson's decision to veto the Burnett Immigration Restriction Bill in 1915 and 1917. The bill's main feature was a literacy test, designed to exclude those who threatened the health and morals of the United States, as Wilson had asked for. He followed the example of Cleveland and Taft in vetoing the bill. In the process, he was standing up to the growing nativist hysteria brought on by the war. The vote to override failed narrowly in 1915; in 1917 the override passed and the Burnett Bill became law.

The movement to restrict immigration had caught Congress's attention in the 1880s, and produced the Chinese Exclusion Act, as well as the later "Gentlemen's Agreement" with Japan. President Cleveland's position was, not surprisingly, very close to that of his protégé's thirty years later. In 1886, Cleveland stated in his annual message to Congress, "In opening our vast domains to alien elements, the purpose of our law-givers was to invite assimilation, and not to provide an arena for endless antagonisms. The paramount duty of maintaining public order and defending the interests of our own people, may require . . . restriction, but they should not tolerate the oppression of individuals of a special race." In his second term, Cleveland did call for legislation to check the "growing evil" of the padrone system, and he voiced concern over the rising illiteracy rates among immigrants. Nevertheless, he vetoed Sen.

Henry Cabot Lodge's literacy test bill as too restrictive in 1897. Taft likewise vetoed a similar bill in 1913.

The earliest champion of the literacy test was [Henry Cabot] Lodge, the Massachusetts Brahmin who became Wilson's nemesis. Wilson and Lodge both held an idealistic, optimistic view of America's past and future greatness, and both upheld the Puritan ideal of a public-spirited, homogeneous society as the only salvation for the morass of self-serving urban politics. Where the infamous antagonism existed between the two leaders was over *how* to achieve that homogeneity. Wilson sought American strength through unity, blending together the best characteristics of every nationality to create the ideal citizenry. Lodge, on the other hand, sought strength through purity, convinced that only the Anglo-American "race" could succeed. Lodge believed in assimilation and Americanization, to be sure, but it could only be successful when immigrants abandoned their ethnic heritage entirely and became Anglo Americans. Where Wilson wanted only for the immigrants to share a common vision, Lodge wanted them to share a common history, common language, and common customs. This subtle contrast between amalgamation and isolation was, of course, also at the heart of the battle over the League of Nations.

Lodge argued for the literacy test bill almost as soon as he was elected to the House of Representatives. As a senator in 1896, he recommended the literacy test to his colleagues precisely because it would discriminate against undesirable Italians, Poles, Hungarians, Greeks, and Asians, while allowing British, German, Scandinavian, and French immigrants to come in. He declared that "illiteracy runs parallel with the slum population, with criminals, paupers, juvenile delinquents of foreign birth or parentage . . . [and] those who bring the least money to the country and come most quickly upon private or public charity for support." Furthermore, the new immigrants were dangerous because they were "changing the quality of our race and citizenship through the wholesale infusion of races whose traditions and inheritances, whose thoughts and whose beliefs are wholly alien to ours." For Lodge, citizenship was directly tied to ethnicity. He could not see Wilson's argument that the American spirit could transcend ethnicity.

The G.O.P. platform of 1896 called for a literacy test, and Roosevelt pressed Congress to ban all anarchists after McKinley's assassination. Roosevelt tried to maintain a balanced position on immigration, however, despite favoring the literacy test. In his 1903 message to Congress, he sounded the theme of Wilson's National Liberal Immigration League (NLIL) which sought to break up the urban slums and spread the immigrants across the nation. "The need is to devise some system by which undesirable immigrants shall be kept out entirely, while desirable immigrants are properly distributed throughout the country." Again in 1905 he called for distribution, suggesting the banning of immigration only in the big Northern cities. It was only during World War I that Roosevelt became the champion of the rabid nationalists.

The Southerners were violently opposed to any immigrants being distributed around Dixie, and it is not surprising to find that most of the literacy test's supporters were Southern Democrats such as Oscar Underwood and John Burnett. They wanted an end to all immigration of non-"Teutonic" foreigners, and thought that the literacy test could accomplish this as well as it kept blacks from voting in their home states. Immigration restriction was also a golden opportunity for Southern Democrats to win back the farmers and unions that had bolted the party for the Populists in the 1890s.

The theme of racial superiority dominated Congressional debates quite as much as economic concerns about wages and jobs. Congressman Everis A. Hayes of California made a motion in 1914 to amend the Burnett Bill by excluding all "Hindoos [sic] and all persons of the Mongolian or yellow race, the Malay or brown race, the African or black race," but it was defeated handily. Sen. James A. Reed of Missouri did get an amendment excluding all blacks (carefully worded so as to bar even black United States citizens who travelled abroad from returning!) to pass the Senate, but it was dropped in conference committee in 1915. The 1917 bill that finally passed over Wilson's veto did include an "Asiatic Barred Zone" that restricted immigration by longitude and latitude.

While Wilson saw the Southerners and the unions as guilty of promoting selfish special interests, Congressman John L. Burnett of Alabama attacked the foes of his bill as special interests: the "Ship Trust," the "Brewer's Trust." He argued that his bill did exactly what Wilson had called for in his address to the foreign-language editors during the campaign: restricting immigration to maintain American ideals. (However, he contradicted himself immediately by quoting a *Boston Transcript* editorial claiming that the literacy test was *not* a test of character.) Burnett made sure to fill his speeches with the social science statistics that made progressives' ears perk up, and quoted experts such as New York Police Commissioner Bingham: "You will notice that these particular crimes [against women and children] are done by fellows who can't talk the English language; . . . [who] don't know what liberty means, and don't care; don't know our customs; . . . and are in general the scum of Europe." While Burnett was definitely a white supremacist, he urged the House to vote down the amendment restricting all blacks— but only because the amendment would insure the bill's defeat.

The most outspoken opponent of the Burnett Bill was Congressmen James A. Gallivan of Massachusetts. He joined Washington Gladden in denouncing the new "holy wars" between Catholics and Protestants that the debate on immigration was engendering. He also pointed out the hypocrisy of the bill's supporters, noting that the majority of white Southerners, let alone blacks, were as poor as the immigrants, and had much higher rates of illiteracy. He observed, too, that wealth and education had grown in the North along with immigration. Gallivan reminded his colleagues that the twelve Apostles were mostly illiterate when Jesus called them, and that their own colonial ancestors, of whom they were so proud, were largely illiterate, too. As he said: "Then, as now, the men who faced the hazards of the tempestuous ocean and the perils of the savage continent were usually the bravest and most enterprising of their class; they had courage, strength, common sense, native ability, and a willingness to work out their own salvation in a new country . . . ," but not a good education. Gallivan pleaded always for a true test of character, noting that anarchists and socialists were almost always well-educated, and so a literacy test would not keep them out. He concluded that "we have grown fat and foolish in our progress; we forgot our origins; we imagine that the eternal verities will change and that the letters and scripts that man has made have, by some curious alchemy, become greater and more worthy than the gifts God has given us."

In Wilson's first veto message, he called the bill, "a radical departure from the traditional and long-established policy of this country . . . in which our people have conceived the very character of their government to be expressed, the very mission and spirit of the Nation . . ." because it greatly curtailed the right to political asylum in the United States. In addition, the bill was unsound because it would, "turn away from tests of character and of quality and impose tests which exclude and restrict; for the new tests are . . . tests of opportunity. Those who come seeking opportunity are not to be admitted unless they have already had one of the chief opportunities they seek, the opportunity of education." Wilson's second veto message basically reiterated the first. Ironically, however, he criticized an amendment put in to answer his objections about the elimination of asylum, saying that it would lead to diplomatic difficulties. The ever-approaching war no doubt contributed to this seeming about-face.

Wilson did not desire the severe repression of the wartime years, although he did condone it. The Burnett Immigration Restriction Bill, on the other hand, was a measure that he opposed from the start. Not only did Wilson deem it unnecessary (as he remained confident that the majority of immigrants were loyal Americans) but more importantly, it violated the foundational principles of America. Wilson consistently saw America as more of a spiritual concept than a physical reality, a mental device used by most Americans to reconcile the image of America that they have been socialized to accept with the far-from-perfect reality which they can plainly see. Wilson recognized that it was vital to keep the spiritual concept of America, symbolized by the Statue of Liberty, not too far out of line with the reality of Ellis Island.

This spiritual concept called America was in reality the old Puritan dream of the New World as the new Jerusalem, the "city set on a hill" of which Jesus spoke, and of the American people as the new Israel, a people set apart by God to be an example and inspiration to all the world. The biblical texts and the writings of Calvinist preachers were all familiar to the son of a Presbyterian minister and a devout Christian in his own right, and his allusions clearly drew on them. In a Thanksgiving Day address to the Har Sinai Temple of Trenton, New Jersey in 1910, he quoted the old New England divine William Stoughton on the subject of God sifting the nations of the world to plant the choicest seed in America, and he went on to say, "And so, apparently God is sifting the nations yet to plant seed in America." He described the American people as a "conglomerate," with each ethnic group contributing necessary characteristics, "I will not say, out of alien stocks, for these stocks are bound by adoption, by mixture and by union." One can hear St. Paul saying, "Theirs is the adoption as sons; theirs the divine glory, the covenants, the receiving of the law, the temple worship and the promises." Wilson then said, "I don't regard these national elements, that is, race elements, that make up American life as something outside America for they have come in and been identified with her. They are all instantly recognizable as Americans and America is enriched with the variety of their gifts and the variety of their national characterization."

His campaign speeches in 1912 emphasize this spiritual concept as the force which motivated most immigrants to come to the United States. In part, this was because Wilson was trying to mollify hyphenate groups who were outraged over the infamous passage in Wilson's *History* by arguing that the quote was taken out of context, and that he referred only to those immigrants who were "forced" to come over as contract labor. By contrast, the majority of immigrants came over voluntarily, literally "moved by the spirit."

But this defense merged in Wilson's mind with what he considered to be the more important reason to emphasize the spiritual concept of America: the unity of believers that it implied. Wilson believed that he could reunite the divided American people by teaching them that the past no longer mattered, save to teach them the necessity and inevitability of their being all as one now in the American spirit. It is as if Wilson was paraphrasing St. Paul again: "Here there is no Greek or Jew, immigrant or native, Pole, Italian, slave or free, but America is all, and is in all." It also calls to mind the motto of King Louis XVIII of France after the French Revolution: "L'union et l'oublie" ("Union and Forgetfulness").

We can hear this cry in Wilson's address to a Polish-American crowd in Chicago's South Side:

> When we speak of America, we speak not of race; but of a people. After we have enumerated the Irish-Americans, the Jewish-Americans, the German-Americans, and the Polish-Americans who will be left? Settlers and descendants of settlers constitute the minority in America, and the people of all the races of Europe a majority. The term America is bigger than

the continent. America lives in the hearts of every man everywhere who wishes to find a region somewhere where he will be free to work out his destiny as he chooses.

Wilson, indeed, began to protest wherever he spoke against the very hyphenated terms with which the immigrants were labelled. He realized that the use of such terms fostered the lack of unity felt by Americans of different ethnic backgrounds, and prevented the full flowering of united American power that he predicted for this century. He declared, "I am looking forward to an era of unprecedented national action. We are now coming to an era where there will be but one single expression and but one common thought." In order for this era to be brought about, the usages of thought and expression had to be changed, however. Thus he went on, "I protest against speaking of German-Americans, or Irish-Americans or Jewish-Americans, for these nationalities are becoming indistinguishable in the general body of Americans. Drop out the first words, cut out the hyphens and call them all Americans."

The importance of language in communicating this spiritual concept of America was stressed to a group of approximately one hundred editors of foreign-language newspapers in 1912. Wilson explained to them his view of America, and stated that immigrants should only be restricted to exclude those who did not have the spirit of American idealism which caused people to voluntarily emigrate. He then protested against their designation as foreign-language editors, arguing that whatever language was used to convey American ideals was the language of America: "All my interest is that you shouldn't regard the language in which you print your periodicals as a foreign language when printed in America for the conveyance of American thinking." This was indeed a radical statement of the American spirit of unity erasing even the most obvious ethnic divisions.

True American faith was limited to the elect, however. There were certain languages that simply could not convey the American spirit. Wilson thought that the key to a successful immigration policy was assimilation. Indeed, it was on this basis that Wilson supported the Chinese Exclusion Act. Oriental people, like the blacks in the South, were simply incapable of conforming to the ideal, Wilson believed. Therefore, they were obviously heathen intruders in the Kingdom of God, who should be tolerated, but kept in their place.

Despite the fact that Europeans emigrated to the United States because they were already Americans at heart, assimilation was not an automatic experience. Immigrants needed to work out their salvation with fear and trembling, and it was up to the "native" citizens to aid them in the assimilation process. The key was education. Wilson heartily approved the naturalization classes and night school movements started by progressive social workers during this time period. But, he believed that "the chief school that these people must attend after they get here is the school which all of us attend, which is furnished by the life of the communities in which we live and the Nation to which we belong. . . . It is easy . . . to communicate physical lessons, but it is very difficult to communicate spiritual lessons." The ideal American community (i.e., small and rural) was the best school for instilling American ideals, not crowded cities where those ideals had been corrupted.

The chief spiritual lessons which immigrants needed to learn were American political ideals. Wilson was very upset that the immigrants kept the urban political machines running by exchanging votes for jobs and other favors. This process corrupted Wilson's, and America's, ideals of both the statesman and the electorate. His views on the ideal statesman have been discussed above. It needs to be pointed out here that although Wilson saw the party as a powerful tool, he demanded that elected officials act as individually responsible trustees, and not as mere delegates, blindly following party dictates. As early as 1876 he wrote:

> Although there are principles of duty to his party and to the cause he has espoused, still no statesman should allow party feeling to bias his opinions on any point which involves truth or falsehood, justice or injustice. He should search for truth with the full determination to find it, and in that search he should most earnestly seek aid from God, who will surely hold him responsible for the course he pursues.

In a 1912 campaign speech, Wilson cautioned his audience to, "always distinguish a boss from a political leader. Party organization is absolutely legitimate and absolutely necessary," but only when the political leader uses the party to serve the commonweal. "A boss is a man who uses this splendid open force for the secret processes of selfish control."

Voters must vote for the good of the nation as a whole, and politicians must serve that greater good. In Wilson's speech accepting the Democratic nomination in 1912, the man who had defeated the bosses in New Jersey called on his party to do the same nationwide: "We are servants of the people, the whole people. *The nation has been unnecessarily, unreasonably at war within itself.* Interest has clashed with interest when there were common principles of right and of fair dealing which . . . should have bound them all together. . . . As servants of all, we are bound to undertake the great duty of accommodation and adjustment." Thus the call once more to end the civil war and unite in patriotic homogeneity of belief and practice.

Wilson explicitly linked this homogeneity of American idealism to the assimilation of immigrants during the campaign. He argued that America had always opened its doors and extended hospitality to all the "modern civilized peoples," that they might share in our ideals and enrich our melting pot. America must be careful to live up to the ideals which persuaded the immigrants to come here, the vision of "a place of close knit communities, where men think in terms of the common interest, where men do not organize selfish groups to dominate the fortunes of their fellow men, but where, on the contrary, they, by common conference, conceive the policies which are for the common benefit." Once more, the image of special interest groups as an evil, divisive force emerges, as well as the image of small-town community life as the ideal force to Americanize and unify the diverse elements of the population.

Although he believed that Americans came with, and because of, this ideal vision, they did not always realize it. Often they continued to act politically in the manner that they learned in the Old World, giving loyalty on the basis of debts owed and blood ties. Wilson saw a need to educate immigrants to accept that in the United States, the people, and not the State, were sovereign. He told the Conference on Americanization, "When you ask a man to be loyal to a government, if he comes from some foreign countries, his idea is that he is expected to be loyal to a certain set of persons like a ruler or a body set in authority over him. . . . Our idea is that he is to be loyal to certain objects in life." Not only must they be taught that idealism is allowed in the United States, they must be taught that idealism is mandatory in the United States.

> Loyalty means nothing unless it has at its heart the absolute principle of self-sacrifice. Loyalty means that you ought to be ready to sacrifice every interest that you have, and your life itself, if your country calls upon you to do so, and that is the sort of loyalty which ought to be inculcated into these newcomers, . . . that, having once entered this sacred relationship, they are bound to be loyal whether they are pleased or not; and that loyalty which is merely self-pleasing is only self-indulgence and selfishness.

Education was necessary for assimilation. But, as noted above, Wilson believed that the best education came from everyday community life. The healthiest communities were naturally the rural ones. Wilson therefore supported efforts to get the immigrants out of the crowded, squalid cities in which most of the immigrants stayed, and spread them out in the great expanse of American country. To this end he became a director of the National Liberal Immigration League. In fact, he asked for legislation to facilitate such assimilation by dilution instead of the Burnett Bill in 1915.

Seen now in the context of Wilson's overall attitude towards immigration, these two vetoes make much more sense. Wilson saw himself as another Lincoln or Cleveland, trying to heal the divisions of civil war and reunify the country to carry on its God-ordained mission. The literacy test may have been useful in keeping blacks and Asians out of American political life, because they were patently unassimilable to Wilson. However, it constituted an arbitrary restriction on thousands of European immigrants, who had the spirit of America in their hearts,

and could only help build the glorious empire of the United States in the twentieth century, and spread the gospel of political freedom to all the world.

More importantly, the rhetoric of Woodrow Wilson reveals several foundational myths in American life. The myth of America as the chosen people of God, building His Kingdom on Earth, rings forth in Wilson's religious imagery. This myth requires logically the myth of homogeneity, that all cultural differences must blend away in the melting pot, and that education will lead all rational men to recognize and strive only for the commonweal. "E pluribus, unum," thundered Wilson from the classroom and the bully pulpit of the Presidency. And the people responded by silencing all opposition to the war, by staging race riots, by abandoning the very ideals which Wilson had said unity would serve.

In this decade of the 1990s, when "multiculturalism" is the watchword of the universities, and cultural pluralism continues to increase rather than decrease, America needs to examine closely her foundational myths. Can, or should, the divided Puritan ideal be reunified? Does the concept of a nation still require a set of shared values and cultural experiences? The message of Woodrow Wilson is therefore a challenge to our society to redefine our national character, and examine anew our complex reactions to immigration. We can harshly suppress all differences, and thus destroy the very ideals we seek to preserve. We can abandon all hope of cultural cohesiveness, and either Balkanize our society or water down our ideals to meaninglessness. Or we can try to follow the middle road that Wilson attempted to lay down: teaching immigrants what it means to be Americans, but at the same time learning and adopting from them what their cultures have to offer.

Silent Cinema as
Historical Mythmaker

John Hope Franklin

From its beginning, the nation has lived, along with its philosophical commitment to freedom and equality, a contrary existence of white privilege. American race relations have been laced with complex strains of myth. Racial ideology, legal segregation, and political disfranchisement have all carried its taint. In conspiracy with social practices such as lynching, economic subordination, and habitual day-to-day discrimination, myth helped shape by the end of the nineteenth century an articulated white supremacy in place of slavery. In the early decades of the twentieth century, notes African-American scholar John Hope Franklin, James B. Duke Professor of History at Duke University, a vital new ingredient of American popular culture—motion pictures—profoundly influenced and further prejudiced the country's race relations. The efforts of a Baptist minister, Thomas Dixon; an aspiring filmmaker, David Wark Griffith; and President Woodrow Wilson combined the forces of religion, art, and politics to advance the cause of racism through their involvement with the film spectacular, *The Birth of a Nation* (1915). Out of common cultural ancestry rooted in the white South of the Reconstruction era, they used propaganda as history, and history as propaganda. Together, they inspired, shaped, and condoned a racial romance of white supremacy, "a travesty against truth." The progressive mentality, akin in its energies to this new cinematic art form, had ideological connections to a racism that after the death of slavery had found other forms of cultural expression.

The fact that certain scholars specialize in studying the past does not mean that the past as an area of serious inquiry is beyond the reach of the layman with even the most modest intellectual and professional equipment. One must respect the efforts of anyone who seeks to understand the past; but it does not follow that one must respect or accept the findings of all who inquire into the past. Nor does it follow that the curiosity seekers of one brand or another can speak for those who by training and commitment devote their major attention to a study of the past. The decades and centuries that have receded from contemporary view are too important to all of us to leave their study to those who do not bring to the task all the skills available and present

their findings with a clear understanding of what history means to the present and to the future.

The study of the past may mean many things to many people. For some it means that the effort to reconstruct what actually happened in an earlier era demands an honesty and integrity that elevate the study of history to a noble enterprise. For some it means that the search for a usable past provides instruction that may help to avoid the errors of their forefathers. It is not necessary to enumerate each of the many uses of the past, but it is worth noting that not all such quests are characterized by a search for the truth. Some of the most diligent would-be historians have sought out those historical episodes that support some contemporary axe they have to grind.

Others look for ways to justify the social and public policy that they and like-minded persons advocate. Others even use the past to hold up to public scorn and ridicule those who are the object of their own prejudices.

The era of Reconstruction after the Civil War is an excellent example of a period that attracts historians—laymen and professionals alike—who seek historical explanations for certain contemporary social and political problems. And Thomas Dixon, Jr. is a peerless example of a historian—in his case a layman—who has mined the era of Reconstruction to seek a historical justification for his own social attitudes and who has exerted as much influence on current opinions of Reconstruction as any historian, lay or professional. Born in 1864 in a farmhouse near Shelby, North Carolina, Dixon was eight years old when he accompanied an uncle to a session of the state legislature in South Carolina where he saw in that body "ninety-four Negroes, seven native scalawags [white South Carolina Republicans] and twenty-three white men [presumably carpetbaggers from the North]." The impression on young Dixon of blacks and unworthy whites sitting in the seats of the mighty was a lasting one and ostensibly had a profound influence on his future career.

Dixon's Reconstruction experience was not unlike that which he had in 1887 when he heard Justin D. Fulton speak in Boston's Tremont Temple on "The Southern Problem." He was so outraged at Fulton's strictures against the South, based on a visit of six months, that he interrupted the distinguished minister midway through his lecture to denounce his assertions as "false and biased." It was on this occasion that Dixon decided to tell the world what he knew about the South firsthand and thus he began seriously to study the Civil War and Reconstruction.

The road that led Dixon to write about the Reconstruction era took him on a long and eventful journey. It led to Wake Forest College, where he was a superior student and leading debater. Then, for a brief sojourn he was at the Johns Hopkins University, where he became friendly with a graduate student, Woodrow Wilson, with whom he would later exchange favors. At the age of twenty young Dixon was a one-term member of the North Carolina legislature, which he quit because he was sickened by the conduct of the politicians whom he called "the prostitutes of the masses."

Incidentally, the number of black members of the Assembly was so small in 1884 that they could not possibly have been the cause of Dixon's disillusionment. Successively, this restless and talented young man became an actor, lawyer, clergyman, essayist, and lecturer. None of these pursuits satisfied Thomas Dixon as long as he was consumed with the desire to "set the record straight," as he would put it, regarding Reconstruction. Consequently, he forsook his other activities and proceeded to write the first volume of his Reconstruction trilogy. He called it *The Leopard's Spots: A Romance of the White Man's Burden.* The title was derived from the Biblical question "Can the Ethiopian change his skin, or the leopard his spots?"

Dixon sent his first novel to his old Raleigh, North Carolina friend, Walter Hines Page, then a partner in the publishing house, Doubleday, Page and Company. Page accepted it immediately and optimistically ordered a first printing of fifteen thousand copies. The success of the work when it appeared in 1903 was instantaneous. Within a few months more than one hundred thousand copies had been sold, and arrangements made for numerous foreign translations. Highly touted as a general history of the racial problem in the South and especially in North Carolina from 1885 to 1900, *The Leopard's Spots* established Dixon as an authority whom many were inclined to take seriously. His "luxuriant imagination" gave him the power to create "human characters that live and love and suffer before your eyes," a critic in the *Chicago Record-Herald* exclaimed. If there were those who were adversely critical—and there were—their voices could scarcely be heard above the din of almost universal praise.

Fame and fortune merely stimulated Dixon to greater accomplishments. He was in constant demand as a lecturer and writer; and soon his tall, commanding figure was on the platform in many parts of the country, constantly pressing his case as if in an adversary relationship with his audience. Within a few years he was ready to begin the second of his works on the Reconstruction, and thirty days after he began the writing he completed *The Clansman: An Historical Romance of the Ku Klux Klan.* Two years later, in July, 1907, he finished the last of the volumes in the Reconstruction trilogy which appeared under the title of *The Traitor: A Story of the Rise and Fall of the Invisible Empire.*

The great success of *The Clansman* as a novel caused Dixon to consider its possibilities as a drama.

In a matter of months, in 1905, Dixon had converted his second Reconstruction novel into a dramatic play whose script won the praise of John Hay, the Secretary of State, and Albert Bigelow Paine, who was to become the literary executor of Mark Twain. When the play went on tour, it was acclaimed as "The Greatest Play of the South . . . A Daring Thrilling Romance of the Ku Klux Klan . . ." and it drew enormous crowds even though some critics thought it a bit excessive in its strictures against blacks and the way in which it aroused emotions and animosities that many hoped were abating. But *The Clansman* remained as thrilling on the stage as it had been as a best-selling novel.

On a voyage from Europe in 1912, Dixon, proud of what he had accomplished, began once more to think seriously about his future. By that time he had completed his trilogy on Reconstruction as well as a trilogy on socialism. *The Clansman* had been a success on the stage, and everywhere he was acclaimed as a near-genius. He began to wonder if he should return to acting, but he rejected such a career as being too prosaic. Likewise, he rejected the idea that he should remain a playwright on the thoroughly defensible ground that the endless repetition of plot and scene before relatively small audiences was not a very effective medium for the dissemination of ideas. Books, likewise, were limited in their appeal, and although Dixon would continue to write them, they would never claim all of his attention.

By this time, however, there was a new medium, called motion pictures, just becoming known. This novel method of communication lured Dixon "like the words of a vaguely-heard song," as his biographer put it. If this new medium, still scorned by most actors, most religious groups, and many "respectable" people, could be dignified by some great statement—like a historically vital story—would it not be the means of reaching and influencing millions of people? This could be an exciting, new venture, and this adventuresome man answered his own question in the affirmative.

In the months following his return from Europe, Dixon tried to persuade some producer in the infant motion picture industry to take on his scenario of *The Clansman*, but none would accept the offer. The movies were popular only as low comedies, light farce, and short action sequences with little plot. All the producers whom Dixon approached insisted that *The Clansman* was too long, too serious, and too contro-

versial. Finally, late in 1913, Dixon met Harry E. Aitken, the head of a small company, and through him he met David W. Griffith who had enough daring and imagination to turn from his one-reel productions at least to consider the possibility of producing a large work like *The Clansman*. When Griffith's own company, The Epoch Producing Corporation, was unable to pay Dixon the ten thousand dollars he asked for his work, the author had to content himself by accepting a 25% interest in the picture. Armed with Dixon's blessings and thousands of his suggestions, Griffith set out for Hollywood to find a cast and to proceed with production. The actual filming occupied nine weeks, between July and October, 1914.

Prior to this time the motion picture had been composed of a series of stilted poses taken at random distances and tagged together with little continuity. The motion, not the play, was the thing. Griffith now introduced principles of shooting that were to make the motion picture a new and important art form. "His camera became a living human eye, peering into faces of joy and grief, ranging over great vistas of time and space, and resolving the whole into a meaning flux, which created a sense of dramatic unity and rhythm to the story." It was this living human eye that gave the Reconstruction story a new dimension.

It has been suggested that the film was more Griffith than Dixon. This is patently not the case. To be sure, Griffith was from Kentucky, and he had a certain sympathy for the Southern cause. And in the flush of success, Dixon would say, on opening night between the acts, that none but the son of a Confederate soldier could have directed the film. But Griffith's knowledge of history was scant, and he was much too occupied with the technical aspects of filming the picture to interpose his views regarding its content. Even a casual comparison of the texts of *The Leopard's Spots* and *The Clansman* with the film itself will convince one that "Birth of a Nation" is pure Dixon, all Dixon!

When the twelve-reel drama was completed, Joseph Carl Breil composed a musical score for it that was essentially adaptations from Negro folk songs and passages from Wagner's "Rienzi," and "Die Walkure," and Bellini's "Norma." In February, 1915, there were private showings in Los Angeles and New York. Dixon first saw the film at the New York showing. He sat in the balcony alone, fearing that he would be hooted and jeered by the seventy-odd people on the first floor. There was no such likelihood. Dixon said that his own experience of seeing the film was "uncanny." "When the last scene had faded," he later recounted, "I wondered vaguely if the emotions that had strangled me were purely personal. I hesitated to go down to the little group in the lobby and hear their comments. I descended slowly, cautiously, only to be greeted by the loudest uproar I had ever heard from seventy-five people." It was at that time that Dixon shouted to Griffith across the auditorium and exclaimed that "The Clansman", was too tame a title for such a powerful story. "It should be called 'The Birth of a Nation,' ' he exclaimed.

There is a great deal of overlap in the characters and plots of the works in the Dixon Reconstruction trilogy, but "Birth of a Nation" draws more heavily on *The Clansman* than on the others. The first part of the film introduces the Stoneman brothers, Phil and Tod, from Pennsylvania, who are visiting their school friends, the Cameron brothers, in Piedmont, South Carolina. They are the sons of Austin Stoneman, a member of Congress. Phil falls in love with Margaret Cameron, while Ben Cameron falls in love with Elsie Stoneman. When the war erupts, the Stonemans return north to join the Union Army while the Camerons enter the Confederate Army. During the war the two younger Cameron brothers and Tod Stoneman are killed. Ben Cameron is wounded and is nursed by Elsie Stoneman as he lies a prisoner of Phil Stoneman in Washington. Meanwhile, Elsie and Phil's father, Austin Stoneman—in real life Thaddeus Stevens, the North's most unreconcilable radical—is busy urging Southern blacks to rise up against the Southern whites. Dixon does not fail to make the most of the fact that Stoneman has a mulatto housekeeper, and, because of Stoneman's power as leader of Congress and the alleged intimacy of Stoneman and his housekeeper, Dixon in *The Clansman* dubs her "The First Lady of the Land."

As the story of Reconstruction unfolds there is, of course, much corruption, much black presumption and arrogance, much humiliation of whites by black troops, and much looting and lawlessness. In order to avenge the wrongs perpetrated against his people, Ben Cameron becomes the leader of the Ku Klux Klan. It is not in time, however, to save his younger sister from the advances of Gus, a Negro roustabout, from whom she escapes by jumping from a cliff to her death. There are other would-be interracial trysts. When Elsie Stoneman asks Silas

Lynch, a leader in the Black League, to save her brother Phil from the Negro militia that had besieged him in a log cabin, Lynch demands that Elsie marry him. The situation is resolved when the clansmen, under the leadership of Ben Cameron, put the black militia to flight, free Elsie from Lynch, and kill Gus. Then, a double wedding takes place between the Stoneman and Cameron families, symbolic of the unification of the North and South. Thus, the long, dark night of Reconstruction ends, and the white people of the South take on an optimistic view of their future as their nation, Phoenix-like, arises from the ashes of war and reconstruction.

The euphoria that Dixon and his friends experienced at the New York theatre in February, 1915, was not sufficient to sustain "The Birth of a Nation" in the face of strong opposition from unexpected quarters. Despite strong criticism of his earlier works on Reconstruction, Dixon had been able to cope with it. When *The Leopard's Spots* appeared, Kelly Miller, the Negro Dean of Howard University, wrote to Dixon, "Your teachings subvert the foundations of law and established order. You are the high priest of lawlessness, the prophet of anarchy." Sutton E. Griggs, the Arkansas black lawyer, asserted that Dixon "said and did all things which he deemed necessary to leave behind him the greatest heritage of hate the world has ever known." Dixon countered by saying, "My books are hard reading for a Negro, and yet the Negroes, in denouncing them, are unwittingly denouncing one of their best friends."

The opposition to "Birth of a Nation" was more formidable. Oswald Garrison Villard, editor of the *New York Evening Post*, and Moorfield Storey, President of the American Bar Association, were both founders and active leaders in the National Association for the Advancement of Colored People. They were representative of a large number of Americans, black and white, who thought that the film was a travesty against truth as well as an insult to an entire race of people. (Villard called it "improper, immoral, and unjust.") They were determined to prevent the showing of the film and began to work assiduously to bring about its doom. But they had not assayed the resourcefulness of Thomas Dixon, Jr., who was equally determined to secure a nationwide showing of his masterpiece. He proved to be a formidable and, indeed, an invincible adversary.

If the President of the United States should give his approval to the film, Dixon thought, perhaps the opposition would be silenced. And so, in February, 1915, Thomas Dixon decided to visit his old schoolmate, Woodrow Wilson, who now occupied the White House. When Dixon called, Wilson was pleased to see his old friend. The two were soon reminiscing about their days at the Johns Hopkins University and about the manner in which Dixon had been instrumental in securing an honorary degree for Wilson at Wake Forest College. When Dixon told Wilson about his new motion picture, Wilson immediately expressed an interest, but indicated that since he was still mourning the death of his wife he could not attend the theatre. Wilson then suggested that if Dixon could arrange to show the film in the East Room of the White House he, his family, and members of the cabinet and their families could see it. The President said, "I want you to know, Tom, that I am pleased to do this little thing for you, because a long time ago you took a day out of your busy life to do something for me. It came at a crisis in my career, and greatly helped me. I've always cherished the memory of it."

On February 18, 1915, "The Birth of a Nation" was shown at the White House, and at the end of the showing President Wilson is said to have remarked that "It is like writing history with lightning. And my only regret is that it is all so terribly true."

Dixon's next scheme was to show the film to the members of the Supreme Court. With the help of the Secretary of the Navy, Josephus Daniels of North Carolina, Dixon secured an appointment with Chief Justice Edward D. White. The Chief Justice told Dixon that he was not interested in motion pictures, and indicated that the members of the Supreme Court had better ways to spend their time. As Dixon was taking his leave he told the Chief Justice that the motion picture was the true story of Reconstruction and of the redemption of the South by the Ku Klux Klan. Upon learning this, the Chief Justice leaned forward in his chair and said, "I was a member of the Klan, sir," and he agreed to see the picture that evening. Not only were members of the Supreme Court at the ballroom of the Raleigh Hotel to see the picture but many members of the Senate and House of Representatives were also there with their guests.

When opposition to the film persisted, Dixon let it be known that the President, the Supreme Court, and the Congress had seen the film and liked it. When this was confirmed by a call to the White House, the censors in New York withdrew their objection and

the film opened there on March 3, 1915, and played for forty-seven weeks at the Liberty Theatre. Although the picture showed to huge audiences in New York and in every city and hamlet across the country, there was always great opposition to it. In New York, Rabbi Stephen Wise, a member of the city's censorship board, called "Birth of a Nation" an "indescribably foul and loathsome libel on a race of human beings. . . . The Board of Censors which allowed this exhibition to go on is stupid or worse. I regret I am a member." In Boston a crowd of 500 persons, including firebrands such as William Monroe Trotter, demonstrated on the grounds of the state capitol, demanding that the governor take steps to ban the film. A bill to that end was rushed through the lower house of the legislature only to be found unconstitutional by the judiciary committee of the upper house.

The President of Harvard University said that the film perverted white ideals. Jane Addams, the founder of Hull House, was greatly disturbed over the picture and wrote vigorously against it. Booker T. Washington denounced the film in the newspapers. Branches of the NAACP protested its showing in cities across the nation. But the film was seldom suppressed anywhere, and the reviews by drama critics were almost universally favorable. Burns Mantle said that there was an "element of excitement that swept a sophisticated audience like a prairie fire in a high wind." Hector Turnbull of the *New York Tribune* called it a "spectacular drama" with "thrills piled upon thrills." But Francis Hackett's review in the *New Republic* conceded that as a spectacle "it is stupendous," but its author was a yellow journalist because he distorted the facts. The film, Hackett insisted, was aggressively vicious and defamatory. "It is spiritual assassination." That may well be, Dixon seemed to think, but to the charges that he had falsified history, Dixon offered a reward of one thousand dollars to anyone who could prove one historical inaccuracy in the story.

I do not know of any person's having proved to Dixon's satisfaction that there were any inaccuracies in the film. I do know that many critics besides Hackett, convinced that it was filled with distortions, half-truths, and outright falsifications, challenged the truth of "Birth of a Nation." Francis J. Grimke, distinguished Negro minister in Washington, published a pamphlet entitled "Fighting a Vicious Film" that was a virtual line-by-line refutation of the Dixon-Griffith work. *Crisis Magazine,* the official organ of the NAACP, ran a series of monthly reports under the heading "Fighting Race Calumny." The film soon became the object of scathing criticism in mass meetings held by Negro religious, educational, and civil groups across the nation. The only concession that Dixon made after the film had been running for several months was to add a reel on the industrial work being done by blacks at Hampton Institute in Virginia. And for cooperating with Dixon in this undertaking, the white President of Hampton was bitterly criticized by the same blacks and whites who had so severely criticized the film.

It is not at all difficult to find inaccuracies and distortions in "Birth of a Nation." Ostensibly a first-hand account of the events that transpired between 1865 and 1877, it could hardly have been firsthand when one recalls that Dixon was one year old when Reconstruction began and was only thirteen when the last federal troops were withdrawn from the South in 1877. That was one reason, though not the principal reason, for Dixon's failure to include anything on Reconstruction in the South between 1865 and 1867, when not one black man had the vote, when all Southern whites except the top Confederate leaders were in charge of all Southern state governments, and when white Southerners enacted laws designed to maintain a social and economic order that was barely distinguishable from the antebellum period. There is not a shred of evidence to support the film's depiction of blacks as impudent, vengeful, or malicious in their conduct toward whites. As pointed out by Francis B. Simkins, a Southern white historian who specialized in Reconstruction in South Carolina where most of "Birth of a Nation" takes place, freedmen manifested virtually no hostility toward former masters. The evidence is overwhelming, although not necessarily commendable, that the vast majority of freedmen worked energetically and peacefully on their former masters' plantations during the entire period of Reconstruction.

The film makes a great deal of the alleged disorderliness, ignorance, and mendacity of the blacks in the South Carolina legislature. It also depicts Silas Lynch, the black lieutenant governor, as an audacious, arrogant, cheap politician whose only interest in life was to marry the blonde daughter of Austin Stoneman, the prototype of Thaddeus Stevens, Pennsylvania's Radical leader in Congress. It did not fit Dixon's scheme of things to acknowledge that the most important black political leader in South Carolina was Francis Cordozo, a graduate of Glasgow University, or that blacks were never in control of the machinery of government in the state. Nor did it matter to Dixon that the two black lieutenant governors of South Carolina during Reconstruction were Richard Gleaves, a Pennsylvania businessman who enjoyed a reputation as an excellent president of the Senate, and Alonzo Ransier, a shipping clerk in antebellum Charleston who was never accused of dishonesty, arrogance, or of harboring any antipathy toward whites. Which of these men, the only two available, did Dixon use as a model for his Silas Lynch? In any case, there was no black lieutenant governor in the closing years of Reconstruction when Dixon gloats over black lieutenant governor Silas Lynch being killed by the Ku Klux Klan for making advances to blonde Elsie Stoneman.

If Southern blacks had a competitor for the most degraded and depraved place in "Birth of a Nation" it was Austin Stoneman, a very thin disguise for Thaddeus Stevens of Pennsylvania. As the member of Congress most deeply committed to racial equality, Stevens was the most hated Northerner in the South. Dixon was so determined to use Thaddeus Stevens for his purposes that he committed every possible violence to the facts of Stevens's life. First, he presented Stoneman (Stevens) as a widower, though Stevens was never married. This was necessary in order to provide Stevens with a son and daughter. That would set the stage for a North-South reconciliation through the double wedding of his son and daughter with two young Southerners. This, in turn, was necessary in order to make Stevens's conversion to Southern principles complete when his black protege sought to marry his daughter.

Secondly, Dixon presented Stevens as being intimate with his black housekeeper, although there is no evidence to support it except that they lived in the same house. For the ultimate proof, Dixon could have had Lydia Brown become pregnant by Stevens, as actually happened in some other instances of intimacies between white leaders and their black "friends." Apparently, this would have interfered with some of the other contrivances. Finally, Dixon was not content until he had Stevens traveling to South Carolina at the climax of Reconstruction in order to experience the ultimate humiliation both from the black lieutenant governor Silas Lynch, who attempted to marry his daughter, and from the Ku Klux Klan, who rescued his daughter from Lynch.

It seems unnecessary to add that Thaddeus Stevens never went to South Carolina and had, indeed, died in 1868, when Dixon was four years old and several years before the high drama of South Carolina Reconstruction actually began. Even so, Thomas Dixon could write as follows: "I drew of old Thaddeus Stevens the first full length portrait of history. I showed him to be, what he was, the greatest and the vilest man who ever trod the halls of the American Congress." This was followed by his customary challenge: "I dare my critic to come out . . . and put his finger on a single word, line, sentence, paragraph, page, or chapter in 'The Clansman' in which I had done Thad Stevens an injustice."

Were it not for other considerations "Birth of a Nation" would be celebrated—and properly so—as the instrument that ushered the world into the era of the modern motion picture, a truly revolutionary medium of communication. Mantle called the pictures "wonderful"; to Charles Darnton, Griffith's work was "big and fine"; while the *New York Times* called it an "impressive new illustration of the scope of the motion picture camera." There were, however, other considerations. By his own admission Dixon's motives were not to discover the truth but to find a means by which to make a case for the South that, regardless of the facts (one is tempted to say, in spite of the facts), would commend itself to the rest of the country. "The real purpose back of my film," Dixon wrote in May, 1915 to Joseph Tumulty, Woodrow Wilson's secretary, "was to revolutionize Northern sentiments by a presentation of history that would transform every man in my audience into a good Democrat! . . . Every man who comes out of one of our theatres is a Southern partisan for life." A few months later he wrote President Wilson, "This play is transforming the entire population of the North and West into sympathetic Southern voters. There will never be an issue of your segregation policy."

Thus, Thomas Woodrow Wilson, twenty-eighth President of the United States and a professionally trained historian, lent the prestige of his high office and the hospitality of the Executive Mansion to promote this unseemly piece of propaganda as history. Dixon was never interested in the truth in history. He was interested in "selling" a particular promotion piece as history. That in itself is not the supreme tragedy, bad as it is. The supreme tragedy is that in *The Clansman* and in "Birth of a Nation," Thomas Dixon succeeded in using a powerful and wonderful new instrument of communication to perpetuate a cruel hoax on the American people that has come distressingly close to being permanent.

In the same year, 1915, that "Birth of a Nation" was showing to millions across the United States, the Ku Klux Klan was reborn. When the film opened in Atlanta that fall, William J. Simmons, who had considered a Klan revival for several years, sprang into action. He gathered together nearly two score men, including two members of the original Klan of 1866 and the speaker of the Georgia legislature. They agreed to found the order, and Simmons picked Thanksgiving eve for the formal ceremonies. As the film opened in Atlanta, a local paper carried Simmons' announcement next to the advertisement of the movie. It was an announcement of the founding of "The World's greatest Secret, Patriotic, Fraternal, Beneficiary Order." With an assist from "Birth of a Nation," the new Ku Klux Klan, a "High Class order of men of Intelligence and Order" was launched. It would spread all across the South and into the North and West in the 1920's and spread terror among Jews and Catholics as well as among blacks.

In the fall and winter of 1915–1916, thousands of Southerners thrilled to the stirring scenes of "Birth of a Nation." "Men who once wore gray uniforms, white sheets and red shirts wept, yelled, whooped, cheered—and on one occasion even shot up the screen in a valiant effort to save Flora Cameron from her black pursuer." They were ripe for enlistment in the new Ku Klux Klan. Thus, "Birth of a Nation" was the midwife in the rebirth of the most vicious terrorist organization in the history of the United States.

When Dixon was writing *The Clansman*, several others were actively competing with him for the title as the most uncompromising racist writer to appear on the American scene. In 1900 Charles Carroll published *The Negro a Beast*, a scurrilous attack on the nature and immorality of blacks which was expanded two years later in his *The Tempter of Eve; or The Criminality of Man's Social, Political and Religious Equality with the Negro*. In 1902 William P. Calhoun continued the attack in *The Caucasian and the Negro in the United States*. In 1907, two years after Dixon's *The Clansman* appeared, Robert W. Shufeldt published *The Negro, a Menace to American Civilization*.

These, however, were mere books, as *The Clansman* was; and Dixon had already concluded that books were limited in their appeal. The diabolical genius of Dixon lay in his embracing the new medium, the motion picture, and thus using that medium to persuade and even to convince millions of white Americans, even those who could not read books, that his case against Negro Americans was valid and irrefutable. It was not merely that illiterate and unthinking Americans were convinced by Dixon's propaganda. It was also that vast numbers of white Americans, searching for a rationale for their own predilections and prejudices, seized on Dixon's propaganda, by his own admission propaganda designed to win sympathy for the Southern cause, and transformed it into history as the gospel truth.

As one reads *The Tragic Era*, published in 1929 by Claude Bowers, surely one of the country's most respected journalist-historians, one is impressed if not awed by its faithful adherence to the case as argued in "Birth of a Nation." It is all there—the vicious vindictiveness of Thaddeus Stevens, the corruptibility of every black legislator, and the nobility of the Ku Klux Klan in redeeming a white civilization threatened with black rule. It was the scum of Northern society that inflamed "the Negro's egotism," said Bowers, "and soon the lustful assaults began. Rape is the foul daughter of Reconstruction," he exclaimed. And even Dixon must have been forced to concede that an inflammatory book like *The Tragic Era*, selected by the prestigious Literary Guild, was in a position to wield enormous influence. *The Tragic Era* remained the most widely read book on Reconstruction for more than a generation, thus perpetuating the positions taken in "Birth of a Nation."

If one seeks a more recent Dixonesque treatment, he can read *The South During Reconstruction*, published in 1948 by E. Merton Coulter, the Regents Professor of History at the University of Georgia and the first president of the Southern Historical Association. Once again, it is all there—the unwashed, drunken, corrupt black legislators; the innocent disfranchised whites; and the resort to desperate measures by the Klan in order to save the South from complete disaster. There are, moreover, Alistair Cooke's book and television programs that, even in their polish and

sophistication, follow, to an incredible degree, the argument set forth in "Birth of a Nation." Pick up almost any elementary or secondary textbook in American history used in our schools and you will discover much about corruption, white oppression by blacks, and the overthrow of Reconstruction by the socially responsible and morally impeccable whites in the South. You will not find there as you will not find in Bowers, Coulter, or Cooke and certainly not in "Birth of a Nation" anything about the oppression of freedmen by Southern whites, the reign of Southern white terror that followed the close of the Civil War, the persistence of white majority rule even during Radical Reconstruction, and the establishment of the first public schools and other social institutions during the period.

Obviously, one cannot place all the blame for [this] view of Reconstruction on "Birth of a Nation." There were too many others who shared Dixon's views when he wrote and too many who have held to those views since that time. As an eloquent statement of the position of most white Southerners, using a new and increasingly influential medium of communication, and as an instrument that deliberately and successfully undertook to use propaganda as history, the influence of "Birth of a Nation" on the current view of Reconstruction has been greater than any other single force. There have been many revivals of "Birth of a Nation" and through them the main arguments Dixon set forth have remained alive. The film is shown in many places today as a period piece. It has achieved the status of an antique and its value is supposed to be in what it tells us about the evolution of the technique of film making. But as one sits in a darkened hall viewing the period piece as this writer recently did, one is a bit perplexed by the nervous laughter and scattered applause as the Klan begins its night ride. One can only surmise—and hope—that these reactions are to "Birth of a Nation" as a period piece and not to "Birth of a Nation" as a powerful instrument in promoting propaganda as history.

The Myth of the Disillusioned American Soldier

David M. Kennedy

World War I, or the Great War as it is more often called, did much to crush European idealism. Shocking in its brutality, its carnage both military and civilian, postwar Europe concluded that the war had triggered a "decline of the West" and that despite its imagined hope and glory war was a Grand Illusion after all. A literature of regret, guilt, despair, and mourning was a predictable aftermath to a war that had been unexpected and tragic. The American experience in World War I, however, was in many respects profoundly different—at least in the judgment of the Stanford University historian David M. Kennedy. Having played the neutral from 1914 to 1917, American involvement in the war was rather brief and far different psychologically. American doughboys landing in France to the fragrance of spring found much of their war experiences fascinating fun. The war of attrition that had so negatively beat upon European consciousness is noticeably absent from the way American fighting men report the war. They could sustain and indulge romantic patriotism, personal idealism, and male fantasy in seeing the war as a special time. For America's soldiers the First World War was one more of euphoria than disillusionment.

Two million American soldiers served in World War I. The experience struck nearly all of them as an extraordinary moment in their lives, while they passed through it, and when they later remembered it. That they considered it an extraordinary interlude at the time is evidenced by the diaries and journals and strikingly "literary" letters so many of them wrote during their period of service. Americans in 1917, especially those of the age and class who qualified for the AEF, were not the diary-keeping people they had once been. Yet thousands of men who had never before recorded in writing their daily doings, and never would again, faithfully kept journals while they were in the Army. Most of these records began with induction and ended with discharge, neatly delineating the time spent in uniform as a peculiar interval, a moment stolen from ordinary life and forever after sealed off in the memory as a bundle of images that sharply contrasted with the "normal"experience. The reactions to France and to war were, of course, as varied as the men who recorded them. But even a modest sampling of the personal documents left behind—a few of them published, many deposited in libraries, more still passed down reverently as family heirlooms to later generations—reveals common responses to the shared enterprise, and common conventions or perception and language to which these men resorted in the effort to comprehend their experience and relate it to others.

They were, first of all, as much tourists as soldiers. Later reflections, governed by the masculine need to emphasize prowess at martial exploits, would tend to blot that fact from the record. But the average doughboy spent more peacetime than wartime in France. And, though as many as 1.3 million Americans came under enemy fire, few saw sustained or repeated battle. Virtually none was subjected to the horror and tedium of the trench warfare for years on end, the typical lot of the European soldier. The Americans fought no major defensive battles. Their two chief engagements were relatively brief, mobile attacks in the closing weeks of the conflict.

Hence, to a remarkable extent—remarkable at least when compared with the war writings of European combatants—the doughboys' accounts deal with topics other than war. It was AEF policy to rotate leave zones in order to give all an equal chance to see as much of France as possible. Most coveted of all were the pink tickets that permitted a trip to Paris. *Stars and Stripes* felt obliged to caution arriving troops against the "oo-la-la" idea of France as a great tourist playground. Too many men, said the journal, came over expecting to find a sort of international Coney Island, a universal pleasure resort. "We have been all over France and seen and learn [sic] a lot," said one awestruck New Yorker. After the Armistice, the Army organized sporting events and provided educational opportunities for the idle troops. It also endlessly compelled them to solve "problems"— sham attacks against an imaginary enemy. Many men fought more of these mock battles than real ones. One long-suffering soldier reported in April 1919 that "every hill in this vicinity has been captured or lost at least ten times." But the same enlisted man spoke the sentiments of many when, in describing his post-Armistice leave to Nice and Monte Carlo, he called it "the most important event in my life over here (from a social standpoint)."

Like previous generations of their traveling countrymen, the doughboys were impressed with the age of the Old World. "Its old cathedrals, chateaux and ancient towns have been quite wonderful to my eyes so accustomed to the look of the New World," said one. In countless diaries and letters the soldiers dwelt upon the quaint antiquity of this town, or that church or chateaux, their imaginations especially fired by the evocation of names from history books. "The church here," wrote another doughboy, "is very, very old, probably built sometime in the 12th or 13th century. Saint Louis the Crusader, King of France, attended service there on three occasions and Jeanne d'Arc was there several times." "The architecture for the most part seems to represent a period several hundred years past," wrote another. "We are living, for the present, in barracks built about the time of Louis XIV, though no one here knows anything about them prior to Napoleon."

The France they described was rich with history, an old country inhabited by old people. No observation of the French life was more common than remarking the elderly women in black who seemed to be the only residents of the ruined towns behind the front. A tired people in a blighted land, the French pursued antiquated ways. "My but the people are old fashioned," observed one enlisted man. "They still harvest with cradles and sickles. Once in a while you see a binder or mower. I've never saw [sic] a real wagon, they use carts." All signs, in short, confirmed the American myth of the Old World as an exhausted place, peopled by effete and even effeminate races. All this, of course, served as a useful foil for the image of American energy and "pep." "What an impression our boys are making on the French," enthused Raymond Fosdick, head of the Commission on Training Camp Activities. "They are the greatest lot of sheer boys you ever saw. . . . The French, who love to sit and meditate, are constantly gasping at the exuberance and tirelessness of our fellows." "Never was there such a spectacle in all of history," exclaimed a *New York Times* correspondent, "as that of the fresh millions of free Americans flocking to the rescue of beleaguered and exhausted Europe."

But if Europe was exhausted, it was still splendid to behold. Numerous accounts expressed rapt wonder at the sheer physical beauty of France. "Picturesque" was perhaps the most commonly used word in these descriptions. One is struck by the frequency of panoramic portraits of nature, of efforts to translate a long sweep of the eye into a string of words. If sunrise and sunset were the characteristic themes in the writings of trench-bound British troops in Flanders, as Paul Fussell has observed in his study *The Great War and Modern Memory*, it was the panoramic landscape that most attracted the eye of the Americans.

There were good reasons for these divergent motifs. In the flatness of Flanders, sunup and sundown provided the only natural relief from the monotonous landscape. And twice-a-day British stand-to's on the trench firing step, year after year, in season and out, were timed to take advantage of the long, silhouetting light when the sun was low on the horizon. But the American troops, by contrast, were doubly "summer soldiers." They were not only civilians temporarily in uniform, but the bulk of them came to France in the late spring and summer months of 1918. Behind the front, at least, the forests were indeed verdant, the fields aripple with grain, the roadsides in bloom. "The country is green and covered with flowers. It is a continuous garden," said a soldier who arrived in April 1918. Moreover, again unlike the British, the American troops were on the move, all the way across France from the Bay of Biscay to their training areas in the north and east. They traversed the rolling country of north-central France, and when they at last saw their assigned portion of the front it ran along the undulating hills from Verdun to Vosges. From the prominence of Montfaucon, for example, one could easily see in clear weather virtually the entire American battle line on the Romagne heights, stretching several miles east to west. Even the seasons and the terrain conspired to sustain an image of France as a kind of grand open-air arena suited to staging battles of operatic movement and theatrical visibility.

Common to many Americans' perceptions of France was a sense of ceremony, which often had religious overtones. *Stars and Stripes* declared that France was "holy ground," and that more than once in history the French "at Chalons, at Tours, at the Marne . . . saved the soul of the world." To many of the doughboys, the great war in which they were now engaged amounted to a ritual reenactment of those historic dramas. To the largely Protestant Americans, the exotic rites of French Catholicism fittingly exemplified the ceremonial attitude they deemed appropriate to the occasion. Alan Seeger had noted that "the Catholic religion with its idealization of the spirit of sacrifices makes an almost universal appeal in these times," and many members of the AEF agreed with him. The "Marseillaise," too, had the power to "set you quivering." When French religion and patriotic music were combined, the effect was deeply moving. One American soldier attended high mass on Bastille Day, 1918, and a band at the flag-draped church played the "Marseillaise": "Rene, talk about throwing up your hat and shouting 'To Hell with the Kaiser.' The scene and music impressed me so much that I could hardly get my breath. I cannot describe how grand the whole thing was."

Time and again in the personal narratives of these touring provincials one suddenly hears a different voice. The rough and often wise-cracking American idiom abruptly gives way to a grandiloquent tone that speaks, for example, of the "red-tiled roofs resplendent in the sunlight, resembling huge cameos set conspicuously on the vine covered slopes." This strange diction was the language of the tourist brochures, or of the ubiquitous YMCA guides who shepherded the gawking troops about the various sights. It was not a natural voice. Those wondrous foreign scenes often exceeded the native American capacity for authentic speech, and the confrontation with the unfamiliar was thus almost automatically rendered in cliches and highly stylized prose. To a significant degree, the same was true of descriptions of the war itself.

Reverence toward France and the "cause" was not carried over to the Army. Fellowship of arms gave certain consolation, but the physical conditions of life and the restrictions of the military regime were constant causes of complaint. Most pestiferous were the lice—"cooties"—that occasioned frequent trips to the delousing stations, and almost daily "shirt readings," or close inspections of clothing for nits. Equally wearing on men's bodies and spirits was army food—or lack of it. In vivid contrast with the wooden descriptions of those rare meals eaten somewhere—anywhere—other than the military mess. The careful recording of menus, indeed, took up a great deal of space in many soldiers' diaries and letters. Men frequently noted losses of more than ten percent of their body weight in the weeks after arrival in France. These accounts confirmed Field Marshall Haig's observation that the Americans "hardly knew how to feed their troops." They also suggest that undernourishment may have dulled the fighting effectiveness of the AEF.

But the worst feature of military life was the discipline. Military hierarchy and subordination chafed against ingrained American values of equality and individualism. Anti-German propaganda harped on the supposedly slavish subservience of the "Hun" in order to enhance the image of the German soldier as an eminently bayonetable alien. The American resentment of martial authority could be found in all ranks, and sometimes manifested itself in striking ways. Even a pillar of traditional authority such as once and future Secretary of War Henry L. Stimson complained to his diary, while a staff officer in France, that "I am getting a little tired of kow-towing to regulars just because they are regulars." On the returning troop carriers in 1919, the doughboys enacted a ritual "funeral of Sam Browne." To the throaty cheers of the enlisted men, the officers solemnly marched to the ship's rail and threw their leather girth-and-shoulder "Sam Browne" belts, hated symbols of military caste, into the sea. Even the hierarchy of different services prompted resentment, as infantry officers often took potshots at airborne American pilots, the elite and haughty "Knights of the Air." "It is just a gesture of irritation at the air service," opined the commander of an observation balloon squadron, "something like boys throwing a rock at a limousine which is dashing by when they are having to work."

Long idle behind the lines, and then only briefly exposed to battle, the great mass of the American soldiers in France were spectators in the theater of war. They had come to see the "Big Show," and were not disappointed. Nothing in that show was more exciting than the aerial battles. Men approaching the front strained their eyes and ears for signs of aircraft, more out of curiosity than fear. Always they referred to aerial "duels," or "wonderful air battles," or "thrilling air fights." One balloonist described seeing "Richthofen's circus." The famed "Red Baron's" formation approached, "some of the planes with red bodies, and they fly along with some planes climbing and some dropping and give the effect of being on the rim of a giant wheel which is rolling through the sky."

What most strikes the reader of these personal war records is their unflaggingly positive, even enthusiastic, tones. [The poet Alan] Seeger's sanguine reflection that war was affording him "the supreme experience" was reiterated countless times by those who followed him to France. Raymond Fosdick, arriving overseas during the German offensive in the spring of 1918, wrote that he was "having an experience . . . which dwarfs anything I have ever lived through or seen before. . . . I am just back from a four days' trip at the Front. . . . Needless to say I had a wonderful time—a most exhilarating time." One volunteer wrote from France in mid-1917 that "I never enjoyed life as much as I have since I have been over here and if one must be killed to enjoy life—Well. It has already been a wonderful thing for me." After the Armistice the same man could only reflect "what a glorious adventure it has all been to me."

These experiences of exhilaration, wonder, and glory are notable not only for what they say but also for the way in which they say it. The sights from France elicited mostly tourist-brochure boilerplate from the doughboy writers. Similarly, the war itself seemed to overwhelm the power of the imagination to grasp directly, and of language to describe authen-

tically. It is not especially surprising to find *Stars and Stripes* assuring a soldier-reader that he was the "spiritual successor" to the "Knights of King Arthur's Round Table." But it is to be remarked when countless common soldiers wrote privately of themselves in the same vein, American war narratives, with unembarrassed boldness, speak frequently of "feats of valor," of "the cause" and the "crusade." The memoirs and missives penned in France are shot through with images of knight-errantry and of grails thrillingly pursued. A truck driver in the aviation section of the AEF exclaimed that "war's great caldron of heroism, praise, glory, poetry, music, brains, energy, flashes and grows, rustles and roars, fills the heavens with its mighty being . . . Oh! War as nothing else brings you back to the adventurous times of old."

Faced with the unfamiliar reality of modern war, many young American soldiers tried to comprehend it in the comfortably familiar verbal formulae of their childhood storybooks. In the homeliest lines scribbled by the humblest privates, the war was frequently couched in language that appears to have been lifted verbatim from the pages of G.A. Henty or, more often, those of Sir Walter Scott. That language echoed, however pathetically, the epic posturings of George Creel and the elaborately formal phrasing of Woodrow Wilson. Those accents may ring strangely in the modern ear, but they flowed easily from the tongues and pens of the doughboys in 1918. The ubiquity of that idiom, from the White House to the trenches, suggested a widely made equation between the official and personal definitions of war's significance. If the war was to redeem Europe from the barbarism, it would equally redeem individual soldiers from boredom; if the fighting in France was the "Great Adventure," the doughboys were the great adventurers; if Creel and Wilson could speak of the "Crusade," then it followed that American troops were crusaders. Not only did many doughboys accept without reflection the official definition of the war's meaning, but, perhaps more important, they translated that meaning into their understanding of their personal experiences, and described those experiences in language transported directly from the pious and inflated pronouncements of the spokesmen for traditional culture. That language pervaded all the vast "literature" produced during the war by members of the AEF.

Almost never in contemporary accounts do

themes of wonder and romance give way to those of weariness and resignation, as they do in the British. The narrative devices most characteristic of American war novels were adopted not from proscenium theater but from cinematic film—a source more appropriate to the American experience of movement and rapt incredibility. And while the American narratives may occasionally reflect on the immenseness and incomprehensibility of the war's evil, they much more often crackle with positive excitement—what the authors themselves would likely call "zest" or "peptomism." "Our boys went [to] the battlefield last night singing," recorded a Regular Army veteran; "you can't beat them they are surely [a] game and happy bunch."

No doubt the objective circumstances of the AEF's relation to the war helped to sustain this cheerful attitude: the season and the terrain, the lateness and brevity of American belligerency, the relatively open warfare that characterized action all along the front in the final weeks when the American army at last saw combat. But one should note, too, the precise character of American good cheer, the imaginative constructs in which it found expression. English war writing showed the heavy impress of the long and rich tradition of English literature. *The Oxford Book of English Verse* traveled in many a Tommy's rucksack to the trenches, and provided a fund of literary models and allusions in which the scene at the front could be mentally encompassed. By contrast, says Paul Fussell, "American writing about the war tends to be spare and one-dimensional," devoid of allusion, without the shaping mold of tradition to give it proper form. Of Seeger's most famous poem, "I Have a Rendezvous with Death," Fussell notes that it "operates without allusion, without the social instinct to invite a number of canonical poems into its vicinity for comparison or ironic contrast."

This is a telling observation, but it can be carried too far. The canon of English literature, after all, had not been embargoed in the British Isles. It had been exported in bulk to the United States, and consumed avidly by generations of readers (the doughboys may have carried few copies of *The Oxford Book of English Verse*, but *Stars and Stripes* carried Kipling's poems on page one). Thus, in one sense American war writing was different from British only in that its life cycle was truncated. It sprang from the same sources but never, or only later, completed the cyclical devolution from mimesis to irony that British writing ac-

complished. In another sense, the contemporary American war literature was more attenuated than the British: it drew on a narrower range of allusions, traced its literary lineage to fewer forbears. Why this should have been so is a question whose pursuit would carry well beyond the boundaries of the present subject. But suffice it to say that, Fussell notwithstanding, the contemporary American imaginative response to the war unmistakably took its inspiration from a branch of English literature: the medieval romantic tale. To be sure, the immediate source of this inspiration was most often the nineteenth-century author Sir Walter Scott, a "popular" writer perhaps not of "canonical" stature. But at the level of popular culture, the mind-set of the great mass of doughboys, Scott's influence was prodigious—and lasting.

Raymond Fosdick showed Scott's tutelage, for example, when he wrote: "I saw one of our divisions going into action the other afternoon. . . . The men had decorated their helmets with red poppies from the fields and they swept by like plumed knights, cheering and singing. I could have wept not to be going with them." Heywood Hale Broun, a correspondent for the New York *Tribune*, was still more explicit: "Verdun and Joffre, and 'they shall not pass,' and Napoleon's tomb, and war bread, and all the men with medals and everything. Great stuff! They'll never be anything like it in the world again. I tell you it's better than 'Ivanhoe.' Everything's happening and I'm in it."

Graphic attempts to invest the war with meaning drew from a similar stock of imagery. Cartoons and posters depicted the spike-helmeted Germans as human gargoyles. Against them stood the lantern-jawed doughboys, fighting for the honor of a fair lady —Dame Victory and Dame Liberty were favorites of *Stars and Stripes*, which also counseled its readers to "hold all women sacred."

In his discussion of British war writing, Fussell concludes that "it is their residence on the knife-edge" between the low mimetic and ironic modes "that gives the memoirs of the Great War their special quality." But the contemporary American accounts reside along a different frontier of the low mimetic mode: the boundary that separates it from the "high mimetic" style of epic, romance, and myth, in which the hero's power of action exceeds that of ordinary people in everyday life.

By war's end, in November 1918, little had happened to dislodge the American imagination from that exotic territory. The Armistice had come so swiftly after Pershing's army at last took the field that many troops in fact registered a desire to continue to dwell in that fantastic landscape. "I have a rather peculiar feeling," wrote one doughboy the day after the Armistice. "Heaven knows I am enormously thankful the war is over, but nevertheless I feel as tho my occupation was entirely gone, and the idea of turning back to civilian life seems like an awful jump. I really have got accustomed to fighting, life in the open, running a balloon company with a lot of men, trucks, etc., and it is going to leave a rather gone feeling for a while." A year later, a marine wrote: "I know how we all cried to get back to the States. . . . But now that we are here, I must admit for myself at least that I am lost and somehow strangely lonesome. These our own United States are truly artificial and bare. There is no romance or color here, nothing to suffer for and laugh at."

For men like these, the war had provided a welcome relief from ordinary life. It had to a large measure lived up to the romantic expectations encouraged by spokesmen for traditional culture like Holmes and Roosevelt. Like the legendary American West, wartime France was a place where men lived in the open, on the move, in the intensely male comradery of adventure and misery and threatening violence. Like the frontier West, "over there" was a distant land, where men could give vent to dangerous impulses that must be suppressed in civil society. For women, by contrast, wartime heroism consisted in preserving their civilian demeanor. Thus did Raymond Fosdick praise the YMCA girls and the "Salvation Army lassies" for being "just as cool and calm as if they were pouring tea at home." This constancy, frequently attributed to women at the front, bespoke an ideal vision of the true feminine character. But for many men, the true male character, including the fancied immemorial imperative to hunt and to kill, could only be released in war. The mystery and allure of the battleground derived largely from the fact that it was *not* home. France figured as a kind of equivalent to Huck Finn's "Territory," a place to light out to in flight from the artificial constraints of civilized life.

The war, like the American West, became mythic in the minds of many who were to remember it. The process of mythicizing began even before most of the troops had returned home. On February 15, 1919, Colonel Theodore Roosevelt, Jr., presided over a meeting in Paris of twenty officers from the AEF. These men formally launched the American Legion, among whose purposes were "to preserve the memories and the incidents of our association in the great war . . . to consecrate and sanctify our comradeship." The Legion, in fact, did not simply spring spontaneously from sentiments like these. It grew from a prewar preparedness society and was subtly encouraged by members of Pershing's staff. They feared that left-wing doctrines might infect the restless troops idled by the Armistice, and that radicalized returning soldiers might link hands with dangerous "bolshevik" elements at home. Far better to promote a "safe" veteran's organization dedicated to commemorating the war and combating reds—which, along with "bonus" agitation, fairly accurately described the bulk of the Legion's activity in the postwar years.

But the ordinary Legionnaires knew little of those designs in the minds of their senior officers. One of the Legion's brilliant organizational strokes was to prohibit military titles, opening membership on an equal footing to all veterans. The Legion thus shrewdly blotted from mind rankling recollections of military hierarchy and discipline, freeing the memory to dwell on more positive wartime themes. And the very name "Legion" perpetuated the romantic idiom in which the official culture had taught the doughboys to think of themselves. (Significantly, the only alternative title seriously proposed for the veterans' organization was "Crusaders.")

Increasingly in the post-Armistice period a younger generation of authors wrote of the devolution of soldiers themselves from a kind of parentally instilled enthusiasm and idealism to bitter disillusionment. John Dos Passos developed this theme in *One Man's Initiation*, 1917, published in 1920, and pursued it further the following year in *Three Soldiers.* In the same year as *A Son at the Front*, Thomas Boyd's *Through the Wheat* appeared, depicting combat which did not ennoble the hero, but made him an insensate zombie. In 1924, *What Price Glory?* Opened to extravagantly favorable reviews, even though it largely ignored a romantic view of the war and instead portrayed its principal characters as cussing and quarrelsome though amiable drunks. Stallings openly mocked the wartime rhetoric of chivalry in his novel of the same year, *Plumes.* Its Walter Scot-like chapter ("Tourneys, The Caitiff Knight") and medieval nomenclature—the hero's full name is Richard Coeur de Lion Plum—provide ironic contrast to the downbeat story line about a wounded doughboy come home from the war. Plume befriends a "wiry little wild Jew" who has been imprisoned for his anti-war agitation. The ex-soldier ends up re-breaking his own shattered knee in the furious roundhouse swing at four men in uniform singing "My Country 'Tis of Thee." In 1929 came Ernest Hemingway's *A Farewell to Arms*, in which the action moves away from war and into the "civilian" pursuits of love, marriage, and childbirth—a precise reversal of the standard plot line in the romantic war literature.

These and several other novels, including e e cumming's *The Enormous Room* (1922), William Faulkner's *Soldier's Pay* (1926), and William March's *Company K* (1933), are usually taken to represent a literature of protest against the war, a collective expression of "disillusionment" with the war's official meaning. These writings have cast a deep shadow over the historical memory of the war, consigning to the darkness of unfathomable obsolescence those sensibilities that had entertained "illusions" about the war's adventure, or romance, or poetry, or idealism.

But the term "disillusioned" as applied to those postwar writers has troubled more than one critic. Cowley, generally regarded as a leading representative of the orthodoxy of disillusionment, himself observed in 1948 that "I have always felt that the adjective was badly chosen. They (these writers) were something quite different; they were *rebels* in art and life." Stanley Cooperman concluded that "The World War I literary protest was far more *dynamic* than the simple tag of 'disillusion' or 'negation' would seem to indicate." And Alfred Kazin offered the important reminder that Europe "now lay paralytic after four shattering years, where Americans were *merely disillusioned* by the *aftermath*. . . . If it was America that 'had won the war for Europe,' as the popular legend had it, it was the new American literature, seizing the *vitality* that was left in the world, that made the victory its own."

"Rebels," "dynamic," "vitality,"—these terms do not harmonize with the chord that the word "disillusionment" usually strikes in the mind. Nor do they seem remotely applicable to European war writing, such as Erich Maria Remarque's *All Quiet on the Western Front*, in which the hero at the end is "so alone, and so without hope." They suggest, rather, that much of the same energy that is naively dis-

played in the romantic war literature is equally present in the "protest" novels, though harnessed to a different wheel. What John Aldridge said of one of those protest novels, Dos Passos's *One Man's Initiation, 1917*, might be said about the entire body of literature of which it is considered to be a part: "The excitement which Dos Passos seems to have felt when he conceived of war as a great adventure and crusade has apparently been transformed . . . into an immense energy of denunciation." The strong feeling of outrage that dominates the last half of the book springs from the same sources of enthusiasm that inform the first half: "it has simply been reinforced now by hurt feelings and has changed direction."

Toward what objects were that outrage and that "immense energy for denunciation" directed? It is misleading and insufficient to reply that they were directed simply at the brutal facts of battlefield violence. Hemingway and Stallings, for example, maintained a life-long fascination with things military. They both contrived to get into the Second World War, and Stallings in 1963 wrote an anecdotal history of the AEF that was heavily invested with nostalgia and peppered with good old soldier-boy stories. Faulkner's *Soldier's Pay*, in which the grotesquely wounded Lieutenant Mahon drifts mutely through the novel to his waiting grave, might be taken as a rather turgid statement against the war's violence. But it is worth noting that Faulkner himself never got beyond Canada in his quest to see the "Big Show," and that *Soldier's Pay* is formally a long anti-climax, with all the violence preceding the action of the novel. cumming's *The Enormous Room* concerns the war only in the most indirect and allegorical sense. The story takes place far from any battlefield, and the book as a whole invites a reading as a kind of impish *jeu d'esprit*, a clever exercise that draws only incidental coloration from the proximity of its action to a great historical catastrophe. cummings himself commented that "When *The Enormous Room* was published, some people wanted a war book; they were disappointed."

Of the overt facts of the military experience that drew these writers' rage, it was not so much violence and suffering that provoked them as *authority*. In this they were at one with the least literate of doughboys. Thus cummings wrote about the arbitrariness of the French military prison at La Ferte Mace, Chrisfield in *Three Soldiers* grenades his hated sergeant, Frederic Henry in *A Farewell to Arms* shoots a retreating Italian, runs afoul of the military police, expiates himself with a drunk in the Tagliamento, and deserts. So too does Dos Passos's John Andrews desert, and one is reminded here of the persistence in American fiction of the imagery of flight, the anti-social rebellion against authority and convention familiar to readers of the *Leatherstocking Tales* and *Huckleberry Finn*. This imagery had been vivid in the minds of many dough-boys. Whether or not they actually read Cooper and Twain, they had nevertheless mentally figured their own flight into the AEF along lines long ago traced in the escape to the western woods by Natty Bumppo and Huck. The theme of desertion simply rotated this traditional American fictional device 180 degrees, making civil society the hero's ultimate refuge.

In the end, the power of the postwar literature of disillusionment principally derived not from de-nouncing the violence of the actual, historical war, nor simply from exploiting the traditional American motif of resentment at authority. It came, rather, from the enlistment of that literature in another war alto-gether—a war between two concepts of culture, a conflict whose first skirmishes had been fought even before 1914. An older generation attempted to carry intact into the twentieth century traditional nine-teenth-century definitions of morality, the rationality of human nature, and the civic utility of "high cul-ture." Against them were pitted younger intellectu-als attracted by notions of absurdity, irrationality, and the possible subversive implications of art. The youthful John Dos Passos in 1916 scorned the older culture's literary tastes as "wholesome rice-pudding fare . . . a strangely unstimulating diet. . . . Our books are like our cities," he complained, "they are all the same. . . . The tone of the higher sort of writing in this country is undoubtedly that of a well brought up and intelligent woman, tolerant, versed in the things of this world, quietly humorous, but bound tightly in the fetters of 'niceness,' of the middle-class outlook." America, he feared, might "stagnate forever, the Sic-ily of the modern world, rich in this world's goods, absorbing the thought, patronizing the art of other peoples, but producing nothing from amid our jum-ble of races but steel and oil and grain." World War I neither initiated that conflict nor set its terms. But both groups of combatants seized upon the war as an occasion to advance the arguments of their respective

sides. Behind the attack was the cultural authority of the Old Guard—the Old Guard that had promoted American entry into the war, and employed the full force of its rhetorical power to describe the war in terms compatible with its ancient values.

The initial victories undoubtedly went to the custodians of the older culture. Their most spectacu-lar triumph was their success in upholding an ideal-ized view of war, a success that Pershing's policies had abetted. Their achievement was everywhere evi-dent in the war years, and for some time thereafter, in the very language that ordinary soldiers used to describe themselves and their exploits—the inflated rhetoric of an archaic literature of romance.

The postwar writers of disillusionment pro-tested less against the war itself than *against a way of seeing and describing the war*. As writers, they naturally focused their fire on the verbal conceits of the older generation. They insisted over and over again that the war experience—and by extension all modern human experience—could not be contained in the stilted shibboleths and pieties of the traditional cul-ture. This was the field of energy—its poles being two separate cultures, even two distinct systems of speech—across which arced the most kinetic prose of the postwar writers. This was the source of power in Hemingway's famous passage about being "embar-rassed by the words, sacred, glorious, and sacrifice and the expression in vain," and finding dignity only in the names of places and the numbers of the roads. This was the thrust of cumming's opposition of "vul-gar American idiom" to a parody of Wilsonian rheto-ric in the opening chapter of *The Enormous Room*: "To borrow a characteristic cadence from Our Great President: the lively satisfaction which we might be suspected of having derived from the accomplish-ment of a task so important in the saving of civiliza-tion from the clutches of Prussian tyranny was in some degree inhibited, unhappily, by a complete absence of cordial relations between the man whom fate had placed over us and ourselves. Or, to use the vulgar American idiom, B and I and Mr. A didn't get on well." This was the point of cumming's describ-ing, again with telling rhetorical juxtaposition, a conversation with Mexique: " 'I t'ink lotta bullsh-t,' which upon copious reflection, I decided absolutely expressed my own point of view."

What Sadie Knew: The Immigrant Working Girl and the Emergence of the Modern Young Woman

John McClymer

In this excerpt from The Birth of Modern America, 1919–1939 (Brandywine Press, 2005), John McClymer explores the emergence of a new ethos of pleasure and consumption—based then, as now, on a great measure of middle class marketing mythology. He looks first at the immigrant work girl and her male counterpart of the early twentieth century and at the new urban institutions—amusements parks, dance halls, movies—where they developed new modes of behavior, such as going steady, and a new source of moral authority, the peer group. McClymer examines, the unsuccessful efforts of upholders of traditional morality, from evangelical preachers to settlement house workers, to suppress the new "animal" dances, the new jazz, and the new sexual freedom. More successful were pastors and rabbis of immigrant and African American congregations who provided supervised venues where tame versions of the dances were permitted and where young people could date but in a controlled setting. Powerfully reinforcing the new ethos was the emergence of Madison Avenue. By the 1920s advertising campaigns explicitly targeted evangelical morals and celebrated the "sane" pursuit of pleasure.

"Sadie" is Sadie Frowne, a sixteen-year-old New York City garment worker whose autobiography appeared in *The Independent* shortly after the turn of the century as part of a series of "Life Stories of Undistinguished Americans." Hers is one of the few voices of the working girls, as they were then called, we can hear not filtered through the moral comment of a middle-class progressive reformer. Sadie's view of the good life goes counter to the beliefs of several reformers, most notably Jane Addams, and that of the most important evangelical preacher of the era, Billy Sunday. Historians have nearly always heeded Addams' views but never Sunday's. Sadie Frowne did not listen to either of them. Instead she did a lot of thinking for herself and she talked things over with her peers. And she spoke most loudly not in the pages of *The Indepen-*

dent but through her actions. She and her peers pioneered a cultural ethos that prized pleasure, and a set of mores—dating, treating, going steady—that would come to characterize the "modern young woman" of the 1920s and thereafter.

Two Views of the Permissible

An article in *The Ladies' Home Journal* of August 1921 by Anne Shaw Faulkner, head of the Music Department of the General Federation of Women's Clubs, asks in its title, "Does Jazz Put the Sin in Syncopation?" Her answer was an emphatic *YES*:

Jazz originally was the accompaniment of the voodoo dancer, stimulating the half-crazed barbarian to the vilest deeds. The weird chant, accompanied by the syncopated rhythm of the voodoo invokers, has also been employed by other barbaric people to stimulate brutality and sensuality. That it has a demoralizing effect upon the human brain has been demonstrated by many scientists. . . .

Dancing to Mozart minuets, Strauss waltzes and Sousa two-steps certainly never led to the corset-check room, which now holds sway in hotels, clubs and dance halls. Never would one of the biggest fraternities of a great college then have thought it necessary to print on the cards of invitation to the "Junior Prom" that "a corset check room will be provided." Nor would the girl who wore corsets in those days have been dubbed "old ironsides" and left a disconsolate wallflower in a corner of the ballroom. Now boys and girls of good families brazenly frequent the lowest dives in order to learn new dance steps. Now many jazz dances have words accompanying them which would then never have been allowed to go through the mail. Such music has become an influence for evil.

Eight years later came an ad campaign for Modess sanitary napkins that measures the distance popular culture had traveled from the old rules Anne Faulkner would want restored. The J. Walter Thompson advertising agency gave the campaign a name, "Modernizing Mother." It heralded the triumph of the "modern young woman" in a series of cultural battles that roiled the 1920s.

Episode one sets the theme. "Millions of daughters," the copy begins, "are teasing mothers back to youth—slamming doors on the quaint ways of the nineties. One by one the foolish old drudgeries and discomforts pass." Life, under the leadership of these daughters, is becoming "easier, more pleasant—sensibly modern." In episode two, the "modern daughter" coaxes her mother up onto the ski slopes. The daughter, confident, fearless, happy, "sane of outlook, wholesome," leads the way. Not just mother but "the world" is having a "hard time" keeping up. The daughter "will not tolerate the traditions . . . [that] . . . kept her mother in bondage." Each episode follows the same format. The "modern" daughter liberates her mother from the constraints of the past by teaching her the latest dance steps, replacing her cotton nightgown with silk pajamas, or taking her for a jaunt in a plane. Mother looks a bit frightened in several scenes but gamely goes along. She is, she recognizes, a product of those "old-fashioned ways" which "cannot withstand the merry onslaught of the modern girl," as episode nine puts it. The daughter's victory, according to the same ad, is complete:

> Her enthusiasm is so sane and contagious, she is so everlastingly right in refusing the drudgeries and repressions of her mother's girlhood that the whole world is approving her gay philosophy which demands the best and nothing but the best.

The changes that the ads advocated were not primarily intellectual and owed little or nothing to the popularization of Freudian psychoanalysis. The changes were behavioral and reflected a new ethos and a new set of expectations.

The short skirts, the bobbed hair, the rolled stockings, the smoking: All went with jazz to frighten, tantalize, or delight the public. The flappers created by John Held, Jr., such as that reproduced here, became one of the visual icons of the twenties. By the end of the decade, the flapper had gone from iconoclast to trendsetter. Millions of women wore skirts whose hemlines ended at the knee, wore their hair cut short, and smoked. Petting had become acceptable behavior. Chaperones went the way of the corset. All of this was, by decade's end, "sensible" as well as "gay." And the heroine of the hour was the modern young woman.

The Working Girl Leads the Way

A few historians have looked at the cultural world of the immigrant working girl, but to find the predecessors of the modern young woman, scholars go primarily to the cultural radicals of the 1910s such as Crystal Eastman, an attorney and women's rights activist. Their behavior did indeed anticipate much that would characterize the modern young woman of the twenties and thirties. These cultural radicals smoked, drank, explored their sexuality, and disparaged Victorianism. Studies of them have clarified much about the rise of the modern young woman. Much, however, remains obscure. How did the kinds of behavior embraced by Eastman and her associates become diffused throughout the larger society? Clustered in Greenwich Village, they formed a narrow circle. Eastman's brother Max edited *The Masses* but the magazine's name reflected its left-wing politics, not its readership. It is not that the radicals were unknown as a group. Lots of people had heard of Greenwich Village and knew, in a vague sort of way, that people there flouted conventional rules of behavior. Walter Lippmann, a member of their set, popularized some of their ideas in *The New Republic*. But it was the Sadie Frownes who shaped the larger culture beyond the salons of the Village.

A typical urban working girl of the early twentieth century might be an immigrant or the daughter of newcomers. She probably worked for a very small wage, but exercised a degree of independence neither her female ancestors in the Old World nor the American daughters of well-born families enjoyed. She seems an unlikely cultural pioneer, for the usual portrayals of the flapper, whether in F. Scott Fitzgerald's *This Side of Paradise* or in movies like *Our Dancing Daughters*, invariably show her to be from so-called old-stock families. Much of the discussion of the flapper fixes on college students, the majority of whom came from northern European backgrounds. The process whereby customs originating in ethnic and racial communities became an invisible presence in the portrayal of first the flapper and then the modern young woman is a startling phenomenon of popular culture in the first half of the twentieth century.

Above is John Sloan's "The Return from Toil." He described a "bevy of boisterous girls with plenty of energy left after a hard day's work." One such might have been Sadie Frowne. Sadie was born in Poland to Jewish parents. Her father died when she was ten, and when she was thirteen her mother decided to emigrate. Both worked and earned about fifteen dollars a week, enough to afford a decent tenement apartment. But then the mother contracted tuberculosis and died. "I had saved a little money," Sadie wrote in *The Independent*, "but mother's sickness and funeral swept it all away and now I had to begin all over again." She and a friend roomed together, paid $1.50 a week rent and spent $3.92 per week on food.

It cost me $2 a week to live, and I had a dollar a week to spend on clothing and pleasure, and saved the other dollar. . . .

Some of the women blame me very much because I spend so much money on clothes. They say that instead of a dollar a week I ought not to spend more than twenty-five cents a week on clothes and that I should save the rest. But a girl must have clothes if she is to go into high society at Ulmer Park or Coney Island or the

theater. Those who blame me are the old country people who have old-fashioned notions, but the people who have been here a long time know better. A girl who does not dress well is stuck in a corner, even if she is pretty, and Aunt Fanny says that I do just right to put on plenty of style.

However exploited on the job, working girls frequently made their own choices about pleasure. Sadie worked long hours, went to night school several evenings a week, and did her own cooking, cleaning, and laundry.

[A]t the end of the day one feels so weak that there is a great temptation to lie right down and sleep. But you must go out and get some air, and have some pleasure. So instead of lying down I go out, generally with Henry [her boyfriend]. Sometimes we go to Coney Island, where there are good dancing places, and sometimes we go to Ulmer Park to picnics. I am very fond of dancing, and, in fact, of all sorts of pleasure. I go to the theater quite often, and like those plays that make you cry a good deal.

Sadie and her coworkers occasioned as much concern and consternation as the flapper would later, and for much the same reason. Many working girls lived outside of a family setting. Many who did live at home were the primary breadwinners. In the wake of the Triangle Shirtwaist Factory fire of 1911, which claimed the lives of 146 young workers like Sadie, the American Red Cross in coordinating relief efforts for the families of the victims found that almost a third of the Italian and Jewish women who had died were the main or sole support of their families. Another third lived alone or with roommates and subsisted entirely upon their own earnings. Their wages, however meager, allowed them some modicum of discretionary spending. Sadie spent a dollar a week on clothes and pleasure and saved another dollar. Some criticized her. She paid them no mind.

Complementing this autonomy was the emergence of new urban institutions that catered to the working woman and man. Working-class women in New York, Chicago, and other urban centers could not receive suitors in their parlors. They lived in crowded tenements or apartment blocks with no space for entertaining. Like Sadie Frowne, they had no family member to act as chaperone. But now there were dance halls, nickelodeons, and amusement parks. These encouraged encounters between young men and women that served and reinforced their social freedom. Such places offered occasions for sexual play. And the immigrant working woman, and man, pioneered there a new set of social norms. They created ways of behaving—dating, going steady, treating; they took their standards of proper behavior from their peer group; and they paid little attention to the traditional upholders of cultural standards. Such women and men chose their own romantic interests, their own friends, their own pleasure, as Sadie put it. In all of this they flouted convention. Yet they were inventing conventions that in time would reach the whole of society.

To the right is John Sloan's 1907 painting, "Movies, five cents." It captures the diversity of the viewers and the titillation of the entertainment. Sadie Frowne loved melodramas, especially sad ones that made you cry. Many early silent films catered to her tastes. Others, like the one Sloan pictures, emphasized romance and featured what was, for the time, daring behavior. Anyone with a nickel could go to "the pictures" and forget the troubles of the day. You could also go to meet a potential romantic partner. Young men and women looked each other over in the waiting line and decided whether they would go in together. Once in the darkened theater, they negotiated the degree to which they would emulate the couple on the screen.

Sadie had a steady beau who took her to dances and other amusements. Many young women did not. Since they also did not have much money and since, like Sadie, they believed that "you must go out and get some air, and have some pleasure," they and their male counterparts and local entrepreneurs—many of them immigrants striving to get out of the working class and in need of working-class customers—together developed the system of treating.

There were some four hundred moving picture theaters in New York City. Young women would wait on line for a young man to offer to treat them to the show. In dance halls, owners would let women in for free or for a smaller charge than the men. At the dance hall, the treat often was a drink from the bar. As for the dances themselves: In Jewish neighborhoods dancing was called "spieling," spinning.

The woman put her arms around the male's neck, he put his around her waist, and the couple spun in a tight circle to the tempo of the music.

Amusement parks also invited customers to engage in sexual play. Some of the pleasures they offered were innocent enough. You could have yourself photographed as a mermaid or King Neptune by sticking your head through a cardboard cutout. Others openly appealed to more robust wishes. Customers who ventured to Luna Park or Dreamland at Brooklyn's Coney Island encountered a fantastic world of spectacles such as "The Fall of Port Arthur" at Luna Park in 1905. They encountered as well a set of rides designed to appeal to working-class young men and women such as the "Helter Skelter." It was a ride for couples. You took an escalator to the top of a huge chute. There were two separate paths to the bottom. The couple slid down through various curves, initially side-by-side, then separated, and then together again, and landed on a mattress in front of a crowd. Perhaps most riders were onlookers first. Part of the thrill was seeing the clothing of the female riders in disarray as they slid down.

The Defenders of Propriety: Fundamentalist and Progressive

The new ways were taking shape at a time when evangelical Protestantism, a major buttress of Victorian propriety, had lost much of its credibility. Billy Sunday, the best-known revivalist of his time, was enormously popular. He also was a cheerful, self-identified reactionary. "To Hell with the twentieth century!" he proclaimed. For him the goal of the revival was individual salvation, pure and simple. "I believe that a long step toward public morality will have been taken when sins are called by their right names." Hence Sunday's much repeated Booze sermon. "Whiskey is all right in its place," goes one famous line, "but its place is hell." Prohibition was the only reform Sunday supported. For the rest he professed indifference. "You can't raise the standard of women's morals by raising their pay envelope. It lies deeper than that" was a typically dismissive remark. Dancing was a graver threat to a woman's morals than low wages.

Sure it is harmful, especially for girls. Young men can drink and gamble and frequent houses of ill fame, but the only way a girl can get recreation is in a narrow gauge buggy ride on a moonlight night or at a dance.

If you can't see any harm in this kind of thing, why I guess the Lord will let you out as an idiot. . . .

The dance is simply a hugging match set to music. The dance is a sexual love feast. . . .

Where do you find the accomplished dancers? In the brothels. Why? They were taught in dancing schools. Listen to me, girls. I have never yet, and never will, flatly contradict the man or the woman who tells me that he or she dances and never knew of premature incitement of passion. I say that I will never contradict them, but I will say then: "Thank God; and get out of it right now, for next time you may."

Yet despite the appeal that what Sunday called "Old Time Religion" held for vast numbers, his message did not work any social transformation. No one was more eager to point this out than Sunday himself.

Sadie Frowne probably heard of Billy Sunday but she certainly did not listen to him. Nor did he attempt to get his message across to her. Sunday's revivals were carefully planned. An advance team would arrive weeks before to organize publicity. All of the posters and handbills were in English. No effort was made to canvass immigrant neighborhoods. Sadie existed for Sunday only as a cliché. She was one of the multitude he thought likely to fall into a life of degradation through the dance. That evangelical Protestantism had little, if any, influence over immigrant working men and women is as important as it is obvious. Evangelicals would shape the emerging ethos only from the outside via efforts at prohibition of various sorts.

Sunday did not even try to reach the immigrant working woman and man, but other upholders of Victorian propriety did. Especially important are the "New Women" of the late nineteenth and early twentieth centuries who went into settlement work and then into a host of new professions. The worldly, in some cases politically radical, Jane Addamses seem at poles from Sunday. Yet their recoil from the emergent manners of their time was less colorful but almost as severe.

Here is a comment of a sort common among progressive reformers. Entitled "DIVERTING A PASTIME: How Are We To Protect the City's Youth and Yet Provide for the Natural Demand for Entertainment?" it appeared in *Leslie's Weekly* in 1911. Belle

Lindner Israels, a former settlement worker at the Educational Alliance and a regular contributor to *The Survey*, a leading reform weekly, told the story, supposedly typical, of a young immigrant named Frieda:

When Frieda went out to do errands she noticed that there were streets with places other than stores. There were brightly lighted halls, from whose open windows strains of music floated and across which forms flitted in rhythmic motion. One evening she drifted in. She found that she did not need to know English to be welcome. At once she found the things that she missed at home—life, joy, laughter and young people. It was easy here. She was pretty, and as girls are always in demand at dances she soon was being shown the dance by a youth whose evident business it was to give her some return for the twenty-five cents she had paid for a "lesson." Quickly she learned the value of knowing how to dance—and still more quickly did her popularity grow with the boys who came to the hall. From that hall she learned to go to others—others where she was taught that to be really popular it was also essential to learn to drink "stylish drinks" and that dancing without drinking was "slow." Then, one night, when her head was whirling from excitement and dazed with drink, the man who had been playing with her for weeks in order to gain that end took her not home, but to a place where she offered on the altar of her "good time" the sacred gift of her girlhood—all she had to lose. She never turned again from the path that began in the kitchen of the tenement, longing for the birthright of her youth. She followed it through the mazes of wretched slavery to men and walked to its end five years later in a reformatory to which she had been committed and where her nameless baby was born. It was the price paid.

While Sunday condemned the quest for pleasure as sinful, New Women who came of age at the end of the nineteenth century accepted the desire for entertainment among the working poor. Yet their view of the sorts of pleasure the poor indulged in differed little from Sunday's idea of the matter. Addams wrote:

As these overworked girls stream along the street, the rest of us see only the self-conscious walk, the giggling speech, the preposterous clothing. And yet through the huge hat, with its wilderness of bedraggled feathers, the girl announces to the world that she is here. She demands attention to the fact of her existence, she states that she is ready to live, to take her place in the world.

But there were no wholesome outlets for the working girl's desire for pleasure:

In every city arise so-called "places"—"gin-palaces," they are called in fiction; in Chicago we euphemistically say merely "places,"—in which alcohol is dispensed, not to allay thirst, but, ostensibly to stimulate gaiety, it is sold really in order to empty pockets. Huge dance halls are opened to which hundreds of young people are attracted, many of whom stand wistfully outside a roped circle, for it requires five cents to procure within it for five minutes the sense of allurement and intoxication which is sold in lieu of innocent pleasure. . . . We see thousands of girls walking up and down the streets on a pleasant evening with no chance to catch a sight of pleasure even through a lighted window, save as these lurid places provide it. Apparently the modern city sees in these girls only two possibilities, both of them commercial: first, a chance to utilize by day their new and tender labor power in its factories and shops, and then another chance in the evening to extract from them their petty wages by pandering to their love of pleasure.

Reform literature contains many stories like Israels' account of Freida. Working girls who went to dance halls learned that the young men who treated might assume the right to some sexual favor in return. If they did not oblige, they could expect no treat the next time. Doubtless there was the woman who "offered on the altar of her 'good time' the sacred gift of her girlhood." But unless the police records of the time are remarkably incomplete, most did not follow "the mazes of wretched slavery to men." There were Sadie Frownes as well as Friedas among the working girls.

Sadie was no moral lightweight. She worked sixty or more hours a week during the busy seasons. She did not earn much money. Of that little she not only supported herself but also put more than $200 in the bank. She intended to save more before deciding whether or not to marry Henry, who was only nineteen. She was a loyal member of her union. She attended night school.

Plenty of my friends go there. Some of the women in my class are more than forty years of age. Like me, they did not have a chance to learn anything in the old country. It is good to have an education; it makes you feel higher. Ignorant people are all low. People say now that I am clever and fine in conversation.

Sadie was resilient and resourceful. She and her friends wanted to make something of themselves, to feel "higher." So in seeking pleasure she was by no means a libertine. Pleasure was simply an element of an essentially serious and well-regulated life. That gives to the Sadies of the early twentieth century an influence that a mere pleasure seeker would not have possessed.

Sadie Frowne's sense of entitlement to pleasure and to self-esteem marks a critical difference between the modern woman of the 1920s and the New Woman of the late nineteenth and the early twentieth century. The New Woman was the first to attend college. She longed, as Addams put it in *Twenty Years at Hull House*, for an outlet for her active faculties. Addams herself burned to find something to do, some way of playing an active part in the life around her. She tried medicine, rejected Christian missionary work, and then discovered the settlement house while on a grand tour of Europe. Back in Illinois she and a college friend opened Hull House. Addams, Florence Kelley, founder of the National Consumers' League, Alice Hamilton, who pioneered public health as a medical specialty, and hundreds of others who followed Addams' example discovered myriad ways of inserting themselves into the life about them. These New Women justified their new roles by the ideal of service to others. They could be, and were, as aggressive and ambitious as the men they dealt with. But their aggression and ambition were not for themselves.

Yet the New Woman had only somewhat more success reaching the working girl than Billy Sunday had. Many joined settlement houses. In *I Came a Stranger: The Story of a Hull-House Girl* (1989) Hilda Satt, like Sadie a Jewish immigrant from Poland, described the many ways in which Hull House deepened and shaped her life:

This oasis in a desert of boredom and monotony became the university, the opera house, the theater, the concert and lecture hall, the gymnasium, the library, the clubhouse of the neighborhood. It was a place where one could become rejuvenated after a day of hard work in the factory.

Thousands benefited from Hull House; hundreds of thousands benefited from the hundreds of other settlements. But this had little effect on the pursuit of pleasure. Wholesome alternatives did not avail any more than did condemnations of dance halls or amusement parks. Evangelical and reform efforts to protect had almost no impact on the emerging popular culture.

The Affluent Discover Working-Class Ways

Dance halls, nickelodeons, and amusement parks started with clear class markers but quickly lost them. The initial clientele of nickelodeons consisted largely of immigrants and their children, as noted in the caption to the *Outlook* illustration (on the right). Dance halls also sought the patronage of the working girl and her male counterpart. Many dance halls were located above saloons. Amusement parks too, starting with Luna Park and its imitators, lured the masses with promises of spectacles, all for a small admission price. Soon, however, the working girl and her boyfriend shared these spaces with middle-class and upper-class pleasure-seekers. These new urban settings became crucial areas of cultural diffusion, as Mrs. Shaw Faulkner bemoaned. "Now boys and girls of good families brazenly frequent the lowest dives in order to learn new dance steps." The phrase "good families" had both a class and an ethnic or racial meaning. Children of affluence, children whose ancestors had helped found the colonies, were frequenting these "dives." There were dives in working-class neighborhoods or, worse yet, in Harlem or other African-American communities. Dance halls provided instructors who, for a quarter, would give a private lesson. But most newcomers probably stood and watched and then went out on the floor and tried the steps themselves. Something quite similar took place at Luna Park and other amusement parks. If a middle-class couple left Luna Park or Dreamland for one of the dance halls frequented by Sadie and Henry, they heard ragtime music, perhaps for the first time, and saw people doing the new "animal dances" and other species of rough dancing. They might declare their disapproval and leave. Many did not. They stayed, learned the steps, and enjoyed themselves. At dance halls, at Coney Island, at the movie houses, young men and women of the more affluent ranks of society were the pupils, not the condescending moral instructors, of the youth of the laboring classes. Many of the rides had spaces where prospective patrons could watch others as they shrieked and clutched at their companions for balance. This too was instruction. Such informal but powerful learning went on at the movie houses as well.

In part, then, this diffusion of working girl behavior was owing to Addams' "most evil-minded" and "most unscrupulous" providers of commercialized pleasure. But commercialization will explain only so much. Consider the popularity of dances that would strike Addams and her colleagues, as well as Billy Sunday, as coarse and illicit. In addition to the cakewalk and the two-step were the Bunny Hug, the Chicken Scratch, the Grizzly Bear, the Snake, the Drab Step, and the Fox Trot. Later came the One Step and the Texas Tommy. As the lyric of one novelty dance tune put it: "Everybody's doin' it./Doin' what?/ Turkey trot." The Turkey Trot, the Bunny Hug, and the other dance crazes swept the nation because people enjoyed doing them, not because wily entrepreneurs enticed them into "lurid places."

James Reese Europe's Society Orchestra accompanied the white Irene and Vernon Castle. Their dance act topped the bill at the Palace and other vaudeville theaters, and they popularized many of the dances. Most were African American in origin. The Castles insisted on Reese's Society Orchestra because, they argued, only black musicians could play the music properly. Yet they offered toned-down, almost decorous versions. This is part of the explanation of how diffusion of cultural practices and values took place. The Castles removed class, ethnic, and racial associations that had served to stigmatize both the music and the dances in the judgment of middle- and upper-class Americans of northern European backgrounds. They did not seek to disguise the origins of the dances. Indeed, by insisting upon Europe's Society Orchestra, they emphasized where the steps had begun. What they offered were elegant, graceful performances of "animal" dances. It was every working girl's dream to dance like Irene Castle. And many a working boy wished he were Vernon Castle. These were the dreams of many of the more affluent as well. But they could not learn to dance like the Castles by taking lessons at the dance academies that did not teach the new steps. The Castles published in 1914 a manual, *Modern Dancing*, but following a diagram in a book was no substitute for having an experienced teacher or watching others. Hence Faulkner Shaw's lament that "boys and girls of good families brazenly frequent the lowest dives in order to learn new dance steps." An added reason, of course, was the attraction of the forbidden.

White musicians, like the Original Dixieland Jass Band, soon began to play versions of the new music. In 1917 the band recorded "Darktown Strutters Ball" for Victor. It was one of the most popular songs of the day. The sheet music displayed black couples, viciously stereotyped, in formal dress, doing the latest dance. It would not take long, however, for black musicians to begin to attract white listeners. Phonograph records originally marketed only to African Americans were selling more broadly by the mid-1920s.

Working-Class Arbiters of the Permissible

Meanwhile, the immigrant Catholic Church, alongside synagogues and the black American churches, had been reaching the people that neither the evangelicals nor the New Woman could. Just as the new ethos of pleasure came out of the ethnic working class, so did the new inhibitions that reined it in. This dialogue within the ethnic communities was vital to shaping the popular attitudes and behavior of the twentieth century.

The churches' relative success in resisting, restraining, and yet giving some place and decorum to the new ethos is not easy to document. The American Catholic Church did not act on a national basis until World War I. Instead each diocese and, in many cases, each parish operated autonomously. In some instances there are relatively full records of their programs. In others there are not. This makes generalizations hazardous. With this in mind, there are well-documented case studies that suggest the ways in which churches came to terms with new practices like dating.

Chicago's Poles, for example, created dense institutional networks with local parishes as the centers of community life. Parishes sponsored organizations for all kinds of social activities. There were choirs, bands, drama societies, athletic teams. The city's Poles put on plays and dances and concerts.

They published newsletters. In each parish a small professional class of doctors, lawyers, and undertakers joined with a small entrepreneurial class of saloonkeepers and contractors to provide leadership. Many of them along with their wives led societies that visited the sick or distributed alms to the needy. Swedish Lutherans, Orthodox Jews, and A.M.E. Zion and other African American churchgoers maintained comparably dense communities.

The closeness of community life meant that canons of respectable behavior were reinforced at every point. School children wore uniforms. Dances did not feature the new jazz or the latest steps. And there were chaperones. Drama societies offered wholesome plays. The example of the Irish schoolteacher or the Polish physician or lawyer modeled behavior. Not everyone within these communities agreed with Victorian values. But such proprieties served numerous functions. One is that they expressed deeply held moral beliefs, especially regarding sexuality. Another is that they provided a means of gaining respectability to people who could not expect to receive it from the larger society. The woman who became president of the Ladies' Sodality or the man who chaired the youth baseball council attained a real measure of status. And given the very large number of parish organizations and the very large number of offices in each, this sort of respectability was within the reach of anyone willing to take the time and trouble to gain it. Status afforded its own pleasures.

From World War I on, as Catholics began to form national organizations, the church's commitment to propriety became more definable. Particularly well documented is its role in movie censorship. Protestant and Jewish groups protested the amount of sexuality, violence, and lawlessness in movies at least as outspokenly as did Catholics. But it was the Catholic Church that could muster millions of members, organized in the Legion of Decency and committed to boycotting any film that the Legion declared objectionable. The new Motion Picture Production Code of 1934, a compendium of Victorian standards broadened to accommodate a degree of the new social freedoms, reflected a Catholic presence. The code then served as a template for radio and television networks. Movies and broadcast media followed Catholic rules throughout the middle third of the century.

Density of parish life made the black and ethnic

churches and the synagogues uniquely powerful socializing agencies. Members of highly articulated parish communities found their friends inside the community, socialized at events sponsored by the parish, played in church leagues. Sadie and her friends were much less integrated into the social networks of their ethnic communities. Sadie was a Jew but made no mention of the place of any Jewish organization in her description of her daily life. In this she had any number of nominally Catholic, Greek or Russian Orthodox, Jewish, and Protestant counterparts. Every American city had its population of young people living on their own. Some of their fellow workers did belong to family, church, and ethnic communities. But the unattached had a certain glamour, "plenty of style," as Sadie would put it. Many had nicer clothes because they did not turn their pay envelopes over to their mothers. They went to exciting places. They had sweethearts they could see whenever they wanted. They knew the newest dance steps. So while the immigrant and black churches had far more success in reaching the working girl than did either the evangelical Protestant churches or the New Woman, the new ethos Sadie Frowne expressed so naively continued to gain ground.

Standard-Setters: Peers and the Ethos of Consumption

As it did so, it established a new moral authority, the peer group, to challenge that of the churches and synagogues. If a young woman accepted a treat at a dance hall, just what should she do in return? Churches could hardly attempt to answer. Doing everything would be immoral. But if doing everything was immoral, yet the girl had to do something, how was she to decide? She talked with her friends. They decided collectively what was appropriate. So too in dancing. How high could a young woman lift her skirt in doing the cakewalk? So too with alcohol and a host of other matters. Friends helped decide, and then decisions set limits at the same time that they widened the choices.

The dance halls and amusement parks the New Woman reformers so loathed were early signs of a profound shift in the workings of the American economy. By 1920, for the first time in human history, consumer demand would provide the principal impetus to economic growth. The radio provided a new, and extremely powerful, medium of

cultural diffusion. Respectable, middle-class whites could now hear the blues in their own living rooms. As consumer choice determined the rides at Luna Park, it dictated what programs would air. There would be relatively decorous programs featuring Rudy Vallee or Fred Waring and His Pennsylvanians. And there would be stations aiming programming at black or Jewish or Polish listeners. In the nature of the medium, anyone could listen to anything, provided the signal was accessible. Recognizing this as a vital selling point, advertisers stressed their product's unique ability to bring in distant programs.

In promoting the range of choices offered by New Era capitalism, advertisers were acting on the same principle as the department store merchants of the prewar years. Department stores were palaces of consumption. Their display windows tempted passersby with visions of luxury and glamour. The message the displays sent was the one Sadie Frowne articulated so emphatically: If a girl wanted to be popular, she needed to put on plenty of style. The message had innumerable variants. John Wanamaker, the Philadelphia and New York department store pioneer, was a devout Presbyterian. But his stores preached the gospel of consumption. Restraint, abstinence, deferred gratification, those cornerstones of Victorian propriety had no place in the successful marketing of the thousands of different products Wanamaker sold. In addition to the great stores were many more modest enterprises for consumers like Sadie Frowne, who could not afford the goods at Wanamaker's. In "Picturesque America," printed in 1909, Harry Grant Dart made fun of the proliferation of stores and their slogans and signs.

The ethos of consumption strikingly reinforced the views expressed by Sadie and her friends. More is better. Pleasure is good. Life is hard so you should enjoy yourself when you can. This meant clothes, dancing, and plenty of style. Advertisers directly attacked Victorian values. That is plain in the Modess campaign that took on a whole series of issues of the 1920s and dismissed the upholders of traditional views. Consider another ad in the Modernizing Mother campaign, "Don't Fuss, Mother, This Isn't So Fast." The daughter takes her mother for a ride in a speedboat. In the parlance of the day, a girl who was fast broke the sexual rules. She went beyond flirting and petting. Mothers and daughters had for years argued about whether wearing skirts at the knee, rolling stockings below the knee, taking off her corset at a dance, smoking cigarettes, using rouge and lipstick made the daughter look fast. How many of those daughters who said "Don't Fuss, Mother" had remonstrated that what they wanted to do wasn't "so fast"? Modess endorsed their side of the argument with this ad on the right:

> Speed! Life is all a-tingle at twenty. The girl of today travels without an anchor. There's too much fun ahead for thought of fear—too many prizes to be won to be satisfied with common things. Do older people really object—are they not just as eager in spirit to escape drabness and drudgery and feel again the thrill of being young?

The modern young woman of the Modess ads bore no visible resemblance to the working girl. Students of advertising have shown that almost all of the faces and names in the ads suggest northern European origins. Blacks appear, except when the ads explicitly target them, only as menials. Immigrants from southern and eastern Europe show up rarely, and then as sources of danger. To the extent that an advertiser wanted millions to identify with the imaginary consumer in an ad, racial, ethnic, and working class features disappeared. Affluent consumers would not identify with any figure so marked. Yet these ethnic and racial communities are invisibly present, in the customs and activities the lily-white figures in the ads are shown engaging in. The excluded had captured the privileged.

The Mythic Meaning of Lindbergh's Flight

John William Ward

Historians have increasingly come to see that the meaning of America has often been reflected in the individuals the nation selects as its heroes. This insight seems to be particularly true regarding the 1920s. By then, for example, Thomas A. Edison's inventive genius had led many to view him as a classic example of the Horatio Alger dream come true. And Henry Ford, a twentieth-century edition of Benjamin Franklin, captured much the same spirit. In the opinion of the late John William Ward, former president of Amherst College and professor of history at Princeton, it was Charles A. Lindbergh, Jr.—the Lone Eagle—who most fully symbolized the spirit of his age. His flight in 1927 from Roosevelt Field, New York, to Le Bourget airport near Paris made him the first aviator to fly solo across the Atlantic Ocean. Lindbergh became an instant legend and his feat triggered "magic on a vast scale" in the American mind. Some viewed him as but the latest representative of the American pioneer tradition, the trailblazer of a new frontier who had found inspiration for his deeds among the legendary frontiersmen of old. For others, he was the new hero of the machine age, his exploits representing a triumph of technology over nature. At one and the same time, then, Lindbergh symbolized the tensions between nostalgia and progress. He symbolized America's continuing love affair with its mythic past and its visions of the future.

On Friday, May 20, 1927, at 7:52 a.m., Charles A. Lindbergh took off in a silver-winged monoplane and flew from the United States to France. With this flight Lindbergh became the first man to fly alone across the Atlantic Ocean. The log of flight 33 of "The Spirit of St. Louis" reads: "Roosevelt Field, Long Island, New York, to Le Bourget Aerodrome, Paris, France. 33 hrs. 30 min." Thus was the fact of Lindbergh's achievement easily put down. But the meaning of Lindbergh's flight lay hidden in the next sentence of the log: "(Fuselage fabric badly torn by souvenir hunters.)"

When Lindbergh landed at Le Bourget he is supposed to have said, "Well, we've done it." A contemporary writer asked "Did what?" Lindbergh "had no idea of what he had done. He thought he had simply flown from New York to Paris. What he had really done was something far greater. He had fired the imagination of mankind." From the moment of Lindbergh's flight people recognized that something more was involved than the mere fact of the physical leap from New York to Paris. "Lindbergh," wrote John Erskine, "served as a metaphor." But what the metaphor stood for was not easy to say. The *New York Times* remarked then that "there has been no complete and satisfactory explanation of the enthusiasm and acclaim for Captain Lindbergh." Looking back on the celebration of Lindbergh, one can see now that the American people were trying to understand Lindbergh's flight, to grasp its meaning, and through it, perhaps, to grasp the meaning of their own experience. Was the flight the achievement of a heroic, solitary, unaided individual? Or did the flight represent the triumph of the machine, the success of an industrially organized society? These questions were central to the meaning of Lindbergh's flight. They were also central to the lives of the people who made Lindbergh their hero.

The flight demanded attention in its own right, of course, quite apart from whatever significance it might have. Lindbergh's story had all the makings of great drama. Since 1919 there had been a standing prize of $25,000 to be awarded to the first aviator who could cross the Atlantic in either direction between the United States and France in a heavier-than-air craft. In the spring of 1927 there promised to be what the *New York Times* called "the most spectacular race ever held—3,600 miles over the open sea to Paris." The scene was dominated by veteran pilots. On the European side were the French aces, Nungesser and Coli; on the American side, Commander Richard E. Byrd, in a big tri-motored Fokker monoplane, led a group of contestants. Besides Byrd, who had already flown over the North Pole, there were Commander Davis, flying a ship named in honor of the American Legion which had put up $100,000 to finance his attempt, Clarence Chamberlin, who had already set a world's endurance record of more than fifty-one hours in the air in a Bellanca tri-motored plane, and Captain Rene Fonck, the French war ace, who had come to America to fly a Sikorsky aircraft. The hero was unheard of and unknown. He was on the West Coast supervising the construction of a single-engined plane to cost only ten thousand dollars.

Then fate played its part. It seemed impossible that Lindbergh could get his plane built and east to New York in time to challenge his better equipped and more famous rivals. But in quick succession a series of disasters cleared his path. On April 16, Commander Byrd's "America" crashed on its test flight, crushing the leg of Floyd Bennett who was one of the crew and injuring Byrd's hand and wrist. On April 24, Clarence Chamberlin cracked up in his Bellanca, not seriously, but enough to delay his plans. Then on April 26, Commander Davis and his co-pilot lost their lives as the "American Legion" crashed on its final test flight. In ten days, accidents had stopped all of Lindbergh's American rivals. Nungesser and Coli, however, took off in their romantically named ship, "The White Bird," from Le Bourget on May 8. The world waited and Lindbergh, still on the West Coast, decided to try to fly the Pacific. But Nungesser and Coli were never seen again. As rumors filled the newspapers, as reports came in that the "White Bird"

was seen over Newfoundland, over Boston, over the Atlantic, it soon became apparent that Nungesser and Coli had failed, dropping to their death in some unknown grave. Disaster had touched every ship entered in the trans-Atlantic race.

Now, with the stage cleared, Lindbergh entered. He swooped across the continent in two great strides, landing only at St. Louis. The first leg of his flight established a new distance record but all eyes were on the Atlantic and the feat received little notice. Curiously, the first time Lindbergh appeared in the headlines of the New York papers was Friday, the thirteenth. By this time Byrd and Chamberlin were ready once again but the weather had closed in and kept all planes on the ground. Then, after a week of fretful waiting, on the night of May 19, on the way into New York to see "Rio Rita," Lindbergh received a report that the weather was breaking over the ocean. He hurried back to Roosevelt Field to haul his plane out onto a wet, dripping runway. After mechanics painfully loaded the plane's gas by hand, the wind shifted, as fate played its last trick. A muddy runway and an adverse wind. Whatever the elements, whatever the fates, the decisive act is the hero's, and Lindbergh made his choice. Providing chorus to the action, the *Herald Tribune* reported that Lindbergh lifted the overloaded plane into the sky "by his indomitable will alone."

The parabola of the action was as clean as the arc of Lindbergh's flight. The drama should have ended with the landing of "The Spirit of St. Louis" at Le Bourget. That is where Lindbergh wanted it to end. In *We*, written immediately after the flight, and in *The Spirit of St. Louis*, written twenty-six years later, Lindbergh chose to end his accounts there. But the flight turned out to be only the first act in the part Lindbergh was to play.

Lindbergh was so innocent of his future that on his flight he carried letters of introduction. The hysterical response, first of the French and then of his own countrymen, had been no part of his careful plans. In *We*, after Lindbergh's narrative of the flight, the publisher wrote: "When Lindbergh came to tell the story of his welcome at Paris, London, Brussels, Washington, New York, and St. Louis he found himself up against a tougher problem than flying the Atlantic." So another writer completed the account in the third person. He suggested that "the reason Lindbergh's story is different is that when his plane came to a halt on Le Bourget field that black night in

Paris, Lindbergh the man kept on going. The phenomenon of Lindbergh took its start with his flight across the ocean; but in its entirety it was almost as distinct from that flight as though he had never flown at all."

Lindbergh's private life ended with his flight to Paris. The drama was no longer his, it was the public's. "The outburst of unanimous acclaim was at once personal and symbolic," said the *American Review of Reviews*. From the moment of success there were two Lindberghs, the private Lindbergh and the public Lindbergh. The latter was the construction of the imagination of Lindbergh's time, fastened on to an unwilling person. The tragedy of Lindbergh's career is that he could never accept the role assigned him. He always believed he might keep his two lives separate. But from the moment he landed at Le Bourget, Lindbergh became, as the *New Republic* noted, "ours. . . . He is no longer permitted to be himself. He is US personified. He is the United States." Ambassador Herrick introduced Lindbergh to the French, saying, "This young man from out of the West brings you better than anything else the spirit of America," and wired to President Coolidge, "Had we searched all America we could not have found a better type than young Lindbergh to represent the spirit and high purpose of our people." This was Lindbergh's fate, to be a type. A writer in the *North American Review* felt that Lindbergh represented "the dominant American character," he "images the best" about the United States. And an ecstatic female in the *American Magazine*, who began by saying that Lindbergh "is a sort of symbol. . . . He is the dream that is in our hearts," concluded that the American public responded so wildly to Lindbergh because of "the thrill of possessing, in him, our dream of what we really and truly want to be." The act of possession was so complete that articles since have attempted to discover the "real" Lindbergh, that enigmatic and taciturn figure behind the public mask. But it is no less difficult to discern the features of the public Lindbergh, that symbolic figure who presented to the imagination of his time all the yearnings and buried desires of its dream for itself.

Lindbergh's flight came at the end of a decade marked by social and political corruption and by a sense of moral loss. The heady idealism of the First World War had been succeeded by a deep cynicism as to the war's real purpose. The naïve belief that virtue could be legislated was violated by the vast discrepancy between the law and the social habits of prohibition. A philosophy of relativism had become the uneasy rationale of a nation which had formerly believed in moral absolutes. The newspapers agreed that Lindbergh's chief worth was his spiritual and moral value. His story was held to be "in striking contrast with the sordid unhallowed themes that have for months steeped the imaginations and thinking of the people." Or, as another had it, "there is good reason why people should hail Lindbergh and give him honor. He stands out in a grubby world as an inspiration."

Lindbergh gave the American people a glimpse of what they liked to think themselves to be at a time when they feared they had deserted their own vision of themselves. The grubbiness of the twenties had a good deal to do with the shining quality of Lindbergh's success, especially when one remembers that Lindbergh's flight was not as unexampled as our national memory would have it. The Atlantic was not unconquered when Lindbergh flew. A British dirigible had twice crossed the Atlantic before 1919 and on May 8 of that year three naval seaplanes left Rockaway, New York, and one, the NC-4 manned by a crew of five, got through to Plymouth, England. A month later, Captain John Alcock, an Englishman, with Arthur W. Browne, an American, flew the first heavier-than-air land plane across the Atlantic nonstop, from Newfoundland to Ireland, to win twice the money Lindbergh did, a prize of $50,000 offered by the London *Daily Mail*. Alcock's and Browne's misfortune was to land in a soft and somnolent Irish peat bog instead of before the cheering thousands of London or Paris. Or perhaps they should have flown in 1927.

The wild medley of public acclaim and the homeric strivings of editors make one realize that the response to Lindbergh involved a mass ritual in which America celebrated itself more than it celebrated Lindbergh. Lindbergh's flight was the occasion of a public act of regeneration in which the nation momentarily rededicated itself to something, the loss of which was keenly felt. It was said again and again that "Lindy" taught America "to lift its eyes up to Heaven." Heywood Broun, in his column in the *New York World*, wrote that this "tall young man raised up and let us see the potentialities of the human spirit." Broun felt that the flight proved that, though "we are small and fragile," it "isn't true that there is no health in us." Lindbergh's flight provided the moment, but the meaning of the flight is to be found in the deep and pervasive need for renewal which the flight brought to the surface of public feeling. When Lindbergh appeared at the nation's capital, the *Washington Post* observed, "He was given that frenzied acclaim which comes from the depths of the people." In New York, where 4,000,000 people saw him, a reporter wrote that the dense and vociferous crowds were swept, as Lindbergh passed, "with an emotion tense and inflammable." The *Literary Digest* suggested that the answer to the hero-worship of Lindbergh would "throw an interesting light on the psychology of our times and of the American people."

The *Nation* noted about Lindbergh that "there was something lyric as well as heroic about the apparition of this young Lochinvar who suddenly came out of the West and who flew all unarmed and all alone. It is the kind of stuff which the ancient Greeks would have worked into a myth and the medieval Scots into a border ballad. . . . But what we have in the case of Lindbergh is an actual, an heroic and an exhaustively exposed experience which exists by suggestion in the form of poetry." The *Nation* quickly qualified its statement by observing that reporters were as far as possible from being poets and concluded that the discrepancy between the fact and the celebration of it was not poetry, perhaps, but "magic on a vast scale." Yet the *Nation* might have clung to its insight that the public meaning of Lindbergh's flight was somehow poetic. The vast publicity about Lindbergh corresponds in one vital particular with the poetic vision. Poetry, said William Butler Yeats, contains opposites; so did Lindbergh. Lindbergh did not mean one thing; he meant many things. The image of itself which America contemplated in the public person of Lindbergh was full of conflict; it was, in a word, dramatic.

To heighten the drama, Lindbergh did it alone. He was the "lone eagle" and a full exploration of that fact takes one deep into the emotional meaning of his success. Not only the *Nation* found Sir Walter Scott's lines on Lochinvar appropriate: "he rode all unarmed and he rode all alone." Newspapers and magazines were deluged with amateur poems that vindicated one rhymester's wry comment, "Go conquer the perils / That lurk in the skies—/ And you'll get bum poems / Right up to your eyes." The *New York Times*, that alone received more than two hundred poems, observed in trying to summarize the

poetic deluge that "the fact that he flew alone made the strongest impression." Another favorite tribute was Kipling's "The Winners," with its refain, "He travels the fastest who travels alone." The others who had conquered the Atlantic and those like Byrd and Chamberlin who were trying at the same time were not traveling alone and they hardly rode unarmed. Other than Lindbergh, all the contestants in the trans-Atlantic race had unlimited backing, access to the best planes, and all were working in teams, carrying at least one co-pilot to share the long burden of flying the plane. So a writer in the *New York Sun*, in a poem called "The Flying Fool," a nickname that Lindbergh despised, celebrated Lindbergh's flight: ". . . no kingly plane for him; / No endless data, comrades, moneyed chums; / No boards, no councils, no directors grim—/ He plans ALONE . . . and takes luck as it comes."

Upon second thought, it must seem strange that the long distance flight of an airplane, the achievement of a highly advanced and organized technology, should be the occasion for hymns of praise to the solitary unaided man. Yet the National Geographic Society, when it presented a medal to Lindbergh, wrote on the presentation scroll, "Courage, when it goes alone, has ever caught men's imaginations," and compared Lindbergh to Robinson Crusoe and the trailmakers in our own West. But Lindbergh and Robinson Crusoe, the one in his helmet and fur-lined flying coat and the other in his wild goatskins, do not easily co-exist. Even if Robinson Crusoe did have a tidy capital investment in the form of a well-stocked shipwreck, he still did not have a ten thousand dollar machine under him.

Lindbergh, in nearly every remark about his flight and in his own writings about it, resisted the tendency to exploit the flight as the achievement of an individual. He never said "I," he always said "We." The plane was not to go unrecognized. Nevertheless, there persisted a tendency to seize upon the flight as a way of celebrating the self-sufficient individual, so that among many others an Ohio newspaper could describe Lindbergh as this "self-contained, self-reliant, courageous young man [who] ranks among the great pioneers of history." The strategy here was a common one, to make Lindbergh a "pioneer" and thus to link him with a long and vital tradition of individualism in the American experience. Colonel Theodore Roosevelt, himself the son of a famous exponent of self-reliance, said to reporters at his home in Oyster Bay that "Captain Lindbergh personifies the daring of youth. Daniel Boone, David Crocket [sic], and men of that type played a lone hand and made America. Lindbergh is their lineal descendant." In *Outlook* magazine, immediately below an enthusiastic endorsement of Lindbergh's own remarks on the importance of his machine and his scientific instruments, there was the statement, "Charles Lindbergh is the heir of all that we like to think is best in America. He is of the stuff out of which have been made the pioneers that opened up the wilderness, first on the Atlantic coast, and then in our great West. His are the qualities which we, as a people, must nourish." It is in this mood that one suspects it was important that Lindbergh came out of the West and rode all alone.

Another common metaphor in the attempt to place Lindbergh's exploit was to say that he had opened a new "frontier." To speak of the air as a "frontier" was to invoke an interpretation of the meaning of American history which had sources deep in American experience, but the frontier of the airplane is hardly the frontier of the trailmakers of the old West. Rather than an escape into the self-sufficient simplicity of the American past, the machine which made Lindbergh's flight possible represented an advance into a complex industrial present. The difficulty lay in using an instance of modern life to celebrate the virtues of the past, to use an extreme development of an urban industrial society to insist upon the significance of the frontier in American life.

A little more than a month after Lindbergh's flight, Joseph K. Hart in *Survey* magazine reached back to Walt Whitman's poem for the title of an article on Lindbergh: "O Pioneer." A school had made Lindbergh an honorary alumnus but Hart protested there was little available evidence "that he was educated in *schools.*" "We must look elsewhere for our explanation," Hart wrote and he looked to the experience of Lindbergh's youth when "everything that he ever did . . . he did by himself. He lived more to himself than most boys." And, of course, Lindbergh lived to himself in the only place conceivably possible, in the world of nature, on a Minnesota farm. "There he developed in the companionship of woods and fields, animals and machines, his audaciously natural and simple personality." The word, "machines," jars as it intrudes into Hart's idyllic pastoral landscape and betrays Hart's difficulty in relating the setting of nature upon which he wishes to insist with the fact that its product spent his whole life tinkering with machines, from motorcycles to airplanes. But except for that one word, Hart proceeds in uncritical nostalgia to show that "a lone trip across the Atlantic was not impossible for a boy who had grown up in the solitude of the woods and waters." If Lindbergh was "clear-headed, naif, untrained in the ways of cities," it was because he had "that 'natural simplicity' which Fenimore Cooper used to attribute to the pioneer hero of his Leatherstocking Tales." Hart rejected the notion that any student "bent to all the conformities" of formal training could have done what Lindbergh did. "Must we not admit," he asked, "that this pioneering urge remained to this audacious youth because he had never submitted completely to the repressions of the world and its jealous institutions?"

Only those who insist on reason will find it strange that Hart should use the industrial achievement of the airplane to reject the urban, institutionalized world of industrialism. Hart was dealing with something other than reason; he was dealing with the emotion evoked by Lindbergh's solitude. He recognized that people wished to call Lindbergh a "genius" because that "would release him from the ordinary rules of existence." That way, "we could rejoice with him in his triumph and then go back to the contracted routines of our institutional ways [because] ninety-nine percent of us must be content to be shaped and moulded by the routine ways and forms of the world to the routine tasks of life." It is in the word "must" that the pathos of this interpretation of the phenomenon of Lindbergh lies. The world had changed from the open society of the pioneer to the close-knit, interdependent world of a modern machine-oriented civilization. The institutions of a highly corporate industrial society existed as a constant reproach to a people who liked to believe that the meaning of its experience was embodied in the formless, independent life of the frontier. Like Thomas Jefferson who identified American virtue with nature and saw the city as a "great sore" on the public body, Hart concluded that "certainly, in the response that the world—especially the world of great cities—has made to the performance of this midwestern boy, we can read of the homesickness of the human soul, immured in city canyons and routine tasks, for the freer world of youth, for the open spaces of the pioneer, for the joy of battling with nature and clean storms once more on the frontiers of the earth."

The social actuality which made the adulation of Lindbergh possible had its own irony, for the notion that America's strength lay in its simple uncomplicated beginnings. For the public response to Lindbergh to have reached the proportions it did, the world had by necessity to be the intricately developed world of modern mass communications. But more than irony was involved. Ultimately, the emotion attached to Lindbergh's flight involved no less than a whole theory about American history. By singling out the fact that Lindbergh rode alone, and by naming him a pioneer of the frontier, the public projected its sense that the source of America's strength lay somewhere in the past and that Lindbergh somehow meant that America must look backward in time to rediscover some lost virtue. The mood was nostalgic and American history was read as a decline, a decline measured in terms of America's advance into an urban, institutionalized way of life which made solitary achievement increasingly beyond the reach of ninety-nine per cent of the people. Because Lindbergh's ancestors were Norse, it was easy to call him a "Viking" and extend the emotion far into the past when all frontiers were open. He became the "Columbus" of another new world to conquer as well as the "Lochinvar" who rode all alone. But there was always the brute, irreducible fact that Lindbergh's exploit was a victory of the machine over the barriers of nature. If the only response to Lindbergh had been a retreat to the past, we would be involved with a mass cultural neurosis, the inability of America to accept reality, the reality of the world in which it lived. But there was another aspect, one in which the public celebrated the machine and the highly organized society of which it was a product. The response to Lindbergh reveals that the American people were deeply torn between conflicting interpretations of their own experience. By calling Lindbergh a pioneer, the people could read into American history the necessity of turning back to the frontier past. Yet the people could also read American history in terms of progress into the industrial future. They could do this by emphasizing the machine which was involved in Lindbergh's flight.

Lindbergh came back from Europe in an American man-of-war, the cruiser *Memphis*. It seems he had contemplated flying on, around the whole world perhaps, but less adventurous heads prevailed and dictated a surer mode of travel for so valuable a piece of public property. The *New Republic* protested against bringing America's hero of romance home in a warship. If he had returned on a great liner, that would have been one thing. "One's first trip on an oceanliner is a great adventure—the novelty of it, the many people of all kinds and conditions, floating for a week in a tiny compact world of their own." But to return on the *Memphis*, "to be put on a gray battleship with a collection of people all of the same stripe, in a kind of ship that has as much relation to the life of the sea as a Ford factory has! We might as well have put him in a pneumatic tube and shot him across the Atlantic." The interesting thing about the *New Republic*'s protest against the unromantic, regimented life of a battleship is that the image it found appropriate was the Ford assembly line. It was this reaction against the discipline of a mechanized society that probably led to the nostalgic image of Lindbergh as a remnant of a past when romance was possible for the individual, when life held novelty and society was variegated rather than uniform. But what the Ford Assembly Line represents, a society committed to the path of full mechanization, was what lay behind Lindbergh's romantic success. A long piece in the Sunday *New York Times*, "Lindbergh Symbolizes the Genius of America," reminded its readers of the too obvious fact that "without an airplane he could not have flown at all." Lindbergh "is, indeed, the Icarus of the twentieth century; not himself an inventor of his own wings, but a son of that omnipotent Daedalus whose ingenuity has created the modern world." The point was that modern America was the creation of modern industry. Lindbergh "reveres his 'ship' as a noble expression of mechanical wisdom. . . . Yet in this reverence . . . Lindbergh is not an exception. What he means by the Spirit of St. Louis is really the spirit of America. The mechanical genius, which is discerned in Henry Ford as well as in Charles A. Lindbergh, is in the very atmosphere of [the] country." In contrast to a sentiment that feared the enforced discipline of the machine there existed an attitude of reverence for its power.

Lindbergh led the way in the celebration of the machine, not only implicitly by including his plane when he said "we," but by direct statement. In Paris he told newspapermen, "You fellows have not said enough about that wonderful motor." Rarely have two more taciturn figures confronted one another than when Lindbergh returned to Washington and Calvin Coolidge pinned the Distinguished Flying Cross on him, but in his brief remarks Coolidge found room to express his particular delight that Lindbergh should have given equal credit to the airplane. "For we are proud," said the President, "that in every particular this silent partner represented American genius and industry. I am told that more than 100 separate companies furnished materials, parts or service in its construction."

The flight was not the heroic lone success of a single daring individual, but the climax of the cooperative effort of an elaborately interlocked technology. The day after Coolidge's speech, Lindbergh said at another ceremony in Washington that the honor should "not go to the pilot alone but to American science and genius which had given years of study to the advancement of aeronautics." "Some things," he said, "should be taken into due consideration in connection with our flight that have not heretofore been given due weight. That is just what made this flight possible. It was not the act of a single pilot. It was the culmination of twenty years of aeronautical research and the assembling together of all that was practical and best in American aviation." The flight, concluded Lindbergh, "represented American industry."

The worship of the machine which was embodied in the public's response to Lindbergh exalted those very aspects which were denigrated in the celebration of the flight as the work of a heroic individual. Organization and careful method were what lay behind the flight, not individual self-sufficiency and daring romance. One magazine hailed the flight as a "triumph of mechanical engineering." "It is not to be forgotten that this era is the work not so much of brave aviators as of engineers, who have through patient and protracted effort been steadily improving the construction of airplanes." The lesson to be learned from Lindbergh's flight, thought a writer in the *Independent*, "is that the splendid human and material aspects of America need to be organized for the ordinary, matter of fact service of society." The machine meant organization, the careful rationalization of activity of a Ford assembly line, it meant planning, and, if it meant the loss of spontaneous individual action, it meant the material betterment of society. Lindbergh meant not a retreat to the free life

of the frontier past but an emergence into the time when "the machine began to take first place in the public mind—the machine and the organization that made its operation possible on a large scale." A poet on this side of the matter wrote, "All day I felt the pull / Of the steel miracle." The machine was not a devilish engine which would enthrall mankind, it was the instrument which would lead to a new paradise. But the direction of history implicit in the machine was toward the future, not the past; the meaning of history was progress, not decline, and America should not lose faith in the future betterment of society. An address by a Harvard professor, picked up by the *Magazine of Business*, made all this explicit. "We commonly take Social Progress for granted," said Edwin F. Gay, "but the doctrine of Social Progress is one of the great revolutionary ideas which have powerfully affected our modern world." There was a danger, however, that the idea "may be in danger of becoming a commonplace or a butt of criticism." The speaker recognized why this might be. America was "worn and disillusioned after the Great War." Logically, contentment should have gone with so optimistic a creed, yet the American people were losing faith. So Lindbergh filled an emotional need even where a need should have been lacking. "He has come like a shining vision to revive the hope of mankind." The high ideals of faith in progress "had almost come to seem like hollow words to us—but now here he is, emblematic of heroes yet to inhabit this world. Our belief in Social Progress is justified symbolically in him."

It is a long flight from New York to Paris; it is a still longer flight from the fact of Lindbergh's achievement to the burden imposed upon it by the imagination of his time. But it is in that further flight that lies the full meaning of Lindbergh. His role was finally a double one. His flight provided an opportunity for the people to project their own emotions into his act and their emotions involved finally two attitudes toward the meaning of their own experience. One view had it that America represented a brief escape from the course of history, an emergence into a new and open world with the self-sufficient individual at its center. The other said that America represented a stage in historical evolution and that its fulfillment lay in the development of society. For one, the meaning of America lay in the past; for the other in the future. For one, the American ideal was an escape from institutions, from the forms of society, and from limitations put upon the free individual; for the other, the American ideal was the elaboration of the complex institutions which made modern society possible, an acceptance of the discipline of the machine, and the achievement of the individual within a context of which he was only a part. The two views were contradictory but both were possible and both were present in the public's reaction to Lindbergh's flight.

The Sunday newspapers announced that Lindbergh had reached Paris and in the very issue whose front pages were covered with Lindbergh's story the magazine section of the *New York Times* featured an article by the British philosopher, Bertrand Russell. The magazine had, of course, been made up too far in advance to take advantage of the news about Lindbergh. Yet, in a prophetic way, Russell's article was about Lindbergh. Russell hailed the rise to power of the United States because he felt that in the "new life that is America's" in the twentieth century "the new outlook appropriate to machinery [would] become more completely dominant than in the old world." Russell sensed that some might be unwilling to accept the machine, but "whether we like this new outlook or not," he wrote, "is of little importance." Why one might not was obvious. A society built on

the machine, said Russell, meant "the diminution in the value and independence of the individual. Great enterprises tend more and more to be collective, and in an industrialized world the interference of the community with the individual must be more intense." Russell realized that while the co-operative effort involved in machine technology makes man collectively more lordly, it makes the individual more submissive. "I do not see how it is to be avoided," he concluded.

People are not philosophers. They did not see how the conflict between a machine society and the free individual was to be avoided either. But neither were they ready to accept the philosopher's statement of the problem. In Lindbergh, the people celebrated both the self-sufficient individual and the machine. Americans still celebrate both. We cherish the individualism of the American creed at the same time that we worship the machine which increasingly enforces collectivized behavior. Whether we can have both, the freedom of the individual and the power of an organized society, is a question that still haunts our minds. To resolve the conflict that is present in America's celebration of Lindbergh in 1927 is still the task of America.

IV

Myths of Politics & Foreign Affairs

A culture especially receptive to myth typified the age of Franklin Roosevelt, the New Deal, and beyond. The crisis conditions of the country, combined with the engaging personal style and special leadership abilities of FDR, rather guaranteed it.

Masterfully sensing the temper of the times, Franklin Delano Roosevelt came to the presidency in 1933 with ideas, slogans, and myths uniquely shaped to the needs of Depression America. "Let it be symbolic," he advised the Democratic party's nominating convention that presented him to the American people, "that I broke tradition." The New Deal's turn to federal action for dealing with the nation's ills broke with American mythic adherence to laissez-faire. The legendary belief that the nation must always resign its fate to the "inevitable" business cycle was swept into the dust heap.

More slowly, Roosevelt came to dominate American foreign policy. Against strong opposition from isolationists, he ultimately pursued an internationalist course. His intention became increasingly evident after the outbreak of war in Europe in September 1939. On the isolationist side was the America First Committee; on the internationalist side, the Committee to Defend America by Aiding the Allies. The argument over the legitimacy of intervention acted as an incubator for enduring opinions and myths concerning American involvement in the war and the role that Roosevelt took in that involvement. Since then, many of these myths have been incorporated into historical works on FDR and American entry into what has been called the Good War. How can anyone be against a war that stopped genocide?

FDR's legacy and legend have conditioned presidencies ever since. Postwar politics in general did much to distort the atmosphere and realities of American political culture. Major mythologies triggered American involvement in Vietnam. The especially "mythic presidencies" of John F. Kennedy and, later, Ronald Reagan, both revalidated much past mythology while creating and fashioning their own.

Like the mythic FDR, JFK was often referred to by his initials. *(Courtesy, Library of Congress)*

Franklin Roosevelt: Hero of the Workingclass. *(Cartoon by Burris Jenkins, January 30, 1934)*

Ingrid Bergman and Humphrey Bogart star in
Casablanca. (Courtesy, Library of Congress)

The Lengthening Shadow of FDR: An Enduring Myth

William E. Leuchtenburg

In every recent poll taken among historians ranking the performance of past Presidents, Franklin Delano Roosevelt invariably ranks as great. The most recent survey puts him with George Washington, Andrew Jackson, Abraham Lincoln, and Woodrow Wilson, only Lincoln reaching higher stature. Roosevelt is the most recent of the great leaders, and subsequent presidential expectations have been measured against the achievement—ultimately the mythic image—of FDR, idol to professor and public, Democrat and Republican. In the estimation of William E. Leuchtenburg, William Rand Kenan Professor of History at the University of North Carolina, Chapel Hill, the nature of Roosevelt's greatness resides in large measure in his confident enlargement of the presidency and his "leading the nation to accept the responsibilities of world power." Roosevelt's contagious optimism spiritually mobilized the nation to confront the Depression and World War II. Having an intuitive sense of the new media politics, which would so much define the conduct of national affairs in the decades to come, Roosevelt reshaped the office he occupied in its relation to an attentive public, an expectant press corps, and (at least initially) a charmed Congress, making it into what is often called the "imperial presidency." Some Americans thought him a usurper king whose reign laid the foundations for a questionable extension of executive power. For the great many, however, FDR was a personal hero, an "event-making man."

When the American people got their first look at the entries in the 1988 presidential race, they sensed immediately that not one of the contenders measured up to their highest expectations. The Republican heir apparent was dismissed as a "wimp," and the original Democratic field as the "seven dwarfs." Asked whom in either party they preferred, a huge proportion of respondents replied, "None of the above." And if inquirers had gone on to ask what sort of nominee voters had in mind, not a few would have answered without hesitation, "Franklin Delano Roosevelt."

That sentiment cut across party lines. Predictably more than one Democrat sought to associate himself with his party's four-time winner. At the 1984 Democratic National Convention in San Francisco, Jesse Jackson had drawn a roar of approval when he said that FDR in a wheelchair was better than Ronald Reagan on a horse, and in the 1988 contest Senator Paul Simon of Illinois offered any number of New Deal solutions to contemporary problems. More surprisingly, Franklin Roosevelt has attracted no little favorable comment from Republicans, most conspicuously President Reagan. In his 1980 acceptance address Reagan spoke so warmly of FDR that the *New York Times* editorial the next morning was entitled "Franklin Delano Reagan," and thereafter he rarely missed an opportunity to laud the idol of his opponents.

Indeed, so powerful an impression has FDR left

on the office that in the most recent survey of historians, he moved past George Washington to be ranked as the second greatest President in our history, excelled only by the legendary Abraham Lincoln.

This very high rating would have appalled many of the contemporaries of "that megalomaniac cripple in the White House." In the spring of 1937 an American who had been traveling extensively in the Caribbean confided, "During all the time I was gone, if anybody asked me if I wanted any news, my reply was always—'there is only one bit of news I want to hear and that is the death of Franklin D. Roosevelt. If he is not dead you don't have to tell me anything else.' " "And at one country club in Connecticut, a historian has noted, "mention of his name was forbidden as a health measure against apoplexy."

Roosevelt, his critics maintained, had shown himself to be a man of no principles. Herbert Hoover called him a "chameleon on plaid," while H. L. Mencken declared, "If he became convinced tomorrow that coming out for cannibalism would get him the votes he so sorely needs, he would begin fattening a missionary in the White House backyard come Wednesday."

This reputation derived in good part from the fact that Roosevelt had campaigned in 1932 on the promise to balance the budget but subsequently asked Congress to appropriate vast sums for relief of the unemployed. Especially embarrassing was the memory of his 1932 address at Forbes Field, home of the Pittsburgh Pirates, in which he denounced Hoover as a profligate spender. The presidential counsel Sam Rosenman recalled how FDR asked him to devise a way to explain this 1932 speech in one he planned to make in his 1936 campaign. After careful consideration, Rosenman had one suggestion: "Deny categorically that you ever made it."

Historians, too, have found fault with FDR. New Left writers have chided him for offering a "profoundly conservative" response to a situation that had the potential for revolutionary change, while commentators of no particular persuasion have criticized him for failing to bring the country out of the Depression short of war, for maneuvering America into World War II (or for not taking the nation to war soon enough), for permitting Jews to perish in Hitler's death camps, and for sanctioning the internment of Japanese-Americans.

Roosevelt has been faulted especially for his fail-

ure to develop any grand design. The political scientist C. Herman Pritchett claimed that the New Deal never produced "any consistent social and economic philosophy to give meaning and purpose to its various action programs." Even harsher disapproval has come from Undersecretary of Agriculture Rexford Tugwell, who in many ways admired FDR. "He could have emerged from the orthodox progressive chrysalis and led us into a new world," Tugwell said, but instead, FDR busied himself "planting protective shrubbery on the slopes of a volcano."

Given all this often very bitter censure, both at the time and since, how can one now account for FDR's ranking as the second-greatest President ever? We may readily acknowledge that polls can be deceptive and that historians have been scandalously vague about establishing criteria for "greatness." Yet there are, in fact, significant reasons for Roosevelt's rating, some of them substantial enough to be acknowledged even by skeptics.

To begin with the most obvious, he was President longer than anyone else. Alone of American Presidents he broke the taboo against a third term and served part of a fourth term as well. Shortly after his death the country adopted a constitutional amendment limiting a President to two terms. Motivated in no small part by the desire to deliver a posthumous rebuke to Roosevelt, this amendment has had the ironic consequence of assuring that Franklin Roosevelt will be, so far as we can foresee, the only chief executive who will ever have served more than two terms.

Roosevelt's high place rests, too, on his role in leading the nation to accept the responsibilities of a world power. When he took office, the United States was firmly committed to isolationism; it refused to join either the League of Nations or the World Court. Roosevelt made full use of his executive power to recognize the USSR, craft the good-neighbor policy with Latin America, and, late in his second term, provide aid to the Allies and lead the nation into active involvement in World War II. So far had America come by the end of the Roosevelt era that the Secretary of War, Henry Stimson, was to say that the United States could never again "be an island to herself. No private program and no public policy, in any sector of our national life, can now escape from the compelling fact that if it is not framed with reference to the world, it is framed with perfect futility."

As wartime President, FDR demonstrated his

executive leadership by guiding the country through a victorious struggle against the Fascist powers. "He overcame both his own and the nation's isolationist inclination . . . ," the historian Robert Divine has concluded. "His role in insuring the downfall of Adolf Hitler is alone enough to earn him a respected place in history."

Whatever his flaws, Roosevelt came to be perceived all over the globe as the leader of the forces of freedom. The British political scientist Sir Isaiah Berlin wrote that in the "leaden thirties, the only light in the darkness was the administration of Mr. Roosevelt . . . in the United States."

For good or ill, also, America first became a major military power during Roosevelt's Presidency. As late as 1939 the U.S. Army ranked eighteenth in the world, and soldiers trained with pieces of cardboard marked "Tank." Under FDR, Congress established peacetime conscription and after Pearl Harbor put millions of men and women in uniform. His long reign also saw the birth of the Pentagon, the military-industrial complex, and the atomic bomb. At the conclusion of FDR's Presidency, one historian has noted, "a Navy superior to the combined fleets of the rest of the world dominated the seven seas; the Air Force commanded greater striking power than that of any other country; and American overseas bases in the . . . Atlantic, the Mediterranean, and the Pacific rimmed the Eurasian continent."

*　　*　　*

But there is an even more important reason for FDR's high ranking: his role in enlarging the presidential office and expanding the realm of the state while leading the American people through the Great Depression.

Roosevelt came to office at a desperate time, in the fourth year of a worldwide depression that raised the gravest doubts about the future of the Western world. "In 1931," commented the British historian Arnold Toynbee, "men and women all over the world were seriously contemplating and frankly discussing the possibility that the Western system of Society might break down and cease to work." And in the summer of 1932, the economist John Maynard Keynes, asked by a journalist whether there had ever been anything before like the Great Depression, replied, "Yes, it was called the Dark Ages, and it lasted four hundred years."

By the time Roosevelt was sworn in, national income had been cut in half and more than fifteen million Americans were unemployed. Every state in the Union had closed its banks or severely restricted their operations, and on the very morning of his inauguration, the New York Stock Exchange had shut down. For many, hope had gone. "Now is the winter of our discontent the chilliest," wrote the editor of *Nation's Business*.

Only a few weeks after Roosevelt took office, the spirit of the country seemed markedly changed. Gone was the torpor of the Hoover years; gone, too, the political paralysis. "The people aren't sure . . . just where they are going," noted one business journal, "but anywhere seems better than where they have been. In the homes, on the streets, in the offices, there is a feeling of hope reborn." Again and again, observers resorted to the imagery of darkness and light to characterize the transformation from the Stygian gloom of Hoover's final winter to the bright spring-time of the Hundred Days. People of every political persuasion gave full credit for the revival of confidence to one man: the new President.

In April the Republican senator from California, Hiram Johnson, acknowledged: "The admirable trait in Roosevelt is that he has the guts to try. . . . He does it all with the rarest good nature. . . . We have exchanged for a frown in the White House a smile. Where there were hesitation and vacillation, weighing always the personal political consequences, feebleness, timidity, and duplicity, there are now courage and boldness and real action." On the editorial page of *Forum*, Henry Goddard Leach summed up the nation's nearly unanimous verdict: "We have a leader."

*　　*　　*

The new President had created this impression by a series of actions—delivering his compelling inaugural address, summoning Congress into emergency session, resolving the banking crisis—but even more by his manner. Supremely confident in his own powers, he could imbue others with a similar confidence. Moreover, he had acquired an admirable political education: state senator, junior cabinet officer, his party's vice-presidential nominee, two-term governor of the most populous state in the Union. As the political scientist Richard Neustadt has observed, "Roosevelt, almost alone among our Presidents, had no conception of the office to live up to; he was it. His image of the office was himself-in-office."

FDR's view of himself and his world freed him from anxieties that other men would have found intolerable. Not even the weightiest responsibilities seemed to disturb his serenity. One of his associates said, "He must have been psychoanalyzed by God."

A Washington reporter noted in 1933: "No signs of care are visible to his main visitors or at the press conferences. He is amiable, urbane and apparently untroubled. He appears to have a singularly fortunate faculty for not becoming flustered. Those who talk with him informally in the evenings report that he busies himself with his stamp collection, discussing in an illuminating fashion the affairs of state while he waves his shears in the air."

The commentator Henry Fairlie has remarked: "The innovating spirit . . . was [FDR's] most striking characteristic as a politician. The man who took to the radio like a duck to water was the same man who, in his first campaign for the New York Senate in 1910, hired . . . a two-cylinder red Maxwell, with no windshield or top, to dash through (of all places) Dutchess County; and it was the same man who broke all precedents twenty-two years later when he hired a little plane to take him to Chicago to make his acceptance speech. . . . The willingness to try everything was how Roosevelt governed."

This serenity and venturesomeness were precisely the qualities called for in a national leader in the crisis of the Depression, and the country drew reassurance from FDR's buoyant view of the world. Secretary of Labor Frances Perkins remarked on his feeling that "nothing in human judgment is final. One may courageously take the step that seems right today because it can be modified tomorrow if it does not work well. . . ."

FDR's self-command, gusto, and bonhomie created an extraordinary bond with the American people. Millions of Americans came to view him as one who was intimately concerned with their welfare. In the 1936 campaign he heard people cry out, "He saved my home"; "He gave me a job." In Bridgeport, Connecticut, he rode past signs saying, "Thank God for Roosevelt," and in the Denver freight yards a message in chalk on the side of a boxcar read, "Roosevelt Is My Friend."

*   *   *

Roosevelt made conscious use of the media almost from the moment he entered the White House, with his press conferences serving to educate news-paper writers and, through them, the nation on the complex, novel measures he was advocating. He was fond of calling the press meeting room in the White House his "schoolroom," and he often resorted to terms such as *seminar* or, when referring to the budget, *textbook*. When in January 1934 the President invited thirty-five Washington correspondents to his study, he explained his budget message to them "like a football coach going through skull practice with his squad."

FDR's performance at his first press conference as President on March 8, 1933, the journalist Leo Rosten has written, has "become something of a legend in newspaper circles. Mr. Roosevelt was introduced to each correspondent. Many of them he already knew and greeted by name—first name. For each he had a handshake and the Roosevelt smile. When the questioning began, the full virtuosity of the new Chief Executive was demonstrated. Cigarette-holder in mouth at a jaunty angle, he met the reporters on their own grounds. His answers were swift, positive, illuminating. He had exact information at his fingertips. He showed an impressive understanding of public problems and administrative methods. He was lavish in his confidences and 'background information.' He was informal, communicative, gay. When he evaded a question it was done frankly. He was thoroughly at ease. He made no effort to conceal his pleasure in the give and take of the situation."

Jubilant reporters could scarcely believe the transformation in the White House. So hostile had their relations become with FDR's predecessor that Hoover, who was accused of employing the Secret Service to stop leaks and of launching a campaign of "terrorism" to get publishers to fire certain news-papermen, finally abandoned press conferences altogether. Furthermore, Hoover, like Harding and Coolidge before him, had insisted on written questions submitted in advance. But to the delight of the Washington press corps, Roosevelt immediately abolished that requirement and said that questions could be fired at him on the spot. At the end of the first conference, reporters did something they had never done before: they gave the man they were covering a spontaneous round of applause.

The initial euphoria continued long afterward. Roosevelt could sometimes be testy—he told one reporter to go off to a corner and put on a dunce cap—but mostly, especially in the New Deal years of

1933 to 1938, he was jovial and even chummy, in no small part because he regarded himself as a longtime newspaperman, since he had been editor in chief of the *Harvard Crimson*. The first President to appoint an official press secretary, he also made clear that members of the Fourth Estate were socially respectable by throwing a spring garden party for them at the White House.

Above all, FDR proved a never-ending source of news. Jack Bell, who covered the White House for the Associated Press, has written of him: "He talked in headline phrases. He acted, he emoted; he was angry, he was smiling. He was persuasive, he was demanding; he was philosophical, he was elemental. He was sensible, he was unreasonable; he was benevolent, he was malicious. He was satirical, he was soothing; he was funny, he was gloomy. He was exciting. He was human. He was copy."

One columnist wrote afterward, "The doubters among us—and I was one of them—predicted that the free and open conference would last a few weeks and then would be abandoned." But twice a week, with rare exceptions, year after year, the President submitted to the crossfire of interrogation. He left independently minded newspapermen like Raymond Clapper with the conviction that "the administration from President Roosevelt down has little to conceal and is willing to do business with the doors open." If reporters were 60 percent for the New Deal, Clapper reckoned, they were 90 percent for Roosevelt personally.

Some observers have seen in the FDR press conference a quasi-constitutional institution like the question hour in the House of Commons. To a degree, it was. But one should keep in mind that the President had complete control over what he would discuss and what could be published. He used the press conference as a public relations device he could manipulate to his own advantage.

Franklin Roosevelt also was the first Chief Executive to take full advantage of radio as a means of projecting his ideas and personality directly into American homes. When FDR got before a microphone, he appeared, said one critic, to be "talking and toasting marshmallows at the same time." In his first days in office he gave a radio address that was denominated a "fireside chat" because of his intimate, informal delivery that made every American think the President was talking directly to him or her. As the journalist and historian David Halberstam has

pointed out: "He was the first great American radio voice. For most Americans of this generation, their first memory of politics would be sitting by a radio and hearing *that* voice, strong, confident, totally at ease. If he was going to speak, the idea of doing something else was unthinkable. If they did not yet have a radio, they walked the requisite several hundred yards to the home of a more fortunate neighbor who did. It was in the most direct sense of government reaching out and touching the citizen, bringing Americans into the political process and focusing their attention on the presidency as the source of good. . . . Most Americans in the previous 160 years had never even seen a President; now almost all of them were hearing him, *in their own homes*. It was literally and figuratively electrifying."

* * *

By quickening interest in government, Roosevelt became the country's foremost civic educator. One scholar has observed: "Franklin Roosevelt changed the nature of political contests in this country by drawing new groups into active political participation. Compare the political role of labor under the self-imposed handicap of Samuel Gompers' narrow vision with labor's political activism during and since the Roosevelt years. The long-run results were striking: . . . public policy henceforth was written to meet the needs of those who previously had gone unheard."

Roosevelt and his headline-making New Deal especially served to arouse the interest of young people. When Lyndon Johnson learned of FDR's death, he said: "I don't know that I'd ever have come to Congress if it hadn't been for him. But I do know that I got my first desire for public office because of him—and so did thousands of other men all over this country."

FDR's role as civic educator frequently took a decidedly partisan turn, for he proved to be an especially effective party leader. In 1932, in an election that unraveled traditional party ties, he became the first Democrat elected to the White House with a popular majority since Franklin Pierce eighty years before. Yet this heady triumph, reflecting resentment at Hoover more than approval for FDR and the Democrats, might have been short-lived if Roosevelt had not built a constituency of lower-income ethnic voters in the great cities tenuously allied with white voters in the Solid South.

He brought into his administration former Republicans such as Henry Wallace and Harold Ickes; enticed hundreds of thousands of Socialists, such as the future California congressman Jerry Voorhis, to join the Democrats; worked with anti-Tammany leaders like Fiorello La Guardia in New York; backed the independent George Norris against the Democratic party's official nominee in Nebraska; and forged alliances with third parties such as the American Labor party. In 1938 he even attempted, largely unsuccessfully, to "purge" conservative Democrats from the party and in World War II may even have sought to unite liberal Republicans of the Wendell Willkie sort with liberal Democrats in a new party, though the details of that putative arrangement are obscure.

* * *

Roosevelt won such a huge following both for himself and for his party by putting together the most ambitious legislative program in the history of the country, thereby considerably enhancing the role of the President as chief legislator. He was not the first chief executive in this century to adopt that role, but he developed the techniques to a point beyond any to which they had been carried before. He made wide use of the device of special messages, and he accompanied these communications with drafts of proposed bills. He wrote letters to committee chairmen or members of Congress to urge passage of his proposals; summoned the congressional leadership to White House conferences on legislation; used agents like the presidential adviser Tommy Corcoran on Capitol Hill to corral maverick Democrats; and revived the practice of appearing in person before Congress. He made even the hitherto mundane business of bill signing an occasion for political theater; it was he who initiated the custom of giving a presidential pen to a congressional sponsor of legislation as a memento. In the First Hundred Days, Roosevelt adroitly dangled promises of patronage before congressmen, but without delivering on them until he had the legislation he wanted. The result, as one commentator put it, was that "his relations with Congress were to the very end of the session tinged with a shade of expectancy which is the best part of young love."

To the dismay of the Republican leadership, Roosevelt showed himself to be a past master not just at coddling his supporters in Congress but at disarm-ing would-be opponents. The conservative Republican congressman Joseph W. Martin, who had the responsibility of insulating his party members in the House from FDR's charm, complained that the President, "laughing, talking, and poking the air with his long cigarette holder," was so magnetic that he "bamboozled" even members of the opposition. Martin resented that he had to rescue opposition members from the perilous "moon glow."

To be sure, FDR's success with Congress has often been exaggerated. The Congress of the First Hundred Days, it has been said, "did not so much debate the bills it passed . . . as salute them as they went sailing by," but in later years Congress passed the bonus bill over his veto; shelved his "Court-packing" plan; and, on neutrality policy, bound the President like Gulliver. After the enactment of the Fair Labor Standards law in 1938, Roosevelt was unable to win congressional approval of any further New Deal legislation. Moreover, some of the main New Deal measures credited to Roosevelt were proposals originating in Congress that he either outrightly opposed or accepted only at the last moment, such as federal insurance of bank deposits, the Wagner Act, and public housing. In fact, by latter-day standards, his operation on the Hill was primitive. He had no congressional liaison office, and he paid too little attention to rank-and-file members.

Still, Roosevelt's skill as chief legislator is undeniable. A political scientist has stated: "The most dramatic transformation in the relationship between the presidency and Congress occurred during the first two terms of Franklin D. Roosevelt. FDR changed the power ratio between Congress and the White House, publicly taking it upon himself to act as the leader of Congress at a time of deepening crisis in the nation. More than any other president, FDR established the model of the most powerful legislative presidency on which the public's expectations still are anchored."

As one aspect of his function as chief legislator, Roosevelt broke all records in making use of the veto power. By the end of his second term, his vetoes already represented more than 30 percent of all the measures disallowed by Presidents since 1792. According to one credible tale, FDR used to ask his aides to look out for a piece of legislation he could veto, in order to remind Congress that it was being watched.

So far did Roosevelt plumb the potentialities of the chief executive as legislative leader that by the end of his first term, the columnist Raymond Clapper was writing, "It is scarcely an exaggeration to say that the President, although not a member of Congress, has become almost the equivalent of the prime minister of the British system, because he is both executive and the guiding hand of the legislative branch."

In 1938, in his annual message to Congress, Roosevelt made his philosophy about the duty of the state still more explicit: "Government has a final responsibility for the well-being of its citizenship. If private co-operative endeavor fails to provide work for willing hands and relief for the unfortunate, those suffering hardship from no fault of their own have a right to call upon the Government for aid; and a government worthy of its name must make fitting response."

Starting in the electrifying First Hundred Days of 1933, Roosevelt brought the welfare state to America, years after it had come to other lands. He moved beyond the notion that "rights" embodied only guarantees against denial of freedom, to the conception that government also has an obligation to assure certain economic essentials. In his State of the Union message of January 1944, he declared: "This Republic had its beginning, and grew to its present strength, under the protection of certain inalienable political rights—among them the right of free speech, free press, free worship, trial by jury, freedom from unreasonable searches and seizures. . . .

"As our Nation has grown in size and stature, however—as our industrial economy expanded—these political rights proved inadequate to assure us equality in the pursuit of happiness.

"We have come to a clear realization of the fact that true individual freedom cannot exist without economic security and independence. 'Necessitous men are not free men.' People who are hungry and out of a job are the stuff of which dictatorships are made.

"In our day these economic truths have become accepted as self-evident. We have accepted, so to speak, a second Bill of Rights under which a new basis of security and prosperity can be established for all—regardless of station, race, or creed."

In expanding the realm of the state, Roosevelt demanded that business recognize the superior authority of the government in Washington. At the time, that was shocking doctrine. In the pre–New Deal period, government often had been the handmaiden of business, and many Presidents had shared

the values of businessmen. But FDR clearly did not. Consequently the national government in the 1930s came to supervise the stock market, establish a central banking system monitored from Washington, and regulate a range of business activities that had hitherto been regarded as private.

As a result of these measures, Roosevelt was frequently referred to as the "great economic emancipator" (or, conversely, as a traitor to his class), but his real contributions, as the historian James MacGregor Burns has said, were "a willingness to take charge, a faith in the people, and an acceptance of the responsibility of the federal government to act."

After a historic confrontation with the Supreme Court, Roosevelt secured the legitimization of this enormous increase in the growth of the state. As a consequence, not once since 1936 has the Court invalidated any significant statute regulating the economy.

*   *   *

Roosevelt quickly learned that enacting a program was one thing; getting it carried out was something altogether different. He once complained: "The Treasury is so large and far-flung and ingrained in its practices that I find it almost impossible to get the action and results I want. . . . But the Treasury is not to be compared with the State Department. You should go through the experience of trying to get any changes in the thinking, policy, and action of the career diplomats and then you'd know what a real problem was. But the Treasury and the State Department put together are nothing compared with the Na-a-vy. The admirals are really something to cope with—and I should know. To change something in the Na-a-vy is like punching a feather bed. You punch it with your right and you punch it with your left until you are finally exhausted, and then you find the damn bed just as it was before you started punching."

To overcome resistance to his policies in the old-line departments, Roosevelt resorted to the creation of emergency agencies. "We have new and complex problems," he once said, "Why not establish a new agency to take over the new duty rather than saddle it on an old institution?"

Roosevelt also departed from orthodoxy in another way. In flat defiance of the cardinal rule of public administration textbooks—that every administrator ought to appear on a chart with a clearly stated assignment—the President not only deliberately disarranged spheres of authority but appointed men of clashing attitudes and temperaments. The historian Arthur Schlesinger, Jr., has maintained: "His favorite technique was to keep grants of authority incomplete, jurisdictions uncertain, charters overlapping. The result of this competitive theory of administration was often confusion and exasperation on the operating level; but no other method could so reliably insure that in a large bureaucracy filled with ambitious men eager for power the decisions, and the power to make them, would remain with the President."

To ensure trustworthy information, Roosevelt relied on a congeries of informants and personal envoys. Though there were times when one man had an especially close relationship to him—Louis Howe early in the New Deal, Harry Hopkins in the war years—Roosevelt never had a chief of staff, and no single individual was ever permitted to take the place of what one historian called the "countless lieutenants and supporters" who served "virtually as roving ambassadors collecting intelligence through the Executive Branch," often unaware that more than one man had the same assignment. "He would call you in, and he'd ask you to get the story on some complicated business," one of FDR's aides later said, "and you'd come back after a couple of days of hard labor and present the juicy morsel you'd uncovered under a stone somewhere, and *then* you'd find out he knew all about it, along with something else you *didn't* know."

So evident were the costs of FDR's competitive style—not only bruised feelings but, at times, a want of coherence in policy—and so harum-scarum did his methods seem, that it became commonplace to speak of Roosevelt as a poor administrator. A British analyst has commented that though the "mishmash" Roosevelt put together was "inspired," it resulted not in a "true bureaucracy" but in "an ill-organized flock of agencies with the sheep dogs in the White House snapping at their heels as the President whistled the signals."

Not a few commentators, though, have concluded that Roosevelt was a superior administrator. They point out that he vastly improved staffing of the Presidency and that he broke new ground when he assigned Henry Wallace to chair a series of wartime agencies, for no Vice-President had ever held administrative responsibilities before. Granted, there was

no end of friction between subordinates such as Hopkins and Ickes, or Cordell Hull and Sumner Welles, but Wallace once observed, in a rare witticism, that FDR "could keep all the balls in the air without losing his own."

Furthermore, his admirers maintain, if the test of a great administrator is whether he can inspire devotion in his subordinates, FDR passes with flying colors. Even Ickes, the most conspicuous grumbler of the Roosevelt circle, noted in his diary, "You go into Cabinet meetings tired and discouraged and out of sorts and the President puts new life into you. You come out like a fighting cock."

An even better test of an administrator is whether he can recruit exceptional talent, and Roosevelt broke new ground by giving an unprecedented opportunity to a new corps of officials: the university-trained experts. Save for a brief period in World War I, professors had not had much of a place in Washington, but in his 1932 presidential campaign FDR enlisted several academic advisers, most of them from Columbia University, to offer their thoughts and to test his own ideas. The press called this group the Brain Trust. During the First Hundred Days of 1933, droves of professors, inspired by that example, descended on Washington to take part in the New Deal. So, too, did their students—young attorneys fresh out of law school and social scientists with recent graduate degrees who received an unprecedented open-arms reception from the federal government.

The sudden change of personnel was discountenanced by the President's critics, not least H. L. Mencken. "You Brain Trusters," he complained, "were hauled suddenly out of a bare, smelly classroom, wherein the razzberries of sophomores had been your only music, and thrown into a place of power and glory almost befitting Caligula, Napoleon I, or J. Pierpont Morgan, with whole herds of Washington correspondents crowding up to take down your every wheeze."

Roosevelt had such success in recruiting this new cadre of administrators because of his openness to groups that had long been discriminated against. Before the New Deal, the government had largely been the domain of a single element: white Anglo-Saxon Protestants. Under FDR, that situation altered perceptibly, with the change symbolized by the most famous team of FDR's advisers: Tommy Corcoran and Ben Cohen, the Irish Catholic and the Jew. Nor did ethnic diversity end there. Though some patterns of racial discrimination persisted, the President appointed enough blacks to high places in the government to permit the formation of what was called the "black cabinet."

For the first time, also, women received more than token recognition. In appointing Frances Perkins Secretary of Labor, Roosevelt named the first woman ever chosen for a cabinet post. He also selected the first female envoy and the first woman judge of the U.S. Circuit Court of Appeals. As First Lady, Mrs. Roosevelt, in particular, epitomized the new impact of women on public affairs. One of the original Brain Trusters, Rexford Tugwell, has written, "No one who ever saw Eleanor Roosevelt sit down facing her husband, and . . . say to him, 'Franklin, I think you should' . . . or, 'Franklin, surely you will not' . . . will ever forget the experience." She became, as one columnist said, "Cabinet Minister without portfolio—the most influential woman of our times."

*   *   *

In addition to attracting hitherto neglected talent to government service, Roosevelt, for all his idiosyncratic style, also made significant institutional changes. For instance, by an executive order of 1939, he moved several agencies, notably the Bureau of the Budget, under the wing of the White House and provided for a cadre of presidential assistants. This Executive Order 8248 has been called a "nearly unnoticed but none the less epoch-making event in the history of American institutions" and "perhaps the most important single step in the institutionalization of the Presidency."

Harold Smith, who served in the pre-war era and throughout the war years as FDR's budget director, later reflected: "When I worked with Roosevelt—for six years—I thought as did many others that he was a very erratic administrator. But now, when I look back, I can really begin to see the size of his programs. They were by far the largest and most complex programs that any President ever put through. People like me who had the responsibility of watching the pennies could only see the five or six or seven per cent of the programs that went wrong, through inefficient organization or direction. But now I can see in perspective the ninety-three or -four or -five percent that went right—including the winning of the biggest war in history—because of unbelievably skillful or-

ganization and direction. . . . Now, I think I'd say that Roosevelt must have been one of the greatest geniuses as an administrator that ever lived. What we couldn't appreciate at the time was the fact that he was a real *artist* in government."

It has become commonplace, even among Roosevelt's admirers, to view the President as an intellectual lightweight. He read few books, and these not very seriously. "He was neither a philosopher, like Jefferson, nor a student of government, like Wilson, the two Presidents he most admired," one writer has said. He had small talent for abstract reasoning, although perhaps no less than most men in public life. He loved brilliant people, commented one of his former aides, but not profound ones. The Brain Trustee Raymond Moley has observed that a picture of Teddy Roosevelt, "regaling a group of his friends with judgments on Goya, Flaubert, Dickens, and Jung, and discussions of Louis the Fat or the number of men at arms seasick in the fleet of Medina Sidonia—this could never be mistaken for one of Franklin Roosevelt. F.D.R.'s interests have always been more circumscribed. His moments of relaxation are given over exclusively to simpler pleasures—to the stamp album, to the Currier and Ives naval prints, to a movie or to good-humored horseplay."

Roosevelt kept himself informed not by applied study but by observation and conversation, and his particular qualities of mind served him reasonably well in the thirties. True, he was not well versed in economic theory, but had he accepted the greater part of what went for economic wisdom in 1932, he would have been badly misguided. Furthermore, contrary to the general notion, he knew far more about economic matters—utilities regulation, agriculture, banking, corporate structure, public finance—than was usually recognized.

He impressed almost everyone who worked with him with his knowledge of detail and, more important, with his grasp of the interrelationship of the larger aspects of public policy. "Never, at least since Jefferson," a prominent jurist wrote Justice Brandeis in 1937, "have we had a President of such constructive mind as Roosevelt."

*   *   *

Indeed, so manifest has been FDR's mastery of the affairs of state and so palpable his impact on the office as chief administrator, chief legislator, and tribune of the people that in recent years a separate, and disturbing, line of inquiry has surfaced: Does the imperial Presidency have its roots in the 1930s, and is FDR the godfather of Watergate? For four decades much of the controversy over the New Deal centered on the issue of whether Roosevelt had done enough. Abruptly, during the Watergate crisis, the obverse question was raised: Had he done too much? Had there been excessive aggrandizement of the executive office under FDR?

The notion that the origins of Watergate lie in the age of Roosevelt has a certain plausibility. In the First Hundred Days of 1933, Roosevelt initiated an enormous expansion of the national government with proliferating alphabet agencies lodged under the executive wing. Vast powers were delegated to presidential appointees with little or no congressional oversight. In foreign affairs Roosevelt bent the law in order to speed aid to the Allies, and in World War II he cut a wide swath in exercising his prerogatives. FDR was the first and only President to break the barrier against election to a third term, and for good measure he won a fourth term too. Only death cut short his protracted reign.

Those captivated by the historical antecedents of the Watergate era allege that Roosevelt showed no more sensitivity about Congress than did Nixon. When Roosevelt was asked in 1931 how much authority he expected Congress to grant him when he became President, he snapped, "Plenty." In office he ran into so much conflict with the legislators that on one occasion he said he would like to turn sixteen lions loose on them. But, it was objected, the lions might make a mistake. "Not if they stayed there long enough," Roosevelt answered.

Many have found Roosevelt's behavior on the eve of America's intervention in World War II especially reprehensible. Senator J. William Fulbright accused Roosevelt of having "usurped the treaty power of the Senate" and of having "circumvented the war powers of the Congress." On shaky statutory authority the President, six months before Pearl Harbor, used federal power to end strikes, most notably in sending troops to occupy the strikebound North American Aviation plant in California, his detractors assert. In this era, too, they point out, Roosevelt dispatched American forces to occupy Iceland and Greenland, provided convoys of vessels carrying arms to Britain, and ordered U.S. destroyers to shoot Nazi U-boats on sight, all acts that invaded Congress's war-making authority.

After the United States entered the war, Roosevelt raised the ire of his critics once more by his audacious Labor Day message of 1942, "one of the strangest episodes in the history of the presidency." In a bold—many thought brazen—assertion of inherent executive prerogative, Roosevelt, in demanding an effective price-and-wage-control statute, sent a message to Congress on September 7, 1942, saying: "I ask the Congress to take . . . action by the first of October. Inaction on your part by that date will leave me with an inescapable responsibility to the people of this country to see to it that the war effort is no longer imperiled by threat of economic chaos.

"In the event that the Congress should fail to act, and act adequately, I shall accept the responsibility, and I will act. . . .

"The President has the powers, under the Constitution and under Congressional acts, to take measures necessary to avert a disaster which would interfere with the winning of the war. . . .

"The American people can be sure that I will use my powers with a full sense of my responsibility to the Constitution and to my country. The American people can also be sure that I shall not hesitate to use every power vested in me to accomplish the defeat of our enemies in any part of the world where our own safety demands such a defeat.

"When the war is won, the powers under which I act automatically revert to the people—to whom they belong."

Congress quickly fell into line, and Roosevelt never had to make use of this threat.

It has also been contended that Nixon's overweening privy councillors wielded their inordinate power as a consequence of a reform brought about by Roosevelt. The 1937 report of the President's Committee on Administration Management called for staffing the executive office with administrative assistants "possessed of . . . a passion for anonymity." That job description sounded tailor-made for the faceless men around Nixon, for Haldeman and Ehrlichman seemed so indistinguishable that they were likened to Rosencrantz and Guildenstern.

Yet the parallels between Roosevelt and Nixon need to be set against the dissimilarities. "To Roosevelt, the communications of a President had to be . . . lively, intimate, and open," the journalist and Republican speech writer Emmet Hughes has observed. "He practiced an almost promiscuous curiosity." In marked contrast with the obsessively reclusive Nixon regime, the New Deal government went out of its way to learn what the nation was thinking and to open itself to questioning. Each morning the President and other top officials found a digest of clippings from some 750 newspapers, many of them hostile, on their desks, and before Roosevelt turned in for the night, he went through a bedtime folder of letters from ordinary citizens. During the First Hundred Days he urged the press to offer criticism so that he might avoid missteps, and then and later he solicited everyone from old friends to chance acquaintances outside the government to provide information that would serve as a check on what his White House lieutenants were telling him.

Roosevelt differed from Nixon, too, in creating a heterogeneous administration and encouraging dissenting voices within the government. "What impresses me most vividly about the men around Roosevelt," wrote the historian Clinton Rossiter, "is the number of flinty no-sayers who served him, loyally but not obsequiously."

Furthermore, even in the crisis of the Second World War, Roosevelt most often acted within constitutional bounds, and any transgressions have to be placed within the context of the dire challenge raised by Hitler and his confederates. Winston Churchill was to tell the House of Commons: "Of Roosevelt . . . it must be said that had he not acted when he did, in the way he did, had he not . . . resolved to give aid to Britain, and to Europe in the supreme crisis through which we have passed, a hideous fate might well have overwhelmed mankind and made its whole future for centuries sink into shame and ruin."

Such defenses of Roosevelt, however impressive, fall short of being fully persuasive. As well disposed a commentator as Schlesinger has said that FDR, "though his better instincts generally won out in the end, was a flawed, willful and, with time, increasingly arbitrary man." Unhappily, of FDR's many legacies, one is a certain lack of appropriate restraint with respect to the exercise of executive power.

*   *   *

The historian confronts one final, and quite different, question: How much of an innovator was Roosevelt? Both admirers and detractors have questioned whether FDR's methods were as original as they have commonly been regarded. Some skeptics have even asked, "Would not all of the changes from 1933 to 1945 have happened if there had been no Roosevelt, if someone else had been President?" Certainly trends toward the centralization of power in Washington and the White House were in motion well before 1933.

FDR himself always refused to answer what he called "iffy" questions, but this iffy question—would everything have been the same if someone else had been in the White House?—invites a reply, for it came very close to being a reality. In February 1933, a few weeks before Roosevelt was to take office, he ended a fishing cruise by coming to Bay Front Park in Miami. That night an unemployed bricklayer, Giuseppe Zangara, fired a gun at him from point-blank range, but the wife of a Miami physician deflected the assassin's arm just enough so that the bullets missed the President-elect and instead struck the mayor of Chicago, fatally wounding him. Suppose he had not been jostled and the bullets had found their mark. Would our history have been different if John Nance Garner rather than FDR had been President? No doubt some of the New Deal would have taken place anyway, as a response to the Great Depression. Yet it seems inconceivable that many of the more imaginative features of the Roosevelt years—for example, the Federal Arts Project—would have come under Garner, or that the conduct of foreign affairs would have followed the same course, or that the institution of the Presidency would have been so greatly affected. As the political scientist Fred Greenstein has observed, "Crisis was a necessary but far from sufficient condition for the modern presidency that began to evolve under Roosevelt."

The conclusion is one with which most scholars would agree: that Franklin Roosevelt was, to use the philosopher Sidney Hook's terminology, an "event-making man" who not only was shaped by but also shaped his age. He comprehended both the opportunity that the Great Depression offered to alter the direction of American politics and the menace Hitler posed to the nation, and as a consequence of both perceptions, America, and indeed the world, differed markedly in 1945 from what it had been in 1933, to no small degree because of his actions.

Roosevelt is one of the few American Presidents who loom large not just in the history of the United States but in the history of the world. The economist John Kenneth Galbraith has spoken of the "Bismarck–Lloyd George–Roosevelt Revolution," and Lloyd George himself called FDR the "greatest reforming statesman of the age."

*   *   *

Because Roosevelt "discovered in his office possibilities of leadership which even Lincoln had ignored," wrote the Oxford don Herbert Nicholas, it is hardly surprising that he continues to be the standard by which American Presidents, more than forty years after his death, continue to be measured. When the stock market slumped in the fall of 1987, the White House correspondent of the *Washington Post*, Lou Cannon, wrote a column that appeared under the headline REAGAN SHOULD EMULATE FDR, NOT HOOVER. Cannon, noting that "President Reagan has spent much of his public career emulating the style and cheerful confidence of his first political hero, Franklin D. Roosevelt," maintained that in dealing with the financial crisis, Reagan could "dodge the legacy of Roosevelt's luckless predecessor, Herbert Hoover," only "if he is willing to behave like FDR."

Even in an era when the country is said to have moved in a more conservative direction and the FDR coalition no longer is as potent as it once was, the memory of Franklin Roosevelt is still green. As the political scientist Thomas E. Cronin has observed, "With the New Deal Presidency firmly fixed in memory . . . we now expect our Presidents to be vigorous and moral leaders, who can steel our moral will, move the country forward, bring about dramatic and swift policy changes, and slay the dragons of crisis. An FDR halo effect has measurably shaped public attitudes toward the Presidency, persisting even today. . . . So embellished are some of our expectations that we virtually push . . . candidates into poses akin to the second coming of FDR."

The Myth of New Deal Radicalism

Paul K. Conkin

Even before Franklin D. Roosevelt's death in April 1945, assessment of his New Deal was already well under way. Viewpoints and opinions were expressed on subjects ranging from Roosevelt's personality to the legitimacy of New Deal legislation. Many politicians, citizens, and historians then and since have volunteered their commentary on the meaning of the New Deal for America. Predictably, interpretations have differed widely, creating many myths in the process. While it is traditional to see the New Deal as fundamentally liberal and democratic, some historians questioned the alleged "revolutionary" nature of FDR's programs. One of these historians, Professor Paul K. Conkin of Vanderbilt University, finds the conventional image of "Roosevelt as radical" mostly legend. In seeking an evenhanded assessment of the Age of Roosevelt and the New Deal, he fails to find evidence that New Deal legislation in any appreciable way destroyed such cherished American ideals as free enterprise, individual initiative, or laissez-faire capitalism. Though the hero-president succeeded in giving America a "transfusion of courage," his programs in the long run failed to bring economic recovery, did little to end poverty, largely ignored the plight of minorities, and in general brought little significant change to American society. The New Deal, in short, was conservative in its intent and its outcome.

The New Deal was an exceedingly personal enterprise. Its disparate programs were unified only by the personality of Franklin D. Roosevelt. Every characterization, every evaluation of governmental innovations from 1933 to 1938 terminates and often flounders in this personality. Characterization is ever hazardous: least so for a person who matures a coherent, articulate system of beliefs; most so of one who, like Roosevelt, operates within conventional, unarticulated beliefs and, in addition, retains a disarming simplicity. Even in the best of circumstances, biography reflects the catalyzing influence of the biographer and thus usually reveals the often fascinating chemical compound of two interacting personalities.

Today only a small minority of Americans remember Franklin Roosevelt, at least with more than vague images of childhood. Unswayed by his vital presence, even less impressed by his recorded speeches, unmoved by his increasingly dated political concerns, young Americans are baffled by the continued passion of their parents or grandparents, by the subdued fervor of professors, by all oldsters who still dare confess their love or who ever yet vent their hate. They note the touch of reverence in the books of Arthur M. Schlesinger, Jr., the adulation of an aged or departed court—Rosenman, Tully, Tugwell, Perkins, Morgenthau. They also note the last echoes of bitterness from right-wing critics, who continue to identify an almost unbearably conventional Roosevelt with both domestic and foreign treason. Surely the sympathetic portraits are more revealing.

Hate is a poor vehicle for communicating personality. But even the best portraits, conceived in love, often seem unlovely to another generation.

Roosevelt, as president, gave millions of Americans a transfusion of courage. They still remember. From his confidence, his optimism, they gleaned bits of hope in times of trouble and confusion. This was Roosevelt's only unalloyed success as president. It was a pervasive aspect of his administration, yet tied to no policies and no programs. It was the magic of a man, based as much on illusion as on reality. There was much to fear in 1933, as there is today. Only fools or gods believed otherwise.

. . . The New Deal, as a varied series of legislative acts and executive orders dealing either with the problems of depression or with problems created or aggravated by depression, lasted only five years. Most of the important legislation came in brief spurts in 1933, 1935, and, least important, in 1938. But the volume of important legislation so exceeded any earlier precedents, so overwhelmed the immediate capacity for full comprehension, that even today no one can more than begin to make sense out of the whole.

Most New Deal legislation was, in a broad sense, economic. The early legislation was directed at early economic recovery. Some of it, as well as much later legislation, dealt directly with the overall structure of our market system and with the relationship of the federal government to this system. After 1934 the most significant New Deal measures dealt more directly with the immediate economic needs of individuals, families, or exploited groups. These efforts failed to gain complete recovery but significantly modified the American economy. After the New Deal innovations, major producers enjoyed more security in their property, more certainty of profits, less vulnerability to economic cycles, and both more federal subsidies and more extensive federal regulation. Laborers had clearer rights to organize unions and gained new political leverage in the Democratic party. Finally, new welfare policies guaranteed at least a minimum of subsistence for many people excluded from, or unable to compete effectively for, the benefits of a corporate and highly centralized system of production.

By habit, historians often divide the New Deal into two parts. The identification of a second New Deal goes back to contemporary newspaper articles, which noted a policy shift in 1935 toward welfare legislation and a divisive class appeal. Some major changes did occur in 1935, but they overlay continuities in agricultural policy and in resource management. Also, the crucial Court-packing issue in 1937, and other Roosevelt efforts to attain a more directly responsive democracy, might even lend credence to a third New Deal. But all such categories have an arbitrary aspect and are justified only by their usefulness.

In 1932 Roosevelt asked for only one clear mandate—bold action. In what seemed a terribly dangerous and callous demagoguery to an exasperated Hoover, an unseasoned immaturity to commentators, Roosevelt refused to use his campaign to chart a coherent economic program, with all its demands and costs and promised rewards. In many cases he could not. On the central problem of recovery he was lost, although the outlines of the National Recovery Administration (NRA) and the Agricultural Adjustment Administration (AAA) were already forming. But even in areas where his commitments were firm, he preferred general to specific recommendations and refused to join Hoover in a serious dialogue either on the causes of the depression or on basic American ideals. He balanced suggestive speeches on forgotten men, concert of interests, planning of production and distribution, administered resources, and restored purchasing power with traditional pledges of a lower budget and complete fiscal integrity. Most of the time he simply berated the Hoover administration, condemned Republican mistakes, or promised to drive the evil money-changers from the temple. His concealed pack seemed to be full of aces, with something for almost everyone but the financiers. Even his devils were vague enough to be almost empty. At times every ambiguous label of the American political repertoire seemed to fit—left or right, liberal or conservative, socialist or capitalist, individualist or collectivist. His technique proved a political success. Even much of the vagueness, much of the ambiguity, was unavoidable. It was Roosevelt, an unbeatable Roosevelt, at work. But, of course, only some of the cards could be played. Many newly aroused hopes could never be fulfilled.

The overwhelming concern of almost everyone in 1933 was recovery, the most attractive but elusive god of the thirties. This was Roosevelt's clearest commitment. If he had quickly attained this goal much of the later New Deal, including the relief and welfare programs, would have seemed unnecessary. For this reason the NRA, with its permissive monopolies in each industry, its elaborate code system, and its fanfare and promotional excesses, was the most important agency established during the famous hundred-day legislative session of 1933. Complementing this was a complex agricultural act, which established the AAA and inaugurated several lasting programs looking toward both recovery and structural changes. These two efforts represented Roosevelt's earliest response to unprecedented economic maladies which he blamed on Hoover and the Republican party.

. . . The legislative climax of 1935 preceded the political climax of the New Deal in 1936. But again, as in 1932, Roosevelt won no mandate for specific new programs. Then, in the Court fight and the new depression, both in 1937, he lost much of his political leverage. By 1938 he was frustrated in his domestic policies and imprisoned by neutrality legislation in his early ventures into international diplomacy. After a desperate attempt at party realignment, he began buying congressional help in foreign policy at the expense of further domestic innovation. . . .

. . . The Court fight wasted a congressional session, helped destroy the Roosevelt myth of invincibility, disillusioned many of his former disciples, divided the Democratic party, gave the Republican party a new lease on life, and left Roosevelt bitter and hurt. As always, he became deeply involved in the battle and scarcely remembered wht was at issue. In his frustration he exhibited his worst and most militant character traits and thus further aided his opponents. But there was partial redemption for Roosevelt. Some of his most bitter enemies came out even worse. Their onslaught of cheap propaganda, including shabby tricks, outright lies, and fantastic charges, made Roosevelt look like a gentleman.

The Court fight was followed by a new economic collapse, by an increasingly hostile Congress, and by few significant legislative achievements. In the wake of this, Roosevelt renewed his battle for popular democracy. As a consistent postlude to the Supreme Court battle, he used the campaign of 1938 to attempt a minor but controversial rationalization of his own political party. Later, in an overture to Wendell Willkie, he would try to get a new party system, with what he called a progressive-conservative realignment. In the Court fight Roosevelt lost control of congressional Democrats. Just as effectively as the courts, large numbers dared oppose him and, as he saw it, the people who elected him. Roosevelt felt that a national mandate, won by a single party leader and on a party platform, should bind the party in Congress, both to himself and to the platform (he easily blurred the two). Thus he wanted to be prime minister and control a loyal legislative majority. He correctly believed this necessary for responsive democracy. In this case he battled not the written Constitution, with its strict separation of powers, but an unwritten one—the vast, entrenched apparatus of broad-interest, nonideological political parties, rooted in thousands of local machines, local power structures, and local economic interests. This loose, undisciplined party system, except in crisis, made complete party discipline impossible and invited all manner of shifting coalitions, often against the president and against popular majorities. . . .

The New Deal stopped growing. It did not disappear. A subsidized, regulated welfare capitalism still stands . . . as the core of American domestic policy. The United States has neither moved beyond it nor tried other alternatives, despite the varied and often confused protest movements of the sixties. At best, subsequent presidents have patched a few holes, repaired a few loose shingles, and added some new rooms to the welfare state. Thus the changes of the thirties were not only numerous but prophetic, setting the themes for subsequent political discourse. The welfare measures—social security, labor protection, housing—have all been expanded. None has been repudiated. Both conservation and advisory types of planning have remained as generally accepted ideals, however compromised in practice. Whatever the internal inequities, agriculture, our greatest economic success story, still functions under a subsidized price system and, when needed, production controls. Large business enterprise has learned to accept, if not to love, the protective and only mildly restrictive role of government in maintaining growth and high profits. Likewise, organized labor has shrugged off its earlier militancy and, like a happy but protected lamb, finally lain down beside the business lion.

The same continuity is evident at the political level. Whatever the limitations of Roosevelt, America's political parties have not discovered or created another political leader who could tear away, with the wisdom or the foolishness of a child, so many traditional articles of faith, and thus open up so many pregnant possibilities. Instead, many of his successors have turned fragile New Deal policies into new, binding articles of faith. None has been able to step into the inviting flux, the confused and discordant flux of New Deal policies, and provide what Roosevelt so often lacked—a mature comprehension of complexity, a scholar's ability to make clear and careful distinctions, and a teacher's ability to lift the level of popular understanding.

Within the one inescapable context of the thirties—the need for economic growth—the New Deal was a short-run failure, but it did initiate changes that led to long-run success. It began the final maturation of our economic system, and at least pointed toward the political economy most capable of maximizing production, consumption, profits, and jobs. We are as yet only beginning to exploit the full potential of government credit, incentives, and subsidies, even as we glimpse the sometimes disturbing promise of advertising, automation, and more careful political indoctrination, and even as we finally begin to appreciate some of the unanticipated social costs of unending economic growth.

To emphasize the eventual economic results of New Deal policies is not to evaluate the New Deal as a whole. Almost no one in the New Deal, almost no one in the thirties, even dared predict such long-term economic gains. But, superb irony, few New Dealers expected quite so little in other areas. The fervent New Deal bureaucrats dreamed of a much greater level of social justice, of a truer community, than the United States has as yet achieved. They, of course, wanted more production and more jobs, but they also wanted everyone to have a sense of meaningful involvement and worth. They wanted everyone to be able to consume more, but desired consumption not as a balm of meaninglessness but as a necessary adjunct of a sense of real achievement and fulfillment. They wanted industrial growth and even restored profits, not as ends but as corollaries of widespread opportunities for creative and socially beneficial enterprise.

As these more idealistic New Dealers grew older, they often became tragic figures, seemingly out of touch with things. They looked back in nostalgia to what they had dreamed, and what they had all shared, and what they had longed for. The prosperous but callous fifties seemed a mockery. They talked of how Roosevelt, had he lived, would at last have led them into the kingdom. Like lonely and unneeded soldiers, they cried aloud for their old commander and for the old crusade. If anything seemed clear to them, it was that their dreams and hopes had been betrayed. Instead of responding to the greater efficiency, the accelerating growth, even the new welfare measures of the sixties, they looked on sadly, as if the substance, the moral heart, had been removed from things.

For some of the most perceptive social critics of the thirties, for an Edmund Wilson or a John Dewey, the New Deal was not a promise betrayed; it was essentially misdirected from the beginning. It began and ended with conventional or oversimplified half-answers, answers which the more alienated, more sensitive, and more analytic intellectuals all too easily repudiated. But the more radical critics, despite the early hopes of someone like Tugwell, had no pathway to power. In fact, they can never attain power in a democracy unless conditions produce a passive resignation on the part of citizens, a willingness to relinquish responsibility to angry but largely incomprehensible prophets. In a working democracy the penetrating critic, like a lonely Jeremiah, must teach and often suffer. He cannot dictate. Neither can he win elections. His ringing voice must be heard from the lectern and pulpit. He will never master the soothing art of the fireside—and should not. He is too honest and too clearheaded.

For the historian, every judgment and every evaluation of the past has to be tinged with a pinch of compassion, a sense of the beauty and nobility present even in the frustration of honest hopes and humane ideals. He sees that, from almost any valuative perspective, the thirties could have brought so much more, but also so much worse, than the New Deal. No diverse political movement, responding to multiple pressures, can come close to matching the expectations of any sensitive social critic. The limiting political context has to be understood—the safeguards and impediments of our political system, Roosevelt's intellectual limitations, and most of all the economic ignorance and philosophic immaturity of the American electorate. The plausible alternatives to the New Deal are not easily suggested, particularly if one considers all the confining and limiting circumstances.

From almost any perspective, the New Deal solved a few problems, ameliorated others, obscured many, and created unanticipated new ones. This is about all our political system can generate, even in crisis. If the people knew better and chose better, if they shared similar goals, there would be few crises anyway. If they must know better to have better, then our conventional politics is no answer, except as a perennial interim accommodation with incompatible goals and with ignorance. Even this permits more thorough criticism its long day of persuasion and education.

Only with trepidation will the student of history try to judge the results of the New Deal. He will not do it with a sense of heartless criticism. Not only would it be unfair, but too much is involved. But judge he must, not to whip the past but to use it. For so much that originated or at least matured in the policies of the Roosevelt administration lives on in our present institutions. Thus his rightful criticism is directed at himself, his country, his institutions, his age. If so directed, his evaluation must be just, thorough, and honest; otherwise, he practices only self-deceit.

The Myth of the Good War

Richard Polenberg

War has been a major ingredient in the history of civilization. It has reinforced Americans' attitude toward war that for a long time we won them all (oh, we had to fudge a bit occasionally: for example, Mr. Madison's War of 1812). When finally we clearly lost one in Vietnam, it became therapeutically necessary to find scapegoats, send motion picture Rambos back to 'Nam selectively to fight, and also, under President Reagan, to balance the ledger by invading the Caribbean island of Granada (a Cuban labor brigade had better not mess with us there). Of all the nation's "just" wars, World War II, at least in recent historical memory, stands at the pinnacle. The enemy was clear, present, and evil—personified by Adolph Hitler, and we declared war only after we had been attacked. It was good, and we won decisively. All this excepting, of course, those who lost loved ones. Major historical subjects are ultimately targets for revisionists and that includes even the Good War. In this article, Richard Polenberg, Goldwyn Professor of American History at Cornell University, critically examines World War II by addressing government censorship in the motion picture industry while considering that medium's towering influence on the public mind, the acquiescence of liberals to wartime "imperatives," the furthering of those "imperatives" by many academic liberals, the subordination of organized labor's interests by its own leadership to government policies, the active reinforcement of gender stereotypes, and the governmental sanctioning of racism. Polenberg's work, along with that of Paul Fussell and other revisionists, is beginning to give the lie to the combat soldiers' phrase, "The real war will never get into the books." For Fussell, it was a "war and nothing else, and thus stupid and sadistic." In the end, perhaps the ultimate irony of the "Good War" was that in order to defeat fascism we became rather semi-fascist ourselves.

A recent cartoon in *The New Yorker* depicts a young man sitting on a barstool, looking slightly dazed, saying to the bartender, an older man, "I remember the Second World War. That's the one that kind of flickers on the screen, right?" As the years go by and the war recedes further into the past, as the number of Americans old enough to have any memory of the conflict dwindles, perceptions of it are indeed increasingly shaped by the motion pictures and newsreels of the era. Those flickering images, however, were carefully fashioned to present a certain view of the war. Simply put, that view held that World War II was "the good war."

This phrase served as the title of Studs Terkel's oral history of the war, which became a best-seller in 1984 and won a Pulitzer Prize. Terkel took the precaution of placing the words between quotation marks because he considered it "incongruous" to attach the adjective *good* to the noun *war*. Yet most Americans have not been much bothered by the incongruity; nor, until recently, have most scholars. One historian even labeled World War II the "perfect" war, although he, too, used quotation marks.

This concept of the war rests on six assertions, all well substantiated, about the nature and consequences of the conflict:

First, World War II was a just war. Even discounting the official view that the war was fought only for the right of people everywhere to live in freedom and security, it is nevertheless true that the United States was fighting a defensive war, was not motivated by a desire for conquest, and was combating fascism, an evil and expansionist system.

Second, the war was fought by a largely united people, whose shared purpose not only led them to make sacrifices for the common good but also enabled them to transcend ethnic divisions and religious differences. Americans engaged in many forms of cooperative endeavor, such as community service, civil defense, volunteer work, war bond campaigns, and scrap and salvage drives.

Third, the war brought prosperity to a nation still bogged down in depression. Manufacturing output doubled, and there were jobs for all. The war meant good pay—workers' weekly earnings increased by some 70 percent—and a somewhat more equitable distribution of a much larger national income. Membership in trade unions climbed from 10.5 to 14.75 million, and labor began to flex its political muscle. The GI Bill of Rights provided millions of veterans with generous college tuition benefits, allowances to assist in readjusting to civilian life, and federally guaranteed low-cost mortgage loans.

Fourth, the war benefited African-Americans. Fought against Nazi doctrines of Aryan supremacy, the war advanced the civil rights movement by discrediting the racist assumptions on which segregation depended. Defense industries lowered barriers to hiring blacks, who made up more than 8 percent of war workers in 1945, up from 3 percent in 1942. During the war, too, a Committee on Fair Employment Practices attempted, however haltingly, to end job discrimination by federal contractors.

Fifth, the war provided women with unprecedented opportunities in the war industries, in civil service, and in the military. Six million women joined the labor force between 1940 and 1945, and the percentage of women holding jobs rose from 28 to 37. Public opinion polls revealed a startling decline, from 80 to 13 percent, in the number of people who thought married women should not work outside the home, a decline to be expected at a time when three of every four new women workers were married.

A final reason why the war seemed to be "good" had less to do with what happened than with what did not happen. The war did not lead to the harsh curtailment of civil liberties that many had feared. Freedom of speech, press, and assembly were widely protected; there were few prosecutions for sedition; there was no public hysteria or mob violence; and critics of the war were, in general, treated leniently.

One of the people interviewed by Studs Terkel succinctly summed up many of these themes. "The war was fun for America," a retired Red Cross volunteer recalled, adding that for Americans who did not lose a loved one in combat—and most did not—"the war was a hell of a good time." That retrospective comment accurately captured the wartime outlook. Early in 1945, when pollsters asked whether the war had required people to make "any real sacrifices," 64 percent of those surveyed replied, "No."

For many years historians have recognized that this rosy interpretation of World War II is flawed. Even the good war had its manifestly less appealing sides: military and foreign policy decisions based on expediency rather than morality, the persistence of anti-Semitism and ethnic discord, the continuing disparity between the conditions of the working poor and the corporate rich, the stubborn resistance to gains by blacks, the rapid erosion of women's wartime gains after 1945, and such indefensible restrictions on civil liberties as the relocation and incarceration of 110,000 west coast Japanese, two-thirds of them American citizens. By the 1960s and 1970s, scholars routinely noted these defects and offered a more critical assessment of the war. Until recently, however, historians usually accepted the terms in which the argument was originally posed. When the balance sheet was added up, World War II still seemed to have been "the good war."

Only in the last ten years has a body of literature appeared that altered the terms of the discussion and placed the war in a different light. World War II, recent work has suggested, led to a pervasive conformity, in behavior as well as belief, fostered and sometimes imposed by the government, but for the most part eagerly embraced by Americans. The conformity was not something that civil libertarians, or intellectuals, or reformers challenged, but rather something they endorsed. The result was to narrow the scope of individual freedom and to reinforce illiberal tendencies in virtually all areas of life, but especially in class, gender, and race relations.

The war, in this view, bore out Alexis de Tocqueville's warning, sounded more than a century and a half ago, regarding the dangers that any lengthy war posed to democracy. Tocqueville had visited the United States in 1831, ostensibly to study the American prison system and to write a report on it for the French government, but with a more ambitious project in mind: to analyze the very nature of democratic institutions. The two volumes of *Democracy in America*, published in 1835 and 1840, touched on many topics—politics and law, race and religion, literature and the arts, manners and mores, relations between the sexes, and the "tyranny of the majority." Significantly, Tocqueville also presented "some considerations on war in democratic communities."

Tocqueville was of two minds about the subject. On the one hand, he said, war was beneficial, because it "almost always enlarges the mind of a people and raises their character." Although he was not specific, he seemed to think that war could encourage people to make sacrifices for the public good and could serve as a corrective to "the mediocrity of tastes." Yet Tocqueville also believed that a protracted war would "endanger the freedom of a democratic country"—would, indeed, be "the surest and shortest" way to destroy liberty. "War does not always give over democratic communities to military government," he wrote, "but it must invariably and immeasurably increase the powers of civil government, it must almost compulsorily concentrate the direction of all men and the management of all things in the hands of the administration. If it does not lead by despotism by sudden violence, it prepares men for it more gently by their habits."

When Tocqueville spoke of despotism, he had something quite specific in mind: an all-embracing conformity of thought and feeling, deriving not from laws but from public opinion, enforced not by the police but by the desire to be accepted by everyone else. Even in peacetime, the majority did not need laws "to coerce those who do not think like themselves; public disapprobation is enough." Wartime, however, exacerbated the situation. Democratic despotism, Tocqueville thought, not only affected public life but also, and more insidiously, "penetrates from all sides into private life." Under the tyranny of the majority, the "body is left free, and the soul is enslaved." Freedom's forms were maintained, but not its substance. The process by which people came to accept prevailing values would be aided by newspapers, which "can drop the same thought into a thousand minds at the same moment."

Democracy in America was translated into English shortly after its publication, and a revised translation appeared in 1862. The first modern translation, however, was not made until 1944. The editor, Phillips Bradley, asserted that the work "speaks to our condition, while we are in the midst of war . . . as freshly as when it was written." Yet Bradley, in a lengthy historical essay, breezily dismissed Tocqueville's warnings about war. He emphasized, instead, that the United States, guided by strong presidential leadership, was coping marvelously well with wartime problems. Tocqueville had simply not foreseen "the ability of a democratic people to stick together and to fight." Completed in the summer of 1944 and published in April 1945, Bradley's essay reflected the widespread assumption that World War II did not threaten democratic values.

That view, which once governed most historians' accounts of the war and still dominates the public's perception, is no longer viable. To explain why it is not, this essay will show, first, how the government imposed effective censorship on the motion picture industry; second, how liberals acquiesced in the suppression of freedom; third, how some academics betrayed their professional responsibilities to aid the war effort; fourth, how labor organizations subordinated the interests of their members in order to back the government, and how business sometimes took advantage of the war emergency to control workers; fifth, how the war reinforced gender stereotypes, especially the notion that women belonged at home, and promoted new restrictions on the rights of homosexuals; and sixth, how the war sanctioned racist beliefs and racist practices. This essay will conclude with comments on Paul Fussell's 1989 volume, *Wartime: Understanding and Behavior in the Second World War*, which reflects the newly emerging historical consensus.

* * *

When Tocqueville feared that the same thought could be dropped into a thousand minds at the same moment, he had no way of knowing that, a century later, the same thought could be dropped into eleven million minds at more or less the same moment. That was the seating capacity of American movie theaters, and during the war the Office of War Information's Bureau of Motion Pictures assumed responsibility for making sure that moviegoers left those theaters only with government-approved thoughts in their minds. In *Hollywood Goes to War*, Clayton R. Koppes and Gregory D. Black assert that the OWI's supervision of Hollywood filmmaking was "the most comprehensive and sustained government attempt to change the content of a mass medium in American history." Another scholar adds that the level of supervision illustrated "the pervasive and unprecedented power of the state in the private sector."

Lacking statutory authority to censor motion pictures, the government accomplished its objective through a combination of broad hints, appeals to patriotism and profits, and implied threats. The OWI told filmmakers to ask themselves, in each case, a deceptively simple question: "Will this picture help win the war?" Would it help, that is, by "contribut[ing] something new to our understanding of the world conflict," or would it hurt "by creating a false picture of America, her allies, or the world we live in"? In November 1942 Lowell Mellett, the head of the Bureau of Motion Pictures, warned Hollywood executives that they must eliminate "carelessness and false conceptions" that might leave audiences with the mistaken impression that victory would come easily thus doing "a very great disservice to the country." A month later, Mellett suggested to the studios that "it would be advisable" to submit finished scripts at a stage when changes could be made easily. The OWI's most effective threat, however, was that films falling short of expectations would be denied export licenses, thereby cutting into their margin of profitability. As an OWI memo noted, "[i]t would hurt like hell" to deny studios such a license.

Faced with these strictures, Koppes and Black conclude "Hollywood became a compliant part of the American war machine." In all, the Bureau of Motion Pictures reviewed 1,652 movie scripts. It often suggested alterations in dialogue and occasionally persuaded studios not to make a particular film. The OWI wanted movies to extol the virtues of the American way of life and to portray the Allies as models of righteousness and the Axis as embodiments of evil. The kinds of films that the government wanted the studios to make seemed to be the kind the public wanted and, eventually, came to expect. The government never threatened to prosecute a studio for making an unwanted film. On the contrary, the studios were so anxious to please that, in describing its new release *Joe Smith, American* to the OWI, a Metro-Goldwyn-Mayer official pointed out that it was exactly the kind of film "which the Administration would wish to make." Little wonder that an OWI official could boast in 1942 that "the effect of our efforts . . . becomes more apparent every day."

The OWI's concerns, method of operation, and success were illustrated in the changes made in another MGM film, *An American Romance*. In its original version, this movie depicted an immigrant, Steve Dangos, who became a successful automobile magnate and who gave up a comfortable retirement to help build airplanes to win the war. The script, however, sang the praises of individual entrepreneurship and seemed downright hostile to labor unions. As the OWI put it, the screenplay expressed "the Ford philosophy" and "the classic but discredited" Horatio Alger myth. Officials convinced the studio to make revisions to emphasize labor-management cooperation. The final version, therefore, "invoked the liberal vision of a harmony of interests in society." The OWI was, presumably, delighted that the Dangos family had four sons named George Washington Dangos, Thomas Jefferson Dangos, Abraham Lincoln Dangos, and Theodore Roosevelt Dangos, the equivalent, Koppes and Black observe, of "a living Mount Rushmore."

Similarly, the OWI had a hand in shaping the conventions of the combat film, a wartime genre epitomized by *Bataan*. Released in April 1943, the film focused on thirteen soldiers who bravely resisted the Japanese assault on the Philippine peninsula. To show America's diversity and unity, its righteousness and resolve, the men in the battalion represented a cross section of racial, religious, and geographical backgrounds. All thirteen were eventually killed, but their sacrifice, the film asserted, brought valuable time—"ninety-six priceless days"—for American forces and "made possible our victories in the Coral Sea, at Midway, on New Guinea and Guadalcanal. Their spirit will lead us back to Bataan." On reading the screenplay, the OWI was delighted to find that "superior officers are willing to take suggestions from men under them. . . . Thus the army reflects the democratic way of life—which is one way of demonstrating the difference between our ideology and the Fascist doctrine." The agency successfully urged the studio to play up the prominence of two Filipino soldiers and applauded the inclusion of a black private, although, of course, combat units were not then integrated.

Most of the officials in the Bureau of Motion

Pictures were liberals, and the message they wanted films to convey was a liberal one, that "this is a people's army, fighting a people's war." The last thing the OWI wanted were films that depicted internal disunity or intractable social problems. Accordingly, the agency approved films that "upheld the legitimacy and justice of American politics and society." When presented with a screenplay about life in a squalid, poverty-ridden factory town, the OWI balked. The agency wanted the script changed to demonstrate that problems could be solved through the democratic process, because this scenario would enhance "the glorious story that we have to tell about our country." Such a transformation was beyond even Hollywood's vaunted creative powers, and the studio finally shelved the picture. Koppes and Black conclude that perceptions of wartime needs "alter[ed] the liberal ethos from identification with the working class to support for the needs of the state."

This support for the needs of the state also shaped the attitudes of many liberals toward freedom of speech. They had no difficulty accepting the OWI's censorship of films because, as one Department of Justice official put it, "[t]he question of free speech . . . in the entertainment world is not particularly valid." Sadly enough, the question seemed no more legitimate in other areas, either. Writing in the *Columbia Law Review* in 1942, David Riesman, who had recently clerked for Supreme Court justice Louis D. Brandeis, justified liberal support for the new wartime restrictiveness. In a wide-ranging defense of the use of group libel laws to prosecute antidemocratic forces, Riesman explained the need to "reexamine the liberal pre-conceptions, and discard them where they may be invalid." Those liberal preconceptions held that the chief danger to freedom came from a powerful state, when in fact during the war emergency it came from " 'private' fascist groups." Fortunately, he concluded "the Constitution is not a final bar" to such a reexamination, not when "it has become necessary to consider the possibility of repression."

In February 1942, when President Franklin D. Roosevelt issued the executive order banning all Japanese Americans from the west coast, prominent civil libertarians, including most members of the American Civil Liberties Union executive board, failed to condemn the step. Faced with a choice between two resolutions, one calling for legal challenges to relocation orders not based on "immediate military necessity" and the other supporting evacuation if it had "a reasonable relationship to the danger intended to be met," the ACLU opted for the latter by a margin of two to one, thereby producing what one scholar has called "a clear victory for those who would subordinate civil liberties to wartime considerations and political loyalties." Those who took a principled stand on the issue were in a distinct minority. The majority view was closer to that expressed by Alexander Meikeljohn: "For us to say that they are taking away civil rights, would have as much sense as protesting because a 'measles' house is isolated. The Japanese citizens, as a group, are dangerous both to themselves and to their fellow-citizens."

Leaders of the ACLU, such as Meikeljohn and Roger Baldwin, felt at one, socially and politically, with the government officials in charge of relocation, such as War Relocation Authority director Dillon S. Myer and Assistant Secretary of War John J. McCloy. Baldwin "regularly met with top administration officials" and then returned to New York City to give the ACLU board of directors confidential briefings and to report that officials "are about as much troubled as we ourselves." He wrote to General John L. DeWitt, who, as head of the Western Defense Command, supervised the process of putting 80,000 American citizens in concentration camps, to congratulate him on carrying out evacuation "with a minimum of hardship" and with "comparatively few complaints of injustice and mismanagement." Dillon S. Myer, according to his biographer, Richard Drinnon, maintained an "extraordinary alliance with leading civil libertarians." Calling Baldwin and Meikeljohn into his office on one occasion, Myer "indicated that we needed their sympathetic understanding in the whole process. We have always been very cordial in our relations with the Civil Liberties group, and both men showed a fine understanding."

Liberals showed a similar understanding when the government decided to prosecute a group of pro-fascist extremists. In July 1942, urged on by President Roosevelt, Attorney General Francis Biddle moved to indict twenty-eight "native fascists" for violating the 1917 Espionage Act. Their attacks on government policy, the Department of Justice maintained, amounted to a conspiracy to cause insubordination in the armed forces. Later, at their trial, the prosecutor asserted that the defendants had attempted "to destroy the faith of all of us and have our soldiers not believe in our leaders, in order that we remain weak." An unsavory lot, to be sure, the defendants represented no danger to the United States and surely were not in cahoots with one another. Yet liberals in the Department of Justice favored the prosecution, in part to project an image of toughness. One of Biddle's assistants, James H. Rowe, Jr., informed his chief that the public had begun to regard them as "civil liberties boys" and "softies." "We had better get moving fast," Rowe said, in order to "jack up our public relations." The ACLU refused to aid the defendants. The group decided that, unless due process issues were involved, it would not participate "in cases where, after investigation, there are grounds for a belief that the defendant is cooperating with or acting on behalf of the enemy, even though the particular charge . . . might otherwise be appropriate for intervention." The case dragged on through much of 1944 but ended in a mistrial when the judge died late in the year.

Just as Roosevelt had pushed for action against fascist sympathizers, so he urged Biddle to talk to black newspaper editors "to see what could be done about preventing their subversive language." The language to which the president objected contained harsh condemnations of racial injustice. This type of criticism was an intrinsic element in the Double V campaign—victory over segregation at home as well as over fascism abroad—that African-American newspapers endorsed early in 1942. In this instance, liberals within the federal government, notably Biddle, proved instrumental in blocking any attempt to indict black newspapers for treason. The government, however, accomplished its purpose more subtly by the use of pleas, veiled threats, and hints that a failure to tone down criticism might result in the withholding of newsprint from the offending papers or even in criminal indictments. It became routine practice for FBI agents to visit black editors to complain about reporters who, for example, wrote about discrimination against black soldiers in the South. Unnerved by such visits, the black press retreated and became "subtly less outspoken" as the war progressed. From April to August 1942, the space devoted to the Double V campaign declined by half, and the movement was virtually dead a few months later.

One instance illustrated the larger pattern. In January 1943 a black soldier was court-martialed, convicted of sedition, and given a twenty-year sen-

tence. At his trial, he maintained that he was influenced by articles in two black papers, the *Baltimore Afro-American* and the *Pittsburgh Courier*. Rather than publicize his statement, military officials arranged a meeting with the executive editor of the *Courier* and reported what the convicted soldier had said. The next day, the newspaper's president, Ira F. Lewis, wrote to thank the army for its "liberal attitude" in not releasing the testimony. Lewis added further assurances that his paper stood squarely behind the government, noting proudly that every employee had purchased war bonds. He realized, he said, parroting the official military line, that "the War Department cannot become a laboratory for an analysis of social ills."

The liberals' acceptance of restrictions on freedom, no less than government control of Hollywood films, illustrates, as Stephen Fox has written in another context, that "it is possible for a nation like the United States . . . to come near to losing its soul in a time of crisis, even during a 'good war.'" Fox was alluding to "the unknown internment," for several months in 1942, of a sizable number of German and Italian aliens on the west coast, but his comment can also be applied to scholars who were sometimes willing to sacrifice their professional standards in order to serve the government. Historians, economists, and political scientists worked for the Research and Analysis Division of the Office of Strategic Services, while anthropologists and sociologists cooperated with the War Relocation Authority. The experience of these scholars was, in at least one crucial respect, similar to that of scientists who worked on the atomic bomb.

One of the physicists who played an important part in the Manhattan Project recalled that many of his colleagues had set aside their moral qualms about working at Los Alamos because of "an absolutely Faustian fascination about whether the bomb would really work." The scientists could not resist, any more than Marlowe's Doctor Faustus could, the opportunity to discover forbidden knowledge and the chance to experience "a world of profit and delight[,] of power, of honor, of omnipotence." After the bombs had devastated Hiroshima and Nagasaki, J. Robert Oppenheimer, who headed the Manhattan Project, allegedly said that "the physicists have known sin." As Oppenheimer's friend, Freeman Dyson, has pointed out, however, if the physicists had known sin, it was not because they had built the atomic bomb: "[T]hey did not just build the bomb. They enjoyed building it. They had the best time of their lives while building it." The scientists would always recall Los Alamos as "an ideal republic" and the years they spent there, in the words of Hans Bethe, as "really the great time of their lives."

Like the physicists, the scholars who were recruited by the OSS experienced an exhilarating sense of engagement. They remembered the OSS as fondly as the scientists remembered Los Alamos. As one recalled, "OSS was the most wonderful place to be young! We young ones had everything—belief, enthusiasm, opportunity, victory: Life rushed on in excitement and in confidence that we were a special group of colleagues with an important mission for our country." In the words of another participant, Walt W. Rostow, "[t]he fact that this intellectual process related directly to violent acts of war gave to it, at the time, extraordinary point and vitality." Unlike many physicists, who would eventually have second thoughts about the making of the atomic bomb, social scientists were more likely to have only the warmest memories of "this almost legendary experience." One historian, too young to have participated, lamented that there was "no 'moral equivalent' to the OSS in peacetime."

McGeorge Bundy once commented that the OSS was "a remarkable institution half cops-and-robbers and half faculty meeting." Many professors of history, economics, political science, and literature worked for the Research and Analysis Division, headed by William L. Langer, a Harvard University historian. For the most part, these scholars simply analyzed political and economic trends in various countries and submitted reports, sometimes of great value, to military and civilian authorities. A scholar who reached a conclusion at variance with policies favored by those in charge might be admonished by Langer that "your responsibility is primarily to me" and that it was presumptuous "to stake your judgment against ours." Such conflicts were rare, however, and most scholars in the OSS could reconcile military assignments with professional standards quite comfortably.

The same cannot be said for such undertakings as the Yale Library Project, described so well in Robin W. Winks's *Cloak and Gown.* By 1943 Joseph Toy Curtiss, a member of the Yale English department, had taken up residence in Istanbul, ostensibly to acquire books for the Yale University library, but actually to serve as a cover for an OSS mission in Turkey. To be sure, Curtiss collected books, but he also secretly collected all the information he could for the OSS. In order to conceal the OSS connection from prying eyes, Yale had to keep two sets of payroll accounts. Winks notes that a critic of such clandestine work could say that the library project proved the OSS was "willing to use anyone, to lie, to compromise the integrity of the academic community in order to achieve its ends." Yet even if Yale faculty and administrators had known the library was being used as a cover, Winks adds, "few would have objected, for hostility toward the intelligence agencies was neither great, nor as yet had it been earned."

The OSS did more than use a library as an operational cover. It also contracted out projects to Stanford, Berkeley, Columbia, Princeton, Yale, and other colleges. As Winks says: "No one at the universities appears to have protested these ties, and university presidents and professors courted contracts and consultantships." Not only was the boundary between scholarship and intelligence crossed, but ingenious arguments to rationalize the crossing were also devised. A Committee on Relations between Government Intelligence and Research Work and the American Universities, appointed by Langer, reasoned that because faculty members traveled all over the world and spoke many languages, they could easily serve the purposes of intelligence agencies. Subsidizing scholars' research, in this view, was simply a cost-efficient way for intelligence agencies to obtain valuable information. "There is nothing at all discreditable or dishonorable in the projected activities," the committee concluded. Scholars who "collect intelligence in the course of their legitimate research in a foreign country are in no sense engaged in activities detrimental to that country. . . . Such intelligence work can be done by American academic persons with a completely clear conscience."

Not all scholars had to travel to faraway places to participate in the war effort; anthropologists and sociologists found opportunities closer to home. The War Relocation Authority hired more than twenty anthropologists, including John Provinse, who served as chief of community management, Robert Redfield, and John Embree. One of the anthropologists' chief tasks was to help control the behavior of Japanese Americans in the relocation centers. To this end, they studied the camps as if they were examining any other "developing communities"—as if, that is, the camps were appropriate subjects of ethnographic investigation. Their goal was to discover the sources of unrest that had led to strikes, labor stoppages, and riots and to recommend ways of reducing such conflicts and restoring order.

The anthropologists treated acts of resistance by internees, by definition, as evidence of maladjustment, as dysfunctional or pathological behavior. Having useful skills to put "at the disposal of [administrative] authority," these scientists served as agents of social control by seeking to dampen unrest, never conceding that such disturbances might be a rational response to poor conditions or to the injustice inherent in confinement. With the best of intentions—these scholars, after all, wanted to combat racism—they became part of an administrative apparatus that enforced a racist executive order and thereby helped legitimize it.

The anthropologists' ready acceptance of "notions of social control with repressive implications" was illustrated by their willingness to employ a -government-approved vocabulary. According to one WRA directive, Japanese Americans "should always be referred to as 'evacuees,' never as 'internees' or 'prisoners' "; the work areas "should be referred to as 'relocation centers' or 'relocation projects,' not as 'internment centers' or 'concentration camps.' " Similarly, Japanese Americans were subjected only to "registration," not urged to sign "loyalty oaths." As Peter T. Suzuki has argued, the anthropologists assimilated "the categories of thought and the perspectives of the bureaucracy" and took seriously such concepts as "community government," which were, in truth, little more than figments of the WRA's imagination. "Instead of confronting power with truth," another critic has concluded, "anthropology was to supply information to power."

The subject of power—economic power—offers yet another avenue for exploring the implications of the war for American society. If some scholars and scientists had made a Faustian bargain during the war, so, too, did leaders of organized labor. By backing government policies designed to maximize war production and curb strikes, CIO and AFL officials gained real benefits for their members, solidified their authority, and extended their influence. Yet they also paid a price for obtaining this "Rooseveltian seal of patriotic orthodoxy," a price nearly as heavy, in its own way, as that exacted of Doctor Faustus. During the war, according to one historian, the CIO

moved into a "filial-dependent relationship with the government."

In December 1941, shortly after the United States entered the war, representatives of labor and management had agreed on a no-strike, no-lockout pledge. By 1943, however, many workers, dissatisfied with wages and job conditions, pressed for a more militant policy. They called for revoking the pledge (which was not, in any event, legally binding) and often resorted to wildcat strikes. Union leaders, on the other hand, nearly always advised caution and adherence to the agreement. "Let our slogan be WORK, WORK, WORK, PRODUCE, PRODUCE, PRODUCE," said CIO official Philip Murray in 1942, and other leaders reiterated that motto even when members had legitimate grievances. In March 1944, for example, when automobile workers at Henry Ford's River Rouge plant discovered that management was planning to provoke a strike, they caused a violent disruption at the factory's labor-relations office. In retaliation, Ford dismissed twenty workers, some of whom had not even taken part in the disturbance but were union activists. United Automobile Workers' representative R. J. Thomas nevertheless backed the company's decision. "Public opinion has become inflamed against our union," he said. "There can be no such thing today as a legitimate picket line. Any person who sets up picket lines is acting like an anarchist, not like a disciplined union man."

Labor willingly accepted a system of economic regulation that placed decision-making authority in the hands of business leaders. True enough, union officials were consulted on most matters, and they even held positions in such agencies as the War Manpower Commission and the National War Labor Board. Yet business executives, not labor leaders, had the expertise the government wanted. As a result, "virtually all major decision makers in war production were drawn from the business community," while "organized labor had little say as to the administration of war production." The consequences were predictable. Tax laws "were rewritten and administered to facilitate profit making," military orders were channeled to the nation's largest corporations (with the leading 100 firms receiving 70 percent of war contracts), and, in general, "the relevant capitalists got most of the concessions on profits and taxes that they desired."

The war enabled employers, in a few specialized cases, to impose brutally coercive controls on powerless employees. To ensure an adequate supply of agricultural labor in the South and Southwest, the government created an emergency farm labor program. In the Arkansas and Mississippi deltas, cotton planters used the program "to secure a large pool of cheap and unskilled labor to harvest their crops." Planters not only dominated the local committees that decided whether farm workers would be permitted to leave the area but also sat on draft boards that sometimes "refused to defer those who would not work on their terms."

In Hawaii, where martial law had been declared and remained in force until October 1944, the army controlled wages, working conditions, and the allocation of labor to plantations. By criminalizing job switching, and even absenteeism, the army won the approval of local business groups. Speaking for the Honolulu Chamber of Commerce, one official said his membership "was not interested in the courts or the rights of civilians, but was only interested in the obtaining of priorities and the freezing of labor." Sometimes the army even permitted plantation managers to preside at the courts-martial of their own employees and to exercise "an insidious form of labor control." A Department of Labor representative in Hawaii reported that workers, threatened with jail or the draft if they did not follow orders, had become "virtual 'slaves' of private individuals."

During the war, the labor movement retreated from the class politics that had marked the 1930s and moved toward what Nelson Lichtenstein has termed "consensual politics and social homogeneity." The wartime outlook, popularized by the government and endorsed by the unions, held that any form of internal discord threatened national unity. That was as true for class conflict as for racial, religious, or ethnic conflict. Derogatory remarks about Catholics or blacks sabotaged wartime unity, in this view, but so did such assertions as "Capital is profiteering." Gary Gerstle's study of textile workers in Woonsocket, Rhode Island, maintains that confrontation between workers and employers came to be seen as dangerously divisive. The union forsook its militant rhetoric, which accepted class antagonism as a fact, and emphasized instead what labor and capital had in common.

"In the case of the World War II mobilization," a recent study concludes, "the expansion of the state's power simultaneously reinforced the dominant so-

cial classes in industry and agriculture." That seems an accurate assessment of the war's effect on class relations. More surprisingly, the war acted as a conservative force in the area of gender relations. Even though millions of women entered the work force, many in jobs that had traditionally been reserved for men, and even though the public came to accept the idea of women, especially wives and mothers, working outside the home, the consensus among historians is that the war thwarted any potential for a significant alteration in gender roles.

The war usually reinforced sex segregation in the workplace. Studies of the automobile and electrical equipment industries show that men and women invariably did different kinds of work. As one writer concludes, "Rosie the Riveter did a 'man's job,' but more often than not she worked in a predominantly female department or job classification." Work assignments on the Pennsylvania Railroad exhibited a similar pattern. The number of female employees rose during the war from 2,400 to nearly 24,000, but women overwhelmingly filled traditional female jobs as clerks, stenographers, and switchboard operators. Management and the railroad brotherhoods outdid one another in their patronizing approach to women, who were denied seniority and paid less than men. "Even during the wartime emergency," Michael Nash has noted "it was almost impossible for working women to break the traditional barriers of labor market segregation." In the shipyards, too, "the basic distribution between men's work and women's work was not altered. To a great extent, women and men in the shipyards were doing different types of jobs. Women filled in where men were unavailable or unwilling to work."

Women who entered the work force were supposed to be motivated by "feminine" ambitions—the desire to help win the war so their men could return quickly and their children could grow up in a safe world. It was acceptable for women to take jobs for reasons of patriotism, altruism, and self-sacrifice, but not merely because they enjoyed working or needed the money. A war job was a vehicle through which a woman shouldered her civic and moral duties. Any suggestion of individualistic or self-interested motives was disapproved. These attitudes inevitably prepared the ground for the mass layoff of women once the war was over. As one shipyard union newspaper put it, "The Kitchen—Women's Big Post-War Goal." Although women were expected to take on new responsibilities, they were also supposed to pre-serve their identities as wives, mothers, and home-makers. Susan M. Hartmann therefore concludes: "Along with its potential for refashioning sex roles, World War II also contained powerful forces which put checks upon women's aspirations and options."

Those forces were patently revealed in stories appearing in popular magazines during the war. Inspired by the Office of War Information's Maga-zine Bureau, short-story writers invented plots de-signed to encourage women to take war jobs but, at the same time, to see their own needs as subordinate to those of their husbands, children, and communi-ties. A typical story in the *Saturday Evening Post*, "The Winning of Wentworth Jones, Jr.," involved a young woman, Lois Neeley, with romantic designs on a Princeton graduate who worked in the town's bank. Unable to gain Jones's attention, much less his af-fection, Neeley enlisted in the WACs, performed bravely overseas, and became a local celebrity. Natu-rally, Jones noticed her, fell in love with her, and proposed marriage. The ultimate reward for any woman, in this view, was male approval. Maureen Honey, who has studied this brand of popular fic-tion, describes it as a "reactionary aspect of home-front propaganda."

The war saw the introduction in many places of "social protection" programs. Ostensibly designed to stop the spread of venereal disease, they also regulated "promiscuous" or "deviant" behavior. In other words, they restricted women's sexual and even social freedom. The Social Protection Division of the Office of Community War Services urged that all women arrested or held for investigation on mor-als charges be detained for mandatory testing for syphilis and gonorrhea. In 1944 the Seattle police arrested more than 2,000 women, all of whom were required to spend four or five days in the county jail awaiting the results of medical tests, though the great majority were not infected. A woman might be charged with prostitution if she had sexual relations with a man who was not her husband, even if no money changed hands. Some communities modified their disorderly conduct and vagrancy laws to per-mit the arrest of women whose behavior was deemed inappropriate, who patronized bars without male escorts, for example, or who registered at hotels un-der aliases.

Allan Bérubé's *Coming Out Under Fire*, a study of gay men and women, shows that, in the armed forces

at least, wartime pressures strengthened sexual stereotypes and led to a more repressive environ-ment. Before the war, the army did not seek to de-termine the sexual orientation of recruits. Acts of sodomy, however, were considered criminal and if discovered could lead to a court-martial and a result-ing prison sentence. During the war, however, the policy changed drastically. Psychiatrists introduced the concept of the homosexual as a personality type unfit for military service and combat—as, in fact, mentally ill. Experts devised procedures to screen out men with "feminine bodily characteristics" or who betrayed an "effeminacy in dress and manner" and to disqualify them. This supposedly more hu-mane approach sought to avoid formal trials and imprisonment; instead, homosexuals were commit-ted to hospital psychiatric wards and, eventually, discharged as psychopathic undesirables. From 1941 to 1945, more than four thousand sailors and five thousand soldiers were so treated. The result, Bérubé reports, was "the widening of the net in which gay men and lesbians could be caught, vastly expanding the military's antihomosexual apparatus and creat-ing new forms of surveillance and punishment."

The current of wartime repression, so treacher-ous in class and gender relations, also exerted a pow-erful pull in the area of race. Even while Americans condemned the Nazis' racial doctrines, they accepted odious stereotypes of the Japanese. Far from discred-iting racism, one scholar has argued, the war merely made it "more subtle and complex." John W. Dower's splendid book, *War Without Mercy*, demon-strates that race hatred, pure and unadulterated, shaped the behavior of the United States and Japan alike. The Japanese emphasized their own racial and cultural superiority and regarded Americans as "the demonic other"—immoral, decadent, and bar-barous. For their part, Americans saw Japanese as subhuman and inherently inferior—primitive, child-ish, and mad. The consequences of racial thinking on both sides, Dower says, were "virtually identical—being hierarchy, arrogance, viciousness, atrocity, and death."

The wartime image of the Japanese was, most commonly, the image of an animal, a reptile, or an insect; they were depicted as monkeys, baboons, go-rillas, dogs, rats, rattlesnakes, cockroaches, and ver-min. It was often said that they hissed, like snakes. In motion pictures, Japanese were called "monkeypeo-ple" and "ringtails" and "slant-eyed rat[s]." In *China*

(1943), an American soldier kills three Japanese soldiers who have raped a Chinese woman and terms them "flies in a manure heap." In *Flying Tigers* (1944), an American soldier says, "I hear those Japs glow in the night like bugs." Films, of course, still had to meet the standards of the Hollywood Production Code, which banned profane and blasphemous language. Consequently, scripts were not approved in which American gunners exclaimed "hell" or "dam 'em" as they shot down Japanese fliers, but it was perfectly acceptable for GIs to shout "stinkin' Nips" or "fried Jap going down!"

When the government decided to relocate Japanese Americans, Dower points out, "[t]hey were not merely driven from their homes and communities on the West Coast and rounded up like cattle, but actually forced to live in facilities meant for animals for weeks and even months before being moved to their final quarters." Confined in stockyards, racetracks, and cattle stalls at fairgrounds, some were even housed for a time in converted pigpens. When they finally got to the concentration camps, they might find that state medical authorities tried to prevent them from receiving medical care, or, as in Arkansas, refused to permit doctors to issue state birth certificates to children born in the camps, as if to deny the infants' legal existence, not to mention their humanity. Later, when the time came to begin releasing them from the camps, racist attitudes often blocked their resettlement. Even so staunch a supporter of minority rights as New York City mayor Fiorello H. La Guardia exhibited a virulent racism and xenophobia when it came to Japanese Americans. He not only defended relocation, but in 1944 he also opposed allowing any of the internees to settle in New York City. He called on Washington to prevent "these alien enemies" from moving about freely. Throughout the war, La Guardia referred to the Japanese as "deceitful Jap monkeys."

Racist doctrines often impute mystical qualities to blood, qualities that, in turn, are linked to concepts of "purity" and "contamination." The pervasiveness of racism during the war, the casual manner in which it was accepted, helps explain the tenacity with which the Red Cross and the armed forces adhered to their policies of segregating the blood plasma of black and white donors. Few official practices seemed better calculated to offend African-Americans, who pointed out that the policy "coincides with the Nazi philosophy of superior blood." Despite the

bitter complaints of William C. Hastie, dean of Howard University Law School, who served as a civilian aide to Secretary of War Henry L. Stimson, the armed forces refused to rescind the policy. Frustrated in this skirmish, as in his general campaign against segregation in the army, Hastie resigned in disgust early in 1943. Not until December 1950 did the armed forces collect blood plasma without regard to race.

Hastie's departure demonstrated that a war in which racial thinking was so prominent was not likely to further the cause of civil rights. True, blacks chalked up significant gains in the workplace because of manpower needs, but the most conspicuous victory for the civil rights movement—the creation of the Committee on Fair Employment Practices following a threatened march on Washington—occurred in the summer of 1941, before the United States entered the war. Thereafter, agitation for equality was confined to a relatively small number of northern, largely middle-class blacks. Recent scholarly research indicates that the war "delayed and stifled black protest activism, that it dampened black militancy." More characteristic than victories for civil rights was an "advancing racial polarization" between blacks and whites that produced deadly riots in Detroit and other cities.

No work better illuminates the overall reappraisal of how World War II affected American society than Paul Fussell's biting, highly controversial *Wartime: Understanding and Behavior in the Second World War*, published in 1989. In Fussell's view, the war was so senseless and destructive, the soldiers—the "faceless young automatons"—who fought it were so expendable and so damaged by the experience, that some "artful narrative" had to be invented to confer purpose on events that were fundamentally meaningless. This was the role, Fussell asserts, played by the war publicists, who were skilled at disingenuous presentation. Critical analysis, evaluation, and satire were suspended for the duration, he continues, to be replaced by celebration, self-satisfaction, and smugness, by an atmosphere of "obligatory goodness." Fussell writes: "Now, fifty years later, there has been so much talk about 'The Good War,' the Justified War, the Necessary War, and the like, that the young and the innocent could get the impression that it was really not such a bad thing after all." In Fussell's view, it was "a war and nothing else, and thus stupid and sadistic."

Fussell also quotes someone else Studs Terkel interviewed, not the person who talked about the war being fun and Americans having a hell of a good time, but a woman whose brother was killed in an airplane crash on a training mission and who resented the wartime propaganda: "The good war? That infuriates me. Yeah, the idea of World War Two being called a good war is a horrible thing. . . . I was lied to, I was cheated. I was made a fool of." Fussell entitles his concluding chapter, "The real war will never get in the books," a slogan of the combat soldiers who knew that patriotic propaganda had so falsified the barbarity of their experience that it could never be adequately communicated.

Yet perhaps the face of the real war, certainly of a different war, is at last beginning to get in the books. That war was closer to the type that Tocqueville had predicted democracies would fight, one that brought undoubted advantages but also prepared people for a democratic despotism "more gently by their habits." Although that is never going to be the image of World War II that we see flickering on the screen, it is nevertheless the more accurate image.

The Myth of the Placid 1950s

Robert D. Marcus

In many ways the decade of the 1950s revitalized old American mythologies. There was renewed commitment, for example, to the economic legend that an unbalanced budget would bring financial ruin to America—even though President Eisenhower succeeded in balancing the budget in only two of his eight years as President. There was as well a reemphasis on the sacred American belief that the public affairs of the nation were best vested in the hands of those of business background and disposition—as stated by a contemporary cabinet member: "What's good for General Motors is good for America." But it is the amiable, nay placid, image of the 1950s which has endured. It was a decade wherein the "bland were leading the bland." It was "quiet time in America," as President Dwight "Ike" Eisenhower waved to the electorate, read western novels, and played golf. Americans, in turn, discovered credit cards, chain stores, strip malls and suburbia, and got seriously at the task of becoming a nation of consumers. Professor Robert D. Marcus, of the State University of New York at Brockport, however, finds another America. The supposedly "placid decade" was vibrant with social, cultural, and political change. It was an energetic period of critical cultural transformation. Its alleged congenial bleakness yields, on closer examination, a cultural landscape of burgeoning cities, an emergent youth culture, significant change within African-American communities signaled by the famous *Brown v. Board of Education* decision of the Supreme Court, and a developing tradition of social criticism which would yield still more profound change in the decades to come. Indeed, "The times they were a'changin."

To a remarkable extent historians and popular writers have agreed on the mood of the 1950s: we had entered upon a placid age, economically secure and pleasantly dull. The affluent, even as they turned from public issues to the suburban pursuit of status, had surrendered their independence to corporations; Americans were absorbing from the media a bland popular culture—"midcult," its critics called it—that was neither vulgar nor serious but simply insipid; they filled churches but made the "American way of life" their religion; and they raised children in large numbers. Commentators noted an increasingly complicated structure of corporation, government, military, and academic bureaucracies in which procedures and methods were more and more standard. America, they observed, was flattening into a single unit as the West gained population, the South industrialized, and indistinguishable suburbs sprang up from one end of the country to the other. Furthermore, as the critics rightly held, Americans were interested in making sure that their behavior was not in any way aberrant. The popularity of the Kinsey reports revealed how far this concern would go. Many people read them—or popularizations of them—avidly, hoping that their sexual life conformed to that of their neighbors.

While Americans were becoming uniform in certain matters, and a large part of the population (not so large as was then thought) had entered upon a remarkably comfortable economic existence, in other respects the American intellect was sharpening, the national conscience becoming more acute, and society was fracturing into new sorts of antagonistic interests and persuasions.

A major object of social and cultural criticism was standardization; and yet standardization held conflicting possibilities. The bleak surfaces of life could correspond, of course, to personalities bare of taste or imagination; and to the degree that they did so, all the talk about "conformity" had significance. Standardization could, however, mean something quite different. As people in increasing numbers moved to different sections of the country, from one suburb or urban development to another set of boxes in glass and brick, and abandoned everything that could sentimentally be called their "roots," they were forced to a flexibility and receptiveness of mind. Technology and the professions themselves demanded openness to new information and techniques. The major institutions set out to create a national and rootless class of managers and professionals; the corporations and the military moved their men about to teach them all phases of their work and to give them a national rather than a local orientation. Stripping away cluttered detail, cutting down the environment to its useful commodities and packaging those in neutral plastic, pulling families from neighborhoods and setting them in cubicles bare of personality, postwar technology could throw suburbanites and apartment dwellers back upon themselves and upon the advanced professional skills that gave them the place and identity their surroundings could not provide.

Standardization provided something more immediate. The repetitive institutions of the credit card, the chain store, and the quickly marketed fashions gave firmness of line to an unstable environment; the similar houses and shops and roads and name brands were little signposts for men and women unsure of their direction. Technology and rationalism cast a broad net over the land, but essential things slipped through.

Politically it was an unsettling age, not so much so as many others, but enough to dispel the myth of its blandness. Eisenhower prosperity was brief; the air of complacency that accompanied the installation of this beloved President was even more short-lived. The early fifties, the time of the Korean War and Joseph McCarthy, was a period of ideological and political stress. The breakdown of the wartime Russian-American alliance, the "fall" of China to the Communists, the Russian nuclear threat, the fear of internal subversion, and the emerging tensions over race marked by a split in the Democratic party—all had contributed to the irritable and sour malaise that Eisenhower's election was supposed to cure, and in fact did for a time. But the Eisenhower tranquillity did not last until the end of the General's administration. The political calm, which began only with the conclusion of the Korean War in mid-summer 1953, ended in October 1957 with the beeps from space of the Russian earth satellite. Criticisms of American politics grew all through the later fifties, and after the successful launching of a second vastly heavier Russian sputnik, the American public was quite ready to listen, as it demonstrated by electing a more liberal Congress in 1958.

Technology and economics put the continuing American phenomenon of migration, geographical and occupational, to a new point of activity in the fifties; communities were broken and others tentatively formed, and shifted populations congealed along dangerous fault lines—how dangerous would not be revealed for a number of years. The dominant continental motion was still westward; but now it was to the new Southwest as well, and into the old South, burgeoning with industries and cities. Of greater social consequence was the pattern of migration both in and out of the urban centers. Already in decay because depression and war had prevented the continual renovation they needed to remain habitable, the cities were undergoing a double movement that would damage them further. During the twenty-five years after 1930 there occurred an enormous movement off the farms and into the cities. By the 1950s twenty million people had flooded the cities; many impoverished rural blacks, country white southerners, Puerto Ricans, and Chicanos were victims of a technological revolution that enabled heavily mechanized farms to feed a nation approaching two hundred million. In the late forties and the fifties an even larger contrary shift was taking place, from the central cities to the peripheries; the urban middle classes, the modest and the affluent, were moving to the suburbs in search of better housing and schools. The passage to the suburbs was financed by wartime savings and postwar prosperity; it drew also on a gigantic federal subsidy to the middle classes in the form of mortgage guarantees, tax deductions, and road-building programs. These two migrations heightened the crisis of the city. The newcomers, poorly equipped culturally and economically for life in the continental metropolis, raised a demand for housing and public services inadequate to begin with, while families able to cope with big-city conditions and solvent enough to bear the tax burdens were leaving to enrich the school systems and the governments of the suburbs.

Suburbia was revealing some curious social patterns. Middle-class women were turning from the place in the world that their predecessors had gained throughout the century, and looking to their homes and kitchens, their car pools and their children. The proportion of women to the total college student population dropped steadily from 47 percent in 1920 to 35 percent in 1958; and the number of these women taking their degrees in secretarial, home economics, nursing, or teaching courses had risen to over half of the women enrolled. The proportion of women among professionals with Ph.D., LL.B., or M.D. degrees declined as well.

This trend admits of no simple explanation. American society has always exerted strong pressure to marry, and postwar prosperity removed inhibitions about wedding young. The median marrying age for women went down into the teens, and early marriages meant early childbearing. Add to this the responsibilities for uncompleted schooling, the isolation in bedroom suburbs where baby-sitting services are a perennial problem, and where time and transportation are major crises, and only special motivation would tempt a woman to combine her socially mandatory marriage with a career. The economy of the fifties, moreover, was not suited to her. Before the great university building boom got under way in the later fifties, there were too few professional schools even for the men who wished to attend them, and the G.I. Bill was, among other things, an act of *de facto* sexual discrimination applied to higher schooling. Women also suffered from the first misunderstandings of the postindustrial economy. Since muscle power was vanishing as a major asset, women were increasingly capable of performing the work the economy demanded; but the expansion of the consumer market was impressive. And the era was more conspicuous for the advertising bent on turning women into energetic consumers than for any attempts on the part of economists to discover job openings for them.

Suburban society was particularly child-centered. In the attenuated communities that extreme mobility produced, children were portable "roots"

that peripatetic adults carried with them. The first social entree a new family might have into the neighborhood could occur when the mother heard of the local baby-sitting cooperative from other carriage-pushing women in the shopping center or the pediatrician's office. Churches grew enormously in membership, and their emphasis on family social services reflected the importance of the children. Suburbs were the milieu of adolescents. And adolescence—that long period of suspension before adulthood, in which the young are thrown together at school into their own society, given much leisure and much regimentation, equipped with records, radios, and cars, and learn that they are in a very particular and intriguing moment of their growing up—is a product of the twentieth century.

Early in the century most people scarcely had an adolescence by our social definition of it. They were children until they finished school (usually grade school), when they got a job and became adults. And child labor compelled some of them into man's or woman's estate even earlier. But in time an extensive adolescent sub-society took form, and by the late forties or earlier a number of its members had developed for themselves, and had received from fascinated adults, the self-image and style of hepcats and bobby-soxers.

It was a generation at school. Between 1900 and 1940 secondary education, once a small enterprise preparing a very few college-bound students and emphasizing grades and intellectual skills, became the nearly universal experience of youth in their teens. It had diluted its old curriculum with industrial and commercial courses, as well as with life-adjustment projects. These were intended to bring into the folkways of an urban industrial society the migrants from Europe and our own countryside, or their children. And then, after dropping for over forty years, the percentage of high school students going on to college began in the late forties to rise steeply, as America moved into a postindustrial economy demanding college graduates. Universities hastily expanded their facilities, first to meet the influx of returning veterans and then to accommodate the rush of students from the high schools and to prepare for the postwar babies. High schools and even primary schools returned to the function they had served before World War I, that of college preparation—but no longer for only a small segment of the people. The high schools, tied to an ideology of progressive education now under heavy intellectual attack and burdened with habits that had matured during the long era of practical, all-purpose secondary schools, strained to meet their new obligations. The attempt to raise standards, which went on through most of the decade but with increased intensity after the Russian space successes of 1957, pressed heavily upon the student population.

The affluent children of the fifties were not a gentry class assured of property and power whether they achieved academically or not, nor were they poor or lower-middle people who might believe that academic success would add increments to their future, a little more education meaning a little more wealth and standing. To the contrary, by the late fifties they were being taught to conceive of the world as an academic sweepstakes, where the very success not only of their own lives, but of their parents' as well, rested on their winning entry into the right college. The high school of the affluent was only the apex of an entire edifice built of educational playthings (not toys), nursery schools, "creative" summer camps, children's encyclopedias, and more homework. Parents invested energy in school budget fights and in parent-teacher associations. The new middle class was making of schooling, as the old had made of property, the ground of all progress; it was constituting itself a meritocracy. In the nineteenth century poverty and wealth had been defined by property, and the poor had been urged to work and save to acquire it; by mid-twentieth century poverty was understood to be qualitatively a lack of education, and one suggestion was to provide, as an incentive to parents and through them to their children, a payment to poor families for the achievements of their offspring at school.

The schools gave the adolescent society much of its character. The large high schools physically brought the young together; by the fifties, schools in affluent neighborhoods were virtually inclusive of youth, for the surrounding society did not siphon off many of the most admirable young people into adult roles as in the past, when school youths could see contemporaries already donning the mantle of the adult in the world of independence and financial reward. The relationships between the school and the student were differing and ambivalent. With the increasing professionalization of American society, college had become for middle-class youth a necessity, and if the teenager did not himself want to think

a great deal about college, he had his parents to hover over his grades and ambitions, especially in the late fifties when competition for entrance into college became stiffer. The high school students who were taking their heroes not from the fields of intellectual and professional achievement but from athletics, modeling, and entertainment were nevertheless forced to base their future to some extent on performance in the classroom. Even the more intellectually relaxed of the schools required from the most relaxed students the persistent tedious business of attendance and at least exterior regimentation. James Coleman has described a passive resistance in which adolescent cliques imposed informal sanctions against excessive work and achievement on the part of their fellows. But in the dramatic rise in social importance that education was gaining during the later fifties some schools were becoming genuinely demanding and some students were getting a positive commitment to their work. For them the tensions of adolescence were increased by their anxieties of study.

Adolescent subsociety discovered and defined itself, though, not in its schooling but in its leisure—which, paradoxically enough, was enlarging in possibilities at a period when the pressures of education were also growing. Parents imposed less control. This was perhaps the first generation with sufficient money at its disposal that it could sustain a whole consumer market of its own. And an important part of that market was rock and roll.

Rock and roll is artistically important in its own right. Forms once distinctive, such as the jazz of the twenties and the swing of the thirties and after, had become by the forties and early fifties simply the common currency of American culture: the show tunes, the popular ballads, the "rhythm" numbers, all related distantly to their origins in Negro music but endlessly bleached by decades of adaptation. Song after song dealt in essentially the same tones, and was timed to fit one 10-inch 78 rpm record, published on the same street in Manhattan—dubbed Tin Pan Alley. Rock and roll was a fresh start. It got back to the rich lode of black music, added the sounds of country music, and devised new techniques for their transformation. The music and songs treated of special interests the young had found: the lovers, the hot rodders, the delinquents, the athletes, later the surfers, and especially the dancers and rockers themselves. Dick Clark's "American Bandstand," a popular television program that began in the summer of 1957, had a large impact; the program announced that the style had come into its own, persuaded young viewers that they could dare to dance in the new manner, and showed that performers need not be any older than they were. The hard beat of the music lent itself to an image and romantic myth that America was evolving about its youth: rock and roll seemed to express a young consciousness that was quick, syncopated, and at once tough and vulnerable. The music also evoked the technological setting, the advanced media and the fast cars, carefully and skillfully tended, for the sound had an almost metallic pace and brokenness.

This adolescent society was comparable only in a limited way to the more advanced youth culture of the sixties and beyond. It had no ideologies, no intentions to achieve permanence or to remake the rest of America; it was so much the object of commercialization that it seems almost to have been the passive recipient of its own self-image designed for it by its commercializers. Though doubtless it still exists, it has been overshadowed by the new culture of the universities and the streets, with their own styles now finding their way back into the high schools. But it did give something of itself to the more recent and more radical culture—beyond, of course, contributing those of its members who actually moved into that culture. It passed on its music, synthesized into folk rock and hard rock, and it hinted just barely at things that the counterculture explicitly believes in—a special consciousness, alien to the rest of civilization, new in perceptions, subsisting in its distinct community.

Beneath the surface of America in the fifties, the lives of black Americans were changing more than almost anyone realized. Their odyssey into the urban ghetto had its beginnings long ago; there had been heavy migration at the time of World War I, and even before. But the greatest influx started with the forties, when World War II cracked the old frozen customs of segregation. In 1940 the percentage of Negroes in occupations above the unskilled had actually been less than in 1890. But suddenly blacks were needed: the armed forces drew many of them, civilian employment opened as workers were pulled into the military services, and other jobs were created by the economic expansion of wartime. The eventual result of their exodus from the southern countryside to the cities would be the massive urban ghettos; but the

war economy and the subsequent prosperity of the forties also gave birth to a new kind of middle class—more numerous and stronger than the older Negro bourgeoisie, more aggressive as it sensed its strength and had its initial provocative tastes of what equality might be like. And it was the first sizable segment of Negro society whose condition unequivocally committed it to the goal of integration.

The new urban, secularized Negro community produced a heady competition for power among a variety of organizations. The church was a declining, though continuing, social and political force in Negro life. Beside it the National Association for the Advancement of Colored People (NAACP) took leadership in the new bourgeoisie. With its continuous history of advocating legal, political, and social equality, the classic goals of integration, rather than the self-help of Booker T. Washington and the various Negro business groups, the NAACP spoke for the aspirations of the new black middle class, which was prepared to enter the white world with the aid of government and education instead of depending on business enterprise and community development. Moreover, the NAACP had achieved results. Its strategy of legal challenge to the edifice of segregation had earned victory after victory, starting with an important decision in 1938 to desegregate a law school and climaxing in *Brown v. Board of Education*, the famous school desegregation case of 1954.

As Negroes migrated northward they also shed their traditional allegiance to the party of Lincoln and became late arrivals in the New Deal coalition. Black Democratic Congressmen such as Oscar S. DePriest and William L. Dawson of Chicago, and Adam Clayton Powell of New York, gave witness that the movement out of the South had created a new political quantity. Under President Truman, Negroes received recognition in public office, several important executive orders banned discrimination in industries related to war and integrated most of the armed forces. In 1948 the Democratic party leadership chose to accept a southern rebellion rather than alienate the liberal and black vote that it correctly diagnosed would provide the margin of victory in the populous northern states. Finally, in 1957, the first civil rights legislation in over eighty years passed through Congress. In that year as well, the crisis at Central High School in Little Rock, Arkansas, demonstrated that even a conservative administration would enforce Supreme Court rulings on the race question.

This political power, combined with the Court's decisions in favor of the Negro and the rise in economic position from the forties into the mid-fifties, brought forth a new temper in the black community, joining militancy about achieving rights to a considerable optimism over recent gains. The result was the remarkably good-natured and buoyant civil rights movement of the late fifties and early sixties, a movement whose main strength was the cooperation of liberal whites with the Negro middle class. Martin Luther King, Jr., emerged during the 1955 Montgomery, Alabama, bus boycott as the leading spokesman of the new mood. He translated legal advances into far wider social and moral energies. His tactics of direct action through nonviolent mass demonstration also made him the first black leader since Marcus Garvey in the 1920s to gain a large base of support in the community.

The fragility of this coalition should have been more obvious than it was. It rested not simply on the ability of white and black to cooperate politically; even more fundamentally it depended on the passive acquiescence of both black and white Americans outside the coalition. Almost certainly the majority of Americans never really approved of direct action as a technique. Northern whites would tolerate such activity only so long as they were not its targets. Any expansion of the civil rights movement beyond its assault on official segregation in the South might awaken their fears. And the passivity of lower-class Negroes lay on still more tenuous grounds. Until the early fifties, migration northward to better jobs had encouraged a sense of progress. But 1952 marked the point of closest parity to the white world, and the gap between white and black incomes began to increase once again. More and more blacks had grown up not in the South but in northern slums and had no memories of worse times by which to measure their progress; advertising and the new medium of television flaunted the affluence that other Americans enjoyed. The civil rights movement could sharpen this discontent, but not offer it an immediate practicable program. For much of the ghetto lived below the economic and social line at which integration is a possibility, unpossessed of skills and knowledge that would gain entrance to open employment, lacking the money to move into better neighborhoods, having access only to schools that would not be decent whether segregated or mixed. The new hopes raised in the fifties and the eroding life of the cities were uniting into a dangerous combination. By the end of the decade, white America discovered the Black Muslims, a small but suddenly growing nationalist sect vigorously opposed to integrating with "white devils." They were the "rainbow sign," as James Baldwin said: "No more water, the fire next time!"

America had a smaller band of rebels whose rebellion was singularly passive, expressing itself only through an engagement in an alternative way of life. Seeking poverty as a state of redemption, finding community among themselves, the "beats" proclaimed free perception and expressiveness—in cool jazz, in handicrafts or high arts, in drugs and sex, in exotic religion or poetry or mystic inspiration. Here were the ancient values of community and of the sensual, impulsive, and immediate life to pit against the abstraction, calculation, and hypocrisy of science, materialism, official religion, and the bureaucratic mind. Such a shrewd liberal publicist as James Wechsler instantly recognized the importance of the beats: although he was not happy with what Jack Kerouac and similar people were saying, he acknowledged them to be the first new voice to challenge his generation, which had come of age in the thirties. A purely personal and deliberately alienated movement like that of the beats could not provide the energies for rebellion, but their lives and their statement were a possible starting point for a more extensive cultural critique.

The citizens who came to be known as the "radical right" moved to the assertion of a separate identity. Those among them who had opposed the New Deal had known what it is to be among a frustrated minority; but for a period, the strident early days of the Cold War when "socialism" was a deadly word and hard-line Americanism was ascendant, the Right could assume that its temperament was the nation's. Many right-wingers have never abandoned that belief. But Dwight Eisenhower's triumph over the conservative Robert A. Taft in the 1952 Republican convention, the General's moderate administration, and the decline of McCarthyism, showed the Right that it no longer had a comfortable home in the Republican party and forced the more militant into a social and political enclave of their own. Particularly after the Cold War had become barren of the aggressive ideological emotion they relished, they formed secret groups like the John Birch Society and separate schools and institutions like the Christian Anti-Communist Crusade of Dr. Fred Schwartz, and published journals like *American Opinion*. In many areas they became active in local politics and on school and library boards, defending their neighborhoods from what they considered Communist penetration, and they maintained important pressures on American society. However far from their times these sour reactionary critics may have been, their fears of totalitarian centralism and their taste for smallness of scale were not unlike the persuasion that many on the Left would later have. The rightists were also suggestive of more recent movements in their coming to political awareness and their breaking away from a major party coalition; for it would be typical of the 1960s that social fragmentation would not remain social only, as it did for the most part in the Eisenhower years, but would find political expression.

The Cold War evoked a distinctive feeling for power: a sense of power in vast contours, the great antagonistic international blocs that were pressed against each other; a conception among informed Americans of the infinite detail, economic and technical, that sustains power; and for thoughtful segments of the public, a patient albeit nervous willingness to allow national policy the small exact moves, unsatisfying to chauvinism, that maintain power without inviting its violent eruption. To live with power so massive and ubiquitous, and learn so sophisticated an understanding of it, induced intellectual paradoxes that would become fully apparent only after about a decade of the Cold War. Civilization was thickening into great structures of technological power; yet in a few respects it was becoming light and spare. Technology itself worked increasingly with the invisible quickness of chemistry and electricity and nuclear fuel rather than with the bulky force of machines; the solid things of industrialism, the machinery and the buildings, continued their progress toward delicacy and perfection of line; and television was beginning to create a community of viewers that exists instantly and magically, in the obliteration of space.

Along with the technocratic rationalism of the Cold War went a careful, if not always successful, tempering of political tone. Even the Eisenhower administration, which was given at moments to describing international communism as a transcendent evil, was learning to speak in quieter tones. It was an age of making up material resources lost in depression and war, of muteness in criticism, and especially of horror over the excesses of political adventures. The memory of naziism traumatized a whole generation against activism and ideology in politics. Ideologies, both communist and fascist, were dangerous and irresponsible romantic visions, "terrible simplifications" that threatened civilized values. They were not only dangerous; they were unworkable, declared a doctrine proclaiming the "end of ideology": the world had become much too complex for simple solutions devised by theory and was now to be put in the hands of management, for piecemeal adjustment and sensible reform. This conception of politics, cool and rational, suited the problems of the Cold War, with its need for protracted and technically elaborate politics and for the avoidance of provocation and overreaction. In fact, the history of the idea was intimately tied to the Cold War. C. Wright Mills, one of its most powerful critics, observed that it "began in the mid-fifties, mainly in intellectual circles more or less associated with the Congress for Cultural Freedom and the magazine *Encounter.* . . . Since then, many cultural gossips have taken it up as a posture and an unexamined slogan." Actually it goes back to the very founding of the Congress for Cultural Freedom in 1950, and that organization, the *New York Times* discovered in April 1966, had been established and supported through its formative years by the United States Central Intelligence Agency. The Cold War had frozen some currents of intellectual life, drawing together government and the intellectual classes usually its critics. This went against a major tradition, for the conflict and tension between national claims and the life of the mind have persisted since the age of the French Revolution.

So unnatural an intellectual acquiescence could not continue. In Europe a recognizably newer Left emerged in both the eastern and NATO countries in a reaction to the events of 1956: the Suez crisis, the Russian invasion of Hungary, and Khrushchev's revelations (at the twentieth party congress) of Stalin's crimes. The whole system of international power politics that was the common creation of the two great foes would soon face major attacks. By the end of the decade, a Marxist radicalism was spreading to a few American campuses. Wisconsin had an active socialist club that began publishing *Studies on the Left* in 1959, the first important journal of the evolving new Left. At Berkeley in that year SLATE was organized to run independent candidates for student government. Graduate students at the University of Chicago began publishing *New University Thought* in 1960. Minor episodes of campus activism occurred.

Further questionings came from professional critics. While the social sciences were in many cases deeply involved with the government in its decision making, and organizations like the Rand Corporation did direct consulting for policy makers, social science was also a ground of social criticism. In fact, the role that journalists had performed earlier in the century, that of "muckraking" the nation to uncover the evils buried beneath the official pieties, was now frequently performed by social scientists. Economists analyzed the poor performance of the American economy in the light of European and Japanese growth rates. Sociologists raised the specter of conformity and the "organization man." They also analyzed and decried status seeking and subliminal advertising. John Kenneth Galbraith exposed poverty and the decline of public services in the midst of affluence. C. Wright Mills described America as a mass society ruled by an interlocking power elite. Mills, the most radical of the sociological muckrakers, aptly described the function he served: "When little is known, or only trivial items publicized, or when myths prevail, then plain description becomes a radical fact, or at least is taken to be radically upsetting." This new sociological muckraking found its popularizers in journalism, and such writers as Vance Packard came to make the social sciences their journalistic beat, presenting the findings of social investigators without the charts, graphs, and qualifications. Late in the decade, after the Russian space achievements, liberal Americans increasingly became willing to listen to the various kinds of criticism; many of the Kennedy programs were a result. Dwight Eisenhower himself, a man of the era that was passing, warned about the existence of a "military-industrial complex" and thereby contributed a phrase that before long would be popular on the Left.

The loosening of debate went back to a number of tangible developments in domestic and international affairs. America's age of renewed social criticism was part of the "thaw" that appeared to envelop the entire world in the late fifties. The postwar era, moreover, the period defined by the problems World War II had created, was coming to an end. The economic and social troubles of the world were increasingly those of the new nations, the new economies, and a new generation growing up since the war. And the lessons of the past, always infinitely malleable, would change as well. Even the central lesson of modern history, the possibility of a regime such as the Nazis', altered its meaning. Watching the trial of Adolf Eichmann in Jerusalem in 1961, the world saw a new side to the horrors of totalitarianism: that it was, as Hannah Arendt explained, the product not only of mad romantic demagogues, but of the rational, pragmatic, sensible bureaucrats who ran the machinery of the state—or, indifferently, the machinery of death. We might avoid madmen with luck, but how were we to escape from the technocrats whom every modern society seemed to need and whose reasoned attitudes we had trusted to save us from the romantic, the irresponsible, and the sinister?

The Kennedy Myth

Herbert S. Parmet

The assassination of President John F. Kennedy provides the historian a ready example of the intersection of political reality and social mythology. The circumstances of Kennedy's death, the media coverage of the nation's emotional response, and the Kennedy élan did much, at least initially, to fashion a stained-glass image of JFK. Though historical revisionists have been active, the image remains tenacious thirty years after the "thousand days." Here, Professor Herbert S. Parmet of the City University of New York examines the Kennedy myth, particularly its relationship to the conduct of American politics. He concludes, among other things, that Kennedy and the LBJ succession took the New and Fair Deal reform movement to its conclusion, sometimes nobly, as in the Peace Corps and the Alliance for Progress. A persistent and consistent carryover of the New Deal would be Kennedy's support of education at all levels. And back to the myth: Parmet concludes with an emphasis on JFK's deep and lasting influence, however devoid of substance, on the perception of the office of the presidency. As Lance Morrow has suggested, its nature was perhaps even "vaguely religious." Symptomatic of this influence was the strong rebuke of Vice President Dan Quayle by his senior, vice-presidential candidate Lloyd Bentsen, in 1988: "You're no Jack Kennedy!" Most discerning Americans believed that they understood that classic putdown.

When Lyndon Johnson began his presidency with the words "Let us continue," his meaning was clear. The idea of America had acquired another shrine. JFK was the apostle of racial and religious equality, compassion toward the underprivileged, and a champion of democracy. Johnson went on to exploit that sentiment by engineering the enactment of key elements in his Great Society legislation. The most significant, civil rights, was hailed as a memorial to Kennedy. The fallen president became transformed in memory as a fighter for the common man.

Trading on that, and utilizing his own considerable skills, President Johnson acted during a time of economic well-being, in contrast to his political "daddy," F.D.R., to create his own distinctive revolution. Before the end of 1966, however, the momentum was almost dead, destroyed by the politics of backlash.

The shape of American politics during the years that followed drew more from a variety of other factors, both domestic and international. The New Frontier became invisible. Kennedy was less an architect of the future than a player at the leading edge of change. Nevertheless, it is appropriate to note that the harshest critics of John F. Kennedy have conceded the place of inspiration as his chief legacy. So sharp a writer as Henry Fairlie has, in fact, charged him with orchestrating "the politics of expectation."

Skepticism about Kennedy was hardly new. Eric Sevareid wrote in 1959 that "Kennedy's candidacy for the nomination" would be a test "of the charm-school theory of high politics," and Fletcher Knebel declared that "Kennedy's political success is based on two foundations—shrewd planning and votes." One Kennedy senatorial colleague, Pat McNamara of Michigan, told Drew Pearson, "As between Kennedy and Nixon if they both were running for President, I would have a hard time making up my mind who to vote for." Political scientist James MacGregor Burns, while working on his campaign biography, jeopardized his relationship with the Kennedyites by daring to raise questions about the young man's commitment to anything other than his own ambitions. The critics were invariably Democrats and liberals. They also shared doubts about the ideological commitment of a son of Joseph Patrick Kennedy and a friend of Joe McCarthy.

Ted Sorensen has agreed that Jack Kennedy "never identified himself as a liberal; it was only after his death," Sorensen added, "that they began to claim him as one of theirs." In fact, Sorensen went on to say, in an interview that took place during the first Reagan term, "on fiscal matters he was more conservative than any president we've had since." If, as has been so widely suggested, Kennedy's liberalism was two-thirds mythology, concocted to suit the tastes of his potential Democratic backers, and only some one-third the product of enlightened progressivism—and if that tepid commitment was held inadequate for the "common good" in a nation besotted by Eisenhower shibboleths—how much does that still leave Kennedy responsible for what happened after his death?

How much was he responsible, in other words, for the Quixotic effort to subdue Indochina, for the unleashing of domestic economic and racial animosities that smoldered in decaying inner cities, for the counter-culture and the counter-counter culture—the revenge of the "forgotten Americans," and the rise of a new conservative majority?

How much was due to the Kennedy mythology? Had he been given more years, how would he have altered future history? Would middle class America have been less determined to safeguard their homes, jobs, and pocketbooks from the menacing poor?

*   *   *

Most Americans thought that Dallas marked a sudden end of stability. Kennedy's years became an interlude between Eisenhower tranquility and Johnson-Nixon turmoil. A Gallup survey in 1983 reported that 65 percent of those canvassed believed that the United States would have been "much different" if Kennedy had not been killed. If only he had lived, went the argument, the storm would not have come. Vietnam would not have become an American trap, there would not have been fires in the streets, and the presidency would have remained untarnished by scandal and bitterness.

Certain points about the Kennedy impact, however, can be made with confidence:

It is true that there was no social and economic transformation. The distribution of income, the extremes of wealth and poverty, were essentially untouched. But it is also true that, despite current tensions in parts of the country, the Jim Crow that lived on until the 1960s belongs to the past.

Kennedy—and the Johnson succession—closed out the New and Fair Deal reform movement. The upheavals of the post-Kennedy '60s and early '70s precipitated a combination of social backlash and inflation. Any future administration devoted to reforms will be compelled to devise a new blueprint.

If certain of our current leaders are "no Jack Kennedys," it should be remembered that neither is the U.S. of 1989 the U.S. of the early 1960s. The Kennedy luster profited not only from its own style but, to a considerable degree, from the relative drabness and inertia of the Eisenhower fifties. Kennedy said he spoke for a new generation, and he seemed plausible in that role. Under his leadership, the national purpose sent a message of clear pragmatic idealism—one filled with such high-minded notions as the Peace Corps and the Alliance for Progress—that inspired a new generation of Americans. Our actions began to fall into line with our propaganda.

The Kennedy image drew added strength from the timely marriage of technology and nature. The contrast of Jack and Jackie with Ike and Mamie was striking, especially in a world not yet accustomed to saturated television coverage. Eisenhower, it is commonly assumed, retained sufficient popularity at the end of his second term to have been able to win another. Kennedy, however, having pulled off his razor-thin victory over Nixon, was quickly hailed as the herald of a new generation, a point he himself encouraged in his Inaugural Address. A nonideological nation succumbed to attractions that were more regal than philosophical. For the next 1,037 days, the American people were treated to more of the same. The Kennedys, with Caroline and her little brother, became *the* royal family.

*   *   *

Richard Goodwin has noted that Kennedy's 1960 campaign began the process of speeding up the "terminal decay" of the Democratic Party. If that party was being reshaped, so was the strength of partisan loyalties. With the help of the newer electronic media, and with a further boost from older government entitlement programs, the influence of local political leaders was gradually weakening. Kennedy, in the 1960 campaign, relied on his own cadre that was independent of the Democratic National Committee. Lyndon Johnson neglected the DNC even more. By 1971, David Broder would write a book called *The Party's Over*. The post-McGovern, post-Watergate election in 1974 brought into positions of power a new group of bright Democrats, such people as Michael Dukakis, Les AuCoin, Toby Moffett, and Paul Tsongas. Perhaps most closely identified with the Kennedy style was Gary Hart, especially in the 1984 campaign.

They and others—James Florio, Bill Bradley, Richard Gephardt, Timothy Wirth, Bruce Babbitt, Albert Gore, Jr., Jim Hunt, Christopher Dodd—and a number of journalists—especially Charles Peters and the staff of *The Washington Monthly*, as well as academics, became the "cool pragmatists" (or "bloodless progressives") of a new political wave. Speaking in the wake of Reagan's 1980 victory, Morton Kondracke of *The New Republic* declared that "what the Democratic Party has to do is adopt some sort of a—what might be called a *neoliberal* ideology." Pressed by a startled Jim Lehrer on his PBS television program for exactly what that meant, Kondracke went on to explain that it was "an attempt to combine the traditional Democratic compassion for the downtrodden and outcast elements of society with different vehicles than categorical aid programs or quota systems or new federal bureaucracies." More privately, over a year earlier, editor Peters, loosened by alcohol, shouted in glee at *The Washington Monthly*'s tenth anniversary party, "We are the neoliberals." They were liberal but called for no crusades. As political scientist William Schneider has written, "A new kind of liberal emerged out of this context: unorthodox, reform-minded, iconoclastic, and staunchly independent of Democratic Party tradition." Many regarded them as a break from the old dominant New Deal liberalism.

They were, in short, Kennedy's children. Several, including Peters as well as Christopher Dodd and Paul Tsongas, had served with the Peace Corps. They followed their symbolic leader in the disavowal of ideological rigidity. Randall Rothenberg, in his *Esquire* article of February 1982 that introduced the world to neoliberalism, stated, "What's more important is that many of these younger Democrats have consciously modeled their political presence on JFK's vision." He then quoted Gary Hart as saying, "I believe that John Kennedy was a bridge from Roosevelt and Truman and the New Deal to something beyond. . . . If you rounded us all up and asked, 'Why did you get into politics?' nine out of ten would say John Kennedy." Hart, George McGovern's former campaign manager in an earlier life, stood out as neoliberalism's most prominent proponent. Along with the others, his economics advocated growth combined with industrial planning policies together with vigorous support for federal aid to education.

Hart, of course, failed to win his party's presidential nomination in 1984; four years later, his personal behavior (another Kennedyesque pattern) crippled a second attempt. Michael Dukakis, of course, embarrassed himself after he got the nomination. The Bush victory appeared to have rendered neoliberalism one of the briefest movements in American politics. Critics had already seen the idea as a corruption of liberalism. Sidney Blumenthal thought it was "Carterism without Carter." Arthur Schlesinger, Jr., a loyal New Frontiersman, came close to denouncing it as "Reaganism without Reagan." Neoliberalism, he wrote, was "a politically futile course for the Democratic Party. . . . Far from rejecting the Reagan frameworks, they would at most rejigger priorities here and there."

It was fitting that Kennedyites should differ about the Kennedy legacy. Much clearer is the establishment of the Kennedy image at the heart of American nationalism. His name has been invoked by such conservatives as Ronald Reagan, Jack Kemp, Richard Nixon, and Jeanne Kirkpatrick. In the New York City mayoralty election of 1989, the fight was between a Republican who had been a Kennedy admirer and worker in his youth, Rudolph Giuliani, and David Dinkins, who used the Kennedy name to assure potential voters of his political purity. Senator Charles S. Robb of Virginia, speaking to the Democratic Leadership Council, advised the rejection by the party of "ideological litmus tests and programmatic rigidity of what some have called 'liberal fundamentalism.'" Calling for a broader, more inclusive liberalism, he made clear that he meant a return to the "forward-looking liberalism" of the New Frontier. His words echoed neoliberal themes.

Neoliberals, sometimes known as "Atari Democrats," high-tech types emphasizing the new technology, voiced both the strengths and weaknesses of the combination of idealism and pragmatism, an attractive credo to all who identified with the Kennedy legacy.

Take, for example, education, a subject about as dear to the heart of the Ataris as economic growth and technology. Their emphasis was on fulfilling the American dream and preparing young people for the coming high technology order. Peters, in his "neoliberal manifesto" of 1983, declared that their concern with the public school system was "at once pragmatic and idealistic."

Theodore Sorensen has agreed that education was "the one domestic subject that mattered most to John Kennedy . . . ," a position that can be easily confirmed by examining his entire political career. Kennedy's commitment was most often justified by America's Cold War needs. The National Defense Education Act that followed the Soviet launching of *Sputnik* was the prime example. Partly as a form of political atonement for his silence about Joe McCarthy, Kennedy became a vigorous advocate of repealing the loyalty oath required of graduate students attempting to qualify for federal funds. Or, as with the position taken by President George Bush in Charlottesville, Virginia, last September, when meeting with governors on the need to overhaul the nation's school system, the importance of international commerce was the compelling rationale. Kennedy often stressed both factors, but he also argued for improved education for the benefit of individuals and the society, especially in a democracy.

As president, his resistance to private school aid was as much of an obstacle as his earlier support, especially when the Rules Committee narrowly defeated his public school education bill in 1961. Kennedy followed that loss with the statement that he considered "it to be the most important piece of domestic legislation." Indeed, his aid to higher education bill of 1963, where assistance to private schools was not a factor, was notable as the first major aid to education proposal that did not carry the defense needs of the cold war as its justification. "No number of setbacks discouraged him," Sorensen reports. "When an omnibus bill failed, he tried for each of its parts, and vice versa. When elementary and secondary school aid was blocked, he worked on higher education."

At the end, the administration's Higher Education Facilities Act was still pending. Aid to education became a more legitimate part of the Kennedy legacy than civil rights—not only in the formal sense but through such programs as the Peace Corps and its domestic imitation, VISTA, as well as through desegregation and the antipoverty program that began to take shape during his final months. Concern for early childhood education was the mission of the administration's Committee on Juvenile Delinquency, which had the close involvement of Robert Kennedy and spawned other programs, most notably such grass-roots efforts as Haryou and Mobilization for Youth. Lyndon Johnson, in his mournful first speech to the joint session of Congress of November 27, 1963, that called for the enactment of Kennedy's program urged passage of "the pending education bills to help bring the light of learning to every home and hamlet in America."

The legislation was signed into law one week before Christmas, with a fulsome tribute to Johnson to his predecessor for having made it possible. Francis Keppel, who was appointed Commissioner of Education by Kennedy in November of 1962, later told an interviewer that the President had been particularly persuasive on the higher levels of education. "He had an effect simply because he lived and breathed intellectual matters. . . . He just represented that whole generation and this devotion touched me about it. He caught that generation. . . . The tone was set for it."

Johnson then went on to the enactment, as part of his Great Society program, of the Elementary and Secondary Education Act. Guided along by Keppel, it contained provisions for aid to private schools, including sectarian institutions. That question had been one of the major obstacles to federal assistance during the entire post-World War II period. The Kennedy-Johnson period did much to keep education on the agenda. More recently, a half dozen years before George Bush declared himself "the education President," alarming reports about the state of the nation's educational system went unheeded. That was true despite the publicity given to the *A Nation at Risk* report by the National Commission on Excellence in Education. Recently, Japanese officials advised Americans to upgrade their schools if they wanted to be competitive in international commerce. Meanwhile, two decades after the Kennedy-Johnson period, the nation's schools continued to decline.

* * *

We should also argue that Kennedy altered the presidency itself. Not since FDR's time had the Executive Branch cast such an intimidating shadow. Successors had to cope with the standards set by Kennedy—his rhetoric, his sparkling press conferences, the attractiveness of the First Family, his sense of style, his efforts to set the tone for American culture.

Kennedy made the public feel good about the man in the White House, thanks in large part to his ability as an image-maker. In 1983, Gallup reported that he was by far the favorite former president, three times as much as the man who placed second, FDR. In 1988, *New York Times* correspondent Michael T. Kaufman wrote that interest in JFK "is surging, and not only because the anniversary of his death falls this week. . . . For many now in middle age," he added, "including those ascending to positions of power, basic political reflexes were established in the early 1960's."

How all this can be separated from the horror at Dallas is beyond understanding, so it will be a trick to step back from that event and find the man who was at the center of "Camelot." One week before Kennedy went to Texas, James Reston devoted his newspaper column to the state of the presidency. "One has the distinct impression that the American people are going to reelect him, probably by a wide margin," he wrote, "but don't quite believe him." Then, in words that were rendered ironic by the assassination, he added, "He has touched the intellect of the country but not the heart. He has informed but not inspired the nation." Reston concluded with the observation that "he has not made the people feel as he feels, or lifted them beyond their private purposes to one of the larger purposes he has in mind . . . this is a far cry from the atmosphere he promised when he ran for the Presidency in 1960." A New Frontiersman, Richard Goodwin, has recently written that "No one ever really knew John Kennedy."

Nevertheless, it should be added, we all think we do, which gives the legend the strength of universality.

'With One Hand Tied Behind Their Back'... and Other Myths of the Vietnam War

Robert Buzzanco

It is too frequently forgotten that Vietnam is a country, not just a war. For "Vietnam" has assumed the status of an American metaphor for *cultural mistake* or *failure*. Moreover, it is a metaphor subject to multiple interpretations—implying either misguided political-military adventurism or problematic patriotism, depending upon one's point of view. To the historical memory of many, America's failure in Vietnam was directly attributable to the Armed Forces having had "one hand tied behind their back." Pursuit of a military solution to the problems in Southeast Asia, so the story goes, was habitually undermined by politicians (especially President Lyndon Baines Johnson) formulating inconsistent policies, and a citizenry in the United States which never forcefully—and patriotically—supported the war effort. Vietnam, it is said, offers an American equivalent of the "stab in the back theory." Reflecting new research into the war, Professor Robert Buzzanco of the University of Houston, rejects the "one hand tied behind their back" interpretation. In fact, he finds, most key military personnel consistently urged a "hands off" policy in Southeast Asia, held few illusions about total victory there, and—even when forced to pursue the war effort largely for political purposes—had use of a staggering repertoire of military hardware and options. More fundamental, the country that American troops were defending—The Republic of Vietnam (RVN), invented at the 1954 Geneva Conference—was never more than an imagined community to begin with.

As he unleashed American air power against the armed forces and people of Iraq in January 1991, President George Bush assured the nation that U.S. soldiers would not be inhibited by craven politicians or an ambivalent public. "Our troops," Bush explained, "will not be asked to fight with one hand tied behind their back." Just six weeks later, after the American destruction of Iraq, Bush explained that "by God, we've kicked the 'Vietnam Syndrome' once and for all."

The president's words were not coincidental. The use of Vietnam as a symbol of a lack of will and weakness has become common in American political discourse over the past two decades. The United States, many politicians, officers, and scholars have argued, did not suffer a military defeat in Indochina but was in fact undermined at home by weak political leaders and a large antiwar movement. "On the battlefield itself," retired Colonel Harry Summers asserted, "the [U.S.] Army was unbeatable," a view shared by many defenders of the war. Others criticized political leaders, particularly President Lyndon B. Johnson and Defense Secretary Robert Strange McNamara, for limiting the war geographically, needlessly restricting the U.S. air war against the Democratic Republic of Vietnam (DRVN) in the north, and failing to take the strategic initiative and employ more firepower more effectively. By the 1980s such views had become commonplace and powerful; thus candidate Ronald Reagan called the American intervention into Vietnam a "noble cause," and Defense Secretary Caspar Weinberger, amid a public discussion over military policy, explained that "we must never again send Americans into battle unless we plan to win."

Such views, though they may produce significant political currency, do not constitute good history. In fact, those individuals charged with conducting the war in Vietnam, senior American military officers, were in fact critical of and divided over U.S. intervention in Indochina throughout the 1950s and early 1960s. Once American combat troops were deployed to Vietnam, the brass remained pessimistic about U.S. prospects there and engaged in serious interservice arguments over the way the war should be fought. In short, the U.S. armed services never agreed on either intervention or strategy. The American failure in Vietnam was thus not a case of "hands tied behind backs," but rather was due to a conscious political decision to go to war in an area of secondary importance where the possibilities for success, as the military itself recognized, were never great.

For over a decade after the end of World War II, American officers remained highly critical of plans to increase U.S. involvement in Vietnam. Although the revolutionary Viet Minh, a nationalist-Communist force led by Ho Chi Minh and supported by the Soviet Union and People's Republic of China, seemed likely victors in its war against French imperialists and Vietnamese collaborators that had begun in 1946, American military leaders urged a "hands off" policy. Indeed, in the early 1950s, service officials developed a critique of Vietnam that would remain valid for two decades. Above all, the brass opposed war in Indochina because the area was not a priority in national security policy and because the military understood the limits of American power. Accordingly, officers such as Air Force Chief of Staff Hoyt Vandenberg—concerned that French stability was the keystone to European security—warned in 1953 that the continued commitment in Vietnam amounted to "pouring money down a rathole."

American officers clearly understood that French imperialism had created an oppressive politi-cal environment for native Vietnamese. Ho Chi Minh enjoyed the support of eighty percent of the population, U.S. Army planners estimated, yet eighty percent of the Viet Minh's followers were *not* communists. Even France's biggest booster inside the military, Pacific Commander and later JCS Chair Admiral Arthur Radford, saw that "the French seem to have no popular backing from the local Indo-Chinese." By late 1954, Army analysts pointed out that the Viet Minh had grown to about 340,000 troops with about one-quarter *below* the seventeenth parallel, which divided North from South Vietnam.

Any American military commitment to Vietnam, ranking service officials added, would face enormous barriers to success. In March 1950, Army intelligence officers recognized that the "rugged terrain" in Vietnam was a great advantage to the Viet Minh, which was well-versed in jungle, guerrilla warfare. Air Force General Charles Cabell, a JCS official, also had a clear understanding of the hazards of combat in Vietnam. "Terrain difficulties, the guerrilla nature of Viet Minh operations, and the political apathy of the population," he explained in 1953, would make it impossible to clear the Viet Minh out of southern villages, unless "physically occupied" by numerous friendly forces. In his debriefing after leaving Vietnam, General Thomas Trapnell, leader of the U.S. military advisory effort there, cited Ho's followers for their "clever war of attrition" and explained that the Viet Minh, believing that time and public opinion was on its side, would simply continue its guerrilla operations. "A strictly military solution to this war," Trapnell warned, "is not possible."

More importantly, Army Chief of Staff Matthew B. Ridgway, who had been the United Nations commander in Korea after the dismissal of Douglas MacArthur, successfully challenged advocates of intervention in the Spring of 1954. President Dwight Eisenhower and Secretary of State John Foster Dulles were seeking support for American intervention to relieve besieged French troops at Dien Bien Phu, a village near the Laotian border. Such a military commitment in Vietnam, Ridgway emphatically charged, would be a "dangerous strategic diversion" because of limited U.S. resources and troops. It therefore made no sense to Ridgway to commit American soldiers to "a non-decisive theatre" where only "non-decisive local objectives" might be gained. More pointedly, General James Gavin, the Army's chief of planning observed that any U.S. commitment to protect Vietnam below the seventeenth parallel "involves the risk of embroiling [the] U.S. in the wrong war, in the wrong place, at the wrong time."

Despite the military's strong reservations about involvement in Vietnam throughout the early 1950s, the United States established a training mission to the nation below the seventeenth parallel it had ostensibly invented at the 1954 Geneva Conference, the Republic of Vietnam (RVN), and, as the American military leadership had warned, escalated the U.S. role there throughout the next two decades. Publicly, Vietnam declined quite a bit as a foreign policy issue after 1955, but in the later 1950s Generals Gavin and Ridgway continued to criticize American involvement in Indochina. Ridgway expressed his opposition to intervention in poignant yet ultimately empty words: "When the day comes for me to face my Maker and account for my actions, the thing I would be most humbly proud of was the fact that I fought against, and perhaps contributed to preventing, the carrying out of some hare-brained tactical schemes which would have cost the lives of thousands of men. To that list of tragic accidents that fortunately never happened, I would add the Indo-China intervention."

By the early 1960s, it was clear that Ridgway would have to change the script for his heavenly talk. Though America's military planners of the early 1950s had anticipated the serious if not insurmountable barriers to effective military action in Vietnam, Presidents John F. Kennedy and Lyndon B. Johnson progressively expanded the U.S. commitment to the RVN and Johnson eventually deployed ground troops and "Americanized" the war in 1965.

John F. Kennedy came to the White House promising to "pay any price" and "bear any burden" in the global fight against Communism. From his inaugural in January 1961 to his assassination in November 1963, the centerpiece of that Cold War policy would be Vietnam. Kennedy, especially after suffering an embarrassing political defeat at the Bay of Pigs in Cuba in April 1961, focused increasing amounts of resources and money on the effort to prevent Ho Chi Minh's victory in Vietnam. As a result, the Kennedy administration supported the corrupt and repressive regime of Ngo Dinh Diem in the RVN; increased the number of military personnel in Vietnam from 800 to 16,000; allowed the military to use defoliation agents and napalm in southern villages; and authorized the use of helicopters and air support against the enemy,

now referred to as the "Viet Cong" (VC). Although Oliver Stone, in his film *JFK*, and many others claim that the president was preparing to withdraw the United States from Vietnam after the 1964 elections, the historical record proves otherwise. Kennedy and McNamara were heading toward war in Vietnam.

U.S. military leaders, however, were not nearly so hawkish. The armed forces, afraid of being unfairly blamed for failure in Vietnam as they had been after the Bay of Pigs disaster, constantly tried to pin down the president regarding Vietnam policy, to make him establish, describe and take responsibility for any military involvement there. As General Charles Bonesteel of the JCS staff put it, the military needed Kennedy to offer an explanation of "real national intent" before developing its own proposals for Indochina. More specific criticism came from the military's Pacific Commander, Admiral Harry D. Felt, who "strongly opposed" the use of American troops in Vietnam out of fear that the United States would be seen as the aggressor in Vietnam and that world opinion would condemn the intervention of Caucasian soldiers in an Asian civil war. Several officers, after touring Vietnam in mid-1962, added that "the military and political situation in South Vietnam can be described in four words, 'it is a mess.'"

Such military pessimism remained in evidence throughout the Kennedy years. American officers, however, did not refuse to implement the president's policies in Indochina or even strongly challenge them. Rather, the military, for the most part, went along with civilian decisions on Vietnam, but always tried to make it clear that Kennedy and McNamara would be responsible if conditions there, as the brass expected, worsened. Perhaps the best example of this came from General Lionel McGarr, the head of the U.S. Advisory Group in Vietnam. McGarr warned that any military involvement would turn out badly and, as early as 1961, he saw a "slimmer and slimmer" chance to succeed in Vietnam. McGarr nonetheless was willing to accept Kennedy's commitment to the RVN, but even more he feared that the military would be blamed for the likely failure. "As I am jealous of the professional good name of our Army," he explained, "I do not wish it to be placed in the position of fighting a losing battle and being charged with the loss."

Despite such military reservations, U.S. policy in Vietnam did not change in the Kennedy years. The young president, convinced that he had to challenge Communism everywhere, kept increasing the American role in Indochina. Indeed, in interviews shortly before his death, Kennedy was still hawkish on Vietnam. Though he understood that the public might be anxious about war there, an American withdrawal "only makes it easier for the Communists." Problems may lie ahead, but "I think we should stay." Lyndon Johnson agreed.

Lyndon Johnson entered the White House committed to "seeing things through in Vietnam"; he would not, he pledged, "be the President who saw Southeast Asia go the way China went" and so he told his advisors to "tell those generals in Saigon that Lyndon Johnson intends to stand by our word." As a result, from late 1963 until the Tet Offensive in early 1968, Johnson daily confronted the growing crisis of the Vietnam War without essentially questioning the U.S. commitment there. During those years three developments characterized military policy with regard to Vietnam. First, U.S. military leaders in the 1960s continued to recognize the dangerous nature of the American role and the serious obstacles to future success in Vietnam. Second, military leaders understood from the war's beginning that—due to both domestic and international political factors— Lyndon Johnson would establish limits (in troop deployments and geographic areas of warfare) beyond which the U.S. combat commitment in Vietnam would not expand. And third, both the military and the president developed their strategies for Vietnam with politics in mind: understanding the limits imposed by the White House, and unsure of success in any case, the brass nonetheless continued requesting an escalated war, thus forcing the president to confront his shifting approach and be responsible for any U.S. failure in Vietnam.

These three factors would converge in the aftermath of the 1968 Tet Offensive. Not only did the military recognize at that point that Tet had exposed the unsound military strategy of attrition employed in Vietnam but, with its request for 206,000 more troops and a massive reserve callup, also made Johnson accountable for an ultimate decision regarding the war, and effectively transferred blame for the debacle in Vietnam to the White House. Accordingly, U.S. military leaders in the mid-1960s had laid the groundwork for the conservative revisionist critique of Vietnam—the "one hand tied behind their backs" argument—which has become so popular since then.

In the early days of the Johnson administration, the military was no more eager for war than it had been earlier. Thus, in 1963 the incoming Marine Commandant, Wallace M. Greene, Jr., feared that U.S. troops were already "mired down in South Vietnam." "Frankly," he told fellow officers at Quantico, "the Marines do not want to get any more involved in South Vietnam. . . . [W]e've got enough business right now." By early 1965, as U.S. leaders began to debate whether to commit combat forces to Vietnam, many military men—especially General Maxwell Taylor, the Ambassador to Saigon at the time—opposed such deployments. Both Taylor and the Commander of the U.S. Military Assistance Command, Vietnam [MACV], General William C. Westmoreland, recognized that large-scale intervention would lead to increased U.S. responsibility for the war, more casualties, and propaganda linking Americans to French imperialists. Combat intervention, a MACV study remarkably, and prophetically, concluded, "would at best buy time and would lead to ever-increasing commitments until, like the French, we would be occupying an essentially hostile foreign country."

Nonetheless, the White House deployed two Marine battalions to Danang in March 1965, the first American combat units to enter the RVN; their commander, General Fredrick Karch, arrived to find fellow officers "dismal" over U.S. prospects, the enemy VC holding the political and military initiative, and the southern Army of the Republic of Vietnam (ARVN) passive and corrupt. Vietnam, Karch would later charge, "was just one big cancer." And it was spreading. Throughout the first part of 1965 American political and military leaders recognized the imperiled U.S. position in Vietnam but nevertheless significantly expanded their commitment in July. The White House had made a "political calculation" that it could not withstand the domestic consequences of the "loss" of Vietnam to Communism, just as earlier the Truman administration had suffered the political fallout of the "loss" of China.

At the same time the Johnson administration did not want a wider war and did not want Vietnam to obstruct its political agenda at home. Such political concerns were evident in a frank 1964 memo from Johnson's advisor Jack Valenti, in which he recommended that the White House "sign on" the JCS before making any final decisions regarding Vietnam. By bringing the military into the process, Valenti pointed out, the Chiefs "will have been heard, they will have been part of the consensus, and our flank will have been covered in the event of some kind of flap or investigation later." Westmoreland understood that such political limits were affecting military policy. In December 1965 he admitted to Ambassador Henry Cabot Lodge that a reserve call-up and extended terms of service would "require drastic action that could be politically difficult for the President." In addition, military leaders continued to recognize that circumstances inside Vietnam were retarding progress. Even Westmoreland's hawkish Chief of Plans, General William DePuy, expected the war to continue indefinitely because the RVN's government "is really bankrupt" while the VC "fight like tigers." Although the General hoped that political leaders would commit more forces to Vietnam, he recognized that additional troops would not be sent "unless there's been progress," which was not terribly likely.

As if DePuy's understanding of the military and political dilemmas of Vietnam was not ominous enough, the MACV was also suffering the effects of a serious interservice rivalry over strategy which began in 1965 and would continue throughout the war. In particular Marine leaders Wallace Greene and Pacific Commander Victor H. Krulak consistently attacked the Westmoreland, and Army, strategy of attrition, and called for an emphasis on pacification and political warfare. In a late 1965 appraisal of U.S. strategy, Krulak thus urged Westmoreland to "put the full weight of our top level effort into bringing all applicable resources . . . into the pacification process." Greene also championed counterinsurgency and compared Westmoreland's strategy of attrition to "a grindstone that's being turned by the Communist side, and we're backing into it and having our skin taken off of . . . our entire body without accomplishing a damn thing because they've got enough to keep the old stone going." The VC could thus tolerate losses twenty or thirty times greater than the U.S. because, the Commandant wisely understood, "in the end, although their casualty rate may be fifty times what ours is, they'll be able to win through their capability to wage a war of attrition." Yet, Greene concluded, "this is a thing that apparently the Army doesn't understand." Krulak agreed, adding that "this is not the strategy for victory."

After barely two years in the White House, Lyn-

don Johnson had committed increasing resources and troops into Vietnam with a clear understanding of the troubles that lay ahead and the limits to future expansion of the war. At the same time, military leaders were equally aware of obstacles to future progress and of the political constraints on military policy, yet they would continue to seek more forces and bombs rather than develop alternative strategies. Thus, political considerations would increasingly determine the course of the war.

The president himself was growing more anxious about the political turmoil affecting policymaking as well. "General," Johnson told Westmoreland at Honolulu in early 1966, "I have a lot riding on you. I hope you don't pull a MacArthur on me." Westmoreland and his staff understood Johnson's concerns, but were aware of many of the problems in South Vietnam as well. In addition to continued instability and manpower shortages within the Vietnamese military, the U.S. Commander did not expect to receive the reinforcements he had been requesting. In fact, Westmoreland developed the American force structure while assuming "that there will be no major call up of reserves." Nevertheless he would continue to make that very request throughout the war. Wheeler was more anxious about the political factors driving the war. The civilian leadership, he understood, remained troubled by the lack of emphasis given to pacification, the continuing lack of military activity by the South Vietnamese, and growing Communist infiltration into southern Vietnam, which was offsetting the VC's huge losses.

Despite such candid and bleak evaluations, Westmoreland's staff continued to emphasize its accomplishments and to expect progress. In a January 1967 evaluation the military stressed that U.S. and ARVN forces were routing the enemy, many VC and Communist supporters were rallying to the RVN, and pacification was likely to improve markedly in the coming year. While the enemy's determination had not weakened, "the conflict has taken a decided turn for the best." At the same time, however, there was serious question as to whether the military expected its own programs to succeed. Westmoreland himself would later speculate that, "even had Washington adopted a strong bombing policy, I still doubt that the North Vietnamese would have relented." "The influx of men and materials" into the south, Admiral U.S.G. Sharp, the Pacific Commander, admitted, "has increased despite considerable air effort expended to hinder infiltration." Sharp also understood that the White House's reluctance to remove even more restrictions from the air war was "based primarily on political considerations."

Wheeler recognized it too. In early March, after revised MACV statistics showed that VC-initiated major unit attacks were actually about 400 percent higher than originally estimated, the obviously alarmed JCS Chair cabled Westmoreland that "if these figures should reach the public domain, they would, literally, blow the lid off of Washington." And surely the president was not ignorant of the reality of the war. Johnson "never intended" to escalate the war as the military was urging, and developments in Vietnam up to early 1967 had reinforced that position.

Nonetheless in April 1967 Westmoreland requested about 200,000 new troops for Vietnam. But McNamara, among others, had soured on the war and believed that attrition would fail "as a military strategy as well as a presidential policy for political survival." The president himself expressed serious misgivings in a meeting with Westmoreland and Wheeler in late April. Although the U.S. Commander claimed that his forces had eroded enemy strength to the "crossover point" at which its losses exceeded northern infiltration into the south, Johnson wondered "when we add divisions, can't the enemy add divisions? If so, when does it all end? . . . [A]t what point does the enemy ask for [presumably Chinese] volunteers?" The General's answers were not reassuring. Maintaining current levels would simply create a "meat grinder" in Vietnam, he told the president. Wheeler added that massive reinforcement might provoke the Soviet Union or China to retaliate in Europe, in Korea, or elsewhere in Southeast Asia. In addition, the JCS Chair admitted that the air war—the military's fundamental answer to the problems of Vietnam—"is reaching the point where we will have struck all worthwhile targets except the ports."

Such evaluations and continued candid reports out of Saigon thus prompted Johnson to reject Westmoreland's plan for full reinforcement. A full year before the crisis of Tet the White House, the JCS, and the MACV had clearly drawn the lines over which civil-military battles would be fought. The civilian leadership recognized that success was not close, but rejected fully unrestrained war. The military too was aware of the continued peril of war in Vietnam and also understood that it would not receive authoriza-

tion to fight without constraints. Earle Wheeler was especially bleak, lamenting the White House's recognition that "the Main-Force war . . . is stalemated . . . and there is no evidence that pacification will ever succeed in view of the widespread rot and corruption of the government, the pervasive economic and social ills, and the tired, passive and accommodation prone attitude of the armed forces of South Vietnam."

Given such judgments it would take a rather great stretch of imagination to expect success in Vietnam. Yet the war continued, with the White House and the brass as concerned with avoiding blame for failure as with actually improving the situation on the battlefield. Army Chief Harold K. Johnson admitted as much, telling Wheeler that the war was being lost and that the military would "take the fall." Indeed, the service chiefs "now believed that they had been betrayed by their civilian leaders, that the war could not continue without an irrational loss of American lives, and that . . . there was little reason to hope for an eventual American victory." Neither the military nor White House, of course, publicly made such statements, and when Westmoreland made a public relations trip to Washington in late November 1967 he concluded that, despite problems, there was "light at the end of the tunnel."

Clearly Lyndon Johnson had to have such good news; his political career depended on it. But the light at the end of the tunnel, Westmoreland's critics later joked, was a train headed toward the general. And at the end of January 1968 it thundered through Vietnam. Taking advantage of a Tet New Year cease-fire, the VC and northern army struck virtually every military and political center of importance, even invading the U.S. embassy grounds. Within sixty days, Tet would bring down the president, finally force a reassessment of the war at the highest levels, and bring to a climax one of the gravest crises in civil-military relations in U.S. history. Tet, as it were, became the U.S. obituary in Vietnam.

Since 1968 the Tet Offensive has attained mythic status, with analysts of virtually every ideological stripe agreeing that Tet was—as Westmoreland and Johnson publicly claimed at the time—a great U.S. military victory, but political and psychological defeat. Such observations, however, neglect the military's own outlook on the war in February and March 1968. Indeed, throughout the Tet crisis, officials in the MACV and JCS as well as political leaders recognized America's perhaps-intractable dilemma in Vietnam. Just days after the attacks began, Westmoreland reported to Wheeler that, "from a realistic point of view, we must accept the fact that the enemy has dealt [South Vietnam] a severe blow," bringing the war to the people, inflicting heavy casualties and damage, and disrupting the economy. The Commander did end on an upbeat note, though, claiming that the enemy's own huge losses and failure to overthrow the southern government constituted the failure of the offensive. But he also recognized that the enemy's objectives "were primarily psychological and political." A week later Westmoreland would candidly explain, "we are now in a new ballgame where we face a determined, highly disciplined enemy, fully mobilized to achieve a quick victory." Such reports would continue throughout February 1968, leading an obviously alarmed Lyndon Johnson to despatch Wheeler to Saigon at the end of the month.

In his well-documented report, Wheeler found the enemy strong and capable of continuing its attacks. The ARVN meanwhile had lost about one-quarter of its pre-Tet strength. The pacification program had been badly undermined. And the government's effectiveness was obviously in question, especially as it confronted the massive problems of refugees and reconstruction. "In short," Wheeler concluded, "it was a very near thing." Harold K. Johnson did not resort to euphemism. "We suffered a loss," he cabled Westmoreland, "there can be no doubt about it." Clearly then, later claims that Tet was a great U.S. victory are essentially moot. American leaders in early 1968 did not have time for the dust to settle in Vietnam for a thorough analysis of the situation. With a barrage of candid and often pessimistic reports flowing from Saigon to Washington, policymakers could do little more than seek an effective way to cut their losses in Vietnam.

Obviously such bleak views disturbed Washington, with the president on 9 February wondering "what has happened to change the situation between then [initial optimism] and now?" At the end of February, however, Johnson received an even greater shock when Wheeler and Westmoreland again requested about 200,000 additional troops for Vietnam and the activation of almost 300,000 reservists. Even when the military's reports out of Vietnam had been optimistic about future progress, such massive reinforcement was never realistically likely. Amid the

crisis of Tet, it was impossible. Westmoreland himself later admitted that he and the JCS Chair "both knew the grave political and economic implications of a major call-up of reserves." Nonetheless the military asked for a remarkable escalation of the war at the very moment it had descended to its nadir.

Within the context of civil-military relations during the Vietnam War, however, the reinforcement request had a certain logic. It was consistent with long-term White House and military patterns of behavior toward the war. By February and March 1968 military and civilian leaders understood that reinforcement, especially in such vast numbers, was not politically feasible. But the military, rather than change course after Tet, sent notice that it would continue its now-discredited war of attrition. In so doing, however, the service leaders forced Lyndon Johnson to finally take decisive action regarding Vietnam and bear responsibility for future failure.

The military realized that the request for more forces would cause a political firestorm. The Army's Pacific Commander, General Dwight Beach, when notified of Westmoreland's proposals, "had commented that it would shock" government officials. Indeed, the military had reason to expect such a reaction from Washington. Not only had the White House rejected Westmoreland's previous proposals for such escalation, but the president himself on 2 February had told reporters that he saw no reason to expand troop levels beyond the 525,000 then deployed to Vietnam. Johnson was also worried that the crisis of Tet might be politically devastating. At a meeting with his advisors, he charged that "all of you have counseled, advised, consulted and then—as usual—placed the monkey on my back again.... I do not like what I am smelling from those cables from Vietnam."

Johnson's outburst may have been disingenuous but it was well-founded. The monkey in fact belonged squarely on his back, but it was true that his advisors had developed even more grave reservations about the Vietnam War as a result of Tet. Thus, the president feared that the military might be able to exploit White House division over Vietnam. "I don't want them [U.S. military leaders] to ask for something," Johnson worried aloud, "not get it, and have all the blame placed on me." Although not expecting such a huge reinforcement request, it was thus clear that the president understood the political implications of any future moves regarding Vietnam.

Ambassador to Saigon Ellsworth Bunker understood as well, warning Westmoreland against asking for so many additional forces because reinforcement was now "politically impossible," even if Johnson had wanted it, which was also more unlikely than ever.

Indeed it was. Within the month, incoming Defense Secretary Clark Clifford would reassess the war, Johnson's informal advisors, the so-called Wise Men, would finally urge de-escalation, and U.S. military leaders would continue to provide candid evaluations of the enemy's capabilities and America's problems. By the end of March the President would lament that *"everybody is recommending surrender."* But it was Johnson himself who surrendered, withdrawing from the 1968 presidential campaign at the end of a 31 March national address. Finally forced to confront his failure to determine a consistent policy on Vietnam by the twin shocks of Tet and the huge reinforcement proposal, the president knew that time had run out on both his political career and the U.S. experience in Vietnam.

Although the United States would remain in Vietnam for five more years, until the Paris Peace Accords of January 1973, Tet in fact constituted the end of American illusions about "victory" in the Indochina War. The United States, after Tet, began its policy of "Vietnamization," which meant that the South Vietnamese themselves would be responsible for the war while American troops began to withdraw. At the same time, however, Johnson's successor Richard M. Nixon would significantly expand the conflict into neighboring Laos and Kampuchea and markedly escalate the air war. In the end, however, the ARVN was not able to withstand continuing pressure from the VC and northern Vietnamese forces and, despite massive American air strikes and aid to the RVN, crumbled before the Communist offensive which reunified the country in April 1975. In the end, Vietnamization, as Senator George McGovern charged, amounted to "changing the color of the corpses."

Nixon and his defenders, however, have steadfastly maintained that a more consistent application of air power and intervention into North Vietnam or Laos and Cambodia might have made a difference.

Again, the military itself challenged such views. Indeed, the military did not seriously consider intervening in North Vietnam; the logistics needs alone would have been massive and troop morale could not have been taken for granted. With regard to the air war, Army Chief of Staff General Harold K. Johnson asserted that "if anything came out of Vietnam, it was that airpower couldn't do the job." Nor did the armed services possess the unity of purpose that would be essential to any successful strategy. The Army and Marines, it seemed, were fighting each other as much as they were jointly fighting against the enemy.

In the end, the United States suffered a military defeat in Vietnam. The "country" that American troops were defending, the RVN, never achieved political stability and its military seemed content to let U.S. soldiers fight and die for it. As for the United States, its political and military leaders often seemed more concerned with avoiding blame for failure as with developing strategy. U.S. troops thus did not fight with "one hand tied behind their back," as a popular myth would have it. The United States, in fact, dropped 4.6 million tons of bombs on Vietnam and another 2 million tons on Kampuchea and Laos (over twice the total dropped by the Allies in all theatres of World War II combined). In addition, U.S. forces sprayed 11.2 million gallons of Agent Orange, a dioxin-carrying herbicide, and dropped over 400,000 tons of napalm. The impact of such warfare was catastrophic. American firepower destroyed 9,000, out of 15,000 southern villages, 25 million acres of farmland, and 12 million acres of forests, while creating over 2.5 million bomb craters and leaving a significant amount of unexploded ordnance throughout Vietnam. The human toll was worse: perhaps 2 to 3 million Vietnamese, mostly civilians, were killed, while an additional 300,000 or so Kampucheans and Laotians died. Over 3 million Indochinese were wounded as well. And by 1975, there were about 15 million refugees in the area. If such activities amounted to fighting in a restrained and limited manner, with "hands tied behind backs," one can hardly imagine what total war in Vietnam would have been like.

The Frontier Myth and the Reagan Presidency

Richard Slotkin

Even before the University of Wisconsin historian Frederick Jackson Turner fully articulated the myth in 1893, the idea of "the frontier" had been a central theme and preoccupation of American life and consciousness. Back when America was the frontier of Europe, extravagant myths about western frontiers animated the imaginations of Europeans. Mythologically enhanced expectations of remote yet enticing frontiers kept the nation on the road west to some or another open land of geography or the spirit. The frontier legacy proved irresistible to a succession of enterprising pathfinders—from leatherstockinged pioneers to leather-lunged politicians. So habitual did such movements of men and imagination become that territorial confusion resulted. In the truest historical sense, the "old west" of New England and the Chesapeake eventually became "the east" and the "Far West" eventually preempted the "Old Northwest," thus creating a vacuum-filling "Middle West." And what the nation ultimately had come to call the "Old West" was, in reality, the newest West of all. In the end, all Americans, after their fashion, are and become westerners. Ronald Reagan knew it and capitalized upon it. After serving a mythic apprenticeship riding the landscapes of Hollywood cinema, he mobilized politics with the myth of the frontier. With the Reagan presidency, argues Richard Slotkin of Wesleyan University, the nation's preeminent historical cultural mythologies, addictions, and icons became one. The cultural conflation of "Cowboy," "star," "fame," and "President" revalidated and reenergized the West and its frontier traditions, all personified by President Ronald Reagan. Cowboy capitalism at home and gunfighter nation abroad were "back in the [cultural] saddle again."

The mythographers of the Reagan Revolution sought to overcome the "malaise" of the 1970s—the breakdown of public myth that prevented consensus on purposeful action in both domestic and foreign affairs—by substituting for the distressing memory of "the Sixties" a fictive replica of a simpler time: the "Happy Days" when the Cold War was young and the world was divided between an "evil empire" and a TV-pastoral, "Leave It to Beaver" America that a few good men could save by fighting dirty wars. The central theme of Reagan's two presidential campaigns, and of his conduct of office, was the system-atic resanctification of the symbols and rituals of "public myth"—a task for which Reagan's experience as an actor was ideal preparation. His 1980 and 1984 campaigns associated him with iconic and idealized American settings drawn from the mythic landscapes of cinema: "Morning in America" (1980) depicted an America of farms, country churches, suburban lawns, the "decent" streets of cities, all seen in a soft early-day light; and many of his most characteristic anecdotes, phrases, and slogans ("Make my day!") were borrowed from movie dialogue. But these patently celluloid backgrounds and gestures seemed both appropriate and authentic as settings for candidate and President Reagan, because they were icons of movie-America, and that imagined space was indeed the historical setting in which Reagan matured and acquired his public identity.

From the beginning of his campaign for the presidency, Reagan was widely (and inaccurately) identified as a "B" Western cowboy actor, particularly (at first) by his detractors. The famous campaign poster, "Bedtime for Brezhnev," which shows a cowboy-clad Reagan holding a six-gun on the Russian leader, illustrates the achievement of the Reagan campaign: it transformed the most ridiculous of pop-culture formulas ("B" Westerns and comedies like *Bedtime for Bonzo*) into recipes for a renewal of the American myth. Reagan acquired a more "serious" heroic aura through images that linked him closely to the two most prominent Western movie stars, John Wayne and Clint Eastwood. The most impressive of these images came at the 1984 convention, when clips of John Wayne introduced a film celebrating Reagan's life and the achievements of his first term.

Reagan had a legitimate claim on this kind of heroic aura. Neither Wayne nor Eastwood had actually been a cowboy or a leatherneck—like Reagan, they had merely played those roles on the screen. The use of mythic allusion to lend a politician the afflatus of a hero was hardly unique to Reagan. William Henry Harrison traded on his Indian-fighting laurels to gain the presidency in 1840, and in 1900 Theodore Roosevelt rode into national office as "The Rough Rider" and "The Cowboy President." But Roosevelt's claim to those titles was proved by reference to his actual deeds as a stockman, sheriff, and Rough Rider, while Reagan's claim to heroic character was based entirely on references to imaginary deeds performed in a purely mythic space. The difference between them indicates the change that has occurred in our political culture over this century: the myths produced by mass culture have become credible substitutes for actual historical or political action in authenticating the character and ideological claims of political leaders. Moreover, the substitution of myth for history serves not only as an advertising ploy for electing the candidate but as an organizing principle for making policy. The obsession of the Johnson and Nixon administrations with symbolic victories was an early exercise in mythopolitics, but Ronald Reagan was the virtuoso of the form. At the height of his powers he was able to cover his actions with the gloss of patriotic symbolism and to convince his audience that—in life as in movies—merely symbolic action is a legitimate equivalent of the "real thing."

The public's favorable response to Reagan's conflation of "cowboy," "star," and "president" suggests that (on some level of awareness) it shared the belief that a refurbishing of public myth was the proper antidote to the demoralization of American culture. That response also suggests that the key terms of the myth will be drawn from the language of mass media and not from the language of the intelligentsia. However one evaluates the substance of Reagan's policies and achievements, during his term of office he enjoyed perhaps the greatest personal popularity of any president in our history—a popularity that was not affected by the public's disapproval of many of the specific measures and policies of his administration. By the conviction with which he performed his public role, enacted the rituals of his office, and voiced the requisite religious and patriotic pieties, and by his convincing display of innocence of and disdain for the criticisms that were leveled against the traditions he espoused, Reagan *dramatized* or *impersonated* the condition of mythic belief. Thus by identifying with the President as *dramatis persona*, one could vicariously enjoy the comforts of credulity.

There was more to the myth/ideology of the Reagan Revolution than mere manipulation of surface imagery. The structuring principles of that revolution represented an authentic recrudescence and revision of the Frontier Myth. According to that myth, a magical growth of American wealth, power, and virtue, will derive from the close linkage of "bonanza economics"—the acquisition of abundant resources without commensurate inputs of labor and investment—with political expansion and moral "regeneration" through the prosecution of "savage war." In the "post-industrial" 1980s a similar economic bonanza was to be achieved through the magic of supply-side economics coupled with a regeneration of the nation's spirit through more vigorous prosecution of Cold War (against Russia as "evil empire") and savage war (against enemies like Ghadafy of Libya, Maurice Bishop of Grenada, and the Sandinista regime in Nicaragua).

"Reaganomics" developed in reaction to the failure of the Carter administration to deal with the economic crisis of "stagflation." The Reagan campaign faulted Carter's policy for its vacillation between conservative pro-business policies and conciliation of those labor and minority groups that formed the Democrats' liberal constituency. But the Republicans were equally effective in challenging the intellectual basis of Carter's conservatism: his acceptance of the idea that we had indeed reached "The End of the Cowboy Economy," and that on "spaceship earth" Americans could no longer look forward to high and ever-increasing rates of growth. The Reagan campaign's praise of the bonanza economies of previous "boom" eras was more than just an exercise in nostalgia: it was the prelude to an attempt to revive the "cowboy economy" under "post-industrial" conditions.

The Reagan version of "supply-side economics" represents a recrudescence (with modifications) of the Turnerian approach to economic development. In its original or primary formulation, Turner's Frontier Hypothesis held that the prosperity and high growth rates of the American economy had been made possible by the continual expansion of the Frontier into regions richly endowed with natural resources. As industrial production replaced agricultural and mineral commodities as the primary source of wealth, a revised or secondary version of Turnerism saw rapid increases in industrial productivity as a viable substitute for the land and resource bonanzas of the past—an idea suggested by Turner himself but codified as historical theory by Beard in the 1930s. The theoreticians of the liberal consensus saw the "affluent society" of postwar America as the vindication of this secondary Turnerism and extrapolated from the American model a universal theory of modernization.

"Reaganomics" in effect proposed a *tertiary* Turnerism, in which the multiplication and manipulation of financial capital replaces both agrarian commodities and industrial production as the engine of economic expansion. A "bonanza" of new capital, released through measures favoring business and the wealthy (tax cuts and deregulation), was to act as the magical guarantor of perpetual and painless economic growth, in just the way that the opening of "vast untapped reserves" of free land or gold or cheap oil on the Frontier had energized the economy in the past. At the ceremonies attending his signature of the St. Germain/Garn bill, which deregulated the savings and loan industry, Reagan hailed the measure as one that would cost the taxpayers nothing but would produce limitless benefits for the whole economy by energizing the banking industry and the crucial investment sectors of housing and real estate: "All in all, I think we've hit the jackpot." Although the poor and the middle classes would not benefit directly, some of the newly generated wealth would "trickle down" through the economy. (Even here the parallel with the Frontier held: the opening of new lands had not only benefited the minority who pioneered them, it had contributed indirectly to the prosperity of others by raising the value of land and labor and lowering the cost of food.)

The enactment of tertiary Turnerism was accompanied by the recrudescence of ideas and behaviors associated with the bonanza economics of the old Frontier. The term "frontier" enjoyed its widest currency since 1960–63. Writers on economic subjects and promoters of particular businesses publicized a range of new "frontiers" in marketing and development, while on the left Robert Reich suggested that The New American Frontier lay in the development of human resources neglected by the "politics of greed" that shaped the Reagan program. Proposals for extraterrestrial colonization (on space stations or in lunar or planetary settlements) transformed "outer space" into The High Frontier; and since every American frontier presupposes the threat of Indians, the same term was used in polemics on behalf of a space-based nuclear warfare system, the Strategic Defense Initiative, or "Star Wars." Closer to home, the unexploited realm of the oceans was dubbed our "Last Earthly Frontier," a potentially inexhaustible source of nutriment, mineral wealth, and energy—and of course, an embattled wilderness whose more intelligent natives (the dolphins) might be enlisted as our allies in warfare.

But perhaps the most characteristic use of "frontier" as a term of cultural significance in the Reagan era occurred in the voice-over by Robin Leach that introduced one of the most popular television programs of the decade, *Lifestyles of the Rich and Famous*. Leach invites his viewers to share with him the privilege of a voyeur's peep into the lives of "super" celebrities and the "super" rich, who inhabit "Fame and Fortune—the Final Frontier!" As on other frontiers, minimal investments of labor yield fabulous returns: the most trivial actions are seen to yield the extravagant perquisites of celebrity, especially a license for excessive consumption and conspicuous waste.

In its celebration of wealth and fame as things

supremely valuable in themselves, *Lifestyles* seems a self-parody. But the show's abstraction of "wealth" from concrete scenarios of labor, savings, and investment highlights the distinctive character of this most recent recrudescence of Turnerian economics, in which vast speculations in the paper values of real-estate developments, Third World debt, junk bonds, and debt-leveraged corporate takeovers replaced productivity and investment as the calculus of economic value. The economic style of the 1980s has been likened to that of the Roaring 20s. But there is an equally good precedent in Mark Twain's description of bonanza economics during the Nevada silver boom of the 1860s:

> It was the strangest phase of life one can imagine. It was a beggar's revel. There was nothing doing in the district—no mining—no milling—no productive effort—no income—... and yet a stranger would have supposed he was walking among bloated millionaires. ... Few people took *work* into their calculations—or outlay of money either; except the work and expenditures of other people. ... You could ... get your stock printed, and with nothing whatever to prove that your mine was worth a straw, you could put your stock on the market and sell out for hundreds and even thousands of dollars. To make money, and make it fast, was as easy as it was to eat your dinner. They burrowed away, bought and sold, and were happy.

Conceiving of our landed, wooded, animal and mineral wealth as inexhaustible, the frontiersmen of the past felt licensed to exploit that wealth without restraint. That same ethic had been applied in the metropolis to the human resource of labor, first in the exploitation of slaves and later in the somewhat more limited exploitation of immigrant and industrial laborers. Under Reaganomics, a marvelous new mother lode of wealth was discovered in the heritage of our society's accumulated savings and in the capital produced by past labor and investment, and a generation of junk-bond financiers and corporate raiders became rich and famous by strip-mining it. As Garry Wills has said,

> Wealth ... became staggeringly *non*-productive in the Reagan era. It was diverted into shelters. It was shuffled through paper deals; it financed its own disappearance; it erased others' holdings, along with the banks that contained them. It depleted rather than replenished. It shriveled where it was supposed to irrigate. Huge sums were bandied about at art auc-

tions while bridges were disintegrating. Money flew in all directions at home, while seeping almost invisibly abroad.

Although the economy expanded under Reagan, the benefits of expansion were distributed so unequally that, while the richest Americans were acquiring a larger share of the national wealth, the number of persons living in poverty increased and the real income and assets of most of the population declined. The savings and loan deregulation, which Reagan had hailed as a "jackpot" in 1982, proved to be the worst financial disaster since the Great Depression. The government's colossal indebtedness—the result of Reagan's insistence on cutting taxes while accelerating defense spending—seems certain to limit for years to come the government's fiscal resources and its ability to pursue needed policies of social and economic reconstruction at home and to take a leading role in the investments that will shape the post-Cold War political and economic order.

Like the "beggar's revel" of Reaganomics, the "savage war" side of Reagan's revived Frontier Myth shows a disparity between nominal values and real values. The center of Reagan's foreign-policy agenda was the more energetic prosecution of the Cold War against the Soviet Bloc, primarily through a massive buildup of military forces and the acquisition of the most advanced military technology. The renewed Cold War also envisioned the nation's resumption of an active counterinsurgency role in the Third World, both as a means of resisting the advance of Communism and as a way of asserting American interests against those of local opponents. Both policies required the discovery of a cure for "Vietnam syndrome": the public's unwillingness to support military engagement in the Third World for fear of becoming trapped in another "quagmire."

To build public support for defense expenditures, government spokesmen and policy-makers pointed with alarm to the continuing growth of the "Soviet menace." They abandoned the rhetoric of détente for an apocalyptic symbolism which labeled the Soviet Bloc an "evil empire" and "the foundation of evil in the modern world." "Vietnam syndrome" presented a more difficult problem, because engagement in Third World conflicts threatened immediate costs in blood instead of the deferred costs of the anti-Soviet buildup. The administration solved the problem by recognizing that "Vietnam syndrome" could be treated as merely a defective symbolism—a tendency to interpret every Third World contest as a metaphor of the Vietnam War and to conceive of that war as a "mistake" and inherently unwinnable. Reagan himself became the chief spokesman for a revisionist history of the Vietnam War. He represented that war as a noble, unselfish struggle that could have ended in victory if only the liberal politicians in Washington had not tied the hands of the military.

This version of the war was supported (and by Reagan explicitly linked) to a contemporary genre-myth of great currency and power which might be called "The Cult of the POWs/MIAs." *The Deerhunter* incorporated this theme in its epic treatment of the war. But the theme reached its widest audience through the films of the *Rambo* and *Missing in Action* series. The concentration of these films on the captivity formula links them to the most basic story-form of the Frontier Myth, and their obsessive repetition of the rescue fantasy makes them seem like rituals for transforming the trauma of defeat into a symbolic victory. The heroes of these films are military vigilantes, ex-Green Berets who cannot fully return to America until they have completed their failed "mission" and canceled the debt of honor owed to comrades they survived or left behind. The American who, as representative of the world's mightiest army, had been defeated by ragtag, Vietnamese guerrillas now gets to play the war movie in reverse: this time he is the guerrilla, and he defeats a rigid, regularized, totalitarian enemy who has him outnumbered and outgunned. But the redemption of national honor in these films also requires the defeat of a domestic, American opponent: the most insidious enemies of these rescuer-heroes are officials of their own government who represent those politicians and "big shots" who (as the Nazis said of the Weimar liberals) "stabbed the army in the back" and prevented it from winning the war.

In these Vietnam-rescue films, mass-culture myth plays its classic role, which is not (as critics of media violence fear) to act as a stimulus to individual violence but to justify social violence through the symbolic enhancement of a tale of personal violence. The belief that numbers of POWs/MIAs are still held by the Vietnamese had been a recurrent preoccupation in every administration since 1975 and remains an important factor in our Southeast Asia diplomacy.

But the most significant political referent of these films was not the Vietnam War but the new crisis in America's relations with the Third World symbolized by the series of hostage crises that began with the *Mayaguez* incident and became a major factor in our politics after Iranian Revolutionary Guards seized our Tehran embassy in 1979. The mythic imperative implicit in any hostage "crisis"—that we must rescue or avenge the captive at all costs—has given such events a fatal attraction for public concern, media attention, and political opportunism. Carter's failure to rescue the Tehran hostages helped bring down his administration, and Reagan's obsession with the Beirut hostages distorted our policy in the Levant and encouraged the CIA and the NSC to undertake a series of scandalously illegal covert actions that tainted the last years of Reagan's presidency.

"Standing tall" in places like Central America required the explicit repair of those counterinsurgency myths that had been discredited by Vietnam. The Reagan administration invested a good deal of time, effort, money, and moral capital in justifying its support of the *"contra"* war against the Marxist regime in Nicaragua: a war fought by "Chicago rules" which breached American moral codes and ultimately (in the Iran-*Contra* affair) federal law as well. More recently, the Bush administration's "War on Drugs" has invoked the traditional myths of savage war to rationalize a policy in which various applications of force and violence have a central role. Here the Myth of the Frontier plays its classic role: we define and confront this crisis, and the profound questions it raises about our society and about the international order, by deploying the metaphor of "war" and locating the root of our problem in the power of a "savage," captive-taking enemy.

Once invoked, the war-metaphor governs the terms in which we respond to changing circumstances. It spreads to new objects; it creates a narrative tension for which the only emotionally or esthetically satisfying resolution is literal rather than merely figurative warfare. What begins as a demand for symbolic violence ends in actual bloodshed and in the doctrine of "extraordinary violence": the sanctioning of "cowboy" or (more properly) vigilante-style actions by public officials and covert operatives who defy public law and constitutional principles in order to "do what a man's gotta do."

The mythic scenarios that rationalize and perhaps govern policy no longer take their language primarily from Western movies. They draw as well on the vocabularies of the vigilante-cop film and the

Vietnam War rescue-revenge fable. Terms and images derived from Vietnam are used to interpret the "drug crisis" and to project a scenario of response. Advisers are sent to Colombia and Peru, and naval and air power is deployed to interdict supply routes and help the native troops conduct search-and-destroy operations. There are projects for defoliation or coca-crop destruction and efforts to win the hearts and minds of the people (both American drug users and Colombian peasants). The invasion of Panama in January 1990, which literalized the metaphor of the "War on Drugs," was framed by the classic rationales of the Frontier Myth: the tyrannical Manuel Noriega (formerly a paid agent of our own CIA) was characterized not only as a dictator but as a physically repellent man (with pocked face and "Indian" blood), a sexual deviant and a drug addict; and the immediate pretext for the invasion itself ("Operation Just Cause") was the need to rescue American civilians from abuse by Noriega's forces and to avenge the assault on an American officer and his wife.

The most triumphant, and the most disturbing, of these exercises in mythography is the Gulf War of 1991. In justifying the largest deployment of American military force since the Vietnam War, President Bush invoked the classic elements of "captivity" and "savage war" mythology. Saddam Hussein's potential dominance of the Gulf oil fields was seen as a danger to the future of "bonanza economics"; defeating Saddam would facilitate long-term development and save American jobs in the present. Hussein himself was the perfect enemy for a modern Frontier-Myth scenario, combining the barbaric cruelty of a "Geronimo" with the political power and ambition of a Hitler. This characterization was made credible by the oppressive character of the Ba'ath regime, the murderous occupation of Kuwait, and Saddam's ill-managed attempts at hostage-holding. The vivid symbolism and the passions it aroused effectively masked the questionable aspects of American policy in the region, including our earlier complicity with Saddam in his war against Iran.

More disturbing still is Bush's assertion that the violence of the Gulf War has regenerated the national spirit and moral character by expiating the defeat in Vietnam. Mythopolitical exercises of this kind are of course inimical to the successful conduct of affairs, to the extent that they palliate or even justify badly conceived policies. But their most harmful effect may be their distortion of the language and logic that

inform the discourses of our political culture. By treating the Gulf War as a ritual of regeneration through violence, and asking us to receive it as redemption for our failure in Vietnam, Bush asks us to conceive our political and moral priorities in *exclusively* mythic terms—with primary reference to the conflicts, needs, desires, and role-playing imperatives that are exhibited in mass-culture mythology, and with secondary or negligible reference to the realities of public and political life. By assuring us that the sentiments we feel when watching a movie-captivity like *Rambo II* or *Missing in Action* are a sufficient basis for engaging in war, the President authorizes the shedding of blood, not as a cruel means to a necessary end, nor as a defense of vital interests or principles, but as a cure for the illness of our imagination—to erase the discomforting memory of our historical experience of error and defeat, and to substitute in its place the lie of "symbolic victory."

The destructive effects of this kind of mythological thinking are not restricted to foreign affairs, but (like counterinsurgency) have their domestic counterpart. The "savage war" paradigm has also been invoked to conceptualize and formulate policy for the social disruption and urban violence that have attended the "drug war" and the "Reagan Revolution" in American cities. The title of a popular novel and film of the early 1980s—*Fort Apache, the Bronx*—vividly captures the public's sense of cities "reverting to savagery" and ruled by semi-tribal youth gangs representing African-American and other Third World "races" or "ethnicities." The policy scenarios implicit in this paradigm emphasize "military" over social solutions: the use of police repression and imprisonment—a variation on free-fire zones and "reconcentration camps" or "reservations"—as policies of first resort preferable to more laborious and taxing projects of civic action or social reform.

The political successes of the Reagan and Bush administrations suggest that in the 1980s there was indeed a renewal of public myth: a general disposition to think mythologically about policy questions, substituting symbol and anecdote for analysis and argument; and a specific revival of the ideological structures of the Frontier Myth (savage war and bonanza economics) abstracted from its traditional association with Western movies and the historical Wild West. However, it would be a mistake to see this recrudescence as proof of the restoration of a true public myth capable of organizing the thought and feeling of a genuine and usable national consensus. The iconography, symbolism, and public ritual associated with American patriotism were indeed given new currency and credibility by Reagan's performance of his role. But his repair of public myth was partial and incomplete. He did not (could not) wholly succeed in effacing either the material consequences of our historical experience or its registration in memory.

The magical effects of Reagan's performance began to dissipate with the departure of the performer and with the discovery that some rather costly "due bills" were left behind. Although the economy had revived between 1982 and 1990, the Reagan "boom" was followed by a prolonged recession, by some measures the longest since 1945. Nor has the refurbished myth/ideology of the Reagan Revolution functioned as a unifying or consensus-making tool. On the contrary, as the 1988 presidential campaign made clear, it has helped to polarize political discourse by reviving (in more polite form) the old symbols and codes of racial prejudice, anti-intellectualism, and red-baiting. Reagan sailed into the presidency by smiling and waving Old Glory; his successor won by brandishing the flag, playing "the race card," and deriding his opponent's Americanism.

Despite such triumphs as the collapse of Communism and victory in the Gulf War, polls taken in 1990–91 indicate that most Americans have not recovered their faith in the most fundamental principles of national ideology: the belief that American democracy offers effective means for expressing the will of the people through political action, and the belief in national and personal progress—the idea that each generation will do better and produce more than the one before. There is widespread public skepticism about the ability of the political leadership, Republican or Democrat, to provide an accurate assessment of our problems, a useful set of predictions and policies, or even an honest set of account books. There is a growing awareness that the real bases of American political and industrial strength have been weakened and our culture undermined by the waste and abuse of our human resources in the last fifteen years, in particular our failure to invest in public health and education, in the restructuring of our displaced industrial workforce, in the improvement of our cities, and in measures for reducing the size and permanency of the "underclass." These failures have undermined our capacity to compete with other industrialized nations and have prolonged the crisis of demoralization that has affected our political culture since the end of the 1960s.

The Myth of Deterrence and the End of the Cold War

Richard Ned Lebow and Janice Gross Stein

Eric Hobshawm has defined the twentieth century as beginning in 1914. American history since then has been mainly crisis-laden, both at home and abroad. The nation, in fact, seems to have come to depend on some level of excitement. The Cold War, coming in the wake of World War II, is a prime example. During the Great Depression and the "Good War" the nation had built up a high tolerance for crisis. War's end in 1945 created a crisis vacuum that beckoned to be filled. General Patton is said to have observed: "Peace is going to be a hell of a bore." Yalta, however, had presaged competition in postwar eastern and central Europe. Moscow and the Communists immediately entered the fray. It was The Red Army, after all, that had defeated the Germans in the east. Old prewar fears of Communist Russia were dusted off; Winston Churchill's Fulton, Missouri, speech emblazoned the phrase "Iron Curtain" on the public mind; George Kennan outlined a policy of containment; all followed by House UnAmerican Activities Committee investigations, McCarthyism, Loyalty Oaths. In the movie "The Russians Are Coming! The Russians Are Coming!" some Russians actually come, but in a submarine. They were not members of the Communist hordes poised for attack on both our Canadian and Mexican borders. The film may be taken as a satiric comment on an American mentality, our unrequited national expectancy. Here, Richard Ned Lebow, Professor of Political Science at the University of Pittsburgh, and Janice Gross Stein, Professor of Conflict Management at the University of Toronto, address the mythology that United States deterrence ultimately forced the Russians to call off the Cold War. The two postulate that deterrence in fact had very little ultimate effect on the Russian decision. Stalin's rigid "command economy" held sway from the 1930s on, calling for twenty-five percent peacetime expenditure on defense, impossible to continue into the 90s. That, added to Mikhail Gorbachev's resolve for reconciliation, brought about the Cold War's demise.

The final claim made for nuclear deterrence is that it helped to end the Cold War. As impeccable a liberal as *New York Times* columnist Tom Wicker reluctantly conceded that Star Wars and the massive military buildup in the Reagan administration had forced the Soviet Union to reorient its foreign and domestic policies. The conventional wisdom has two components. American military capability and resolve allegedly convinced Soviet leaders that aggression anywhere would meet unyielding opposition. Forty years of arms competition also brought the Soviet economy to the edge of collapse. The Reagan buildup and Star Wars, the argument goes, were the straws that broke the Soviet camel's back. Moscow could not match the increased level of American defense spending and accordingly chose to end the Cold War.

We cannot examine these propositions about the impact of deterrence on the end of the Cold War with the same quality of evidence we used to assess the role of deterrence in superpower relations during the Cold War. Nevertheless, the absence of a large body of documents, interviews, and memoirs has not discouraged columnists and scholars from rendering judgments about the end of the Cold War. Nor will it prevent policymakers from using these interpretations as guides to action in the future. It is therefore essential that the conventional wisdom does not go unexamined. The limited evidence that is now available is not consistent with these two propositions about the role of deterrence in ending the Cold War. Within the confines of the available evidence, we sketch the outlines of a very different interpretation.

* * *

Soviet officials insist that Gorbachev's withdrawal of Soviet forces from Afghanistan, proposals for arms control, and domestic reforms took place *despite* the Reagan buildup. Mikhail Sergeyevich Gorbachev came to power in March 1985 committed to liberalizing the domestic political process at home and improving relations with the West so that the Soviet Union could modernize its rigid economy. Within a month of assuming office, he announced his first unilateral initiative—a temporary freeze on the deployment of Soviet intermediate-range missiles in Europe—and in a series of subsequent proposals tried to signal his interest in arms control. President Reagan continued to speak of the Soviet Union as an "evil empire" and remained committed to his quest for a near-perfect ballistic-missile defense.

Gorbachev came to office imbued with a sense of urgency of domestic reform and with a fundamentally different attitude toward the West. He was confident that the United States would not deliberately attack the Soviet Union and that the serious risk was an accidental or miscalculated exchange. In conversations with his military advisors, he rejected any plans that were premised on a war with the United States. "During the period of stagnation," he observed, "we have assumed that such a war was possible, but when I became general secretary, I refused to consider any such plans." Since he saw no threat of attack from the United States, Gorbachev was not

"afraid" of any military programs put forward by the Reagan administration and did not feel forced to match them. Rather, he saw arms spending as an unnecessary and wasteful expenditure of scarce resources. Deep arms reductions were not only important to the reform and development of the Soviet economy, but also an imperative of the nuclear age.

Rather than facilitating a change in Soviet foreign policy, Reagan's commitment to the Strategic Defense Initiative (SDI) complicated Gorbachev's task of persuading his own officials that arms control was in the Soviet interest. Conservatives, much of the military leadership, and captains of defense-related industries took SDI as further evidence of the hostile intentions of the United States and insisted on increased spending on offensive countermeasures. Gorbachev, Eduard Shevardnadze, Aleksandr Yakovlev, and many foreign-ministry officials did not feel threatened by Star Wars but were constrained and frustrated by the political impact of Reagan's policies at home.

To break the impasse, Gorbachev used a two-pronged strategy. In successive summits he tried and finally convinced Reagan of his genuine interest in ending the arms race and restructuring East-West relations on a collaborative basis. When Reagan changed his estimate of Gorbachev, he also modified his assessment of the Soviet Union and became the leading dove of his administration. Gorbachev also worked hard to convince Western publics that he intended a radical departure from past Soviet policies. The withdrawal from Afghanistan, freeing of Soviet political prisoners, and liberalization of the Soviet political system evoked widespread sympathy and support in the West and generated strong public pressure on NATO governments to respond positively to his initiatives.

The first breakthrough—an agreement on intermediate nuclear forces (INF)—was the unintended result of the Reagan administration's need to placate American and European public opinion. American officials were deeply divided on the question of theater arms control and settled on the "double zero" proposal only because they thought that Moscow would reject the offer. The proposal required the Soviet Union, which had already deployed a new generation of nuclear delivery systems in Europe, to make deeper cuts in its arsenal than the United States, which had only just begun to field new weapons in Europe. Washington expected Gorbachev to reject the proposal and hoped thereby to make him appear responsible for the failure of arms control. They were astonished when he agreed in principle. Soviet officials contend that Gorbachev accepted "double zero," not because of Soviet weakness, but in expectation that it would trigger a reciprocal process of accommodation. President Gorbachev subsequently described the INF agreement as a watershed in Soviet-American relations. "Working on the treaty and the treaty itself," he said, "created trust and a network of personal links." To Gorbachev, the absolute gain of accommodation was far more important than the relative distribution of military advantage in any particular arms-control agreement.

Gorbachev's political persistence broke through Reagan's wall of mistrust. At their Reykjavik summit in October 1986, the two leaders talked seriously about eliminating all their ballistic missiles within ten years and significantly reducing their arsenals of nuclear weapons. No agreement was reached because Reagan was unwilling to limit SDI. The Reykjavik summit, as Gorbachev had hoped, nevertheless began a process of mutual reassurance and accommodation. That process continued after an initially hesitant George Bush became a full-fledged partner. In hindsight, it is apparent that Gorbachev's initiatives began the process that brought the Cold War to an end.

*   *   *

The conventional wisdom assumes that the Soviet Union was forced to match American defense spending and to end the Cold War when it could no longer compete. There is no evidence that Soviet defense spending rose or fell in response to American defense spending. Revised estimates by the CIA indicate that Soviet defense expenditures remained more or less constant throughout the 1980s. Neither the Carter-Reagan buildup nor Star Wars had any impact on gross spending levels. Their only demonstrable impact was to shift in marginal ways the allocation of defense rubles. After SDI, more funds were earmarked to developing countermeasures to ballistic defense.

If American defense spending bankrupted the Soviet economy and led Gorbachev to end the Cold War, a sharp decline in defense spending should have occurred under Gorbachev. Despite his rejection of military competition with the United States, CIA statistics show that Soviet defense spending remained relatively constant as a proportion of Soviet gross national product during the first four years of Gorbachev's tenure. The Soviet gross national product declined precipitously in the late 1980s and early 1990s; Gorbachev's domestic reforms had a profoundly negative impact on the Soviet economy. Soviet defense spending was reduced only in 1989 and did not shrink as rapidly as the overall economy. In the current decade, Soviet, and then Russian defense spending has consumed a higher percentage of disposable national income than it did in the Brezhnev years.

From Stalin through Gorbachev, annual Soviet defense spending consumed about 25% of Soviet disposable income. This was an extraordinary burden on the economy. Not all Soviet leaders were blind to its likely consequences. In the early 1970s, some officials recognized that the economy would ultimately stagnate if the military continued to consume such a disproportionate share of resources. Brezhnev, however, was even more heavily dependent on Khrushchev than the support of a coalition in which defense and heavy industry were well represented. In defense, as in other budgetary outlays, allocations reflected the relative political power of different sectors of the economy. Within the different sectors, spending and investment were controlled by bureaucracies with strong vested interests. As a result, not only military but also civilian spending was frequently wasteful and inefficient. Logrolling among competing groups compounded the problem by increasing the aggregate level of spending. Because Soviet defense spending under Brezhnev and Gorbachev was primarily a response to internal imperatives, it is not correlated with American defense spending. Nor is there any observable relationship between defense spending and changes in the political relationship between the superpowers, until the cuts in the American defense budget in 1991.

The proposition that American defense spending bankrupted the Soviet economy and forced an end to the Cold War is not sustained by the available evidence. The critical factor in the Soviet economic decline was the rigid "command economy" imposed by Stalin in the early 1930s. It offered little or no reward for individual or collective initiative, freed productive units from the competition normally imposed by the market, and centralized production and investment decisions in the hands of an unwieldy bureaucracy immune from market forces and consumer demands. The command economy predates the Cold War and was not a response to American deterrence.

To explain the dramatic reorientation of Soviet foreign policy, we need to look first at the domestic agendas of Soviet leaders. Khrushchev's and Gorbachev's efforts to transform East-West relations and Brezhnev's more limited attempt at détente were motivated in large part by their economic objectives.

Khrushchev sought an accommodation with the West to free manpower and resources for economic development. He hoped that success in reducing East-West tensions would enhance his domestic authority and make it more difficult for conservative forces to block his economic and political reforms. Gorbachev had a similar agenda and pursued a similar strategy. *Perestroika* required peaceful relations abroad to succeed at home. Accommodation with the West would permit a shift in resources from the military to productive investment; attract credits, investment, and technology from the West; and weaken the power of the conservatives opposed to Gorbachev and his reforms. Accommodation with the West was especially critical for Gorbachev because the Soviet economy had deteriorated sharply since the early 1970s and the brief détente between the United States and the Soviet Union. The impetus for domestic reform was structural; economic decline, or the threat of serious decline, motivated Gorbachev, like Khrushchev and Brezhnev, to implement domestic reforms and seek accommodation with the West.

The need to arrest economic decline and improve economic performance cannot by itself explain the scope of reforms or the kind of relationship Gorbachev tried to establish with the West. Only a few central Soviet leaders responded to economic imperatives by promoting a radical restructuring of the Soviet relationship with the West. Almost all the fundamental components of Gorbachev's "new thinking" about security were politically contested. Traditional thinkers powerfully placed within the defense ministry and the Soviet General Staff vigorously challenged the new concepts of security. Indeed, Gorbachev had to go outside the establishment to civilian and academic specialists on defense in the policy institutes in Moscow for new ideas about Soviet security. Insofar as senior Soviet leaders and officials in the Gorbachev era disagreed fundamentally about the direction of Soviet foreign and defense policy, structural imperatives alone cannot adequately explain the change in Soviet thinking about security under Gorbachev.

Gorbachev differed significantly from Khrushchev and Brezhnev in his conception of security. Previous Soviet leaders had regarded the capitalist West as the enemy and had feared military aggression against the Soviet Union or its allies. Like their Western counterparts, they measured security in terms of military and economic power; Soviet military prowess and socialist solidarity were necessary to deter attack and restrain the capitalist powers. Khrushchev and Brezhnev wanted to improve relations with the West, but they remained committed to their ideological view of a world divided into two hostile camps. Unlike Stalin, they recognized that nuclear weapons had made war between the superpowers irrational and unlikely, but they believed in the fundamental antagonism between the incompatible systems of capitalism and socialism.

Gorbachev and his closest advisors rejected the traditional Soviet approach to security. In their view, it had helped to create and sustain the Cold War and had placed a heavy burden on the Soviet economy. *Perestroichiks* were especially critical of the domestic consequences of postwar Soviet foreign policy; conflict with the West had been exploited by the Communist Party to justify its monopoly on power and suppression of dissent.

Gorbachev's vision of Soviet security was cooperative rather than competitive. He and Eduard A. Shevardnadze repudiated the class basis of international relations that had dominated Soviet thinking about security since the Soviet state was created. They explicitly condemned as mistaken the thesis developed in the Khrushchev and Brezhnev years that peaceful coexistence was a specific form of class struggle. "New thinking" about security was based on five related propositions: the primacy of universal, "all-human" values over class conflict; the interdependence of all nations; the impossibility of achieving victory in nuclear or large-scale conventional war; the need to seek security in political and economic rather than military terms; and the belief that neither Soviet nor Western security could be achieved unilaterally. Gorbachev called for the development of "a new security model" based on "a policy of compromise" among former adversaries. National security was to be replaced by a "common, indivisible security, the same for all." The goal of the

Soviet Union was to join a "common European house" that would foster security and prosperity through "a policy of cooperation based on mutual trust."

Gorbachev, Shevardnadze, and other committed democrats believed in a complex, two-way relationship between domestic reform and foreign policy. Accommodation with the West would facilitate *perestroika*, but it was more than an instrument of reform and economic rejuvenation. For the Soviet Union to join a family of nations, it had to become a democratic society with a demonstrable respect for the individual and collective rights of its citizens and allies. Granting independence to the countries of Eastern Europe was the international analogue to emptying the gulags, ending censorship in the media, and choosing members of the Supreme Soviet through free elections.

Gorbachev was able to pursue a more far-reaching and dramatic strategy of accommodation than his predecessors because of the evolution in the superpower relationship since the acute confrontations of the 1960s. He was much less fearful of Western intentions than Khrushchev and less concerned that the United States and its allies would exploit concessions as a sign of weakness. Khrushchev's fear of the West severely constrained his search for accommodation. He never considered, as did Gorbachev, that soft words and unilateral initiatives would evoke enough public sympathy and support so that Western governments would be pushed by their own domestic publics to reciprocate. Khrushchev did make some unilateral concessions; he reduced the size of the armed forces and proclaimed a short-lived moratorium on nuclear testing. When his actions were not reciprocated, the militant opposition at home forced him to revert to a confrontational policy. His inflammatory rhetoric in turn strengthened the forces in the West who opposed accommodation with the Soviet Union.

Gorbachev could not have succeeded in transforming East-West relations and ending the Cold War if the West had not become his willing partner. Unlike Khrushchev, whose quest for a German peace treaty frightened France and West Germany, Gorbachev met a receptive audience when he attempted to end the division of Europe. Disenchantment with the Cold War, opposition to the deployment of new weapons systems, and a widespread desire to end the division of Europe, given voice by well-organized peace movements, created a groundswell of support for exploring the possibilities of accommodation with the Soviet Union.

*   *   *

Throughout the Cold War, many leaders in the West argued that the internal structure and foreign-policy goals of the Soviet Union were ideologically determined and largely unaffected by the policies of other states. The West could only restrain Soviet aggression through a policy of strength. Many academic analysts rejected the argument that Soviet domestic and foreign policies were immutable. They maintained that Western policies made a difference, but disagreed among themselves about the nature of the interaction between Soviet and American foreign and domestic policies.

Some scholars contended that the links were reciprocal. Soviet "orthodoxy," which favored heavy industry, restricted individual freedoms, and a strong military, was strengthened by an international environment that appeared to confirm the enemy image of the capitalist West. Conciliatory Western policies could weaken the influence of Soviet militants and strengthen the hand of those officials who favored reform and accommodation with the West. Other scholars subscribed only to the first of these propositions. Citing the Khrushchev experience, they agreed that a threatening international environment undermined reform and accommodation, but, drawing on the Brezhnev years, they denied the corollary that détente encouraged domestic liberalization. The contrast between Gorbachev and Brezhnev led some specialists to argue that reform only came when the leadership confronted the prospect of domestic and foreign-policy disaster.

The available evidence suggests a different proposition about the relationship between American and Soviet foreign policy. The critical factor was the agenda of Soviet leaders. American influence was limited when Soviet leaders were not seriously committed to internal reform. Confrontation then exacerbated Soviet-American tensions, but conciliation did not necessarily improve the relationship, nor did it encourage internal reforms. Jimmy Carter's efforts to transform Soviet-American relations had little effect because they came after Brezhnev had lost interest in domestic reform at home.

When the principal objective of Soviet leaders was economic reform and development, they were anxious to reach some kind of accommodation with the West. Gorbachev, like Khrushchev, was committed to domestic economic reform. Under these conditions, American policy, whether confrontational or conciliatory, had its greatest impact. Confrontation was most likely to provoke an aggressive response because it exacerbated the foreign-policy problems of Soviet leaders, undercut their domestic authority, and threatened their domestic economic goals. Conciliation was most likely to be reciprocated because Soviet leaders expected an improved relationship to enhance their authority at home, free scarce resources for development, and provide access to Western credits and technology.

If American policy did have an impact when Soviet leaders were committed to reform, then the strategy of deterrence likely prolonged the Cold War.

The Cold War ended when Soviet leaders became committed to domestic reform and to a concept of common security that built on the reality of nuclear deterrence, and when Western leaders reassured and reciprocated. We cannot support these propositions with the kind of evidence we marshaled in support of our contention that the strategy of deterrence had complex but largely negative consequences for superpower relations during the Cold War. The same kind of detailed reconstruction of Soviet and American policy during the Gorbachev era will only be possible when documents, memoirs, and interviews of key participants become available. Until then, this alternative interpretation of the impact of the strategy of nuclear deterrence on the end of the Cold War may help to stimulate an important debate about the enduring lessons of the Cold War and its demise.

V

Social Myths of Modern America

Assuring an understanding of a society requires continually thinking that society anew, reexamining the familiar. Much former mythology must be cast aside, even as myth is respected as supplying much of the inner logic of a society's history. And so it must be today, as the nation reinterprets the place within it of women and various minorities—especially African Americans, Chicanos, Asian Americans, and Native Americans. The meaning of the past and the significance of public memory have never been more debated—witness the many controversies surrounding so-called "culture wars," the public exhibition of historical materials, and debates surrounding the teaching of history in the nation's schools.

Mythmaking is an ongoing enterprise of the American mind, as prolific as the current issues of a dynamic society. But American myth is a cultural resource that needs selectively and creatively to be revivified. For as an important component of human existence, myth is at once the process by which human beings order their world and the entity that serves to perpetuate their grandest illusions. As the late American poet Robert Penn Warren once pointedly observed: "The dream is a lie, but the dreaming is true."

A black woman in a southern town during the 1950s watches Klansmen in full regalia. *(Courtesy, AP/Wide world Photos)*

An Indian encampment in front of the Washington state capitol in 1968 was part of the wider Indian movement calling for return of lands. *(Courtesy, State Archives, Washington)*

The mythic torch is passed; young Bill Clinton meets John F. Kennedy in Arkansas in 1960. *(Courtesy, Arnie Sachs, Sygma)*

The Myth of the Feminine Mystique

Joanne Meyerowitz

Perhaps no book did more to mobilize female consciousness in the post World War II period than Betty Friedan's *The Feminine Mystique* which transformed many women's lives from passive to proactive—away from conservative domesticity and the "housewife trap" and toward personal fulfillment. Implicit in Friedan's work was an interpretation of American history over the past half century—that women, like "Rosie the Riveter," had dramatically entered the mainstream of American life during World War II, but had been forced to return to their domestic realm at war's end, and that theirs had been a struggle ever since to recapture the spirit and independence of the war era. Joanne Meyerowitz, professor of history at the University of Cincinnati, here questions this interpretation. Her alternative version of women's postwar history, interestingly drawing from surveys of mass circulation monthly magazines such as *Reader's Digest*, *Coronet*, *Ebony*, and *Ladies Home Companion*, suggests that women after World War II continued in the labor force in large numbers and participated actively in politics and reform. The postwar challenge for women was not so much to defeat "domestic retreat," but rather to render a balance between domestic and public realms—an equilibrium still very much being negotiated by both genders.

In 1963 Betty Friedan published *The Feminine Mystique*, an instant best seller. Friedan argued, often brilliantly, that American women, especially suburban women, suffered from deep discontent. In the postwar era, she wrote, journalists, educators, advertisers, and social scientists had pulled women into the home with an ideological stranglehold, the "feminine mystique." This repressive "image" held that women could "find fulfillment only in sexual passivity, male domination, and nurturing maternal love." It denied "women careers or any commitment outside the home" and "narrowed woman's world down to the home, cut her role back to housewife." In Friedan's formulation, the writers and editors of mass-circulation magazines, especially women's magazines, were the "Frankensteins" who had created this "feminine monster." In her defense of

women, Friedan did not choose a typical liberal feminist language of rights, equality, or even justice. Influenced by the new human potential psychology, she argued instead that full-time domesticity stunted women and denied their "basic human need to grow." For Friedan, women and men found personal identity and fulfillment through individual achievement, most notably through careers. Without such growth, she claimed, women would remain unfulfilled and unhappy, and children would suffer at the hands of neurotic mothers.

The Feminine Mystique had an indisputable impact. Hundreds of women have testified that the book changed their lives, and historical accounts often credit it with launching the recent feminist movement. But the book has also had other kinds of historical impact. For a journalistic exposé, Friedan's work has had a surprisingly strong influence on historiography. In fact, since Friedan published *The Feminine Mystique*, historians of American women have adopted wholesale her version of the postwar ideology. While many historians question Friedan's homogenized account of women's actual experience, virtually all accept her version of the dominant ideology, the conservative promotion of domesticity.

According to this now-standard historical account, postwar authors urged women to return to the home while only a handful of social scientists, trade unionists, and feminists protested. As one recent rendition states: "In the wake of World War II . . . the short-lived affirmation of women's independence gave way to a pervasive endorsement of female subordination and domesticity." Much of this secondary literature relies on a handful of conservative postwar writings, the same writings cited liberally by Friedan. In particular, the work of Dr. Marynia F. Farnham, a viciously antifeminist psychiatrist, and her sidekick, sociologist Ferdinand Lundberg, is invoked repeatedly as typical of the postwar era. In this standard account, the domestic ideology prevailed until such feminists as Friedan triumphed in the 1960s.

When I first began research on the postwar era, I accepted this version of history. But as I investigated the public culture, I encountered what I then considered exceptional evidence—books, articles, and films that contradicted the domestic ideology. I decided to conduct a more systematic investigation. This essay reexamines the middle-class popular discourse on women by surveying mass-circulation monthly magazines of the postwar era (1946–1958). The systematic sample includes nonfiction articles on women in "middlebrow" magazines (*Reader's Digest* and *Coronet*), "highbrow" magazines (*Harper's* and *Atlantic Monthly*), magazines aimed at African Americans (*Ebony* and *Negro Digest*), and those aimed at women (*Ladies' Home Journal* and *Woman's Home Companion*). The sample includes 489 nonfiction articles, ranging from Hollywood gossip to serious considerations of gender. In 1955 these magazines had a combined circulation of over 22 million. Taken together, the magazines reached readers from all classes, races, and genders, but the articles seem to represent the work of middle-class journalists, and articles written by women seem to outnumber ones by men.

My goal in constructing this sample was not to replicate Friedan's magazine research, which focused primarily on short story fiction in four women's magazines. Rather my goal was to test generalizations about postwar mass culture (that is, commodified forms of popular culture) by surveying another side of it. To this end, I chose nonfiction articles in a larger sample of popular magazines. Some of the magazines of smaller circulation, such as *Harper's* and *Negro Digest*, were perhaps outside the "mainstream." But including them in the sample enabled me to incorporate more of the diversity in American society, to investigate the contours of a broader bourgeois culture and some variations within it. Since my conclusions rest on a sample of nonfiction articles in eight popular magazines, they can provide only a tentative portrait of postwar culture. Future studies based on different magazines or on fiction, advertisements, films, television, or radio will no doubt suggest additional layers of complexity in mass culture and different readings of it.

My interpretation of the sample draws in part on recent theories in cultural studies. For Betty Friedan and for some historians, popular magazines represented a repressive force, imposing damaging images on vulnerable American women. Many historians today adopt a different approach in which mass culture is neither monolithic nor unrelentingly repressive. In this view, mass culture is rife with contradictions, ambivalence, and competing voices. We no longer assume that any text has a single, fixed meaning for all readers, and we sometimes find within the mass media subversive, as well as repressive, potential.

With a somewhat different sample and a somewhat different interpretive approach, I come to different conclusions about postwar mass culture than did Friedan and her followers. Friedan's widely accepted version of the "feminine mystique," I suggest, is only one piece of the postwar cultural puzzle. The popular literature I sampled did not simply glorify domesticity or demand that women return to or stay at home. All of the magazines sampled advocated both the domestic and the nondomestic, sometimes in the same sentence. In this literature, domestic ideals coexisted in ongoing tension with an ethos of individual achievement that celebrated nondomestic activity, individual striving, public service, and public success.

This essay first discusses nonfiction that focused on individual women. Despite frequent references to femininity and domesticity, most of these stories expressed overt admiration for women whose individual striving moved them beyond the home. In contrast to the "happy housewife heroine" whom Friedan found in magazine fiction, these "true stories" presented women as successful public figures. Second, this essay examines nonfiction that directly addressed issues of gender. Such articles often applauded housewives, but they also supported women's wage work and urged greater participation in politics. Further, they often expressed ambivalence about domesticity and presented it as a problem. Here Dr. Farnham and her conservative fellow travelers voiced a distinctive minority position that in no way dominated the mass culture.

The postwar mass culture embraced the same central contradiction—the tension between domestic ideals and individual achievement—that Betty Friedan addressed in *The Feminine Mystique*. In this sense, I argue, Friedan drew on mass culture as much as she countered it. The success of her book stemmed in part from her compelling elaboration of familiar themes.

*   *   *

In popular magazines, the theme of individual achievement rang most clearly in the numerous articles on individual women. These articles appeared with frequency throughout the postwar era: they comprised over 60 percent, or 300, of the 489 nonfiction articles sampled. These articles usually recounted a story of a woman's life or a particularly telling episode in her life. In formulaic accounts, they often constructed what one such article labeled "this Horatio Alger success story—feminine version." Of these articles, 33 percent spotlighted women with unusual talents, jobs, or careers, and another 29 percent focused on prominent entertainers. Typically they related a rise to public success punctuated by a lucky break, a dramatic comeback, a selfless sacrifice, or a persistent struggle to overcome adversity. Such stories appeared in all of the magazines sampled, but they appeared most frequently in the African-American magazines, *Ebony* and *Negro Digest*, and the white "middlebrow" magazines, *Coronet* and *Reader's Digest*. Journalists reworked the formula for different readers: In *Negro Digest*, for example, articles returned repeatedly to black performers who defied racism, in *Reader's Digest* they more often addressed white leaders in community service. In general, though, the articles suggested that the noteworthy

woman rose above and beyond ordinary domesticity. Or, as one story stated, "This is the real-life fairy tale of a girl who hurtled from drab obscurity to sudden, startling fame."

At the heart of many such articles lay a bifocal vision of women both as feminine and domestic and as public achievers. In one article, "The Lady Who Licked Crime in Portland," the author, Richard L. Neuberger, juxtaposed domestic stereotypes and newsworthy nondomestic achievement. The woman in question, Dorothy McCullough Lee, was, the article stated, an "ethereally pale housewife" who tipped "the scales at 110 pounds." But more to the point, she was also the mayor of Portland, Oregon, who had defeated, single-handedly it seems, the heavyweights of organized crime. Before winning the mayoral election in 1948, this housewife had opened a law firm and served in the state legislature, both House and Senate, and as Portland's commissioner of public utilities. Despite her "frail, willowy" appearance, the fearless mayor had withstood ridicule, recall petitions, and threatening mail in her "relentless drive" against gambling and prostitution. She was, the article related without further critique, a "violent feminist" who had "intense concern with the status of women." And, according to all, she was "headed for national distinction." The article concluded with an admiring quotation describing Mayor Lee's fancy hats as the plumes of a crusading knight in armor. Here the feminine imagery blended with a metaphor of masculine public service.

The joint endorsement of domestic and nondomestic roles appeared in the numerous stories that offered a postwar version of today's "superwoman," the woman who successfully combines motherhood and career. As Jacqueline Jones has noted, *Ebony* magazine sometimes featured this type of article. One story, for example presented Louise Williams, a mother of two and also the only black mechanic at American Airlines. As *Ebony* reported, "She is a good cook, but an even better mechanic." She was also an inventor and an active member of her union. And, according to *Ebony*, she was "never a lazy housewife." Such stories in African-American magazines clearly provided lessons in surmounting racism. In *Ebony's* female version of racial advancement, women often excelled both in the workplace and at home.

Similar articles appeared regularly in magazines geared to white readers. *Coronet* magazine, for example, presented the "amazing" Dorothy Kilgallen, "star reporter," who wrote a syndicated column, ad-libbed a daily radio program, ran forty charity benefits a year, and had "a handsome and successful husband, a beautiful home, [and] two lovely children." The successful combination of home and career made her "Gotham's busiest glamour girl." Articles of this type resolved the tension between domesticity and public achievement superficially by ignoring the difficulties that women usually faced in pursuing both.

While feminine stereotypes sometimes provided convenient foils that enhanced by contrast a women's atypical public accomplishment, they also served as conservative reminders that all women, even publicly successful women, were to maintain traditional gender distinctions. In their opening paragraphs, numerous authors described their successful subjects as pretty, motherly, shapely, happily married, petite, charming, or soft voiced. This emphasis on femininity and domesticity (and the two were often conflated) seems to have cloaked a submerged fear of lesbian, mannish, or man-hating women. This fear surfaced in an unusual article on athlete Babe Didrikson Zaharias. In her early years, the article stated, the Babe's "boyish bob and freakish clothes . . . [her] dislike of femininity" had led observers to dismiss her as an "Amazon." But after her marriage, she "became a woman," a transformation signaled, according to the approving author, by lipstick, polished nails, and "loose, flowing" hair as well as by an interest in the domestic arts of cooking, sewing, and entertaining. In this article, as in others, allusions to femininity and domesticity probably helped legitimate women's public achievements. Authors attempted to reassure readers that conventional gender distinctions and heterosexuality remained intact even as women competed successfully in work, politics, or sports. It is worth noting that in *The Feminine Mystique*, Friedan adopted this very approach. She attempted to legitimate the early feminists by repeated insistence that most of them were feminine, married, and not man-hating. . . .

In the postwar magazines, marriage also presented problems. Although journalists expected most women to marry, they portrayed the search for a husband as a potentially troubling task. An article in *Ebony* stated, "Most women would rather be married than single but there are many who would rather remain single than be tied to the wrong man." The

magazines gave readers contrasting advice on how to find a good husband. One article told women, "Don't fear being aggressive!," while another considered "aggressive traits" as "handicaps . . . in attracting a husband." Within marriage as well, journalists seemed to anticipate constant problems, including immaturity, incompatibility, and infidelity. They saw divorce as a difficult last resort and often advised both husbands and wives to communicate and adjust.

The issue of "individualism" sometimes arose in the articles on marriage and domesticity. Some authors constructed the housewife problem as a conflict between gender roles and individuality. Often expressed in historical terms, the conflict pitted old-fashioned gender relations in which women were first and foremost doting mothers and submissive wives against modern relations in which women were individual human beings. Postwar authors did not, as Friedan's *Feminine Mystique* would have it, side automatically with "sexual passivity, male domination, and nurturing maternal love." They portrayed the ideal marriage as an equal partnership, with each partner intermingling traditional masculine and feminine roles. One article insisted: "The healthy, emotionally well-balanced male . . . isn't alarmed by the fact that women are human, too, and have an aggressive as well as a passive side. . . . He takes women seriously as individuals." This article and others condemned men who assumed an attitude of superiority. As another article stated, "The dominating husband and submissive wife are things of the past." Yet, to many it seemed that "individualism" could go too far and upset modern marriage. While husbands might do more housework and wives might pursue nondomestic activities, men remained the primary breadwinners and women the keepers of the home. . . .

While all of the magazines endorsed a manicured version of heterosexual appeal, the African-American magazines displayed it most heartily. This may have reflected African-American vernacular traditions, such as the blues, that rejected white middle-class injunctions against public sexual expression. But it also reflected an editorial decision to construct glamour and beauty as political issues in the fight against racism. Articles admired black women's sex appeal in a self-conscious defiance of racist white standards of beauty. In this context what some feminists today might read as sexual "objectification" presented itself as racial advancement, according black womanhood equal treatment with white. Thus, *Ebony*, which in most respects resembled a white family magazine like *Life*, also included some of the mildly risqué cheesecake seen in white men's magazines, like *Esquire*. One editorial explained: "Because we live in a society in which standards of physical beauty are most often circumscribed by a static concept of whiteness of skin and blondeness of hair, there is an aching need for someone to shout from the housetops that black women are beautiful."

In a curious bow to individual striving, popular magazines, both black and white, often portrayed beauty and allure as achievements that any woman could attain if she tried hard enough. As the entertainer Dorothy Dandridge explained in *Ebony*, "Every woman can have some sex appeal." While a woman could achieve allure, she should attain it without "vulgarizing" sex or making an "open display" of it. Similarly, in the *Ladies' Home Journal*, an article proclaimed, "She Turned Herself into a Beauty." This woman's "achievements" included weight loss, better grooming, and medical help for acne, a deformed nose, and a bent back. Another article, in *Coronet*, stated bluntly: "If anything's lacking, she can take immediate steps to remedy it—go to a hairdresser, a psychiatrist, whatever is needed." With a middle-class faith in the individual's ability to rise, articles suggested that individual effort, careful consumerism, and reliance on experts could bring any woman success, even in the realm of beauty and appeal.

Still, despite the magazines' endorsement of feminine beauty and heterosexual allure, Friedan's polemical claim that "American women have been successfully reduced to sex creatures" seems unabashedly hyperbolic. Try as they might, popular magazines could not entirely dictate the responses of readers. In most cases, we have little way of knowing how readers responded to magazine articles, but in the case of sex appeal we have explicit letters of dissent. In the African-American magazines, some readers, women and men both, objected to the photos of semiclad women. One woman complained that the "so-called beauties" were "really a disgrace to all women." And another protested "those girl covers and the . . . so-called realism (just a cover up name for cheapness, coarseness, lewdness, profanity and irreverence)."

In *Ladies' Home Journal*, too, readers responded with rare indignation to one article on sex appeal. In the offending article, "How to Be Loved," movie star Marlene Dietrich lectured housewives on enhancing their allure. Dietrich linked appeal to unadorned self-subordination. "To be completely a woman," she wrote, "you need a master." She advised women to plan their clothes, their conversation, and their meals to please their husbands. After washing their dishes, "like Phoenix out of the ashes," women should emerge "utterly desirable." And they should not grumble. "Some women," Dietrich proclaimed, "could do with a bit of spanking to answer their complaining." The article evoked what the *Journal's* editors called an "intense" response. Sarcastic letter writers objected to Dietrich's call for servile pampering of men and "utterly desirable" behavior. As one writer stated, "How *could* you hand the American woman such an article?" The letter writers portrayed themselves as down-home and unglamorous housewives, "all straight-haired and plain," who could not and would not emulate Dietrich's version of sexual allure. One woman wrote: "I resemble Eleanor Roosevelt more than I do La Dietrich, so that alters the visual effect." Another writer proclaimed: "Pish, tosh and hooey! Could be that Marlene could emerge from a stack of dirty dishes . . . and still be glamorous and desirable, but the housewife and mother I know gets dishpan hands and another twinge in the old back. . . . Marlene should talk about something she understands." For these women, marriage was a working partnership. Their husbands, they claimed, helped with the housework, accepted their scolding, and respected their "whims and fatigue." "Out here where I live," one woman wrote, "reasonably intelligent [married couples] . . . learn to live and work together." These readers used their domestic identities as hardworking housewives, not to berate women of public achievement, but to reject a competing image of women as subservient sexual bait.

A handful of letters, written by only a few readers, scarcely begins to suggest the range of responses that women probably had when reading the magazines. The frequent articles on work, politics, domesticity, and sexuality may have encouraged some women to take pride in, long for, or emulate magazine versions of public participation, home life, or glamour. At the same time, the flood of competing images—of housewives, workers, politicians, and sex bombs—may have inundated women who could not possibly identify with or remake themselves in all of the proffered models.

The response to one article suggests that readers may have chosen among alternative versions of womanhood, appropriating the images that rang true or appealed to them and rejecting the others. In this set of letters, some housewives accepted the "plight of the young mother" as a true description of their experience. They appreciated an article that validated their sense of domestic discontent. For these women, the article was a "morale lifter." "I have no words to tell what it means," one woman wrote, "to have all the facets of housewifery (that seemed to have sprung from my own deficiencies) held up as situations of national import." Other women rejected the article as a "very unfair picture." They resented an article that depicted them as overworked victims who could not cope with their housework. "Oh, for pity's sake," one woman asked, "What old plight am I in that no one has told me about? . . . I have four children . . . and I don't put in a forty-hour week. . . . I think it's a great life." In short, both readers and articles were varied enough and ambivalent enough to enable more than one possible reading. . . .

According to Friedan, the "feminine mystique" emerged full-blown in the mass culture of the late 1940s and 1950s. Friedan compared short story fiction in women's magazines of the late 1930s, late 1940s, and late 1950s, and she also referred to fiction and nonfiction from various magazines of the postwar era. With this evidence, Friedan told a story of declension. In the 1930s, she claimed, women's magazines encouraged women to participate in the wider world outside the home. Short stories featured fictional career women "marching toward some goal or vision of their own." In Friedan's account, this "passionate search for individual identity" ended in the late 1940s. The postwar magazines, she said, narrowed their scope to the housewife in the home and adopted Farnham and Lundberg's antifeminist stance.

My own research suggests a different history. To place my postwar sample in historical context, I supplemented it with comparable samples of nonfiction articles from popular magazines of the Great Depression and World War II. Most striking were the continuities, the themes that recurred throughout the

mid-twentieth century. From the 1930s to the 1950s, magazine articles advocated both domestic ideals and nondomestic achievement for women. In the 1930s and 1940s as well as the 1950s, the women's magazines presented housewives with romantic fiction, marriage advice, recipes, fashions, and ads for household products. And in all three decades, popular magazines, including women's magazines, spotlighted women of public achievement, addressed women as workers, and promoted women's participation in community activism and politics. Throughout the mid-twentieth century, conservatives called occasionally for women's subordination and women's rights advocates insisted occasionally on equality. More frequently, though, the magazines asserted both a long-held domestic ideal and a long-held ethos of achievement.

Beyond the common themes though, postwar magazines differed from earlier magazines in emphasis if not in kind. In my samples, the proportion of articles that focused on motherhood, marriage, and housewifery was actually smaller during the 1950s than during either the 1930s or the 1940s. In the earlier decades, the articles on domesticity often expressed the special concerns of the Great Depression or World War II. During the 1930s, numerous articles praised, advised, and encouraged housewives, as families budgeted their money and adult children returned home. A few articles offered reasons why wives or daughters should not pursue jobs or careers, perhaps reflecting a veiled hostility to women in the depression-era workplace. And several articles presented marriage and domesticity as a "great opportunity" or "the best-paying and most soul-satisfying career that any woman can espouse." During World War II, as expected, the magazines promoted women's participation in war industry, the military, and volunteer service. A couple of articles recommended ways of relieving working women's household burdens, and a few lauded women who combined motherhood and career. But the wartime magazines also lavished extensive praise on devoted mothers and loyal wives. Responding to a wartime fear of family breakdown, they stated explicitly that mothers had a primary duty to their children. The author of one such article called on the government to draft women who neglected their children and assign them "to duty in their own homes." Other articles warned women against taking husbands for granted or lowering housekeeping standards. Placed in this context, the postwar promotion of marriage and motherhood seems neither surprising nor anomalous.

The presentation of women's public lives also shifted with the times. In the postwar era, Rosie the Riveter and her challenge to the sexual division of labor vanished from the mass culture. Magazines rarely presented women in heavy industry or in the armed services. In this sense, the postwar mass culture reverted to prewar assumptions about gender roles. But the sample from the 1950s did not represent domestic retreat. In fact, it included more laudatory stories on women who achieved public success than did the samples from either of the earlier decades. The postwar magazines devoted a greater proportion of space to individual women in business, professions, social service, politics, and entertainment. The concept of public service also seems to have changed. The *Ladies' Home Journal* is perhaps emblematic. In the 1930s, the *Journal* launched a campaign, "It's Up to the Women," inviting women to help end the depression. While the campaign acknowledged the work of local women's clubs, its central theme, repeated in several issues, urged housewives to bolster the economy simply by spending more money. In the 1950s, when the *Journal* again asked housewives to join in public service, it invited them to enter mainstream politics as party workers and politicians. Public service had moved beyond the traditionally female sphere.

Why does my version of history differ from Betty Friedan's? The most obvious, and the most gracious, explanation is that we used different, though overlapping, sources. The nonfiction articles I read may well have included more contradictions and more ambivalence than the fiction on which Friedan focused. But there are, I think, additional differences in approach. Friedan did not read the popular magazines incorrectly, but she did, it seems, cite them reductively. For the prewar era, she seems to have chosen the stories that most embraced public achievement; for the postwar era, she seems to have

chosen the stories that most embodied domestic ideals. A cursory review of some of Friedan's evidence suggests that her account of change over time may be somewhat skewed. For her prewar study, Friedan omitted the fiction that featured housewives and failed to mention that the "career women" heroines she cited relinquished or planned to relinquish their jobs for marriage and housewifery. In this way, she may have projected an imagined feminist past onto the mass culture of the 1930s. For the postwar era, she cited both fiction and nonfiction stories on domesticity. But she downplayed the articles on domestic problems (belittling one by saying "the bored editors . . . ran a little article"), ignored the articles on individual achievement, and dismissed the articles on political participation with a one-sentence caricature. Her forceful protest against a restrictive domestic ideal neglected the extent to which that ideal was already undermined.

My reassessment of the "feminine mystique" is part of a larger revisionist project. For the past few years, historians have questioned the stereotype of postwar women as quiescent, docile, and domestic. Despite the baby boom and despite discrimination in employment, education, and public office, married women, black and white joined the labor force in increasing numbers, and both married and unmarried women participated actively in politics and reform. Just as women's activities were more varied and more complex than is often acknowledged, so, I argue, was the postwar popular ideology. Postwar magazines, like their prewar and wartime predecessors, rarely presented direct challenges to the conventions of marriage or motherhood, but they only rarely told women to return to or stay at home. They included stories that glorified domesticity, but they also expressed ambivalence about domesticity, endorsed women's nondomestic activity, and celebrated women's public success. They delivered multiple messages, which women could read as sometimes supporting and sometimes subverting the "feminine mystique."

Mythology and the Charismatic Leadership of Martin Luther King

Clayborne Carson

The plight of black Americans historically has been that of the "invisible man," kept down on the plantation early in the history of the republic and more recently segregated and ghettoized socially, politically, economically, and educationally. Blacks have been systematically stereotyped, caricatured, mythologized, disenfranchised, discriminated against—not to exclude lynched—by a society claiming to subscribe to principles of freedom, equality, and opportunity. The modern civil rights movement has sought to redress past wrongs, to set aside racial mythology, and to shame American society into recognizing the faulty alignment between its declared values and its legal and factual affection for racism. A critical agent in beginning this process of change was the charismatic leader, the Reverend Martin Luther King, Jr. But even while recognition of Dr. King's greatness is secure, argues Clayborne Carson, Professor of History at Stanford University and a director of the Martin Luther King, Jr., Center for Nonviolent Social Change, his historical significance needs yet to be defined. That means rethinking the King legend. A revision must include tying him to black traditions and institutions and to assessing more closely his relationship to the civil rights movement in its many local manifestations.

The legislation to establish Martin Luther King, Jr.'s birthday as a federal holiday provided official recognition of King's greatness, but it remains the responsibility of those of us who study and carry on King's work to define his historical significance. Rather than engaging in officially approved nostalgia, our remembrance of King should reflect the reality of his complex and multifaceted life. Biographers, theologians, political scientists, sociologists, social psychologists, and historians have given us a sizable literature of King's place in the Afro-American protest tradition, his role in the modern black freedom struggle, and his eclectic ideas regarding nonviolent activism. Although King scholars may benefit from and may stimulate the popular interest in King generated by the national holiday, many will find themselves uneasy participants in annual observances to honor an innocuous, carefully cultivated image of King as a black heroic figure.

The King depicted in serious scholarly works is far too interesting to be encased in such a didactic legend. King was a controversial leader who challenged authority and who once applauded what he called "creative maladjusted nonconformity." He should not be transformed into a simplistic image designed to offend no one—a black counterpart to the static, heroic myths that have embalmed George Washington as the Father of His Country and Abraham Lincoln as the Great Emancipator.

One aspect of the emerging King myth has been the depiction of him in the mass media, not only as the preeminent leader of the civil rights movement, but also as the initiator and sole indispensable element in the southern black struggles of the 1950s and 1960s. As in other historical myths, a Great Man is seen as the decisive factor in the process of social change, and the unique qualities of a leader are used to explain major historical events. The King myth departs from historical reality because it attributes too much to King's exceptional qualities as a leader and too little to the impersonal, large-scale social factors that made it possible for King to display his singular abilities on a national stage. Because the myth emphasizes the individual at the expense of the black movement, it not only exaggerates King's historical importance but also distorts his actual, considerable contribution to the movement.

A major example of this distortion has been the tendency to see King as a charismatic figure who single-handedly directed the course of the civil rights movement through the force of his oratory. The charismatic label, however, does not adequately define King's role in the southern black struggle. The term *charisma* has traditionally been used to describe the godlike, magical qualities possessed by certain leaders. Connotations of the term have changed, of course, over the years. In our more secular age, it has lost many of its religious connotations and now refers to a wide range of leadership styles that involve the capacity to inspire—usually through oratory—emotional bonds between leaders and followers. Arguing that King was not a charismatic leader, in the broadest sense of the term, becomes somewhat akin to arguing that he was not a Christian, but emphasis on King's charisma obscures other important aspects of his role in the black movement. To be sure, King's oratory was exceptional and many people saw King as a divinely inspired leader, but King did not receive and did not want the kind of unquestioning support that is often associated with charismatic leaders. Movement activists instead saw him as the most prominent among many outstanding movement strategists, tacticians, ideologues, and institutional leaders.

King undoubtedly recognized that charisma was one of many leadership qualities at his disposal, but he also recognized that charisma was not a sufficient basis for leadership in a modern political movement enlisting numerous self-reliant leaders. Moreover, he rejected aspects of the charismatic model that conflicted with his sense of his own limitations. Rather than exhibiting unwavering confidence in his power and wisdom, King was a leader full of self-doubts, keenly aware of his own limitations and human weaknesses. He was at times reluctant to take on the responsibilities suddenly and unexpectedly thrust upon him. During the Montgomery bus boycott, for example, when he worried about threats to his life and to the lives of his wife and child, he was overcome with fear rather than confident and secure in his leadership role. He was able to carry on only after acquiring an enduring understanding of his dependence on a personal God who promised never to leave him alone.

Moreover, emphasis on King's charisma conveys the misleading notion of a movement held together by spellbinding speeches and blind faith rather than by a complex blend of rational and emotional bonds. King's charisma did not place him above criticism. Indeed, he was never able to gain mass support for his notion of nonviolent struggle as a way of life, rather than simply a tactic. Instead of viewing himself as the embodiment of widely held Afro-American racial values, he willingly risked his popularity among blacks through his steadfast advocacy of nonviolent strategies to achieve radical social change.

He was a profound and provocative public speaker as well as an emotionally powerful one. Only those unfamiliar with the Afro-American clergy would assume that his oratorical skills were unique, but King set himself apart from other black preachers through his use of traditional black Christian idiom to advocate unconventional political ideas. Early in his life King became disillusioned with the unbridled emotionalism associated with his father's religious fundamentalism, and, as a thirteen-year-old, he questioned the bodily resurrection of Jesus in his Sunday school class. His subsequent search for an intellectually satisfying religious faith conflicted with the emphasis on the emotional expressiveness that pervades evangelical religion. His preaching manner was rooted in the traditions of the black church, while his subject matter, which often reflected his wide-ranging philosophical interests, distinguished him from other preachers who relied on rhetorical devices that manipulated the emotions of listeners. King used charisma as a tool for mobilizing black communities, but he always used it in the context of other forms of intellectual and political leadership suited to a movement containing many strong leaders.

Recently, scholars have begun to examine the black struggle as a locally based mass movement, rather than simply a reform movement led by national civil rights leaders. The new orientation in scholarship indicates that King's role was different from that suggested in King-centered biographies southern communities in which King had little or no direct involvement.

In Montgomery, for example, local black leaders such as E. D. Nixon, Rosa Parks, and Jo Ann Robinson started the bus boycott before King became the leader of the Montgomery Improvement Association. Thus, although King inspired blacks in Montgomery and black residents recognized that they were fortunate to have such a spokesperson, talented local leaders other than King played decisive roles in initiating and sustaining the boycott movement.

Similarly, the black students who initiated the 1960 lunch counter sit-ins admired King, but they did not wait for him to act before launching their own movement. The sit-in leaders who founded the Student Nonviolent Coordinating Committee (SNCC) became increasingly critical of King's leadership style, linking it to the feelings of dependency that often characterize the followers of charismatic leaders. The essence of SNCC's approach to community organizing was to instill in local residents the confidence that they could lead their own struggles. A SNCC organizer failed if local residents became dependent on his or her presence; as the organizers put it, their job was to work themselves out of a job. Though King influenced the struggles that took place in the Black Belt regions of Mississippi, Alabama, and Georgia, those movements were also guided by self-reliant local leaders who occasionally called on King's oratorical skills to galvanize black protestors at mass meetings while refusing to depend on his presence.

If King had never lived, the black struggle would have followed a course of development similar to the one it did. The Montgomery bus boycott would have occurred, because King did not initiate it. Black students probably would have rebelled—even without King as a role model—for they had sources of tactical and ideological inspiration besides King. Mass activism in southern cities and voting rights efforts in the deep South were outgrowths of large-scale social and political forces, rather than simply consequences of the actions of a single leader. Though perhaps not as quickly and certainly not as peacefully nor with as universal a significance, the black movement would probably have achieved its major legislative victories without King's leadership, for the southern Jim Crow system was a regional anachronism, and the forces that undermined it were inexorable.

To what extent, then, did King's presence affect the movement? Answering that question requires us to look beyond the usual portrayal of the black struggle. Rather than seeing an amorphous mass of discontented blacks acting out strategies determined by a small group of leaders, we would recognize King as a major example of the local black leadership that emerged as black communities mobilized for sustained struggles. If not as dominant a figure as sometimes portrayed, the historical King was nevertheless a remarkable leader who acquired the respect and support of self-confident, grass-roots leaders, some of whom possessed charismatic qualities of their own. Directing attention to the other leaders who initiated and emerged from those struggles should not detract from our conception of King's historical significance; such movement-oriented research reveals King as a leader who stood out in a forest of tall trees.

King's major public speeches—particularly the "I Have a Dream" speech—have received much attention, but his exemplary qualities were also displayed in countless strategy sessions with other activists and in meetings with government officials. King's success as a leader was based on his intellectual and moral cogency and his skill as a conciliator among movement activists who refused to be simply King's "followers" or "lieutenants."

The success of the black movement required the mobilization of black communities as well as the transformation of attitudes in the surrounding society, and King's wide range of skills and attributes prepared him to meet the internal as well as the external demands of the movement. King understood the black world from a privileged position, having grown up in a stable family within a major black urban community; yet he also learned how to speak persuasively to the surrounding white world. Alone among the major civil rights leaders of his time, King could not only articulate black concerns to white audiences, but could also mobilize blacks through his day-to-day involvement in black community institutions and through his access to the regional institutional network of the black church. His advocacy of nonviolent activism gave the black movement invaluable positive press coverage, but his effectiveness as a protest leader derived mainly from his ability to mobilize black community resources.

Analyses of the southern movement that emphasize its nonrational aspects and expressive functions over its political character explain the black struggle as an emotional outburst by discontented blacks, rather than recognizing that the movement's strength and durability came from its mobilization of black community institutions, financial resources, and grass-roots leaders. The values of southern blacks were profoundly and permanently transformed not only by King, but also by involvement in sustained protest activity and community-organizing efforts, through thousands of mass meetings, workshops, citizenship classes, freedom schools, and informal discussions. Rather than merely accepting guidance from above, southern blacks were resocialized as a result of their movement experiences.

Although the literature of the black struggle has traditionally paid little attention to the intellectual content of black politics, movement activists of the 1960s made a profound, though often ignored, contribution to political thinking. King may have been born with rare potential, but his most significant leadership attributes were related to his immersion in, and contribution to, the intellectual ferment that has always been an essential part of Afro-American freedom struggles. Those who have written about King have too often assumed that his most important ideas were derived from outside the black struggle—from his academic training, his philosophical readings, or his acquaintance with Gandhian ideas. Scholars are only beginning to recognize the extent to which his attitudes and those of many other activists, white and black, were transformed through their involvement in a movement in which ideas disseminated from the bottom up as well as from the top down.

Although my assessment of King's role in the black struggles of his time reduces him to human scale, it also increases the possibility that others may recognize his qualities in themselves. Idolizing King lessens one's ability to exhibit some of his best attributes or, worse, encourages one to become a debunker, emphasizing King's flaws in order to lessen the inclination to exhibit his virtues. King himself undoubtedly feared that some who admired him would place too much faith in his ability to offer guidance and to overcome resistance, for he often publicly acknowledged his own limitations and mortality. Near the end of his life, King expressed his certainty that black people would reach the Promised Land whether or not he was with them. His faith was based on an awareness of the qualities that he knew he

shared with all people. When he suggested his own epitaph, he asked not to be remembered for his exceptional achievements—his Nobel Prize and other awards, his academic accomplishments; instead, he wanted to be remembered for giving his life to serve others, for trying to be right on the war question, for trying to feed the hungry and clothe the naked, for trying to love and serve humanity. "I want you to say that I tried to love and serve humanity." Those aspects of King's life did not require charisma or other superhuman abilities.

* * *

If King were alive today, he would doubtless encourage those who celebrate his life to recognize their responsibility to struggle as he did for a more just and peaceful world. He would prefer that the black movement be remembered not only as the scene of his own achievements, but also as a setting that brought out extraordinary qualities in many people. If he were to return, his oratory would be unsettling and intellectually challenging rather than remembered diction and cadences. He would probably be the unpopular social critic he was on the eve of the Poor People's Campaign rather than the object of national homage he became after his death. His basic message would be the same as it was when he was alive, for he did not bend with the changing political winds. He would talk of ending poverty and war and of building a just social order that would avoid the pitfalls of competitive capitalism and repressive communism. He would give scant comfort to those who condition their activism upon the appearance of another King, for he recognized the extent to which he was a product of the movement that called him to leadership.

The notion that appearances by Great Men (or Great Women) are necessary preconditions for the emergence of major movements for social changes reflects not only a poor understanding of history, but also a pessimistic view of the possibilities for future social change. Waiting for the Messiah is a human weakness that is unlikely to be rewarded more than once in a millennium. Studies of King's life offer support for an alternative optimistic belief that ordinary people can collectively improve their lives. Such studies demonstrate the capacity of social movements to transform participants for the better and to create leaders worthy of their followers.

The Chicano Image and the Myth of Aztlán Rediscovered

John R. Chávez

Mexican Americans—or, as they would prefer to be called out of a new sense of cultural pride, "Chicanos"—today are the nation's second largest and fastest-growing minority. Their greater visibility dates largely from the political and cultural maelstrom of the 1960s. In that decade, both nonwhites worldwide and nonwhite minorities in America began to assert a cultural independence calculated to free them from what they regarded as the control of Western and American myths, respectively. For Chicanos, this development represented a special opportunity to reattach themselves to their origins and cultural traditions. What they rediscovered and revivified—the "myth of Aztlán"—was of great value, says Professor John R. Chávez of Texas A&M University. With their ancient, mythic past providing inspiration, Chicanos reclaimed their history as an Aztec legend which spoke of ancestral roots in Indian prehistory—an Aztec Eden—when their earliest forebears had inhabited and prevailed in what only later came to be designated the Southwest borderlands. Feeling a new sense of belonging to the region inspired by the Aztlán myth, Chicano political efforts such as César Chávez's farm workers' strikes in California, Reies López Tijerina's land grant struggles in New Mexico, and Rodolfo Gonzales's community efforts in Denver all found special energy and validity in this newly rediscovered "usable past." While the myth of Aztlán, now expressed as Chicano desire to recover a larger measure of control, has not been, and probably cannot be, fulfilled, the power of myth is once again made manifest and continues to persist.

During the middle and late 1960s, the political situation in the United States developed into a crisis that permitted a resurgence of the image of the lost land. The myths of the Spanish Southwest and the American Southwest, which the Mexicans of the region had accepted for much of the twentieth century, were suddenly set aside. During that period when so many myths were being reexamined by U.S. society in general, many Mexican-Americans found it possible to challenge the images of themselves and their region that had been imposed by the Anglo majority. The shattering effect that the civil rights and the antiwar movements had on the Anglo self-image led many Mexican-Americans to believe that their attempts to be like Anglos were against their own interests. They began to feel that perhaps they had more in common with blacks and even the Vietnamese than with the dominant Anglo-Americans. Reviewing their own socioeconomic position after two decades of "Americanization," Mexican-Americans found themselves lower even than blacks in income, housing, and education. Though they were not as discriminated against or segregated as blacks, Mexican-Americans realized that they had in no way become the equals of Anglos. In searching for the causes, the view that all "immigrant" groups initially experienced such problems seemed to explain less and less, for by 1960, 81 percent of Mexicans in the Southwest were United States–born. Furthermore, the condition of longtime residents in New Mexico and Texas was no better and often worse than that of other Mexican-Americans.

The nationalist movements of such peoples as the Vietnamese and the Cubans inspired a significant number of Mexican-Americans to reexamine their own condition through history and conclude that they too had been the victims of U.S. imperialism. As a result, the nineteenth- and early twentieth-century image of the Southwest as lost and of themselves as dispossessed reemerged from the collective unconscious of the region's Mexicans. . . . [T]hat image had persisted, largely because of the intense Mexican nationalism that radiated from across the border, but in the 1960s it was reasserted and reshaped under the influence of contemporary ideas. Increasingly after World War II the former colonies of the world gained political independence and established nonwhite rule. Nonwhites sought to reestablish pride in their own racial backgrounds to combat the feelings of inferiority that colonialism had imposed. In the United States this phenomenon manifested itself in calls for black pride and black power, and also in cries for Chicano pride and Chicano power. The use of the term "Chicano," derived from *mexicano* and formerly used disparagingly in referring to lower-class Mexican-Americans, signified a renewed pride in the Indian and mestizo poor who had built so much of the Southwest during the Spanish and Anglo colonizations. While investigating the past of their indigenous ancestors in the Southwest, activist Chicanos rediscovered the myth of Aztlán and adapted it to their own time.

After gaining independence from Spain and again after the revolution of 1910, Mexicans had turned to their ancient past for inspiration. It is no surprise that Chicano activists did the same thing during the radical 1960s, especially given the example of contemporary nationalist movements. In the ancient myth of Aztlán, activists found a tie between their homeland and Mexican culture that antedated the Republic of Mexico, the Spanish exploration of the borderlands, and even Tenochtitlán (Mexico City) itself. As we have seen, ancient Aztec legends, recorded in the chronicles of the sixteenth and seventeenth centuries, recounted that before founding Tenochtitlán the Aztecs had journeyed from a won-

drous place to the north called "Aztlán." Since this place of origin, according to some of the chroniclers, was located in what is now the Southwest, Chicano activists reapplied the term to the region reclaiming the land on the basis of their Indian ancestry. And although the preponderance of evidence indicates that the Aztlán of the Aztecs was actually within present Mexico, the activists' use of the term had merit. While the Aztlán whence the Aztecs departed for Tenochtitlán was probably in the present Mexican state of Nayarit, anthropological studies suggest that the distant ancestors of the Aztecs centuries prior to settling in Nayarit had inhabited and migrated through the Southwest. Thus, on the basis of Indian prehistory, Chicanos had a claim to the region, a claim stronger than any based only on the relatively brief history of Spanish settlement in the borderlands.

Since Aztlán had been the Aztec equivalent of Eden and Utopia, activists converted that ancient idealized landscape into an ideal of a modern homeland where they hoped to help fulfill their people's political, economic, and cultural destiny. Therefore, though "Aztlán" came to refer in a concrete sense to the Southwest, it also applied to any place north of Mexico where Chicanos hoped to fulfill their collective aspirations. These aspirations in the 1960s, it turned out, were more or less the same hopes Southwest Mexicans had had since the Treaty of Guadalupe Hidalgo. Chicanos sought bilingual/bicultural education, just representation in the government, justice in the courts, fair treatment from the police and the military, a decent standard of living, and ultimately that which controlled the possibilities of all their other aspirations—their share of the means of production, for this, intellectuals at least now believed, was what the Anglo conquest had fundamentally denied Southwest Mexicans. The northern homeland had been lost militarily and politically in the 1840s; the economic loss had come in subsequent decades with the usurpation of individually and communally owned lands that produced the wealth of the region. During Mexican rule the wealth of the land had been largely agricultural, but later the land of the Southwest had also given forth gold, silver, copper, coal, oil, uranium, and innumerable other products that enriched the Anglos but left Mexicans impoverished. In this respect, Chicanos increasingly saw a parallel between themselves and the native peoples of other colonized lands: all had been conquered, all had been reduced to menial labor, and all had been used to extract the natural bounty of their own land for the benefit of the conquerors.

The Chicanos' historic loss of the economic power inherent in the land of the Southwest underlay the manifestations of militant nationalism that erupted in the late 1960s: the farm worker strikes in California, the land grant struggle in New-Mexico, the revolt of the electorate in Crystal City, Texas, the school walkouts in Denver and Los Angeles, and the other major events of what came to be called the Chicano movement. Though these events exploded with suddenness, they were preceded by calmer yet significant developments in the previous decade that prepared a sizable number of Mexican-Americans for the move away from Americanization. . . . [T]he 1950s and early 1960s had been the nadir in the history of Mexican nationalism in the Southwest. But even though Mexican-American organizations had generally been weakened by the assimilation of potential members into the Anglo world, several new groups had managed to establish themselves during that time. The most important of these were the Mexican-American Political Association (MAPA) founded in California in 1959 and the Political Association of Spanish-Speaking Organizations (PASO or PASSO) founded in Arizona in 1960 and most influential in Texas. These two differed from the League of United Latin American Citizens, the G. I. Forum, and other earlier groups because the new organizations believed in activating the political power of Mexican-Americans for the overall good of Mexican-Americans. Earlier groups, more assimilationist in perspective, preferred a defensive posture, protecting the rights of Mexican-Americans in the name of all U.S. citizens. While the difference may seem subtle, the new emphasis on self-interest rather than universality prepared the way for the rebirth of Chicano nationalism. . . .

On 16 September, (Mexican Independence Day) 1965, César Chávez's predominantly Mexican-American National Farm Workers Association (NFWA) voted to join a grape strike initiated in Delano, California, by the Filipino Agricultural Workers Organizing Committee (AWOC). Because of their greater numbers, Mexican-Americans soon dominated the strike and later controlled the United Farm Workers' Organizing Committee (UFWOC), which came into being as a result of the merger of the two original unions. This strike was to lead to the first successful agricultural revolt by one of the poorest groups of Chicanos in the Southwest. Interestingly, this revolt was led by a man who believed in nonviolence, democracy, and religion; who had little faith in government programs; and who distrusted the very Chicano nationalism he inspired.

Chávez, whose grandfather was a "pioneer" in Arizona in the 1880s, was born near Yuma in 1927. "Our family farm was started three years before Arizona became a state," Chávez once remarked. "Yet, sometimes I get crank letters . . . telling me to 'go back' to Mexico!" As a result of the depression the family's land was lost in 1939 because of unpaid taxes, and the Chávezes migrated to California where they became farm workers. After years of such work and a period in the navy, César Chávez joined the Community Service Organization which, though overwhelmingly Mexican-American in membership, stressed the acquisition and exercise of the rights of citizenship by the poor of all ethnic groups. This early influence later helped Chávez gain widespread support for the farm workers, even though it prevented him from becoming a true spokesman for Chicano nationalism. After ten years in the CSO, Chávez in 1962 decided to organize farm workers on his own when the CSO decided the task was beyond its range of activities.

Shortly after the NFWA voted to strike, Chávez appealed to religious and civil rights groups for volunteers. By doing so, he converted a labor dispute into a social movement, and expanded his Mexican-American and Filipino base of support by including all others who wished to help. At the same time he nonetheless acknowledged that race was an issue in the strike. Chávez encouraged nationalism among the farm workers because he knew it could be a cohesive force against the Anglo growers who were accustomed to treating racial minorities as inferiors. Indeed, the Virgin of Guadalupe, the patroness of Mexico, became one of the chief nationalistic symbols used in the movement's demonstrations. Luis Valdez, playwright and propagandist for the farm workers, described her significance:

> The Virgin of Guadalupe was the first hint to farm workers that the pilgrimage [to Sacramento in the spring of 1966] implied social revolution. During the Mexican Revolution, the peasant armies of Emiliano Zapata carried her standard, not only because they sought her divine protection, but because she symbol-

ized the Mexico of the poor and humble. It was a simple Mexican Indian, Juan Diego, who first saw her in a vision at Guadalupe. Beautifully dark and Indian in feature, she was the New World version of the Mother of Christ. Even though some of her worshippers in Mexico still identify her with Tonatzin, an Aztec goddess, she is a Catholic saint of Indian creation—a Mexican. The people's response was immediate and reverent. They joined the march by the thousands, falling in line behind her standard.

Thus, through the Virgin, Chávez and the Chicano workers linked their struggle to their aboriginal Mexican past.

Although the Mexican symbols used by the movement were generally associated with Mexico proper, Chávez was also aware of the Chicano farm workers' indigenous background in the Southwest. He had a personal interest in the history of the California missions and in their treatment of the Indians, the first farm workers. Chávez believed that though the missionaries had indeed used coercion on the Indians, they had saved them from far worse treatment at the hands of the secular authorities and the settlers. They had done this by making the missions sanctuaries where the Indians could work the land communally and by forcing the settlers to treat the Indians as human beings. As a result, Chávez once commented, "The Spanish began to marry the Indians . . . they couldn't destroy them, so instead of wiping out a race, they made a new one." The relative autonomy of the missions, politically and economically, together with the Franciscans' belief in the equality of all human souls, permitted the Indians a certain amount of security and even on occasion complete acceptance through intermarriage with the settlers. Like their Indian predecessors, twentieth-century farm workers, in Chávez's eyes, could only gain their rightful place in society if they believed in their own racial equality with other men and established themselves as an independent political and economic force capable of challenging the new owners of the land.

Chávez fully realized what the historic loss of the land had meant to the Indians and to their Mexican successors. The "Plan of Delano," a Mexican-style proclamation stating the discontent of the farm workers and the aims of Chávez and his movement, reminded society of the oppression Southwest Mexicans had endured: "The Mexican race has sacrificed itself for the last hundred years. Our sweat and our blood have fallen on this land to make other men rich." Chávez knew that the power of the Anglo growers rested on their ownership of the land, and he also realized that Chicanos and the other poor would ultimately achieve full equality only when they had recovered that land: "While . . . our adversaries . . . are the rich and the powerful and possess the land, we are not afraid. . . . We know that our cause is just, that history is a story of social revolution, and that the poor shall inherit the land." Though Chávez stated this belief publicly, he knew land reform was a distant ideal, and he was much too practical to make it a goal for his union. Despite this, the growers claimed that such statements, together with the symbols of Mexican nationalism, revealed Chávez to be communistic and un-American. One rancher remarked,

> Mr. César Chávez is talking about taking over this state—I don't like that. Too much *"Viva Zapata"* and down with the Caucasians, *la raza* [the Latin American race], and all that. Mister César Chávez is talking about *revolución*. Remember, California once belonged to Mexico, and he's saying, "Look, you dumb Mexicans, you lost it, now let's get it back!"

Despite such distortions and in spite of his actual encouragement of nationalism, Chávez feared the divisive effects it could have within the movement. Since the growers were quick to exploit such divisiveness, he would not allow intolerance to split the ranks of his Chicano, Filipino, and liberal Anglo supporters. He was especially concerned that Chicanos not let their incipient nationalism get out of hand: "We oppose some of this La Raza business. . . . We know what it does. When La Raza means or implies racism, we don't support it. But if it means our struggle, our dignity, or our cultural roots, then we're for it." Because of this guarded attitude, however, Chávez could never become a fully committed advocate of Chicano nationalism. His struggle after all was economic, rather than cultural; his concerns were those of the poor as a whole, rather than more specifically Chicano issues, such as bilingual education. On the other hand, Chávez showed Chicanos that their cultural problems could not be solved by politics alone, since these problems were economic at their source:

> Effective political power is never going to come, particularly to minority groups, unless they have economic power. . . . I'm not advocating . . . brown

capitalism. . . . What I'm suggesting is a cooperative movement.

Such power lay in numbers and could best be harnessed if minority groups joined together with liberal Anglos in a broad interracial consumer movement.

During the grape strike, Chávez demonstrated how a cooperative movement could generate economic power, enough power to force the capitulation of the growers in 1970. His major weapon was a grape boycott extending beyond the Chicanos' Southwest, throughout the United States, and even into Europe. Since he had made the strike a moral and civil rights movement, many outsiders were willing to cooperate in the boycott. Within the UFWOC itself, . . . Chávez made the workers understand that the struggle was for human equality, not merely for better wages and working conditions. As a result, in practical terms, the UFWOC itself became more a cooperative than a trade union: "It . . . developed for its members a death benefit plan; a coöperative grocery, drug store, and gas station; a credit union; a medical clinic; a social protest theatre group . . .; and a newspaper. . . ." Such cooperative policies together with the nonviolent, mass protest methods of the civil rights movement (methods Mexican-Americans had earlier disdained to use) effectively countered such traditional grower tactics as the employment of strikebreakers from Mexico. After the grape growers agreed to sign contracts with the UFWOC in 1970, the farm-worker movement in the succeeding decades became an ongoing force as the union entered the lettuce fields, fought for the renewal of old contracts, and expanded to other parts of the nation.

"Across the San Joaquin Valley," proclaimed the "Plan of Delano" in 1966, "across California, across the entire Southwest of the United States, wherever there are Mexican people, wherever there are farm workers, our movement is spreading like flames across a dry plain." Within a short time the farm-worker front of the Chicano movement had indeed spread to Arizona and Texas, but, more important, other fronts of the movement had opened independently throughout the Southwest in other sectors of Chicano life. One of these fronts was the renewal of the land grant struggle in northern New Mexico. . . . [A]fter the Treaty of Guadalupe Hidalgo, Mexicans in the Southwest were gradually deprived of their lands by an Anglo-American legal and economic system that constantly challenged land grants made under previous governments. In his investigation of problems resulting from the land grant issue during the 1960s, Peter Nabokov wrote that in northern New Mexico:

These ancestral holdings had originally been awarded to single people or to communities of at least ten village families. A man had his private home and a narrow rectangular plot which usually gave him access to river water. But the community's grazing and wood-gathering acreage, called *ejido*, was understood to be held commonly, and forever, a perpetual trust. A large percentage of the New Mexico *ejido* lands had been put in the public domain by the surveyors general of the period 1854–1880 because they recognized only claims made on behalf of individuals, not communities.

During the twentieth century much of this "public domain" was turned over to the Forest Service, which in turn was given the authority to lease the lands to private individuals and companies for the use and development of natural resources. Unfortunately for the long-settled small farmers of northern New Mexico, large out-of-state corporations, engaged in mining, logging, and tourism, received preferential treatment in their dealings with the Forest Service. The impoverished small farmers, on the other hand, were gradually denied their grazing rights by an agency that was unconcerned with and even hostile to their needs; in her study of the problem, Patricia Bell Blawis observed that "while logging firms contracted with the Forest Service for immense areas on their ancestral land, the grantees were forbidden to cut stovewood without a permit." Thus, according to Blawis, in the twentieth century the imperialism of the nineteenth continued surreptitiously: "The Forest Service is evidence of the colonial policy of the Federal government. . . . Through this Service, resources of the West are exploited by Washington, D.C. and its friends." . . . [T]he native Mexicans had in the past reacted violently to this colonialism: between the 1880s and the late 1920s, for instance, at least two groups of nightriders, Las Gorras Blancas and La Mano Negra, had burned buildings, torn down fences, and committed other such terrorist acts to protest the seizure of their lands. During the.late 1960s such violence flared again.

In 1963 the militant Alianza Federal de Mercedes (the Federal Land Grant Alliance—always popularly known as the Alianza, even though the official name changed several times) was incorporated under the direction of a dynamic leader named Reies López Tijerina. Tijerina, whose great-grandfather had been robbed of his land and killed by Anglos, was born in Texas in 1926; he lived and moved throughout the Southwest and beyond as a farm worker and later as a poor itinerant preacher. During these wanderings, he came to believe that the problems of his people had resulted from their loss of the land, for as he later stressed, "the ties of our culture with the land are indivisible." As a consequence, he became interested in the land grant issue, spent a year studying the question in Mexico, and in 1960 settled in New Mexico where he felt there was the best hope of recovering the grants. After organizing many of the heirs into the Alianza, Tijerina unsuccessfully petitioned the U.S. government to investigate the land titles for violations of that portion of the Treaty of Guadalupe Hidalgo that guaranteed the property rights of Mexicans in the Southwest. He had also requested the Mexican government to look into the matter, but Mexico, having gradually become economically dependent on as well as ideologically aligned with the United States since the 1930s, had not and would not support any radical claims made by dissident Chicanos. Rebuffed in his efforts to get consideration through regular legal and political channels, Tijerina turned to civil disobedience.

In October of 1966 Tijerina and other *aliancistas* occupied the Echo Amphitheater, a section of the Carson National Forest that had once been part of the land grant of San Joaquín del Río de Chama. Since the original Spanish and Mexican grants had permitted the villagers a good deal of autonomy, the *aliancistas* declared themselves the Republic of San Joaquín and elected as mayor a direct descendant of the original grantee. When several forest rangers attempted to interfere, they were detained by the "republic," tried for trespassing, and released on suspended sentences. By allowing this, Tijerina hoped to challenge the jurisdiction of the Forest Service over the land, thus forcing the land grant issue into the courts, possibly as far as the Supreme Court. Also, the declaration of autonomy would make public the Chicanos' need for self-determination, their need to escape a whole range of problems caused by their incorporation into U.S. society. Not least of these was the war in Vietnam, which even the traditionally patriotic *nuevomexicanos* were beginning to oppose: "The people," as Tijerina had once remarked, "generally feel that our sons are being sent

to Vietnam illegally, because many of these land grants are free city states and are independent." The "liberation" of the Echo Amphitheater had been a dangerous act, but as the increasingly radical Tijerina declared during the occupation: "Fidel Castro has what he has because of his guts. . . . Castro put the gringos off his island and we can do the same." Unfortunately for the Alianza, Tijerina would later serve two years in prison for assault on the rangers at the Echo Amphitheater; furthermore, the courts would refuse to admit discussion of the land grant issue.

During May of 1967, according to Nabokov, "private northern landowners . . . began suffering from the traditional symptoms of unrest—selective cattle rustling, irrigation ditch and fence wreckage, shot-up water tanks, and arson." Although there was no evidence the Alianza had committed these acts, the authorities actually feared that guerrilla warfare might break out in northern New Mexico. When Tijerina revealed that his group planned to have a conference on June 3 at Coyote, a small town near the San Joaquín grant, the authorities anticipated another occupation and prevented the meeting by declaring it an unlawful assembly, blocking the roads to the town, and arresting any *aliancistas* who resisted. This proved to be a mistake, for it brought on the very violence the authorities had feared. Feeling that their right to free assembly had been violated, the *aliancistas* decided to make a citizen's arrest of the district attorney responsible for the police action. On June 5, in the most daring move of the contemporary Chicano movement, Tijerina and about twenty other armed *aliancistas* attacked the courthouse at the county seat at Tierra Amarilla. In the ensuing shoot-out two deputies were wounded, the courthouse was occupied, and the Coyote prisoners were freed. Finding that the district attorney was not present, the *aliancistas* then fled the town with two hostages.

The reaction of the authorities brought the cause of the Alianza to the attention of the entire nation. Imagining "a new Cuba to the north," the state government in Santa Fe sent out four hundred National Guardsmen to join two hundred state troopers in an expedition into northern New Mexico that included the use of helicopters and two tanks. After a few days Tijerina was captured and charged with various crimes connected with the raid, though he was subsequently released on bail. Once in the national spotlight, Tijerina elaborated on the issues and goals of the land grant struggle, issues that were important to Chicanos throughout the Southwest; "Not only the land has been stolen from the good and humble people," he commented, "but also their culture. . . ." And he remarked, "A major point of contention is that we are being deprived of our language. . . ." Tijerina also argued that in addition to property rights, the cultural rights of his people were guaranteed by the Treaty of Guadalupe Hidalgo. Once the guarantees of this treaty were honored and discrimination was ended, Indo-Hispanos, as Tijerina often called his people, would take their rightful place as intermediaries in the pluralistic Southwest:

> We have been forced by destiny to adopt two languages; we will be the future ambassadors and envoys to Latin America. At home, I believe that the Southwest is breeding a special kind of people that will bridge the color-gap between black and white. . . . [Moreover, we] are the people the Indians call their "lost brothers."

While the many charges against him were being handled in the courts, Tijerina continued his activities with the Alianza and also participated in the interracial, antipoverty Poor People's March on Washington in 1968. In 1969, however, the Alianza was deprived of Tijerina's leadership when he was imprisoned for the Echo Amphitheater incident. Suffering from poor health, he was paroled in July 1971, but on condition that he no longer hold office in the Alianza. Deprived of his full leadership and lacking the organized economic power of an institution such as the United Farm Workers, the Alianza lost much of its drive, and not until 1979 was it able to convince the government to give even nominal reconsideration to the land grant issue. Nonetheless, Tijerina and the Alianza did rejuvenate the ethnic pride of a good number of *nuevomexicanos*. Though many Hispanos considered Tijerina an outsider, many others joined his organization, and in doing so reaffirmed their ties to Mexico through reference to the Treaty of Guadalupe Hidalgo, and to their Indian ancestors through acceptance of the facts of *mestizaje* (Indo-Hispano intermarriage). In New Mexico no longer could "Spanish-Americans" easily deny their background. No longer could Spanish-American politicians, who had generally held a representative number of positions in government, ignore their economically depressed constituents without op-

position from Chicano militants around the state—for increasingly among *nuevomexicanos* the image of the Spanish Southwest was giving way to the image of Aztlán.

The person most responsible for the adoption of the term "Aztlán" by the rapidly spreading Chicano movement was Rodolfo "Corky" Gonzales, leader of the Chicano community in Denver, Colorado. In modern times the term was first applied to the Chicano homeland in 1962 by Jack D. Forbes, a Native American professor who argued that Mexicans were more truly an Indian than a mestizo people; his mimeographed manuscript, "The Mexican Heritage of Aztlán (the Southwest) to 1821," was distributed among Mexican-Americans in the Southwest during the early 1960s. The term gained popularity, but was not universally accepted by the Chicano movement until, in the spring of 1969, the first Chicano national conference, in Denver, drafted "El plan espiritual de Aztlán," a document that declared the spiritual independence of the Chicano Southwest from the United States. Paradoxically this sentiment was expressed in a city never legally within the confines of Mexico; however, like arguments for Puerto Rican independence presented in New York, this declaration from Denver signified the desire of a minority group for independence from the colonialism that had subjugated its native land and that continued to affect the individuals of the minority no matter where they resided within the United States.

Born in Denver in 1928, Corky Gonzales was primarily a product of the urban barrios, even though he spent part of his youth working in the fields of southern Colorado. He managed to escape poverty by becoming a successful boxer. As a result of the popularity gained from his career, he became an influential figure in the barrios and was selected to head various antipoverty programs in the early 1960s. By 1965, however, he had become disenchanted with the antipoverty bureaucracy. He concluded earlier than other Chicanos that the War on Poverty was designed to pacify rather than truly help the poor. Had he read it, he would have agreed with a later comment made by a Chicano editor when government and foundation money poured into northern New Mexico in the aftermath of Tierra Amarilla:

> They're trying to create *Vendido* power (sellout power) . . . trying to bring Vietnam to New Mexico and trying

to create "leaders" the system can use as tools. But it hasn't worked with the Vietnamese and it's not going to work with Raza here in the United States.

Disgusted with the strings attached to funds from the government and foundations, Gonzales organized the Crusade for Justice, a community self-help group. Through their own fund-raising efforts, the members established a barrio service center, providing such assistance as child care, legal aid, housing and employment counseling, health care, and other services especially needed in poor urban areas. The Crusade was, moreover, outspoken in its concern for Chicano civil and cultural rights.

More than Chávez and even more than Tijerina, Gonzales felt that nationalism was the force that would get Chicanos to help one another, and that the success of his Crusade exemplified the possibilities of self-determination. Although his participation in the Poor People's March of 1968 revealed his belief in the necessity of interracial cooperation, at heart he felt that Chicanos would have to help themselves and would do so if they became aware of their proud history as a people. Of Chicanos in his state, he once said, "Colorado belongs to our people, was named by our people, discovered by our people and worked by our people. . . . We preach self-respect . . . to reclaim what is ours." Regarding the region as a whole, he commented, "Nationalism exists in the Southwest, but until now it hasn't been formed into an image people can see. Until now it has been a dream. It has been my job to create a reality out of the dream. . . ." The Crusade was part of that reality and so was the Chicano Youth Liberation Conference, called by Gonzales to bring together Chicanos from throughout the nation, but especially from the cities, where 80 percent of all Chicanos lived. In Gonzales urban youth found a leader, unlike Chávez or Tijerina, who had successfully attempted concrete solutions to city problems. Consequently, 1,500 Chicanos

from many different organizations attended the conference of this urban nationalist.

As if in exhibit of the problems of urban Chicanos, the week before the conference riots broke out in the Denver barrios, resulting from events that began with a racist remark made by a teacher at a local high school. A student and community protest led to confrontation with police; according to Gonzales, "What took place . . . was a battle between the West Side 'liberation forces' and the 'occupying army.' The West Side won [police suffered some injuries and damage to equipment]." Although Gonzales opposed violence and tried to stop the rioting, he clearly felt the trouble was justified and was proud that Chicanos were capable of defending themselves against the government he believed had made internal colonies of the city's barrios. After the riots, the conference convened in an atmosphere permeated with nationalism and proclaimed the following in "El plan espiritual de Aztlán":

> Conscious . . . of the brutal "Gringo" invasion of our territories, we, the Chicano inhabitants and civilizers of the northern land of Aztlán, from whence came our forefathers, reclaiming the land of their birth. . . . We [who] do not recognize capricious frontiers on the bronze continent. . . . we declare the independence of our mestizo nation.

In that proclamation the Chicano delegates fully revived their people's tradi tional image of the Southwest and clarified it for their own time: the Southwest was the Chicano homeland, a land paradoxically settled by an indigenous people who were subsequently conquered. Furthermore, these people were now seen as native, not merely because their Spanish ancestors had settled the land hundreds of years before, but because their Indian ancestors had resided on the land thousands of years earlier, tying it permanently to Indian and mestizo Mexico.

Streets of Gold: The Myth of the Model Minority

Curtis Chang

Asian-Americans, it is commonly believed, offer the latest evidence that the American Dream retains its validity and vitality. Popular publications such as *Time* and *Newsweek* have in recent memory celebrated Asian-Americans as a "super minority" that has adopted the Puritan work ethic and outshone even the Anglo majority, and most certainly other ethnic minorities, in both educational achievement and economic success and mobility. This essay, by Curtis Chang a Taiwanese immigrant and Rockefeller Fellow who is now chaplain at Tufts University, challenges almost every sacred notion now rather solidly attached in the public mind to Asian-Americans. He insists on differentiating among Asian-American groups. Conditions and circumstances pertaining to Chinese-Americans, for example, vary greatly from those of Vietnamese-Americans. Japanese-Americans and Filipinos vary in most every category of comparison. "Distortions of status," and other major mythologies related to employment opportunity, job status, and patterns of compensation and promotion, for example, prevent a subtle and textured understanding of Asian-Americans, past and present.

The Model Minority is another "Streets of Gold" tale. It distorts Asian-Americans' true status and ignores our racial handicaps. And the Model Minority's ideology is even worse than its mythology. It attempts to justify the existing system of racial inequality by blaming the victims rather than the system itself.

The Model Minority myth introduces us as an ethnic minority that is finally "making it in America." The media consistently defines "making it" as achieving material wealth, wealth that flows from our successes in the workplace and the schoolroom. This economic achievement allegedly proves a minority can "lay claim to the American dream."

Trying to show how "Asian-Americans present a picture of affluence and economic success," 9 out of 10 of the major Model Minority stories of the last four years relied heavily on one statistic: the family median income. The median Asian-American family income, according to the U.S. Census Survey of Income and Education data, is $22,713 compared to $20,800 for white Americans. Armed with that figure, national magazines have trumpeted our "remarkable, ever-mounting achievements."

Such assertions demonstrate the truth of the aphorism "Statistics are like a bikini. What they reveal is suggestive, but what they conceal is vital." The family median income statistic conceals the fact that Asian-American families generally (1) have more children and live-in relatives and thus have more mouths to feed; (2) are often forced by necessity to have everyone in the family work, averaging *more* than two family income earners (whites only have 1.6); and (3) live disproportionately in high cost of living areas (i.e., New York, Chicago, Los Angeles, and Honolulu) which artificially inflate income figures. Dr. Robert S. Mariano, professor of economics at the University of Pennsylvania, has calculated that when such appropriate adjustments and comparisons are made, a different and rather disturbing picture emerges, showing indeed a clearly disadvantaged group. . . . Filipino and Chinese men *are no better off than black men with regard to median incomes.*

Along with other racial minorities, Asian-Americans are still scraping for the crumbs of the economic pie.

Throughout its distortion of our status, the media propagates two crucial assumptions. First, it lumps all Asian-Americans into one monolithic, homogeneous, yellow skinned mass. Such a view ignores the existence of an incredibly disadvantaged Asian-American underclass. Asians work in low income and low status jobs 2 to 3 times more than whites. Recent Vietnamese refugees in California are living like the Appalachian poor. While going to his Manhattan office, multimillionaire architect I. M. Pei's car passes Chinese restaurants and laundries where 72 percent of all New York Chinese men still work.

But the media makes an even more dangerous assumption. It suggests that (alleged) material success is the same thing as basic racial equality. Citing that venerable family median income figure, magazines claim Asian-Americans are "obviously nondisadvantaged folks." Yet a 1979 United States Equal Employment Opportunity Commission study on Asian-Americans discovered widespread anti-Asian hiring and promotion practices. Asian-Americans "in the professional, technical, and managerial occupations" often face "modern racism—the subtle, sophisticated, systemic patterns and practices . . . which function to effect and to obscure the discriminatory outcomes." One myth simply does not prove another: neither our "astonishing economic prosperity" nor a racially equal America exist.

An emphasis on material success also pervades the media's stress on Asian-Americans' educational status at "the top of the class." Our "march into the ranks of the educational elite" is significant because "all that education is paying off spectacularly." Once again, the same fallacious assumptions plague this "whiz kids" image of Asian-Americans.

The media again ignores the fact that class division accounts for much of the publicized success. Until 1976, the U.S. Immigration Department only admitted Asian immigrants that were termed "skilled" workers. "Skilled" generally meant college educated, usually in the sciences since poor English would not be a handicap. The result was that the vast majority of pre-1976 Asian immigrants came from already well-educated, upper-class backgrounds — the classic "brain drain" syndrome.

The post-1976 immigrants, however, come generally from the lower, less educated classes. A study by Professor Elizabeth Ahn Toupin of Tufts University matched similar Asian and non-Asian students *along class lines* and found that Asian-Americans "did not perform at a superior academic level to non-Asian students. Asian-Americans were more likely to be placed on academic probation than their white counterparts . . . twice as many Asian American students withdrew from the university."

Thus, it is doubtful whether the perceived widespread educational success will continue as the Asian-American population eventually balances out along class lines. When 16.2 percent of all Chinese have less than 4 years of schooling (*four times* that of whites), it seems many future Asian-Americans will worry more about being able to read a newspaper rather than a Harvard acceptance letter.

Most important, the media assumes once again that achieving a certain level of material or educational success means achieving real equality. People easily forget that to begin with, Asians invest heavily in education since other means of upward mobility are barred to them by race. Until recently, for instance, Asian-Americans were barred from unions and traditional lines of credit. Other "white" avenues to success, such as the "old boy network," are still closed to Asian-Americans.

When *Time* (July 8, 1985) claims "as a result of their academic achievements Asians are climbing the economic ladder with remarkable speed," it glosses over an inescapable fact: there is a white ladder and then there is a yellow one. Almost all of the academic studies on the *actual returns Asians receive* from their education point to prevalent discrimination. A striking example of this was found in a City University of New York research project which constructed resumes with equivalent educational backgrounds. Applications were then sent to employers, one group under an Asian name and a similar group under a Caucasian name. Whites received interviews 5 times more than Asians. The media never headlines even more shocking data that can be easily found in the U.S. Census. For instance, Chinese and Filipino males only earned respectively 74 and 52 percent as much as their *equally educated* white counterparts. Asian females fared even worse. Their salaries were only 44 to 54 percent as large as equivalent white males' paychecks. Blacks suffer from this same statistical disparity. We Asian-Americans are indeed a Model Minority—a perfect model of racial discrimination in America.

Yet this media myth encourages neglect of our pressing needs. "Clearly, many Asian-Americans and Pacific peoples are invisible to the governmental agencies," one state agency reported. "Discrimination against Asian-Americans and Pacific peoples is as much the result of omission as commission." In 1979, while the president praised Asian-Americans' "successful integration into American society," his administration revoked Asian-Americans' eligibility for minority small business loans, devastating thousands of struggling, newly arrived small businessmen. Hosts of other minority issues, ranging from reparations for the Japanese-American internment to the ominous rise of anti-Asian violence, are widely ignored by the general public.

The media, in fact, insist to the general populace that we are not a true racial minority. In its attack on affirmative action, the *Boston Globe* (Jan. 14, 1985) pointed out that universities, like many people, "obviously feel that Asian-Americans, especially those of Chinese and Japanese descent, are brilliant, privileged, and wrongly classified as minorities." Harvard Dean Henry Rosovsky remarked in the same article that "it does not seem to me that as a group, they are disadvantaged. . . . Asian-Americans appear to be in an odd category among other protected minorities."

The image that we Asians aren't like "other minorities" is fundamental to the Model Minority ideology. Any elementary school student knows that the teacher designates one student the model, the "teacher's pet," in order to set an example for others to follow. One only sets up a "model minority" in order to communicate to the other "students," the blacks and Hispanics, "Why can't you be like that?" The media, in fact, almost admit to "grading" minorities as they headline Model Minority stories, "Asian-Americans: Are They Making the Grade?" And Asians have earned the highest grade by fulfilling one important assignment: identifying with the white majority, with its values and wishes.

Unlike blacks, for instance, we Asian-Americans have not vigorously asserted our ethnic identity

(a.k.a. [sic] Black Power). And the American public has historically demanded assimilation over racial pluralism. Over the years, *Newsweek* has published titles from "Success Story: Outwhiting the Whites," to "Ultimate Assimilation," which lauded the increasing number of Asian-White marriages as evidence of Asian-Americans' "acceptance into American society."

Even more significant is the public's approval of how we have succeeded in the "American tradition." Unlike the Blacks and Hispanics, we "Puritan-like" Asians disdain governmental assistance. A *New Republic* piece, "America's Greatest Success Story," similarly applauded how "Asian-Americans pose no problems at all." The media consistently compares the crime-ridden image of other minorities with the picture of law abiding Asian parents whose "well-behaved kids" hit the books and not the streets.

Some insist there is nothing terrible about whites conjuring up our "tremendous" success, divining from it model American traits, then preaching, "Why can't you Blacks and Hispanics be like that?" After all, one might argue, aren't those traits desirable?

Such a view, as mentioned, neglects Asian-Americans' true and pressing needs. Moreover, this view completely misses the Model Minority image's fundamental ideology, an ideology meant to falsely grant America absolution from its racial barriers.

David O. Sears and Donald R. Kinder, two social scientists, have recently published significant empirical studies on the underpinnings of American racial attitudes. They consistently discovered that Americans' stress on "values, such as 'individualism and self-reliance, the work ethic, obedience, and discipline' . . . can be invoked, however perversely, to feed racist appetites." In other words, the Model Minority image lets Americans' consciences rest easy. They can think: "It's not our fault those blacks and Hispanics can't make it. They're just too lazy. After all, look at the Asians." Consequently, American society never confronts the systemic racial and economic factors underlying such inequality. The victims instead bear the blame.

This ideology behind the Model Minority image is best seen when we examine one of the first Model Minority stories, which suddenly appeared in the mid-1960s. It is important to note that the period was marked by newfound, strident black demands for equality and power.

At a time when it is being proposed that hundreds of billions be spent to uplift Negroes and other minorities, the nation's 300,000 Chinese Americans are moving ahead on their own — with no help from anyone else . . . few Chinese-Americans are getting welfare handouts—or even want them . . . they don't sit around moaning.

The same article then concludes that the Chinese-American history and accomplishment "would shock those now complaining about the hardships endured by today's Negroes."

Not surprisingly, the dunce-capped blacks and Hispanics resent us apple polishing, "well-behaved" teacher's pets. Black comedian Richard Pryor performs a revealing routine in which new Asian immigrants learn from whites their first English word: "Nigger." And Asian-Americans themselves succumb to the Model Minority's deceptive mythology and racist ideology. "I made it without help," one often hears among Asian circles, "why can't they?" In a 1986 nationwide poll, only 27 percent of Asian-American students rated "racial understanding" as "essential." The figure plunged 9 percent in the last year alone (a year marked by a torrent of Model Minority stories). We "white-washed" Asians have simply lost our identity as a fellow, disadvantaged minority.

But we don't even need to look beyond the Model Minority stories themselves to realize that whites see us as "whiter" than blacks — but not quite white enough. For instance, citing that familiar median family income figure, *Fortune* magazine of May 17, 1982, complained that Asian-Americans are in fact "getting *more* than [their] share of the pie." For decades, when white Americans were leading the nation in every single economic measure, editorials arguing that whites were getting more than *their* share of the pie were rather rare.

No matter how "well-behaved" we are, Asian-Americans are still excluded from the real pie, the "positions of institutional power and political power." Professor Harry Kitano of UCLA has written extensively on the plight of Asian-Americans as the "middle-man minority," a minority supposedly satisfied materially but forever racially barred from a true, *significant* role in society. Empirical studies indicate that Asian-Americans "have been channeled into lower-echelon white-collar jobs having little or no decision making authority." For example, in *Fortune*'s 1,000 largest companies, Asian-American nameplates rest on a mere half of one percent of all officers' and directors' desks (a statistical disparity worsened by the fact that most of the Asians founded their companies). While the education of the upper-class Asians may save them from the bread lines, their race still keeps them out of the boardroom

Our docile acceptance of such exclusion is actually one of our "model" traits. When Asian-Americans in San Francisco showed their first hint of political activism and protested Asian exclusion from city boards, *The Washington Monthly* (May 1986) warned in a long Asian-American article, "Watch out, here comes another group to pander to." *The New Republic* (July 15, 1985) praised Asian-American political movements because

> unlike blacks or Hispanics, Asian-American politicians have the luxury of not having to devote the bulk of their time to an "Asian-American agenda," and thus escape becoming prisoners of such an agenda. . . . The most important thing for Asian-Americans . . . is simply being part of the process.

This is strikingly reminiscent of another of the first Model Minority stories:

> As the Black and Brown communities push for changes in the present system, the Oriental is set forth as an example to be followed — a minority group that has achieved success through adaptation rather than confrontation.

But it is precisely this "present system," this system of subtle, persistent racism that we all must confront, not adapt to. For example, we Asians gained our right to vote from the 1964 Civil Rights Act that blacks marched, bled, died, and in the words of that original Model Minority story, "sat around moaning for." Unless we assert our true identity as a minority and challenge racial misconceptions and inequalities, we will be nothing more than techno-coolies — collecting our wages but silently enduring basic political and economic inequality.

This country perpetuated a myth once. Today, no one can afford to dreamily chase after that gold in the streets, oblivious to the genuine treasure of racial equality. When racism persists, can one really call any minority a "model"?

Revolution in Indian Country

Fergus M. Bordewich

Only recently has a measure of greater awareness, a new consciousness, begun to arise regarding a glaring omission from the nation's history—an adequate incorporation and assessment of the American Indian, the so-called vanishing American. For many decades a measure of understanding seldom transcended the myth of the Indian as either Bloodthirsty Savage or Noble Red Man. Reflecting a more enlightened modern trend is this article by Fergus M. Bordewich, author of the recent book, *Killing the White Man's Indian.* He also demonstrates that mythically-oriented historical dilemmas are rarely completely solved; they too many times display a life of their own involving ancillary complexities, sometimes more problematical than the original issue. A cessation of the results of the Dawes and subsequent Allottment Acts, however well-meant, netted a loss of 70 percent of Indian lands between the 1880s and 1934. Attempts in the 1970s on the part of the president and Congress, along with subsequent Supreme Court decisions, have restored Indian lands, rights and tribal jurisdiction on reservation lands. This has resulted in ironic historical reversals and depredations on whites, many of whom had lived on reservation lands through generations, and now find themselves deprived of democratic rights because, technically, they live on foreign soil. Indians, too, have fared very unevenly, depending on availability of natural resources, quality of leadership, and the opportunities presented by population proximity. Bordewich poses the incisive question whether these developments are good for either whites or Indians. More pointedly from the Indian standpoint, are islands of ultimate isolated sovereignty along with the concommitant driving away of whites the key to successful democratic life? This takes on added importance and resonance in light of how "Indianness" is being steadily and inexorably diffused—that by the year 2080 estimates predict that fewer than 8 percent of native Americans will have one-half or more of Indian blood.

Like no other inhabitants of the United States, Indians have nourished our imagination, weaving in us a complex skein of guilt, envy, and contempt; yet when we imagine we see "the Indian," we often see little more than the distorted reflection of our own fears, fancies, and unhappy longings. This was vividly brought home to me on a visit to the reservation of the two-hundred-member Campo Band of Mission Indians, in the arid hills an hour's drive east of San Diego. This reservation landscape is a profoundly discouraging one. It offers nothing to comfort the eye, produces nothing of value, and provides almost nothing to sustain life as it is enjoyed by most Americans today. The single resource that the Campos possess is wasteland. In 1987 the band learned that the city of San Diego had named the reservation as one of several potential dump sites for the city's refuse.

"We just need this one little thing to get us started," the band's chairman, Ralph Goff, told me as we walked through the redshank and yucca and ocher sand where the first trenches had been cut for the new landfill. "With it we can create our own destiny." Goff, a formidably built man with little formal education, grew up in the 1940s, when the only work available was as a cowhand or day laborer for whites. When there was no work, people went hungry. "You just had to wait until there was some more food." In the 1960s most of the unskilled jobs disappeared, and nearly every Campo family went on welfare. "We needed it, but it really wrecked us as people. It created idleness. People didn't have to do anything in order to get money."

If the Campos have their way, by the end of the decade daily freight trains will be carrying loads of municipal waste to a three-hundred-acre site on a hilltop at the southern end of the reservation. For the privilege of leasing the band's land, a waste-management firm will pay the Campos between two and five million dollars a year. Goff argued that the dump would put an end to the band's dependence on federal largess. It would create jobs for every adult Campo who is willing to work, provide long-term investment capital for the band, supply money for full college scholarships for every school-age member of the band, and finance new homes for the families that now live in substandard housing. The dump would, in short, give the Campos financial independence for the first time in their modern history.

The landfill would be one of the most technically advanced in the United States; to regulate it, the Campos enacted an environmental code more stringent than the State of California's. Nevertheless, the dump generated fierce opposition in towns near the reservation, where thousands of non-Indians live. Geologists hired by the dump's opponents have suggested, but not proved, that seepage from the dump might contaminate the water supply of ranches beyond the reservation boundary. Environmentalists accused the band of irresponsibility toward the earth and charged that the Campos had been targeted in an "assault" on reservations by "renegade" waste-dumping companies. A bill was even introduced in the California legislature that would have made it a crime to deliver waste to the Campo landfill. Goff shrugged away the protests. "It's a sovereignty issue. It's our land, and we'll do what we want to with it."

"How can you say that the economic development of two hundred people is more important than the health and welfare of all the people in the surrounding area?" an angry and frustrated rancher, whose land lay just off the reservation, asked me.

"It's hard making a living here. The fissures will carry that stuff right through here. We'll have all that stuff in our water and blowing down on us off the hills. If our water is spoiled, then everything's spoiled."

There were predictable elements to her rage: the instinctive resistance of most Americans to any kind of waste dump anywhere near their homes and the distress of many white Americans when they realize the implications of tribal sovereignty for the first time and find themselves subject to the will of a government in which they have no say. But there was something more, a sort of moral perplexity at Indians' having failed to behave according to expectation, an imputation that they were guilty of self-interest. Revealingly, I thought, on the wall of the rancher's trailer there was a poster decorated with Indian motifs. Entitled "Chief Seattle Speaks," it began, in words that are becoming as familiar to American schoolchildren as those of the Gettysburg Address once were: "How can you buy or sell the sky, the warmth of the land?" Here, in sight of the dump, the so-called testament of Chief Seattle was a reproach to the Campos, an argument rooted in what the rancher presumably believed to be Indians' profoundest values. "Before all this I had this ideal about Indian people and all they've been through," she told me. "I used to think they had this special feeling about the land."

More than any other single document, Seattle's twelve-hundred-word "testament" lends support to their increasingly common belief that to "real" Indians any disruption or commercialization of the earth's natural order is a kind of sacrilege and that the most moral, the most truly "Indian" relationship with the land is a kind of poetic passivity. Having been translated into dozens of languages and widely reproduced in school texts, the "testament" has attained a prophetic stature among environmentalists: In 1993 Greenpeace used it as the introduction to a scarifying report on toxic dumping, calling it "the most beautiful and profound statement on the environment ever made." Unfortunately, like much literature that purports to reveal the real nature of the Indians, the "testament" is basically a fiction. Seattle was indeed a historical figure, a slave-owning chief of the Duwamishes who sold land to the United States in the mid-1850s and welcomed the protection of the federal government against his local enemies. However, the "testament," as it is known to most

Americans, was created from notes allegedly made thirty years after the fact by a white doctor who claimed to have been present when Seattle spoke, and which then were extravagantly embroidered by a well-meaning Texas scriptwriter by the name of Ted Perry as narration for a 1972 film on the environment, produced by the Southern Baptist Radio and Television Commission. How is it, I wondered, that Americans have so readily embraced such a spurious text, not only as a sacred creed of the ecology movement but also as a central document of "traditional" Native American culture?

Increasingly it became clear to me that to be able to describe the realities of modern Indian life and politics, I would have to strip away the myths that whites have spun around Native Americans ever since Columbus arbitrarily divided the peoples he encountered into noble Arawaks and savage Caribs, conflating European fantasies with presumed native reality and initiating a tradition that would eventually include Montesquieu, Locke, Hobbes, and Rousseau, as well as a vivid popular literature stretching from *The Last of the Mohicans* to *Dances With Wolves.* Untamable savage, child of nature, steward of the earth, the white mans' ultimate victim: each age has imagined its own mythic version of what historian Robert F. Berkhofer, Jr., termed the "white man's Indian."

Typically the Denver *Post* could declare, not long ago, in an editorial attacking the University of Arizona for a plan to build an observatory atop an allegedly sacred mountain: "At stake is the very survival of American Indian cultures. If these sacred places are destroyed, then the rituals unique to those places no longer will be performed and many tribes simply may cease to exist as distinct peoples." Such logic implies both that only Native Americans who profess to live like pre-Columbians are true Indians and that Indians are essentially hopeless and helpless and on the brink of extinction. Apparently it never occurred to the paper's editorialist that the religion of the great majority of Indians is not in fact some mystical form of traditionalism but a thriving Christianity.

In keeping with our essentially mythic approach to the history of Indians and whites, Americans were generally taught until a generation or so ago to view their national story as a soaring arc of unbroken successes, in which the defeat of the Indians reflected the inevitable and indeed spiritual triumph of civilization over barbarism. More recently, but not so differently, numerous revisionist works like Kirkpatrick Sale's *The Conquest of Paradise: Christopher Columbus and the Columbian Legacy* and Richard Drinnon's *Facing West: The Metaphysics of Indian-Hating and Empire Building* have tended to portray the settlement of North America as a prolonged story of unredeemed tragedy and failure, in which the destruction of the Indians stands as proof of a fundamental ruthlessness at the heart American civilization. Such beliefs have steadily percolated into the wider culture—to be embodied in New Age Westerns like *Dances with Wolves* and popular books like the best-selling *Indian Givers: How the Indians of the Americas Transformed the World,* which purports to show how practically every aspect of modern life from potatoes to democracy derives from the generosity of American Indians—and into the consciences of journalists, clergy, and others who shape public opinion.

On the whole the complex and intricate relationship between whites and Indians has been presented as one of irreconcilable conflict between conqueror and victim, corruption and innocence, and Euro-American "materialism" and native "spirituality." The real story, of course, is an often contradictory one, disfigured by periods of harsh discrimination and occasional acts of genocide but also marked by considerable Indian pragmatism and adaptability as well as by the persistent, if sometimes shortsighted, idealism of whites determined to protect Indians from annihilation and find some place for them in mainstream America.

For instance, in contradiction of the notion that Indians were innocent of even the most elementary business sense, it was clear during negotiations over the Black Hills in the 1870s that Sioux leaders had a perfectly good grasp of finance and that indeed they were determined to drive the best bargain they could. "The Black Hills are the house of Gold for our Indians," Chief Little Bear said at the time. "If a man owns anything, of course he wants to make something out of it to get rich on." Another chief, Spotted Tail, added, "I wanted to live on the interest of my money. The amount must be so large as to support us." Similarly, in contrast with the popular belief that the United States government was committed to a policy of exterminating the Indian (no such policy every existed, in fact), Senator Dawes publicly described the history of Indians in the United States as one "of spoilation, of wars, and of humiliation," and he firmly stated that the Indian should be treated "as an individual, and not as an insoluble substance that the civilization of this country has been unable, hitherto, to digest."

Indeed, the impulse behind the allotment of tribal lands and the national commitment to Indians was dramatically (and, with the benefit of hindsight, poignantly) acted out in a rite of citizenship that after 1887 was staged at Timber Lake, in the heart of Cheyenne River Sioux country, and at many other places in the freshly allotted lands of other tribes. In the presence of representatives of the federal government, new allottees stood resplendent in the feathers and buckskins of a by-gone age. One by one, each man stepped out of a tepee and shot an arrow to symbolize the life he was leaving behind. He then put his hands on a plow and accepted a purse that indicated that he was to save what he earned. Finally, holding the American flag, the Indian repeated these words: "Forasmuch as the President has said that I am worthy to be a citizen of the United States, I now promise this flag that I will give my hands, my head, and my heart to the doing of all that will make me a true American citizen." It was the culminating, transformative moment of which Senator Dawes had dreamed.

It is true enough, however, that, as so often in Indian history, reality failed to live up to good intentions. Unscrupulous speculators soon infested the allotted reservations, offering worthless securities and credit in return for land. Within a few years it was found that of those who had received patents to their land at Cheyenne River, 95 percent had sold or mortgaged their properties. When the Allotment Act was passed in 1881, there were 155 million acres of Indian land in the United States. By the time allotment was finally brought to a halt in 1934, Indian Country had shrunk by nearly 70 percent to 48 million acres, and two-thirds of Indians either were completely landless or did not have enough land to make a living from it. In the mid-1990s Indian Country as a whole is still a daunting and impoverished landscape whose inhabitants are twice as likely as other Americans to be murdered or commit suicide, three times as likely to die in an automobile accident, and five times as likely to die from cirrhosis of the liver. On some reservations unemployment surpasses 80 percent, and 50 percent of young Indians drop out of high school, despite progressively increased access to education.

Is the tribal-sovereignty movement a panacea for otherwise intractable social problems? In the cultural sphere, at least, its importance cannot be underestimated. "Our people live in a limbo culture that is not quite Indian and not quite white either," said Dennis Hastings, surrounded by books, gazing out toward the Iowa plains through the window of the sky blue trailer where he lives in a cow pasture. Hastings, a burly former Marine and the tribal historian of the Omaha Nation, which is in northeastern Nebraska, has almost single-handedly led an effort to recover tribal history as a foundation for community renewal that is probably unmatched by any other small tribe in the United States. "It's like living in a house without a foundation. You can't go back to the old buffalo days, stop speaking English and just use our own language, and ignore whites and everything in white culture. If we did that, we'd become stuck in history, become dinosaurs."

Teasing small grants and the help of volunteer scholars from institutions around the country, Hastings has initiated an oral-history project to collect memories of fading tribal traditions. "We go into each family, get an anthropologist to record everything right from how you wake up in the morning," he said. Hundreds of historic photographs of early reservation life have been collected and deposited with the State Historical Society, in Lincoln. A friendly scholar from the University of Indiana recovered a trove of forgotten Omaha songs recorded in the 1920s on wax cylinders. Another at the University of New Mexico undertook a collective genealogy that would trace the lineage of more than five thousand Omahas back to the eighteenth century. Hastings explained, "Until now everything was oral. Some people knew the names of their ancestors, and some knew nothing at all. There was a loss of connection with the past. Now people can come back and find out who their ancestors were." In sharp contrast with the combative chauvinism of some tribes, the Omahas invited scientists from the University of Nebraska and the Smithsonian Institution to examine repatriated skeletons to see what they could discover about the lives of their ancestors. In 1989, astonishing perhaps even themselves, tribal leaders brought home Waxthe'xe, the True Omaha, the sacred cottonwood pole that is the living embodiment of the

Omaha people, which had laid for a hundred years in Harvard's Peabody Museum; at the July powwow that year, weeping hundreds bent to touch it as if it were the true cross or the ark of the covenant.

"We want the benefits of modern society," Hastings told me in his nasal Midwestern drawl. "But America is still dangerous for us. The question is then, How do we take the science that America used against us and make it work for us? The answer is, we try to build on the past. It's like a puzzle. First you see where the culture broke and fragmented. Then you try to build on it where people have been practicing it all along. Then people start to think in a healthy way about what they were in the past. If you can get each person to be proud of himself, little by little, you can get the whole tribe to become proud. We're going to dream big and be consistent with that dream."

In its broadest sense the tribal sovereignty movement is demonstrating that the more than three hundred Indian tribes in the lower forty-eight states (more than five hundred if you count Alaskan native groups) are distinct communities, each with its unique history, traditions, and political environment, for whom a single one-size-fits-all federal policy will no longer suffice. Greater autonomy will surely enable well-governed and economically self-sufficient tribes—mostly those located near big cities and those with valuable natural resources—to manage their own development in imaginative ways. For many others, however, far from airports and interstate highways, populated by ill-trained workers and governed, in some cases, by politicians who do not abide by the most basic democratic rules, the future is much less assured.

There is nothing abstract about such concerns in Timber Lake, South Dakota, which lies a short drive east from Isabel across the rolling plains of the Cheyenne River Sioux Reservation. Like Isabel, Timber Lake has been battered by the general decline of a region that is hemorrhaging jobs and people. Timber Lake is one of the relatively lucky places, kept alive by the presence of the Dewey County offices, the rural electric co-op, the central school, and a cheese factory. Even so, one hundred of the six hundred people who lived there a decade ago have moved away to places with better prospects and more hope. Isabel's population has dropped by half, to three hundred. Trail City has shrunk from three hundred

and fifty to thirty, Firesteel to a single general store, and Landeau has disappeared completely. Entire towns have lost their doctors, banks, and schools. From a certain angle of vision, Sioux demands for the restoration of the reservation to its original nineteenth-century limits are simply an anticlimax.

The people of Timber Lake—the mechanics, the teachers, the co-op clerks, the men who work at the grain elevator, the retired farmers—are the human fruit of allotment, the flesh-and-blood culmination of the cultural blending that Senator Dawes envisioned. "Everyone here has relatives who are Indian," said Steve Aberle, a local attorney whose Russian-German father married into the Ducheneaux, a prominent clan of Cheyenne River Sioux. Aberle, who is thirty-five, is one-eighth Sioux; he is a voting member of the tribe and served for two and a half years as chairman of the tribal police commission. Nevertheless he shares the uneasiness of non-Indians who feel themselves slipping toward a kind of second-class citizenship within the reservation's boundaries. "It would be better to be in a situation where everybody works together and deals with people as people, but it's hard to do that when people know they pay taxes but are excluded from benefits and services," Aberle told me. "When my grandparents came from Russia, the United States government told them that they would be full citizens if they moved out here. Now I see people being told that they can't even take part in a government that wants to regulate them. Something is inherently wrong when you can't be a citizen where you live because of your race. It just doesn't fit with the traditional notion of being a U.S. citizen. At some point there has to be a collision between the notion of tribal sovereignty and the notion of being United States citizens. Anytime you have a group not represented in the political process they will be discriminated against. There's going to be more and more friction. It's going to hurt these communities. People start looking for jobs elsewhere."

The Sioux were the victims of nineteenth-century social engineering that decimated their reservation. But the descendants of the adventurous emigrants who settled the land are also the victims of an unexpected historical prank, the trick of the disappearing and now magically reappearing reservation. Reasonably enough, the rhetoric of tribal sovereignty asks for tribes a degree of self-government that is taken for granted by other Americans. However, the achievement of a sovereignty that drives away taxpayers, consumers, and enterprise may be at best but a Pyrrhic victory over withered communities that beg for cooperation and innovation to survive at all.

With little debate outside the parochial circles of Indian affairs, a generation of policymaking has jettisoned the long-standing American ideal of racial unity as a positive good and replaced it with a doctrine that, seen from a more critical angle, seems disturbingly like an idealized form of segregation, a fact apparently invisible to a nation that has become accustomed to looking at Indians only through the twin lenses of romance and guilt and in an era that has made a secular religion of passionate ethnicity. Much of the thinking that underlies tribal sovereignty seems to presuppose that cultural purity can and ought to be preserved, as if Indian bloodlines, economies, and histories were not already inextricably enmeshed with those of white, Hispanic, and black Americans.

Such concerns will be further exacerbated in the years to come as Indian identity grows increasingly ambiguous. Virtually all Indians are moving along a continuum of biological fusion with other American populations. "A point will be reached . . . when it will no longer make sense to define American Indians in generic terms [but] only as tribal members or as people of Indian ancestry or ethnicity," writes Russell Thornton, a Cherokee anthropologist and demographer at the University of Southern California, in *American Indian Holocaust and Survival*, a study of fluctuations in native populations. Statistically, according to Thornton, Indians are marrying outside their ethnic group at a faster rate than any other Americans. More than 50 percent of Indians are already married to non-Indians, and Congress has estimated that by the year 2080 less than 8 percent of Native Americans will have one-half or more Indian blood.

How much ethnic blending can occur before Indians finally cease to be Indians? The question is sure to loom ever larger for coming generations, as the United States increasingly finds itself in "government-to-government" relationships with tribes that are becoming less "Indian" by the decade. Within two or three generations the nation will possess hundreds of "tribes" that may consist of the great-great-grandchildren of Indians but whose native heritage consists mainly of autonomous governments and special privileges that are denied to other Americans.

Insofar as there is a political solution to the Indian future, I have come to believe that it lies in the rejection of policies that lead to segregation and in acknowledgment of the fact that the racially and ethnically variegated peoples whom we call "Indian" share not only common blood but also a common history and a common future with other Americans. The past generation has seen the development of a national consensus on a number of aspects of the nation's history that were long obscured by racism or shame; there is, for instance, little dispute today among Americans of any ethnic background over the meaning of slavery or of the internment of Japanese-Americans during the Second World War. There is as yet no such consensus, however, with respect to the shared history of Indians and whites, who both still tend to see the past as a collision of irreconcilable opposites and competing martyrdoms.

That history was not only one of wars, removals, and death but also one of calculated compromises, mutual accommodation, and deliberately chosen risks, a story of Indian communities and individuals continually remaking themselves in order to survive. To see change as failure, as some kind of cultural corruption, is to condemn Indians to solitary confinement in a prison of myth that whites invented for them in the first place. Self-determination gives Indian tribes the ability to manage the speed and style of integration but not the power to stop it, at least for long. Integration may well mean the eventual diminishing of conventional notions of "tribal identity," but it must also bring many new individual opportunities, along with membership in the larger human community. "People and their cultures perish in isolation, but they are born or reborn in contact with other men and women, with man and woman of another culture, another creed, another race," the Mexican novelist Carlos Fuentes has written. Tribes will survive, if anything, as stronger entities than they have been for many generations. The question is whether they will attempt to survive as isolated islands or as vital communities that recognize a commonality of interest and destiny with other Americans.

Myth, the Melting Pot, and Multiculturalism

Carl N. Degler

As the world's professed "nation of immigrants," America is by self-definition multicultural. It is the picture we paint of ourselves. Diversity, by choice, necessity, and declaration, has been the byword of the American experience. This is the essential character, and the unique feature, of the great American experiment—a nation like none other, both diverse and free. Yet out of this pluralism a coherent mythic unity of identity—whether "fabric," "salad bowl," "melting pot," or "mosaic"—is said to emerge. Thus stated, the meaning of America, both for itself and the world at large, hinges on its capacity to become the magic kingdom, the "imagined community" it has always envisioned and celebrated. Behind cosmetic differences of speech, appearance, and culture, all might find common ideological ground with their various "cities of gold," "city upon a hill," or their "streets of gold:" a shared, yet very personal, American Dream. Noting that America has enunciated inclusion even while often practicing exclusion, Carl N. Degler, Margaret Byrne Professor of American History Emeritus at Stanford University, here attempts to sift through the chaos and coherence of America's Janus-faced attitude toward its multicultural origins and identity. Despite a historical succession including Alien and Sedition Acts, Know-Nothing political movements, immigrant exclusion and restriction legislation, diatribes against various "hyphenated" Americans, segregation of African Americans, marginalizing of women, reservations for Native Americans, the closeting of gays and lesbians, and other "culture wars," the mythic image of cultural homogeneity sustained itself. America *would be* a "nation of nationalities," ultimately fusing a *United* States. What is needed, Degler concludes, is a more balanced holistic view of the American experience. The telling of the history of America requires a better all-encompassing framework, one that simultaneously allows "a fuller and truer American story." Out of apt comparison with other societies—Argentina, Brazil, and Canada come to mind—at least a comparative understanding of the delicate balance between diversity and unity might emerge. Both the identity and destiny of America demand such self-understanding.

Multiculturalism may be a fashionable neologism of our times, but as a cultural fact of American life it is considerably older than the Constitution. Even worries about its danger to national unity are hardly new. As early as the 1750s, Benjamin Franklin complained about the Germans' flooding into Pennsylvania: "Why should the Palatine boors be suffered to swarm into our settlements, and, by herding together, establish their language and manners to the exclusion of ours?" he asked in 1751. Their large number caused Franklin to wonder why "Pennsylvania, founded by the English," should "become a colony of aliens who will shortly be so numerous as to germanize us, instead of our anglifying them."

Indeed, the diversity of Americans was sufficient at the establishment of the country to impel the founders to break decisively with an age-old European tradition and deliberately sever in their new Constitution any connection between church and state. America was simply too varied in religions to have a national church—a decision whose cultural and political significance becomes clear when comparing the U.S. and Europe, a region in which religious strife has served as its most prominent and enduring source of internal division and conflict.

But if Americans could not be identified by a common or state-supported religion, it was not at all clear that the Union of disparate states created in 1787 was to be anything more than an "experiment." America, a nation both diverse and free, without a standing army or a history of unity, needed some source of national identity.

When the Civil War ended for good that aspect of the search for nationhood, it also established the principle of equality along with freedom as the heart of the American political and social polity. Both ideas, to be sure, had been implicit in the Revolution's declaration of independence from Britain, but only with the Civil War and the Reconstruction of the South, which followed, was inclusion and equality explicitly applied to a racial group, in that case, the recently emancipated slaves of African descent—though Lincoln, it's worth recalling, had doubts that blacks could be integrated into American society, as his Caribbean expatriation experiment reminds us.

Behind that enunciation of inclusion and equality stood the assumption that in time the principle would erase or largely eliminate the differences in demeanor, style, and history between new and established Americans. No matter how different blacks or Irish immigrants might be from native white Americans, equality and freedom in due course would "melt" them together. Equality, to be sure, did not mean sameness; it meant equality of opportunity, which is one reason nineteenth-century Americans led all European countries in providing state-supported education to its citizens including females and, after emancipation blacks. Free schooling, it was believed would level the ground before the competition began.

The nether side of the principle of equality of opportunity, of course, was that the individual rewards of competition, which were also the incentives for competition, would necessarily not be equally distributed. It was expected that some people would do better than others, the acceptance of which explains a great deal about American behavior then and now.

Throughout the nineteenth century a striking but unintended consequence of the idea of equality of opportunity was to make America increasingly multicultural. Millions of Europeans and thousands of Asians poured into the country in order to turn opportunities into a better life. The upshot was a growing fear by those who had preceded them—reminiscent of Franklin's laments—that America was becoming too diverse, too far removed from what it had been earlier, though "earlier" often meant no more than the preceding generation, when the fearful themselves first arrived. Even before the Civil War, apprehensions about what newcomers meant to the "old America" spawned a national party—the so-called "Know-Nothings"—that pledged itself to deny public office to the foreign born and to delay access to citizenship for 20 years.

At that time no one was yet prepared to close the gates on the much needed labor that the immigrants embodied. By the end of the century, however, restrictions on immigrants were in place, first against Asians, then against Europeans. Accompanying the effort to limit numbers was the movement to transform the immigrants through school and workplace into "Americans," that is, wash out their differences in speech, appearance, and culture. Woodrow Wilson and Theodore Roosevelt differed on many things, but they were in agreement in denouncing the "hyphenated" American. Israel Zangwill's 1908 play, *The Melting Pot,* provided the era's motto: "East and West, and North and South, the palm and the pine, the pole and the equator, the crescent and the cross—how the great Alchemist melts and fuses them with his purging flames," the play's hero exclaimed.

*   *   *

During the 1920s, a few scholars suggested that the melting pot was more a hope than a fact, that America was a pluralistic society, a nation of many nationalities living together peaceably without loss of national or racial identity and without denying an American identity. That, however, was not the official view of American life and history appearing in high school and college courses and textbooks. This official view repeated, when it did not celebrate outright, Zangwill's image of a people made homogeneous through the fire of the melting pot. Blacks appeared as slaves and as troublesome figures during Southern Reconstruction and then were lost to view; women rarely appeared at all; immigrants were a problem during the nativist outbursts of the 1850s, 1890s (when anti-Semitism surfaced), and the 1920s, and then silently slipped into the mainstream of American life. The Immigration Restriction Act of 1924, which reduced the number of newcomers from a million a year just before the First World War, to a mere 150,000 a year later, and deliberately screened out certain European nationalities and Asian races, was Congress's way of saying the national "fusing" had been completed.

Yet no sooner had that signal been flashed than contrary signs appeared. The earliest was seen in the election of 1928 when the candidacy of Al Smith, Roman Catholic and Irish, brought out in record numbers the hitherto unrecognized unmeltable ethnics who, for the first time, saw one of their own in Smith. Al Smith lost that election, but the depression and Franklin Roosevelt's New Deal, particularly in its labor and social policies, fostered increased recognition of the country's diversity of immigrant nationalities, as well as acknowledging for the first time the nation's racial diversity. Blacks, after all, had never merged or "melted"; they had simply been held apart, segregated by law or custom, effectively read out of American politics and culture: Reconstruction in the nineteenth century may have proclaimed a policy of equality, but that policy, the Supreme Court pointed out in *Plessy v. Ferguson* in 1896, contemplated no positive means for realizing equality. On the contrary, the court said, any positive support violated the Constitution's conception of equality.

The social and economic changes stemming from the upheaval of the Second World War gave additional prominence to the ethnic diversity of the country. The result was a new sense that the U.S. was "a nation of immigrants," to repeat the title of a book of the late 1950s by a rising young politician, from a prominent Irish family, named John F. Kennedy. By the 1960s, blacks, women, and a variety of national groups began to demand not only recognition in modern America, but also acknowledgment of their presence in the American past. Historians and social scientists responded with alacrity to the call. In a flood of books and scholarly articles they demonstrated that the national ideal of equality of opportunity was far from flawless in practice, that Americans were not typically white and well-off, that women had also shaped the American past, that Amerindians had not become "radishes." By the 1960s, "salad bowl" had replaced "melting pot." Even a half century after the Golden Door had been slammed shut, these scholars were saying, diversity was still a hallmark of American culture.

*   *   *

The upshot of this new social research and understanding was a belated recognition that America had always been more an idea than the locale of a people. Gunnar Myrdal called it "the American Creed" of freedom and equality of opportunity. It was a set of ideas or practices, that both immigrants and those who chose not to leave their homelands accepted as the meaning of America. For the fact was that America could not be like a European nation, the people of which had lived together for countless generations, sharing a slowly evolving culture and history. Americans had to create their identity from scratch, as it were.

Unfortunately, during the nineteenth century the national establishment created a history and culture modeled after the European example, the result of which was a flat, two-dimensional history that left out or suppressed the diversity that today we rightly celebrate and seek to foster in our institutions. There should be no doubt, after all, that diversity in our workplaces, government, military units, and universities is a necessity in a frankly pluralistic nation. However, at the same time, diversity renders more insistent the old question: What is the United States' common history, what is that cluster of ideas and shared experience that constitutes America?

Unfortunately, the wealth of new learning about the diversity of Americans threatens to shunt aside that insistent question. The long overdue recognition of diversity increasingly leaves out the larger story of the U.S. as a whole. The new emphasis on the history of individual national or racial or sexual groups places the national slogan of *E Pluribus Unum* in danger of being transformed into "Out of One, Many."

*   *   *

How the story of diversity can be integrated into the larger story of America; how the Americanness of all groups can be demonstrated—is the challenge the present emphasis on multiculturalism must confront. Only by fitting the two together in a single, overarching whole can we recognize who we are as a people.

For even those who were born abroad are no longer like those left behind. No one was more aware of that fact of life in America than those immigrants during the earlier years of this century who returned to the lands they had left only to find that they themselves and those they returned to perceived them as changed, as Americanized. To say, as some proponents of the new ethnicity do, that *The Federalist* or the writings of Thomas Jefferson have nothing to say to Amerindians or Mexican-Americans is to deny implicitly their membership in the nation. They depend, as we all do, on those historical ideas and institutions in fashioning their own lives and those of their children. Those institutions and ideas, European as they may be in origin, are as much a part of their lives in America as they are in the lives of those whose ancestors originated in England, Germany, or Italy. African-Americans may look more like present-day Africans than like white Americans, but in language, history, and institutions they are indeed Americans, as many African-Americans discover when they return to Africa.

To tell the story of an ethnic or racial group living within the confines of the U.S. without reference to the whole of America is to truncate its identity as well as the identity of all other Americans. Yet, thanks to the recent emphasis on the cultural diversity within the confines of the U.S., we are in danger of doing just that. The irony is heavy here since the original purpose of research into ethnicity, race, and gender was to construct a fuller and truer American story, one that reflected the reality of a pluralistic America.

That much needed holistic view of America has not yet emerged. A framework is still lacking, a theme that will integrate our diversity into an American story. Just because diversity is pervasive in the long American experience, it alone cannot provide that needed theme or framework. Simply because it runs throughout our history, diversity as such will not be able to account for the changes through which Americans have passed. We could, to be sure, write the story around the unfolding of diversity, tracing that evolution from the Dutch, Scots-Irish, English, Swedes, Jews, Catholics, Africans, and Germans in the colonial years down to the arrival of Asians and Latinos and the acknowledgment of women's past in the course of the last two decades. In fact, the history of African-Americans alone would provide a remarkably apt framework, certainly more apt than the experience of any other single national group; including the English. The presence of Africans has helped to shape the law, the Constitution, the politics, and the economy of America, not to mention the greatest single event of all, the Civil War.

Certainly the tale of the evolution of ethnicity, race, and gender would tell a fuller story than a history based on class consciousness and class conflict. Indeed, the very diversity of American society has probably played a crucial role in reducing class as a source of identification for Americans. Groups have found their racial, gender, and ethnic identity stronger than their class roles, especially in a society in which opportunity to acquire property is emphasized. The well-known weakness of socialism and labor unions in the American experience may well be explained, at least in large part, by just that conflict between class and other identities. Nevertheless, complex and developmental as the story of racial and ethnic changes would be, it still would not fully encompass our varied cultural or institutional history, which has been only partly influenced by our diversity in ethnicity, race, and gender.

It would also help to frame the story of Americans by comparing our national development with that of other countries. Out of it could emerge a sense of who we are by seeing how our traversing the path from colony to independence, from agriculture to industry, from frontier to settlement, from village to metropolis, from isolation to world power, from elitist politics to democracy differed from the experience of other peoples. Comparisons with other nations' histories would highlight the nature of our ethnic diversity as well. Like us, Brazil and Argentina are products of large-scale immigration, but they have not exhibited the often violent nativism that has been a recurring part of the *Norteamericano* experience. Moreover, although slavery flourished in several other countries of the New World, only the Americans required a civil war to put an end to it.

Canadians, like Americans, encountered native peoples in their settling of the western territories, but the wars that frequently punctuated the American advance were almost entirely absent in Canada. To Americans the frontier was opportunity; to other peoples it has been threatening and useless. In sum, if we are to understand who we are among the peoples of the world, comparing our experience with that of other native peoples and minorities might be a way to begin.

* * *

Further useful comparison can easily expand beyond ethnicity: although England was the first industrial nation, Big Business emerged first in the U.S.—one consequence of which was that the U.S. was the first industrial nation to fashion an anti-trust law. Is that "first" in Big Business related to the weakness of labor unions and socialism as compared with the experience of many European countries? Do those comparisons mean that Americans are more individualistic than other people, less prone to act collectively? Does that apparent character trait, in turn, help to explain why we were slow to enact Social Security and have yet to establish a national health program or family policy comparable to those of many European nations?

Identity, after all, is at once internal and external: It derives from what our history tells us and from how that history appears when we project it against the background of other nations with comparable experiences. Comparison not only reveals what sets Americans apart from other people, but also offers some suggestions as to what it means to be an American; that is, it provides clues as to the values that Americans as a people hold and how those values may impede or advance our dealing with today's problems.

That the U.S. needs a holistic history seems indisputable. Americans may be a mosaic, as Mayor Dinkens of New York is fond of describing his thoroughly diverse city; but Americans, no less than New Yorkers, are also much more than the loose collection of peoples that term implies. A mosaic, after all, is a picture, a pattern, a whole that integrates and transcends the constituent elements. Similarly, as a people our internal diversity is only a part of the story; each racial and ethnic group has, in turn, been shaped by its interaction with the others and with the past that all have played a part in shaping. We still need a national historical definition that includes our diversity in past and present alike, even as it acknowledges that diversity as peculiarly American. That larger purpose is the proper and necessary goal of multicultural studies.